THE COMMON MADE HOLY

The
COMMON
made
HOLY

NEIL T ANDERSON
AND
ROBERT SAUCY

MONARCH
Crowborough

First published in the USA
by Harvest House Publishers, Eugene, Oregon 97402

First British edition 1997

British Library Cataloguing Data
A catalogue record for this book is available from the British Library

ISBN 1 85424 371 3

Designed and produced by Bookprint Creative Services
P.O. Box 827, BN21 3YJ, England for
MONARCH PUBLICATIONS
Broadway House, The Broadway
Crowborough, East Sussex TN6 1HQ
Printed in Great Britain.

Reproduced from the original text by arrangement
with Harvest House Publishers

Contents

*Dedicated to the memory of
Becky Saucy Hess*

God's Desire for You

A long time ago the infinite and eternal Creator sat down at His potter's wheel as He had so many times before. Everything He had made so far was very good, but this time He had something else in mind. He wanted to create something in His own image. Something, or better, some*one* who could personally relate to Him. The Potter had already fashioned living beings to inhabit planet earth, but this new creation would be different. Far more significant than all other earthen vessels, this new creation would be fruitful and multiply and rule over all the other created beings who flew in the sky, walked on the earth, or swam in the seas.

So He took a glob of clay and placed it on His wheel. As the wheel began to turn, He placed His thumbs in the center of the clay and formed the inward parts. Miraculously the clay began to take shape. As the wheel turned faster and faster, the clay began to rise from the earth from which it was taken. Fearfully and wonderfully He made this new creation which he had planned from the beginning of time. But He wasn't done. Something was missing. The clay had no life. So he breathed into this earthen pot the breath of life and it became a living being. This fusion of divine life and earthly clay would make this new creation different from all the other created beings.

What appeared to be common was indeed holy, and set apart to do His will.

All would have been well if it hadn't been for a previously created spirit being who thought he should be at least equal to the one who made him. That, of course, was an absurd notion, even though he was the most beautiful of all created things. This masterpiece was created to be a light-bearer. But by his own choice, this rebel became the prince of darkness. Not wanting to be alone in his rebellion, this arrogant spirit being persuaded many other lesser spirits to join him. The Potter could not tolerate this sinful rebellion. So He cast the spirits out of His presence, and they fell from their heavenly abode.

The prince of darkness could not stand the thought that a new creation by the Potter would actually rule over him. If only he could get this new creation to act independently of the Potter. *I know what I will do*, thought the evil prince, *I'll get this upstart pot to think that he too could be like the Potter and decide for himself what is good and evil.* What a lie! "Does not the potter have a right over the clay. . . ?" (Romans 9:21 NASB). "Will the clay say to the potter, 'What are you doing?'" (Isaiah 45:9 NASB). This crafty devil actually managed to deceive this new creation by questioning the word of the Potter, enticing him to do his own thing and live independent of the one who fashioned him.

The consequences were swift and immediate. This new creation lost the divine breath that made him spiritually alive and introduced impurities into the clay from which he was made. He no longer had a relationship with the Potter who made him. Because of the impurities in his clay, the earthen vessel would also deteriorate and eventually die. The Potter had designed this new creation and his partner to multiply and fill the earth, and that is what they continued to do, but all their offspring were born dead in their trespasses and sins like their parents. They lost their dominion over all other creation, and the prince of darkness became the rebel holder of the authority that the Potter had intended for the pot and his offspring to have. Now this rebel prince of darkness had his own little kingdom to rule over on planet earth. He was the god of this world and prince of the power of the air. Fallen pots and lesser evil spirits were under his authority and were slaves to his sinful ways.

But the Potter loved what He had created and had a plan to undo the works of this rebel prince—a plan that would do something about the impurities that now characterized all of His creation because He cannot tolerate anything impure in His presence. Through this plan, He would give them His life again. The Potter said, "I will give you a new heart and put a new spirit in you; and I will remove from you your heart of stone and give you a heart of flesh. And I will put my Spirit in you and move you to follow my decrees and be careful to keep my laws" (Ezekiel 36:26,27).

The Potter's plan required He Himself to take on the form of a pot and show the earthly pots how to live a life totally dependent upon the Potter. The prince of darkness threw every possible temptation at this Divine Pot in the hopes that He too would choose to live independent of the Potter, but He stood His ground and declared that pots don't live by the things of this world but by everything that comes from the mouth of the Potter (*see* Matthew 4:4). But He had to do more than just show them how to live, because the consequence of their impurities was certain destruction.

So this Divine Pot who was sent from the Potter had to take all the consequences of the impurities of the fallen pots upon Himself in order that the fallen pots could be pure again. All the forces of evil came against Him and the Potter's just anger against impurity fell on Him and He died. He died to sin once and for all for the fallen pots who would trust in Him. Then three days later, this Divine Pot was resurrected, showing that His death had defeated the prince of darkness and made it possible for all the fallen pots to be forgiven and receive divine life if they would only believe in Him. The law of life in this Divine Pot was greater than the law of the impurities and the law of death.

Although the prince of darkness was defeated, he and all his evil spirits were allowed by the Potter to continue roaming across the planet earth until their final judgment came upon them. Their plan was to blind the minds of the unbelieving pots so that they could never hear the good news that the Divine Pot had come to die for their sins and give them life. Many believed this lie and never received their pardon. Others believed the truth and were instantly forgiven and they received the life offered by the Divine Pot, but the evil one tempted, accused, and did everything within his limited power to get the forgiven pots to believe his lies.

To all the pots that heard the good news and responded to the truth the Potter sent His Spirit of truth to guide and bear witness that they truly were children of the Potter. He said to them, "Like clay in the hand of the potter, so are you in my hand" (Jeremiah 18:6). Because these redeemed pots had been molded by this world, He had to remake them in His image. These new creations could not be remade on their own, but they would have an important part to play in becoming more and more like the Potter. Although they would have many other useful purposes for remaining on planet earth, nothing was more important to the Potter than to have all His redeemed pots free from their awful past and become pure like Him.

This book is about the common made holy by the hands of God. It is about sinners becoming saints, and about children of wrath becoming children of God. The theological term for this change is *sanctification*. The mandate given by God to every one of His children is, "Be holy, because I am holy" (1 Peter 1:16). We are forgiven but we have not yet been perfected. There is no more important work in the church than sanctification. Paul says, "We proclaim him, admonishing and teaching everyone with all wisdom, so that we may present everyone perfect in Christ. To this end I labor, struggling with all his energy, which so powerfully works in me" (Colossians 1:28,29).

"It is God's will that you should be sanctified" (1 Thessalonians 4:3). Everything else is secondary to God. He will certainly guide you concerning career choices, but His primary concern isn't whether you are a carpenter, plumber, or engineer. His primary concern is *what kind* of carpenter, plumber, and engineer you are. In fact, He may find it necessary to sacrifice your career in order to conform you to the image of God. It is character before career, and maturity before ministry. God is more concerned about church purity than church growth, because church purity is an essential prerequisite to church growth.

We are going to show the necessity for growth, and then attempt to define sanctification. We hope to show how God intends for us to conform to His image. With all the moral failure in our churches today, there can be no other doctrine more important to understand than sanctification. The world, the flesh, and the devil will pull out all the stops and make every effort to stop this process in your life, but we are committed to helping you understand God's desire for you to grow in Christ. Everything we have to say could be summarized by one verse, "which is Christ in you, the hope of glory" (Colossians 1:27). We believe the Holy Spirit will lead you into all truth, and that truth will set you free to be all that God called you to be.

Have you made the decision to let God be God and desire nothing more than to be the person He created you to be? Are you convinced that the will of God is good, acceptable, and perfect for you (Romans 12:2) even before you know for certain what it is? Be assured that God loves His children and He has no plans for you that aren't good, although you will surely undergo some times of testing in order that you may be purified. We have been warned in 1 Peter 4:12-14 (NASB):

> Beloved, do not be surprised at the fiery ordeal among you, which comes upon you for your testing, as though some strange thing were happening to you; but to the degree that you share the sufferings of Christ, keep on rejoicing; so that also at the revelation of His glory, you may rejoice with exultation. If you are reviled for the name of Christ, you are blessed, because the Spirit of glory and of God rests upon you.

The Refiner's fire is necessary in order for the Potter to conform His earthen vessels back into His image. You will be
tempted to believe it isn't worth it, but indeed it is. Don't jeop-
ardize your inheritance in Christ for a bowl of soup as Esau did,
or sacrifice eternity to satisfy the flesh. There is a heaven to be
gained and a hell to be shunned. You have been chosen by the
King of kings and Lord of lords to be His child and set aside
from all other creation to do His will, which is good, acceptable,
and perfect. The songwriter said it well:

> Refiner's fire,
> My heart's one desire,
> Is to be holy
> Set apart unto You my Maker
> Ready to do Your will.[1]

1

Designed for Holiness

The heavens declare the glory of God; the skies proclaim the work of his hands.

—Psalm 19:1

The power and energy that can be expended by giant earth movers is fascinating. It's possible to scrape many cubic yards of dirt off the earth's surface in one swipe and skillfully deposit it into a narrow ribbon of land that will become a road to serve mankind. Then more massive machines are used to place a thin layer of concrete over the soil to make the road complete and smooth for convenient driving.

Everything that mankind has made, however, needs a continuous infusion of energy just to maintain what was originally built. The second law of thermodynamics states that all the natural systems of the universe are winding down and becoming more disorderly. The best-made automobile will eventually find its way to the junkyard. Even concrete highways will be reclaimed by nature if left to themselves.

Witness the tiny flowers that somehow grow through the cracks of an abandoned highway. Look closer at each plant as it sets forth its blooms. Marvel at the delicate design and intricate pattern of colors that make up every petal. Who sowed the seed that lay dormant for many years beneath that man-made road?

13

What power is there in the flower that can loosen the soil and break up the concrete that took enormous energy for mankind to make? Who sent the rain and provided the sunshine? Clearly the heavens and earth do indeed show forth the glory of God.

All "created" life is designed to grow. God told Adam and Eve to "be fruitful and increase in number; fill the earth and subdue it" (Genesis 1:28). Every living thing created by God is intended to blossom into full bloom and bear fruit for His glory. From the moment of conception we are destined for growth in every dimension of our existence: physically, emotionally, mentally, socially, and spiritually. Our physical growth is predetermined by a genetic code that scientific minds are just now beginning to understand. We have some influence over our physical development by employing the appropriate disciplines of exercise, rest, and diet, but our basic physical characteristics will not deviate from the genetic information stored in one DNA (deoxyribonucleic acid) molecule found in the chromosomes of every single cell in our bodies.

As mortals, we cannot create anything. That is, we cannot simply speak and bring something into existence out of nothing. We can be creative by skillfully applying paint to a canvas or arranging bricks in an attractive way, but all of our so-called natural talents and abilities should be rightfully credited to God's creation. Whatever seed that mankind sows independent of God will not last for eternity. "Every plant that my heavenly Father has not planted will be pulled up" (Matthew 15:13).

God does, however, allow us to participate in one act of creation, and that is procreation. We have no power or ability to predetermine the genetic code of any DNA molecule or calculate its potential. We can count the seeds in an apple, but only God knows how many apples are in the seed. David must have shaken his head in wonder as he wrote under the inspiration of God, "Thou didst form my inward parts; Thou didst weave me in my mother's womb. I will give thanks to Thee, for I am fearfully and wonderfully made" (Psalm 139:13,14 NASB).

Physically, we are born relatively helpless compared to the creatures in the animal kingdom. You can't help but marvel when you observe a little lamb, who was coiled for weeks in the womb of its mother, wobble to its feet only minutes after being born, or a day-old calf suckling on the udder of a cow. How do they do that? Physically we develop at a much slower pace than animals, a fact that led one person to declare humans the "most orphaned children of nature." Yet proportionately our brain size is immensely larger, which equips us to participate in our own development in many ways that animals cannot.

Growth in the dimension that relates to what the apostle Paul refers to as the "inner man" is quite another matter (*see* 2 Corinthians 4:16). In contrast to animals, whose entire development is controlled by natural capacity or divine instinct, we are created by God to play a much more significant role in our spiritual growth. Although our maturing process is influenced by our parents, friends, and teachers, the most significant role is played by ourselves. Many people will help or hinder us in the pursuit of God and holiness, but nobody can stop us from being the people that God has called us to be. This capacity to participate in the shaping of our own lives is rooted in the biblical truth that we are created in "the image of God" (Genesis 1:26,27).

We are not globs of clay that can be molded into whatever our parents or teachers want us to be. Rather, those who raise or teach us would be wise to discover the gifts, talents, and unique personality that God has already created in each of us. No amount of nurturing can turn a tulip into a rose, but a lot of love and tender care can greatly influence the brilliance of a tulip's blossoms. When it comes to spiritual growth, it is as though we possess a spiritual DNA molecule that God has known from the foundation of the world. "We are God's workmanship, created in Christ Jesus to do good works, which God prepared in advance for us to do" (Ephesians 2:10).

You will never read a birth announcement that says Mr. and Mrs. John Doe gave birth to a doctor, or engineer, or a lawyer.

People achieve their professional status because of God-given abilities, social opportunities, personal choices, and hard work. In a limited sense, God has called each of us to participate in the development of what He intended us to become. This is a great privilege and an awesome responsibility, for no other mortal can determine our ultimate destiny. Created with the capacity to think, we are intricately involved in the process of shaping ourselves and determining our destiny:

> Whoever sows a thought, reaps an action;
>> Whoever sows an action, reaps a habit;
>>> Whoever sows a habit, reaps a lifestyle;
>>>> Whoever sows a lifestyle, reaps a destiny.

The Biblical Challenge to Grow

The parables of the talents (Matthew 25:14-30) and the pounds (Luke 19:12-27) teach that we have all been given a life endowment, and we will be held accountable for what we have done with what God has entrusted to us. Scripture also reveals that apart from Christ we can do nothing (John 15:5). The sovereign grace of God and human responsibility are the essential intertwined catalysts for human growth and potential. In addition, God has provided all the resources we need in order to become all that He created us to be (2 Peter 1:3). We cannot become someone we are not, nor should we try.

The entrance of sin into God's created world brought a destructive power that kills and destroys life and growth. Sin's presence was introduced by a magnificent angel whose prideful rebellion led to his downfall. "How you have fallen from heaven, O morning star, son of the dawn! You have been cast down to the earth, you who once laid low the nations!" (Isaiah 14:12). Satan took many other angelic beings down with him in this unholy rebellion. Then he succeeded in deceiving Eve, which resulted in the fall of mankind. "Therefore, just as sin entered the world through one man, and death through sin, and in this way death came to all men, because all sinned" (Romans 5:12).

Then comes the good news. The prince of darkness, death, and destruction has been defeated by the author of life and light. John writes, "The thief [Satan] comes only to steal and kill and destroy; I have come that [you] may have life, and have it to the full" (John 10:10). God, through Christ, has unleashed an even greater power that allows us to grow toward the fullness of life for which we were created. Paul writes, "For if, by the trespass of the one man, death reigned through that one man, how much more will those who receive God's abundant provision of grace and of the gift of righteousness reign in life through the one man, Jesus Christ. . . . just as sin reigned in death, so also grace might reign through righteousness to bring eternal life through Jesus Christ our Lord" (Romans 5:17,21).

Notice the sucking instinct of a tiny infant and observe the craving that a growing baby has for a bottle of milk. The natural craving that the body has for self-preservation and growth, coupled with the realization that the food is good, causes infants to want more and more and to cry in protest if they don't get it. Even the basic instincts of a child reveal that all created beings are designed to grow. Peter writes, "Like newborn babies, crave pure spiritual milk, so that by it you may grow up in your salvation, now that you have tasted that the Lord is good" (1 Peter 2:2). In a variety of ways, Scripture challenges us to grow. We are to grow in our faith (2 Corinthians 10:15), in the grace and knowledge of our Savior (2 Peter 3:18), and in love (Ephesians 4:16). Also, our growth is not just an individual matter. Rather it takes place with other believers as the church corporately grows into "a holy temple in the Lord" (Ephesians 2:21).

In Scripture, growth is frequently expressed as a process of building. We are told to build ourselves up in our faith (Jude 20) and build up one another (1 Thessalonians 5:11). This building often refers to the church as a whole, which is being "built together into a dwelling of God in the Spirit" (Ephesians 2:22 NASB). The church—or the body—"builds itself up in love" as each part does its share (Ephesians 4:16; *see also* verse 12). The growth of the church collectively takes place only as individuals in the church grow. Of course, all of this building is enabled only by the grace of God (Acts 20:32).

We are being "perfected" (Galatians 3:3 NASB), therefore, "let us purify ourselves from everything that contaminates body and spirit, perfecting holiness out of reverence for God" (2 Corinthians 7:1). We are also being renewed or made new (2 Corinthians 4:16; Ephesians 4:23; Colossians 3:10; Titus 3:5). This renewal includes the transformation of our minds (Romans 12:2), and eventually affects our entire being. "We all, with unveiled face beholding as in a mirror the glory of the Lord, are being transformed into the same image from glory to glory, just as from the Lord, the Spirit" (2 Corinthians 3:18 NASB). Our growth is in every dimension of salvation, but especially in our faith and knowledge of Christ. It is nothing less than a maturity that is described as "attaining to the whole measure of the fullness of Christ" (Ephesians 4:13).[1] In other words, believers are growing toward a destiny characterized by the fullness of Christ's life and character (*see* Colossians 1:28).

Being like Christ means being like God. We are being renewed in the image of our Creator (Ephesians 4:24; Colossians 3:10). It is God's plan to restore a fallen humanity back to its original design. He will faithfully do His part, but what if we don't shoulder our responsibility? Will we grow beyond our salvation experience? If we don't mature, what effect will that have upon the church?

Recognizing True Spiritual Growth

We have often shared with our seminary students that the greatest asset they will have in their first ministry is mature saints. Their relatively young age won't be a problem to these veterans of life and ministry. We advise our students, "Don't alienate yourself from these dear people. They have grown in their knowledge of God and in His likeness and have learned things that only experience can teach." On the other hand, we also warn our students that the greatest liability they will have in their ministry is saints who just got old and didn't mature. All they want to do is censor and control. They are no more loving, kind, or patient now than they were 20 years ago. In other words, they are no more like Christ now than they were two decades ago.

It is not our intention to blame these nongrowing saints or anyone else. They are probably living out what they have been taught. The problem is most likely to originate in Christian leadership and higher Christian education. We can't expect students or church members to rise above their leaders. Scripture teaches that "a student is not above his teacher, but everyone who is fully trained will be like his teacher" (Luke 6:40). The possibility that we may have the wrong goal is the greatest problem in Christian education in both our seminaries and our churches. If we make doctrine or knowledge an end in itself we will distort the very purpose for which it was intended. Jesus said the greatest commandment is to "'love the Lord your God with all your heart and with all your soul and with all your mind' . . . And the second is like it: 'Love your neighbor as yourself.' All the Law and the Prophets hang on these two commandments" (Matthew 22:37,39,40). Proper biblical instruction should result in all of us falling in love with God and each other.

Paul said, "The goal of our instruction is love from a pure heart and a good conscience and a sincere faith" (1 Timothy 1:5 NASB). What's unfortunate is that many Christians measure other people's spiritual growth purely on the basis that they know their Bibles well. Seminary professors usually measure their students' progress in this same way. Yet it's possible for a person to master the Bible's content and not even be a Christian. The greatest evidence that you are a Christian is not your knowledge, but your love. Jesus said, "By this all men will know that you are my disciples, if you love one another" (John 13:35).

Godly leaders and scholars play a vital role in the growth of the church. If they are led of the Lord, they will not intimidate you with their God-given intellect and abilities. They will help you establish your confidence in God and His Word, set you free in Christ, and put you on the right path of knowing Him and conforming to His image. Without godliness and humility, however, even the brightest and best can undermine the work of God because they are operating in the flesh. Paul was a religious zealot and leading candidate for theologian of the year when Christ struck him down. Only when he learned to put no confidence in the flesh was he able to say, "I consider everything a loss compared to the surpassing greatness of knowing Christ Jesus my Lord" (Philippians 3:8). Like Paul before his conversion, we can fill our heads with biblical knowledge about God and not know Him at all.

Don't get us wrong. We are totally committed to knowing the truth of God's Word, but when academia supplants godliness, Christianity is no longer a personal relationship with a living God; rather, it is reduced to an intellectual exercise. The Word of God is not to be intellectually discussed without personal appropriation. It is also counterproductive to intellectually educate a person beyond his or her level of spiritual maturity.

It's important to note that theology is not necessarily divisive, but intellectual arrogance is. "Knowledge puffs up, but love builds up" (1 Corinthians 8:1). If we think we are theologically right, then others ought to know it because of our love, not by our ability to intimidate others and win arguments. That's why godly character is the primary requirement for spiritual leadership (1 Timothy 3:1-13). We can develop our skills, exercise our gifts, and learn better ways to become Christian leaders, yet still miss the mark:

> If I speak in the tongues of men and of angels, but have not love, I am only a resounding gong or a clanging cymbal. If I have the gift of prophecy and can fathom all mysteries and all knowledge, and if I have a faith that can move mountains, but have not love, I am nothing (1 Corinthians 13:1,2).

Viewing God's Holiness

Every child of God begins his or her spiritual pilgrimage as a babe in Christ. It is one thing to "be" in Christ, and yet another to become all that he has created us to be. Personalities, gifts, and talents will determine our own uniqueness in the body of Christ and determine what we should and can do for His glory, but there is one pursuit that we all hold in common: We are to be holy as He is holy (1 Peter 1:16). Because we are in the process of conforming to the image of God, we need to know what we are trying to become like.

The most significant characteristic of God is His holiness. The people of Israel in the Old Testament proclaimed, "Holy is He" (Psalm 99:3 NASB). The psalmist declared, "Holy and awesome is his name" (Psalm 111:9). The "name" of God is His person and reflects all that He is and does. Isaiah especially refers to God as "the Holy One of Israel" (for example, Isaiah 1:4; 5:19,24) or simply, "the Holy One" (40:25; 41:14-16).

Of all of the words used to describe God, "holy" speaks most directly to His deity. Hosea 11:9 says, "I am God and not man—the Holy One among you." There is none or nothing equal to "the Holy One" (Exodus 15:11; Isaiah 40:25). Because God cannot swear an oath by anything higher, He swears by His own self (Amos 6:8; see also Hebrews 6:13), which is the equivalent of swearing by "his holiness" (Amos 4:2; see also Psalm 89:35).

The derivation of the word "holy" is not certain. Many scholars have suggested that the Old Testament Hebrew word *qadash* (usually translated "to be holy," "sanctified," or "dedicated") comes from a root word meaning "to cut" or "to divide" and thus signifies that which is marked off or separate. What is clear from the word's use is that it refers to the realm of the sacred, as distinct from all other things.[2] The Greek word for "holy" (*hagios*) carries this same meaning in the New Testament.

Although the word "holy" carries a strong moral connotation, that is not its primary significance. In the first instance, "holy" simply marks off the sphere of the divine or the sacred.[3]

The same word is used to speak of cult prostitutes who served in pagan shrines. They were men and women "set apart" (that is, "holy ones") in relation to the gods of pagan worship (such as in Deuteronomy 23:17).

To speak of God's holiness is *first* of all to speak of His distinctness or His separateness from all other things. He is holy in His transcendence over all creation. "He is exalted over all the nations," the psalmist declares, and therefore, "He is holy" (Psalm 99:2,3; *see also* verses 5,9). He is "the high and lofty One . . . whose name is holy," and who lives in "a high and holy place" (Isaiah 57:15; *see also* 6:1).

As the holy One who lives above and beyond all creation, God is also separate from all the evil and moral pollution which defiles the creation. His holiness, then, secondarily and climactically refers to His absolute moral perfection. We say secondarily because the concept of separation from sin flows from the first meaning of simply being separate (transcendent) as the Creator. We are not saying that moral perfection is a second meaning of holiness, but that the meaning of holiness climaxes with His separateness from sin. He is separate ontologically as the Creator and therefore he is separate from sin, with the latter being the most dominant thought in most references to God's holiness in Scripture. Isaiah says, "the holy God will show himself holy by his righteousness" (5:16). As the "holy One," His "eyes are too pure to look on evil . . . [or] tolerate wrong" (Habakkuk 1:13). To sin is to spurn "the Holy One" (Isaiah 1:4). Only the person who has "clean hands and a pure heart" can stand in the Lord's holy place (Psalm 24:3,4; *see also* Leviticus 16:30).

Upon reading what Scripture says about God's holiness, we might find ourselves thinking, "We're supposed to be or become holy like God? How?" Obviously we can't do so apart from the grace of God. There is no way humanly possible that we can become like God, much less stand in His presence. We were born dead in our trespasses and sins, and "were by nature objects of wrath" (Ephesians 2:1,3). What hope do we have? He is too pure, too perfect, too awesome! The psalmist declares, "Holy and awesome is his name" (Psalm 111:9). There is none like "the Holy One"—none His equal (Isaiah 40.25). "There is no one holy like the LORD" (1 Samuel 2:2).

The fearful nature of God's holiness is seen in Isaiah's vision of the heavenly beings around God's throne, calling to one another, "Holy, holy, holy is the LORD Almighty; the whole earth is full of his glory" (Isaiah 6:3). The threefold repetition of the word "holy" is the strongest way to express the superlative in the Hebrew language (*see also* the same threefold ascription of holiness to God in Revelation 4:8). Isaiah had partially seen the One who is holy beyond all other gods, the truly other One who is distinct from all else.

No mortal has fully seen God, but Scripture does reveal that some individuals were allowed to experience an unusual sense of His presence. Moses prayed, "Show me your glory. And the LORD said, 'I will cause all my goodness to pass in front of you. . . . But,' he said, 'you cannot see my face, for no one may see me and live'" (Exodus 33:18-20). Moses fell on his face and worshipped God, and his physical countenance radiated the glory of God. Nothing—let me repeat—*nothing* can so immediately and profoundly effect the character and behavior of mankind more than to be confronted with the glory of God, which is a manifestation of His presence. People all over the world have cowered in fear at the presence of demonic manifestations, but their fear would pale in comparison to what they would experience in God's presence.

When Isaiah saw the glory of God's holy nature in his vision, the Temple shook and the prophet became distraught. But it was more than the awesome splendor of God's holy nature that affected the prophet. It was the absolute purity of God's holiness and His character that overwhelmed Isaiah and brought crushing conviction of his own uncleanness and ruination— "Woe to me . . . I am ruined!" (verse 5). Centuries later, when Peter witnessed the awesomeness of God on display in Jesus, "he fell at Jesus' knees and said, 'Go away from me, Lord, I am a sinful man!'" (Luke 5:8). Likewise, if we were brought into the

Lord's presence, we would all crumble at His feet with over-whelming conviction. Christians who are actively aware of God's constant presence in their lives are acutely aware of their own sin. Those who don't practice such awareness often see the sins of others and not their own.

The holiness of God and His acts rightly bring terror on His enemies (*see* Exodus 15:15; Revelation 15:4,5). The writer of Hebrews warned those who turn away from God that "it is a dreadful thing to fall into the hands of the living God" (10:31). Yet it is out of the very nature of this Holy One that salvation comes to us (*see* Isaiah 54:5). What God said to His covenant people in the Old Testament He says to all those who receive Him in His holy nature: "All my compassion is aroused. I will not carry out my fierce anger. . . . For I am God, and not man— the Holy One among you. I will not come in wrath" (Hosea 11:8,9). God's great acts as a redeemer led to awe-inspired praise from His people. Their response is to "acknowledge the holiness of the Holy One of Jacob, and . . . stand in awe of the God of Israel" (Isaiah 29:23). The psalmist similarly declared "Worship the LORD in the splendor of his holiness; tremble before him, all the earth" (96:9).

Set Apart for God

Because God is holy, everything associated with Him is also holy or sanctified. The first use of "holy" in the Scriptures oc-curs when Moses meets God at the burning bush. Moses is warned, "Do not come any closer. . . . Take off your sandals, for the place where you are standing is holy ground" (Exodus 3:5). The second use of "holy" appears in Exodus 12:16 (NASB) in ref-erence to the "holy assembly" of God's people, who were called to celebrate the Passover.

This second use points to Scripture's prominent use of "holy" in connection with God's people. Entering into a covenant with them at Mount Sinai, God declared, "You will be for me . . . a holy nation" (Exodus 19:6). Frequently God re-minds His people that they are to be holy because they belong

DESIGNED FOR HOLINESS   25

to Him who is holy: "Be holy because I, the LORD your God, am holy" (Leviticus 19:2; *see also* 11:44; 20:7, 20:26; 1 Peter 1:16). They were God's holy people because, as God reminds them, "I have set you apart from the nations to be my own" (Leviticus 20:26).

In the Old Testament, the priests who ministered in the worship of God on behalf of the people were "holy." While all were God's holy people, these priests came near to God in a special way and were thus specially holy in comparison to the others. Even the priests' food was holy (Leviticus 22:1,10).

The Tabernacle and Temple where God dwelled among His people along with their furnishings were all considered holy (Exodus 29:43,44; Matthew 23:17,19). The activities associated with worshiping God, including the offerings, were also holy (Exodus 29:27). The firstborn males of both people and animals were all consecrated to God, or made holy (Exodus 13:2; Deuteronomy 15:19). Particular days or years were set apart to God and made holy, such as the Sabbath (Genesis 2:3), fast days (Joel 1:14), and the year of jubilee (Leviticus 25:10). Holiness was attributed to heaven (God's dwelling place— Psalm 20:6), God's throne (Psalm 47:8), Zion, God's "holy mountain" (Psalm 2:6 NASB), and to Scripture (Romans 1:2). Even the kiss of greeting among Christians was called "a holy kiss" (Romans 16:16).

The uses of the word *holy* for many inanimate objects and even animals in the Old Testament shows that it carried a strong emphasis on ritual or ceremonial holiness. That is, things were marked off as related to God without any moral or ethical implications. But there was also an emphasis on holiness in the moral and ethical sphere. On one level God's people kept themselves holy by avoiding "unclean" foods (Leviticus 11:43-47). Although this could be done in a perfunctory manner without one's heart in it, God's intention was always that it be done out of love and fear for Him. God's concern for moral and ethical holiness is evident in the setting apart of the day of atonement for the cleansing of sin (Leviticus 16:30). It is also seen in the psalmist's teaching that only those with "clean hands and a pure heart" may stand in God's "holy place" (Psalm 24:3,4).

That which was set apart or sanctified unto God was distinguished from that which was not holy. The latter belonged to the realm of the profane or common—that is, secular human life outside the sphere of the holy. The profane or common was also considered to be unclean as opposed to that which was clean or holy. The two concepts of holiness and cleanliness and their opposites are closely linked. For example, the altar was said to be both cleansed and consecrated, or made holy (Leviticus 16:19). The two concepts are not, however, synonymous. *Holiness* is a broader concept that is associated with deity. Cleanliness or purity is an aspect of holiness.

It was important for God's people to clearly distinguish the realms of the holy and the profane, and the clean and unclean. The wall around the Temple seen in Ezekiel's vision was "to divide between the holy and the profane" (Ezekiel 42:20 NASB). Stipulations were given to the priests to "distinguish between the holy and the common, and between the unclean and the clean" (Leviticus 10:10). They were responsible to "teach My people the difference between the holy and the common and show them how to distinguish between the unclean and the clean" (Ezekiel 44:23). To fail to maintain this distinction and treat something which was holy as though it were common was to profane or desecrate the holy thing (Leviticus 18:21; *see also* Exodus 31:14). For God's people to live in sin was to profane God's name before others (Proverbs 30:9; Ezekiel 36:20-23).

Called to Be Holy

If all that is associated with God is holy, then the logical and necessary conclusion is that holiness must characterize His people. A personal and intimate relationship with God is the essence of life. This is what Jesus meant when He said, "This is eternal life, that they may know Thee, the only true God, and Jesus Christ whom Thou has sent" (John 17:3 NASB). To "know Thee," as used in this statement, means the knowledge of personal experience. To know a person in this sense is not to have mere knowledge *about* that person; rather, it is to know that person as a friend—to be in an intimate relationship so that your lives influence each other.

To have eternal life is to have an intimate friendship with the holy God, the source of all true life (Psalm 36:9). Because God desires to give His life to His people in abundance, He calls them to holiness and purity and provides instructions for living a holy life. When the Lord told His people in the Old Testament to maintain a distinction between common and holy things, He declared, "I am the LORD, who brought you up from the land of Egypt, to be your God: thus you shall be holy for I am holy" (Leviticus 11:44 NASB).

When God's people pursued holiness, they exalted God's holiness. Just as disobedience profaned God's name, obedience "sanctified" or declared God's name "holy." God said, "You shall keep My commandments, and do them: I am the LORD. And you shall not profane My holy name, but I will be sanctified among the sons of Israel: I am the LORD who sanctifies you" (Leviticus 22:31,32 NASB; *see also* 1 Peter 3:15, "sanctify Christ as Lord in your hearts"). Similarly, when Isaiah warned that relying on foreign powers instead of trusting in the power of God was to rob God of his glory, he said, "The LORD Almighty is the one you are to regard as holy, he is the one you are to fear, he is the one you are to dread" (8:13).

Many of the specific laws about clean and unclean things—such as foods—came to an end with Christ's work on the cross, but the principle of holiness that these laws symbolized remains strong for the New Testament believer. The apostle Peter wrote, "As obedient children, do not conform to the evil desires you had when you lived in ignorance. But just as he who called you is holy, so be holy in all you do; for it is written, 'Be holy, because I am holy'" (1 Peter 1:14-16). The apostle Paul called for us to live a pure life: "This is the will of God, your sanctification" (1 Thessalonians 4:3 NASB); "Therefore, having these promises, beloved, let us cleanse ourselves from all defilement of flesh and spirit, perfecting holiness in the fear of God" (2 Corinthians 7:1 NASB; *see also* 1 Thessalonians 5:23).

Holiness or sanctification is not simply commanded for the believer. It is, as we have noted above, clearly linked to the daily experience of God in our lives. The psalmist asks, "Who may ascend the hill of the LORD? Who may stand in his holy place? He who has clean hands and a pure heart. . . . He will receive blessing from the LORD and vindication from God his Savior" (24:3-5).

God is not only the King who allows the holy one into His presence, He is also the host of His home who invites the believer to dwell with Him: "LORD, who may dwell in your sanctuary? Who may live on your holy hill?" (Psalm 15:1). Eugene Peterson captures the thought of this verse in his paraphrase: "God, who gets invited to dinner at your place? How do we get on your guest list?"[4] The following verse answers the question by citing the qualities of holiness: "He who walks with integrity, and works righteousness, and speaks truth in his heart . . ." (Psalm 15:2 NASB).

The importance of holiness in the believer's life is evident also in the way that holiness is linked to life itself. The apostle Paul declared, "If you are living according to the flesh [that is, according to your own sinful will, which is contrary to God's holiness], you must die; but if by the Spirit you are putting to death the deeds of the body, you will live" (Romans 8:13 NASB). Thus sanctification or growth in holiness is viewed as an essential element in the Christian's life. After stating that the outcome of the things that we did before we came to Christ "is death," Paul goes on to say, "But now that you have been set free from sin and have become slaves to God, the benefit you reap leads to holiness, and the result is eternal life" (Romans 6:21,22). Between the initial salvation of being set free from sin and the final state of eternal life there is the process of growth in holiness or sanctification. The Christian is chosen by God "to be saved through [the process of] the sanctifying work of the Spirit and through belief in the truth" (2 Thessalonians 2:13).

Sanctification or holiness is also seen as essential for entering final glory. Jesus captured this truth in the Beatitude, "Blessed are the pure in heart, for they will see God" (Matthew 5:8). The same thought is elaborated more fully by the writer to the Hebrews when he says, "Make every effort . . . to be holy; without holiness no one will see the Lord" (12:14). The glorious final home of all believers is a place where "nothing impure . . . will ever enter it" (Revelation 21:27).

Clearly Scripture reveals that God has called us to be holy as He is holy. Without this holiness, we will die in hell. But, humanly speaking, why should we be holy? Why should we give up satisfying the natural cravings of the flesh to live a holy life? What fun is there in being a saint? What pleasure is there in living a holy life? What's in it for us? Why should we bow to some higher authority when we can be our own god and determine our own destiny? Frank Sinatra sang the theme song of every humanist, "I did it my way." Tragically, "There is a way that seems right to a man, but in the end it leads to death" (Proverbs 14:12).

It's easy to view the commandments of God as being restrictive, but in actuality, they are *protective*. They protect us from the god of this world and from self-centered living, which can only lead to destruction and death. Only in the will of God can the deep longings of our hearts be fulfilled. And contrary to what some people may think, a holy life is not a boring life. It is an exciting adventure on which we follow God into tomorrow and on into an eternity that is known only by Him. What would you exchange for the fruit of the Spirit—that is, love, joy, peace, patience, kindness, goodness, faithfulness, gentleness, and self-control (Galatians 5:22,23)? A new car or an expensive house? Fame and fortune? An earthly title or academic degree? There is nothing inherently wrong with any of those things, but they will not give you what a Spirit-filled life of holiness can. Only this kind of life can give everybody what they long for. Apart from God, we really don't know what is best for us as this following poem expresses:

I asked God for strength, that I might achieve;
　I was made weak, that I might learn humbly to obey.
I asked for health, that I might do greater things;
　I was given infirmity, that I might do better things.
I asked for riches, that I might be happy;
　I was given poverty, that I might be wise.
I asked for power, that I might have the praise of men;
　I was given weakness, that I might feel the need of God.
I asked for all things, that I might enjoy life;
　I was given life, that I might enjoy all things.
I got nothing I asked for, but everything I hoped for;
　Almost despite myself, my unspoken prayers were
　answered. I am among all men, most richly blessed!

—Author unknown

So how do we grow in holiness or sanctification? What part do we play and what part does God play? What means does God use in our sanctification? Is growing difficult or is it easy? What helps us to grow or hinders us from growing? These questions and others are all part of understanding how we grow as Christians—or, how the common is made holy.

2

Being Saved and Sanctified

*Now that you have been set free from sin and have become
slaves to God, the benefit you reap leads to holiness, and the result is eternal life. For the wages of sin is death, but the gift of
God is eternal life in Christ Jesus our Lord.*

—Romans 6:22,23

Slavery in the United States was abolished by the Thirteenth Amendment on December 18, 1865. How many slaves
were there on December 19? In reality, none, but many still
lived like slaves. They did because they never learned the truth.
Others knew and even believed that they were free, but chose
to continue living as they had always been taught.

Many plantation owners were devastated by this proclamation of emancipation. "We're ruined! Slavery has been abolished. We've lost the battle to keep our slaves." But their chief
spokesman slyly responded, "Not necessarily. As long as these
people think they're still slaves, the proclamation of emancipation will have no practical effect. You don't have a legal right
over them anymore, but many of them don't know it. Keep
your slaves from learning the truth, and your control over them
will not even be challenged."

"But what if the news spreads?"

"Don't panic. We have another barrel on our gun. We may not be able to keep them from hearing the news, but we can still keep them from understanding it. They don't call me the father of lies for nothing. We still have the potential to deceive the whole world. Just tell them that they misunderstood the Thirteenth Amendment. Tell them that they are going to be free, not that they are free already. The truth they heard is just positional truth, not actual truth. Someday they may receive the benefits, but not now."

"But, they'll expect me to say that. They won't believe me."

"Then pick out a few persuasive ones who are convinced that they're still slaves and let them do the talking for you. Remember, most of these newly freed people were born as slaves and have lived like slaves all their lives. All we have to do is to deceive them so that they still think like slaves. As long as they continue to do what slaves do, it will not be hard to convince them that they must still be slaves. They will maintain their slave identity because of the things they do. The moment they try to profess that they are no longer slaves, just whisper in their ear, 'How can you even think you are no longer a slave when you are still doing things that slaves do?' After all, we have the capacity to accuse the brethren day and night."

Years later, many slaves have still not heard the wonderful news that they have been freed, so naturally they continue to live the way they have always lived. Some slaves have heard the good news, but they evaluate it by what they are presently doing and feeling. They reason, "I'm still living in bondage, doing the same things I have always done. My experience tells me that I must not be free. I'm feeling the same way I was before the proclamation, so it must not be true. After all, your feelings always tell the truth." So they continue to live according to how they feel, not wanting to be hypocrites!

One former slave, however, hears the good news, and receives it with great joy. He checks out the validity of the proclamation, and finds out that the highest of all authorities originated the decree. Not only that, but it personally cost that authority a tremendous price, which he willingly paid so that the slave could be free. As a result, the slave's life is transformed. He correctly reasons that it would be hypocritical to believe his feelings and not the truth. Determined to live by what he knows to be true, his experiences began to change rather dramatically. He realizes that his old master has no authority over him and does not need to be obeyed. He gladly serves the one who set him free.[1]

The gospel is the "proclamation of emancipation" for every sinner who is sold into the slavery of sin. Every person that comes into this world is born dead in his or her trespasses and sins (Ephesians 2:1), and is by nature a child of wrath (Ephesians 2:3). The good news is that we who are Christians are no longer slaves to sin. We are now alive in Christ and dead to sin (Romans 6:11). We have been set free in Christ. We are no longer sinners in the hands of an angry God. We are saints in the hands of a loving God. We are forgiven, justified, redeemed, and born-again children of God. We may not feel like it, we may not act like it, and others may tell us that we are not, but we have been sanctified in Christ and are being sanctified in Him.

When we were slaves to sin, we could not free ourselves. And now, as believers, we cannot do for ourselves what Christ has already done for us. Not understanding what Christ has already accomplished for us has resulted in many Christians desperately trying to become somebody they already are. On the other hand, some people are claiming a perfection that has not yet been realized. If we want to mature in our relationship with God, then we need to understand the difference between what Christ has already accomplished for us and what still needs to be done. We also need to know what part Christ plays in our sanctification, and what part we play.

Understanding the Gospel

The idea of freedom is very much a part of the Old Testament meaning of salvation. The primary Old Testament term for *salvation* (Hebrew, *yasa*) meant "to be roomy or broad. . . . Since this (the making spacious for the one constricted) takes place through the saving intervention of a third party in favor of the oppressed and in opposition to his oppressor, we get the sense 'to come to the rescue' and 'to experience rescue'."[2]

The idea of salvation in the New Testament carries over the meaning of deliverance and freedom. Paul said, "It is for freedom that Christ has set us free. Stand firm, then, and do not let yourselves be burdened again by a yoke of slavery" (Galatians 5:1). In other words, don't put yourself back under the law as a means by which you relate to God, because you have been set free in Christ.

The root word for *salvation* (Greek, *sozo*) communicates the notion of wholeness, soundness, and health. This New Testament word for salvation helps us to understand that holiness is not just getting rid of sin. Rather, holiness is freeing us from all the hindrances that would prevent us from being all that we were created to be. Salvation, in its broadest sense, includes deliverance from all that hinders fallen humanity from becoming complete in Christ according to God's creative design.

We dare not miss this important understanding of salvation. What Adam and Eve lost as a result of their sin was life. They died spiritually—that is, they lost their relationship with God and became slaves to sin. Every person since that time has been born physically alive but spiritually dead. Physical death would also be a consequence of Adam and Eve's sin, but not for hundreds of years.

Having no relationship with God, Adam and Eve began a hopeless search for significance. They, like all their descendants, tried to understand the purpose and meaning of life in their natural state of existence. They wondered, as does the natural man today, *Who are we, and why are we here?* In the search for an answer, however, fallen humanity has "exchanged the truth of God for a lie, and worshiped and served created things rather than the Creator" (Roman 1:25). Having no adequate answer, people have accepted their identity from their physical appearance, their social status, and the roles they play.

Trying to make sense of life independently of God is futile, and nobody epitomized that more than Solomon. He appeared to have it all—power, position, status, wealth, and sex (he had 1,000 wives and concubines). He owned the plantation! He had everything that men fight and kill for, but something was missing. Believing that he was the master of his fate and the captain of his soul, he sought to find purpose and meaning in life independently of God. Not only did Solomon have the position and the opportunity to pursue the meaning of life, but he also had at his disposal more God-given wisdom than any other mortal. He wrote his conclusion in the book of Ecclesiastes: "'Meaningless! Meaningless!' says the Teacher. 'Utterly meaningless! Everything is meaningless'" (1:2).

For the most part, the church in the western world has communicated only part of the gospel message. Jesus is presented as the Messiah who died for our sins. If we will receive Him into our hearts, He will forgive us our sins and we will get to go to heaven when we die.

Two things are wrong with that presentation. First, it gives the impression that eternal life is something we get when we die. That is not true. Every born-again child of God has eternal life right now. "He who has the Son has life; he who does not have the Son of God does not have life" (1 John 5:12).

Second, if you were going to save a dead person, what would you do? Give him life? If that were all you did, he would only die again. There are two requirements for saving a dead person: One, you have to cure the disease that caused him to die. The Bible says that the "wages of sin is death" (Romans 6:23a). That's why Jesus went to the cross and died for our sins. Two, the other half of the picture is completed when you finish the verse: "The gift of God is eternal life in Christ Jesus our Lord" (Romans 6:23b).

The coming of the Lord Jesus Christ for our redemption fulfilled a twofold purpose. First, "the reason the Son of God appeared was to destroy the devil's work" (1 John 3:8). Satan had deceived Eve, and Adam sinned. Consequently they lost their relationship with God, and Satan became the rebel holder of earthly authority. Jesus affirmed this when He referred to Satan as the "prince of this world" (John 14:30). Because of what Christ accomplished, "the prince of this world now stands condemned" (John 16:11). Jesus "has rescued us from the dominion of darkness and brought us into the kingdom of the Son he loves, in whom we have redemption, the forgiveness of sins" (Colossians 1:13,14).

The second purpose for Jesus' coming was stated by Christ Himself: "I have come that they may have life, and have it to the full" (John 10:10). He was not talking about our present physical life, which He is going to make full by giving us an abundance of physical things. He was talking about our spiritual life, which is our relationship with God. The fullness of life is the fruit of the Spirit, which is "love, joy, peace, patience, kindness, goodness, faithfulness, gentleness, and self-control" (Galatians 5:22,23). He was talking about a redeemed humanity that is fully alive in Christ. What a wonderful gospel!

Salvation Is Past, Present, and Future

Many Christians are easily confused about the concepts of salvation and sanctification because both are presented in Scripture in the past, present, and future verb tenses. In other words, the Bible says we have been saved, we are presently being saved, and we will someday be fully saved. Notice the past tenses in the following verses declaring that "in Christ" we "have been saved":

> Because of His great love for us, God, who is rich in mercy, made us alive with Christ even when we were dead in transgression—it is by grace you have been saved. . . . For it is by grace you have been saved, through faith—and this is not from yourselves, it is the gift of God (Ephesians 2:4,5,8).
>
> Join with me in suffering for the gospel, by the power of God, who has saved us and called us to a holy life—not because of anything we have done but because of his own purpose and grace (2 Timothy 1:8,9).

When the kindness and love of God our Savior appeared, he saved us, not because of righteous things we had done, but because of his mercy. He saved us through the washing of rebirth and renewal by the Holy Spirit (Titus 3:4,5).

These passages clearly teach that every child of God has experienced salvation. We have been born again; consequently, we are now spiritually alive. Jesus said, "I am the resurrection and the life. He who believes in me will live, even though he dies; and whoever lives and believes in me will never die" (John 11:25). In other words, because of our belief, we are now spiritually alive and will remain so even when we die physically. According to this passage, we will never die spiritually.

Yet Scripture also tells us we are *presently* "being saved," as the following passages indicate:

The message of the cross is foolishness to those who are perishing, but to us who are being saved it is the power of God (1 Corinthians 1:18).

We are to God the aroma of Christ among those who are being saved and those who are perishing (2 Corinthians 2:15).

My dear friends, as you have always obeyed—not only in my presence, but now much more in my absence—continue to work out your salvation with fear and trembling (Philippians 2:12).

We do not work *for* our salvation, but we are called to work *out* what God has borne in us. As we will see later, there is a progressive aspect of sanctification that is similar in concept to the continuing process of salvation. That is, we are "being saved," and we are presently being conformed to the image of God. Bible teacher Charles Hodge makes clear this connection between sanctification and salvation in the following words:

. . . salvation principally consists in . . . transformation of the heart. Jesus is a Savior because He saves His people from their sins. . . . A state of salvation is a state of holiness. The two things are inseparable because salvation is not mere redemption from the penalty of sin, but deliverance from its power. It is freedom from bondage to the appetites of the body and the evil passions of the heart; it is an introduction into the favor and fellowship of God, the restoration of the divine image to the souls, so that it loves God and delights in His service. Salvation, therefore, is always begun on earth.[3]

Our salvation begins on earth, but it is completed in heaven. That is why Scripture speaks about a future aspect of salvation. Look at the following passages, which teach we "shall be saved":

> Since we have now been justified by his blood, how much more shall we be saved from God's wrath (Romans 5:9,10).
> The hour has come for you to wake up from your slumber, because our salvation is nearer now than when we first believed (Romans 13:11).
> Christ was sacrificed once to take away the sins of many people; and he will appear a second time, not to bear sin, but to bring salvation to those who are waiting for him (Hebrews 9:28).

We have not yet been saved from the wrath that is to come, but we have the assurance that we will be. "Having believed, you were marked in him with a seal, the promised Holy Spirit, who is a deposit guaranteeing our inheritance until the redemption of those who are God's possession—to the praise of his glory" (Ephesians 1:13,14).

Just like salvation, the biblical concept of sanctification carries us all the way from our new birth in Christ to the final perfection of glorification. Scripture clearly speaks of the believer's sanctification as already accomplished, as being accomplished, and as finally being completed in the future. These are often referred to as the three tenses of sanctification. In the next chapter, we are going to identify and explain these three tenses, and then we'll devote the rest of the book to looking at how we as Christians conform to the image of God.

3

Being Made Holy

When I was a child, I used to speak as a child, think as a child, reason as a child; when I became a man, I did away with childish things. For now we see in a mirror dimly, but then face to face; now I know in part, but then I shall know fully just as I also have been fully known. But now abide faith, hope, love, these three; but the greatest of these is love.

—1 Corinthians 13:11-13

Every living organism suffers through the three progressive stages of birth, growth, and maturation. Each stage has its own contribution, characteristic, scope, and limits as to what it can supply in the overall purpose of the organism. For example, who or what the person, animal, or plant will be is established at birth. From that stage on, no creature or plant can be anything other than what the Creator intended if it is going to fulfill its purpose. The growth stage cannot alter the organism; it can only ensure that the organism reaches its greatest potential.

Our new birth as Christians—or becoming children of God—is a critical part of our salvation as well as our sanctification. We were identified and set apart as new creatures in Christ from the moment we were born again. Anyone who is a Christian has already been born as a child of God. Next in the process is growth, which calls for us to put off childish things and grow in our relationship with God. As the apostle Paul indicated in 1 Corinthians 13:12, our sanctification is not complete in this lifetime because at this time we see dimly. We are presently growing in sanctification—with each stage of growth building upon the previous one—until the time of our final glorification.

As we consider this growth process, we need to be aware that there are three tenses of sanctification—past, present, and future. It's important for us to understand all three so we can see how God has made us holy, continues to make us holy, and ultimately assures us of perfect holiness.

Past-Tense Sanctification

The past tense is often spoken of as *positional* sanctification because it speaks of the holy position or status that the believer has "in Christ." The *positional* truth of who we are in Christ is real truth and it is the only basis for the *progressive* (present tense) sanctification that follows. Just as the past tense *reality* of salvation is the basis for the present tense *working out* of our salvation, so also is our *position* in Christ the basis for our *growth* in Christ. At salvation the believer is set apart or separated unto God and thus participates in God's holiness. Notice how Peter shows this cause and effect:

> His divine power has [past tense] granted to us everything pertaining to life and godliness, through the true knowledge of Him who called us by His own glory and excellence. For by these He has granted [past tense] to us His precious and magnificent promises, in order that by them you might become partakers of the divine nature, having escaped [past tense] the corruption that is in the world by lust (2 Peter 1:3,4 NASB).

When we hear or read about sanctification, usually it's connected with the present tense—our present Christian growth. But in Scripture, the words "sanctification," "sanctify," "saints," and "holy" are most often used in the past tense. For example, in his opening address to the Corinthian believers, Paul speaks of them as "those sanctified in Christ Jesus" (1 Corinthians 1:2). Describing the change that took place at salvation, Paul says, "You were washed, you were sanctified, you were justified in the name of the Lord Jesus Christ and by the Spirit of our God (1 Corinthians 6:19).

At the same time, Paul wrote sternly to the believers at Corinth because they had many problems. So when Paul said they were sanctified, he did not mean that the Corinthians were living righteously or that they were mature in their character. Rather, they were holy because they were "in Christ."

When we come to Christ, we are given "an inheritance among all those who are sanctified" (Acts 20:32). Similarly, Jesus said to Paul, "I am sending you to them [the Gentiles] to open their eyes and turn them from darkness to light, and from the power of Satan to God, so that they may receive forgiveness of sins and a place among those who are sanctified by faith in me" (Acts 26:17,18). According to both of these passages, by our faith in Christ we belong to the company of believers who are described as *already* sanctified.

The status of those who have been sanctified is especially prominent in the book of Hebrews, where Christ is portrayed as the great High Priest who is superior to the old priesthood of the Levites. As we saw in chapter one, holiness was of prime concern in the Old Testament laws that the Levitical priests served. Thus holiness—sanctification—is central to Christ's priesthood in Hebrews. Through His priestly ministry, believers have been perfected: "We have been made holy through the sacrifice of the body of Jesus Christ once for all" (Hebrews 10:10). Similar statements are made in Hebrews 10:29 and 13:12.

Sinner or Saint?

Believers are not only said to be sanctified, the New Testament also describes them as "saints," which means "holy ones" (for example, Romans 1:7; 2 Corinthians 1:1; Philippians 1:1). Being a saint does not necessarily reflect a person's present measure of growth in character, but it does identify those who are rightly related to God. In the King James Version of the Bible, believers are called "saints," "holy ones," or "righteous ones" more than 240 times. In contrast, unbelievers are called "sinners" over 330 times. Clearly, the term "saint" is used in Scripture to refer to the believer and "sinner" is used in reference to the unbeliever.

Although the New Testament gives us plenty of evidence that a believer is capable of sinning, it never clearly identifies the believer as a sinner. Paul's reference to himself in which he declares, "I am foremost" of sinners is often mentioned as an exception (1 Timothy 1:15 NASB). However, despite Paul's use of the present tense in his words, it's probable that his description of himself as the foremost of sinners is a reference to his preconversion opposition to the Gospel. Taking this as a truthful statement, we can conclude that he indeed was the chief of all sinners. Nobody opposed the work of God with more zeal than Paul in spite of the fact that he could boast, "As for legalistic righteousness, [I am] faultless" (Philippians 3:6). There are several reasons why we believe 1 Timothy 1:15 looks back at what Paul was before he came to Christ.

First, the reference to himself as a sinner is in support of the first part of the verse: "Christ Jesus came into the world to save sinners" (1 Timothy 1:15 NASB). The reference to "the ungodly and sinners" a few verses earlier (verse 9), along with the other New Testament uses of the term "sinners" for those who are outside salvation,[1] show that the "sinners" whom Christ came to save are individuals outside of salvation rather than believers who can still choose to sin.

Second, Paul's reference to himself as a sinner is immediately followed by the words, "And yet . . . I found [past tense] mercy" (verse 16), clearly pointing to the past occasion of his conversion. Paul could not get over the mercy God had shown toward him who was the worst of sinners. Paul makes a similar evaluation of himself based upon the past when he says, "I am [present tense] the least of the apostles, and do not even deserve to be called an apostle, because I persecuted the church of God" (1 Corinthians 15:9). Because of his past actions, Paul considered himself unworthy of what God's grace and mercy had made him: an apostle that was "not in the least inferior to the most eminent apostles" (2 Corinthians 11:4; *see also* 12:11).

Third, although Paul declares that he is the worst sinner, a few verses earlier he also declares that Christ had strengthened him for the ministry, having considered him "faithful"—or trustworthy—for the service to which he was called (1 Timothy 1:12).

All this leads us to agree with Bible commentator George Knight's conclusion: "Paul regards this classification of himself as 'foremost of sinners' as still valid [present tense]; though he is fully forgiven, regarded as faithful, and put into service, he is still the notorious opponent who is so received."[2] The term "sinner" in 1 Timothy 1:15, then, does not describe Paul as a believer, but rather is being used in remembrance of what he was before Christ took hold of him.

The only other places in Scripture that may refer to Christians as sinners are both in the book of James. The first, "Wash your hands, you sinners" (James 4:8), is one of ten verbal commands urging anyone who reads this general epistle to make a decisive break with the old life. We believe this is best understood as calling the reader to repentance and therefore salvation. The second use of "sinner" (James 5:20) appears to be a reference to unbelievers as well. The "sinner" is to be turned from the error of his ways and thus be saved from "death." Since this verse is most likely referring to *spiritual* death, it suggests that the person was not a believer. In both instances, James was using the term "sinner" as it was used particularly among the Jews to speak of those "who disregarded the law of God and flouted standards of morality."

The fact that these sinners are among those addressed by James does not necessarily mean that they are believers, for Scripture teaches that unbelievers can be among the saints (*see* 1 John 2:19), as they surely are today in our churches. Referring to them as sinners fits the usual description of those who have not come to repentance and faith in God, since the rest of Scripture clearly identifies believers as saints who still have the capacity to sin.[3]

The status of "saint" is parallel to the concept of being God's "called" or "elect" ones. Believers are those who are "loved by God . . . called to be saints" (Romans 1:7; *see also* 1 Corinthians 1:2). They are "God's chosen [or elected] people, holy and dearly loved" (Colossians 3:12). They are "chosen . . . through sanctification by the Spirit" (2 Thessalonians 2:13; 1 Peter 1:2 NASB). God chose and separated them out from the world to be His people. As a result, believers are "holy brethren" (Hebrews 3:1).

By the "election" and "calling" of God, we who are believers are set apart unto Him and belong to the sphere of His holiness. Even though we begin our walk with God as immature babes in Christ, we are without question children of God. We are saints who sin, but in Christ, we have all the resources we need in order not to sin. Paul combined these two concepts of holiness when he wrote to the Ephesians. Addressing them as "saints" or "holy ones" in Ephesians 1:1, he goes on in verse 4 to say that God "chose us in him [Christ] . . . to be holy and blameless in his sight." God chose to make these believers already holy in Christ, yet His intent was that they mature in their character as they conformed to the image of God.

Made Holy Through Christ

Our positional holiness as believers is solely because we are a new creation in Christ. Believing faith joins us to Christ so that we now share in all that Christ is, including His holiness. As Paul says, "By His [God's] doing you are in Christ Jesus, who became to us wisdom from God, and righteousness and sanctification, and redemption" (1 Corinthians 1:30).

Our holiness in relation to Christ is illustrated by the high priest in the Old Testament, who was a type of Christ's perfect priesthood to come. The Old Testament priest represented the people before God. On his forehead he wore a plate on which was inscribed "Holy to the Lord" (Exodus 28:36). These words proclaimed that he and the people whom he represented—as well as all of the services that he performed on behalf of the people—were completely holy to the Lord. Similarly, Christ represents His people before God. As one who is totally "holy" (Mark 1:24; Acts 4:27; Revelation 3:7), He represents His people, who are now holy in Him.

When the Old Testament priest came into God's presence representing a people who had sinned, a sacrifice had to be offered. It was only on the basis of atonement to the people's sin that the priest could come before a holy God. So also with Christ. He did not need to make a sacrifice for Himself, but He did in order to bring us into God's holy presence. The writer to the Hebrews emphasizes that our sanctification or relationship to God is based on the perfect sacrifice of Christ for our sins: ". . . We have been made holy through the sacrifice of the body of Jesus Christ once for all. . . . by one sacrifice he has made perfect forever those who are being made holy. . . . Jesus also suffered outside the city gate to make the people holy through his own blood" (Hebrews 10:10,14; 13:12).

Past-tense sanctification, then, means that we as believers have been brought by God into the sphere of His holiness or purity. We have been brought into fellowship with a holy God. Scripture says that only those who are clean and holy can enter His presence to worship and fellowship with Him, and as sinners, we could not enter His holy presence. But by faith in Christ, who sacrificed Himself to cleanse us of our sins, we are joined to Him and have been invited into the very "holy of holies" of heaven to have fellowship with God. Christ's sacrifice for our sins means that God no longer holds the uncleanness of our sins against us. He now welcomes us into His holy presence because we are clothed in Christ's holiness.

What About Sin?

As believers, we still have the capacity to sin when we choose to believe Satan's lies and walk according to the flesh. But because of Christ and His sacrifice, this unfortunate choice does not disbar us from God's presence: "The death he [Christ] died, he died to sin *once for all*" (Romans 6:10, emphasis added). You may ask, "I can accept the truth that Christ has forgiven me for my past sins, but what about my future sins?" Christ died "once for all"—for *all* your sins! Hebrews 10:14 tells us that "by one sacrifice [Christ] has made perfect forever those who are being made holy." Despite the fact that we do sin, God says that "we have confidence to enter the Most Holy Place by the blood of Jesus . . . and since we have a great priest over the house of God, let us draw near to God with a sincere heart in full assurance of faith, having our hearts sprinkled to cleanse us" (Hebrews 10:19-22).

Past-tense sanctification does not mean that we do not sin or have no sin. "If we claim to be without sin, we deceive ourselves and the truth is not in us" (1 John 1:8). It's important to know that "having" sin and "being" basically sinful by nature are two totally different issues. Some people say that making such a distinction denies the doctrine of depravity—the teaching that man is utterly helpless in his sin state. That is not true. The slave was indeed a slave, and there was nothing he could do about it. We must keep in mind that John Calvin's teaching on depravity was a doctrine of the lost, not the saved. To say that Christians are still depraved is like the plantation owner telling his slaves that they really aren't free, but they will be someday.

Some people have suggested that telling people who they are in Christ will give them a license to sin. They insist on identifying Christians as sinners saved by grace, but then expect them to act as saints!

We disagree with such thinking and believe strongly that telling people who they are in Christ actually motivates them toward holy living. "The Spirit himself testifies with our spirit that we are God's children" (Romans 8:16). We surely were sinners and in desperate need of the grace of God, but "now we are children of God, and what we will be has not yet been made known. But we know that when he appears, we shall be like him, for we shall see him as he is. Everyone who has this hope in him purifies himself, just as he is pure" (1 John 3:3).

We were depraved when we were dead in our trespasses and sins, but are we still so depraved? If we are still fundamentally sinners by nature, then shouldn't the dominant pattern of our life be to live in sin? Is that what saints do? No; John says that those who understand they are children of God and have their hope fixed on Jesus purify themselves. They live according to who they really are—children of God.

Present-Tense Sanctification

God performed a gracious work when He called us out of darkness into His marvelous light and granted us the status of holiness by virtue of our union with Christ. He did this so that He could carry on His work of making us holy. The process of growing from carnality to Christlikeness is commonly known as present-tense sanctification, or *progressive sanctification*. It is also sometimes called *experiential sanctification*. Paul says, "Now that you have been set free from sin and have become slaves to God, the benefit you reap leads to holiness [or sanctification], and the result is eternal life" (Romans 6:22).

The concept of progressive sanctification is the present focus of God's work in our lives, so it's important that we understand it. We can define it as God working in the lives of His people, setting them free from sin's bondage and progressively renewing them into the image of His own holiness in attitude, character, and actions of life. The Westminster Catechism defines sanctification as "the work of God's free grace whereby we are renewed in the whole man after the image of God and are enabled more and more to die unto sin and live unto righteousness."

It is important for us to distinguish this sanctification from justification. In justification, God declares the believer righteous because of the righteousness of Christ, which is accounted to the believer. Justification is the act of a judge. It removes from the sinner the condemnation that is deserved because of the *guilt* of sin. Sanctification, however, is more the act of a priest, and deals with the *pollution* of sin. As the Reformed theologian Louis Berkhof explains, it is "that gracious and continuous operation of the Holy Spirit, by which He delivers the justified sinner from the pollution of sin, renews his whole nature in the image of God, and enables him to perform good works."[4]

Justification and sanctification are distinct concepts—the former more related to the guilt of sin, and the latter to its pollution. But they are vitally related. When we are joined to Christ through faith, we are clothed in His righteousness and thereby stand justified before God. In Christ's righteousness we stand in a right relationship to God in relation to His righteous law. As we saw in our discussion about past-tense sanctification, we are also positionally sanctified. We are accepted into God's presence as clean and pure in Christ's holiness. And at the same moment that we became justified and sanctified positionally, the Spirit of God came into our lives and began the process of transforming our character through progressive sanctification, or Christian growth.

Scripture presents progressive sanctification as a challenge to believers. "Having these promises, beloved, let us cleanse ourselves from all defilement of flesh and spirit, perfecting holiness in the fear of God" (2 Corinthians 7:1 NASB). We are urged to sexual purity because "it is God's will that you should be sanctified" (1 Thessalonians 4:3). Elsewhere we are told, "Make every effort to live in peace with all men and to be holy; without holiness no one will see the Lord" (Hebrews 12:14).

Conforming to God's Image

Although the Bible speaks of past-tense sanctification much more frequently than present-tense sanctification, the concept of progressively being made holy is a dominant theme of Scripture. Terms like "growth," "edification," "building up," "transformation," "purification," "renewing," and so on are all related: they refer to the process of conforming to the image of God.

Let's look at two Bible passages that show this conforming process and see what they reveal about it.

> *Colossians 2:6,7*—As you therefore have received Christ Jesus the Lord, so walk in Him, having been firmly rooted and now being built up in Him and established in your faith, just as you were instructed, and overflowing with gratitude (NASB).

The phrase "having been firmly rooted . . . in Him" refers to past-tense sanctification. This shows how necessary it is to first be firmly rooted in Christ before we can be built up in Him. Unfortunately, few people in our churches are firmly rooted in Christ. Most don't have any idea who they are in Christ nor what it means to be a child of God. Many are trying to grow on their own effort, but apart from Christ, they can do nothing (John 15:5). We are all saved by faith, and we are sanctified by faith. We cannot grow spiritually on our own.

Every hope we have for living the Christian life comes solely from the grace and life of God. All of Paul's theology is rooted in Christ. He wrote to the church in Corinth, "I have sent to you Timothy, who is my beloved and faithful child in the Lord, and he will remind you of my ways which are in Christ, just as I teach everywhere in every church" (1 Corinthians 4:17 NASB). Terms like "in Christ," "in Him," or "in the Beloved" are among the most repeated phrases in the epistles. They confirm that we as new creatures are in union with God: we are alive in Christ.

1 John 2:12-14—I write to you, dear children, because your sins have been forgiven on account of his name. I write to you, fathers, because you have known him who is from the beginning. I write to you, young men, because you have overcome the evil one. I write to you, dear children, because you have known the Father. I write to you, fathers, because you have known him who is from the beginning. I write to you, young men, because you are strong, and the word of God lives in you, and you have overcome the evil one.

In Colossians, Paul said you have to be rooted in Christ before you can be built up in Him, and you have to be built up before you can walk in Him. John uses the metaphors of little children, young men, and fathers to describe the process of growing up. Little children are those who have entered into a knowledge of God and have had their sins forgiven. They have overcome the penalty of sin. Fathers, who are more mature, have had a long understanding and knowledge of God. Young men know the Word of God, are strong, and are characterized as those who have overcome the evil one. In other words, they have overcome the power of sin.

How are we going to help fellow believers mature in the faith if they don't know who they are in Christ and are basically ignorant of Satan's schemes? In all the years that we have been helping people find their freedom in Christ, the one common denominator of every person living in defeat was they didn't know who they were as children of God. They were like the slaves who had heard the news that they were free, but were still held hostage by the plantation owner with his double-barreled shotgun. Scripture continually warns against the blinding deceit of the enemy. What he does against the unsaved he continues with us if we let him: "The god of this age has blinded the minds of unbelievers, so that they cannot see the light of the gospel of the glory of Christ" (2 Corinthians 4:4).

A Key Clarification

Paul affirmed both past- and present-tense sanctification in the same epistle. In Colossians 1:28 he said, "We proclaim Him, admonishing every man and teaching every man with all wisdom, that we may present every man complete in Christ" (NASB). Then later Paul wrote, "In Him [Christ] you have been made complete, and He is the head over all rule and authority" (Colossians 2:10 NASB). In the first verse, Paul was admonishing the Colossians to be complete in Christ, and in the second verse he said they were already complete in Christ. How do we reconcile these two verses? In Colossians 1:28 the word "complete" means "mature" or "perfect," and refers to present-tense sanctification. Paul used a different Greek word for "complete" in Colossians 2:10, which means "to fill." The apostle's point is that "in Christ," we are complete—we have everything that pertains to *salvation*. That passage, then, refers to past-tense sanctification.

Scripture clearly presents both the past-tense and present-tense aspects of sanctification. We will confuse our walk with God if we emphasize one truth at the expense of the other. One extreme says our sanctification has already been fully completed. There is no need for any activity on our part to become like Christ. Such an extreme view has led some to believe that they haven't sinned since they became a Christian. These people have failed to see the present-tense teaching of sanctification.

At the other extreme are people who do not understand who they are in Christ. Therefore they fail to believe what has already happened at salvation, or don't recognize past-tense sanctification. These people are trying on their own to become somebody they already are. But we cannot do for ourselves what Christ has already done for us. We are already complete in Christ, and the continuing work of salvation is to "present every man complete in Christ" (Colossians 1:28).

The New Man: Becoming Fully Human

We are so used to sin and imperfection as characteristics of human life that we sometimes think that to be human is to be flawed. But such is not the case. Becoming holy is not simply about being conformed to the likeness of God, it is also about being made fully human. In the present-tense state of salvation, sanctification is the process through which God makes us the whole human beings He created us to be. He is restoring a fallen humanity.

Sin not only distorts the image of God in the human person, it distorts the human person as well. This is the necessary conclusion, since to be human as God created us is to exist in the image of God. At salvation, the believer has put on "the new self," which is literally "the new man" (Colossians 3:9,10; *see also* Ephesians 4:24). We will see later that "the new man" can refer both to the individual and the new humanity of which Christ is the head. What is important now is to see that the newness of sanctification is also a newness of our humanity. It's the renewing of our humanity so that we will be fully human as God intended in His original creation. The seventh-century theologian Maximos the Confessor, explained that we are truly human only in fellowship with our Creator: ". . . communion with the Logos is precisely the natural state of true humanity. Man is truly man when he participates in divine life and realizes in himself the image and likeness of God, and this participation in no way diminishes his authentically human existence, human energy and will."[5]

We see a clear picture of what it means to be humanly holy when we look at Jesus the man. As J.I. Packer says, godliness or holiness "is simply human life lived as the Creator intended—in other words, it is perfect and ideal humanness, and existence in which the elements of the human person are completely united in a totally God-honoring and nature-fulfilling way."[6]

Sanctification or holiness is often pictured as something somber, which is true in the sense that it involves the death of the old sinful life so that the new life can spring forth. But there's great joy in becoming holy because we're entering into the *fullness* of our humanity! Holiness, then, is not about conforming to the rules of an authoritarian rule-maker. Rather, "it is about the celebration of our humanity."[7]

Future-Tense Sanctification

In Scripture, the future tense of sanctification is beautifully expressed in Paul's explanation of the work and goal of Christ's sacrifice for us: "Christ loved the church and gave himself up for her to make her holy, cleansing her by the washing with water through the word, and to present her to himself as a radiant church, without stain or wrinkle or any other blemish, but holy and blameless" (Ephesians 5:25-27). At salvation, Christ set us apart to Himself that He might finally make us perfectly holy.

Paul, in his prayers for other believers, frequently mentioned this ultimate goal. As such, it would also have been the goal of his ministry. His desire was for the ultimate perfection of believers:

> May the Lord make your love increase and overflow for each other and for everyone else, just as ours does for you. May he strengthen your hearts so that you will be blameless and holy in the presence of our God and Father when our Lord Jesus comes with all his holy ones (1 Thessalonians 3:12,13—note love's central place in sanctification).

> May God himself, the God of peace, sanctify you through and through. May your whole spirit, soul and body be kept blameless at the coming of our Lord Jesus Christ. The one who calls you is faithful and he will do it (1 Thessalonians 5:23,24).

This concept of ultimate sanctification is expressed in other ways as well. Paul said this about God in Philippians 1:6: "He who began a good work in you will carry it on to completion until the day of Christ Jesus [that is, his coming again]." This sharing in the glory of God includes that final perfection of separation from sin and participation in the holiness of God (see Romans 8:30; 2 Thessalonians 2:14). Perhaps this is most clearly and climactically stated in terms of being like Christ. The destiny of believers is to "be conformed to the likeness of [God's] Son" (Romans 8:29); to "bear the image of the heavenly [man, or Jesus]" (1 Corinthians 15:49).

The Scope of Sanctification

Scripture reveals to us that becoming holy is all-encompassing. It involves the transformation of every facet of our being. Like growth in the natural realm, healthy spiritual growth involves growth in every part in proper balance. Paul prayed that God would sanctify the Thessalonian believers "entirely," meaning "wholly" or "completely." He prayed that their "spirit, and soul and body be preserved complete, without blame at the coming of our Lord Jesus Christ" (1 Thessalonians 5:23 NASB). When Paul spoke of spirit, soul, and body, he did not intend to emphasize that there were three different parts to a person. Rather, he was simply looking at the person comprehensively. The final sanctification which this verse talks about involves the complete holiness of all aspects of our being. Our sanctification in this life involves the progress of all parts toward that goal. A similar statement of the comprehensiveness of sanctification is found in Paul's prayer for the cleansing of "all defilement of flesh [that is, body] and spirit" (2 Corinthians 7:1 NASB).

The mind is to be transformed in knowledge and disposition (Romans 12:2; Ephesians 4:24; Colossians 3:10). The will is to be more and more bent toward the good and acceptable will of God (Romans 12:2). The feelings are to be purified and transformed in their love. Our physical bodies are to be offered to God for use in actions of love and righteousness (Romans 8:13,23; 1 Corinthians 6:19,20).

Sanctification, then, flows from the new heart of the believer, and since the heart is the center of the person out of which all life flows, true sanctification cannot help but touch every area of life. Bible teacher and commentator Charles Hodge said it well:

> Every thing depends upon this harmonious progress. If the arms retained their infantile proportions, while the

rest of the body advanced to maturity, deformity and help-lessness would be the result. Or if judgment and feeling gained their full force, while memory and conscience remained as in infancy, the mind would be completely deranged. The same law of symmetrical development is impressed upon the life of the soul. If it exists at all, it manifests itself in all the forms of goodness. There may be some kinds of excellence, where others are absent; but then such excellence has not its source in the divine life; or in a new heart; for that, in its very nature, includes all moral excellence. We feel it to be a contradiction to say that he is a good man, who though just, is unkind; because goodness includes both justice and benevolence. And it is no less a contradiction to say that a man is religious who is not honest, because religion includes honesty as well as piety. It is not simply intended that the word religion comprehends and expresses all forms of moral excellence, but that the thing meant by religion, or the new man, the principles of grace or of divine life in the heart, includes within itself all kinds of goodness.[8]

4

A Changed Relationship

Now a righteousness from God, apart from the law, has been made known, to which the Law and the Prophets testify. This righteousness from God comes through faith in Jesus Christ to all who believe.

—Romans 3:21,22

There is only one thing that separates man from a holy God, and this is sin. However, there are two orientations people have to sin that are diametrically opposite to each other, and both are debilitating.

The first category of people are those who seem to have no moral conscience or any awareness of their own sin. "Were they ashamed because of the abomination they have done? They were not even ashamed at all; they did not even know how to blush" (Jeremiah 6:15 NASB). These kind of people obviously have no relationship with God.

What's especially tragic, however, is the other orientation toward sin, which is held by those who have a relationship with God. They know that they are totally justified in the eyes of God, but at the same time they are overwhelmed by their sins and cannot seem to accept God's forgiveness. They feel compelled to earn God's favor by doing good and thus trap themselves in the bondage of legalism, and they are plagued with condemning thoughts by Satan, the accuser of the brethren (Revelation 12:10), and consequently question their salvation. Intellectually they know that "there is now no condemnation for those who are in Christ Jesus" (Romans 8:1), but they can't seem to rest in that truth. The following testimony from a missionary reveals this struggle:

Though I have been a Christian for many years, I never understood God's forgiveness and my spiritual inheritance. I have been struggling for years with a particular sin. I was in Bible college when I began this horrible practice. I never thought this living hell would ever end. I would have killed myself had I not thought that was a sin. I felt God had turned His back on me and I was doomed to hell because I couldn't overcome this sin. I hated myself. I felt like such a failure.

The Lord led me to purchase your book *Victory Over the Darkness*. I now feel like a new Christian, like I've just been born again. My eyes are now open to God's love, and I realize that I am a saint who has chosen to sin. I can finally say I am free—free of Satan's bondage and aware of the lies he has been feeding me.

Before, I would confess to God and beg His forgiveness when I sinned, but the next time I fell deeper into Satan's grasp because I couldn't accept God's forgiveness and I couldn't forgive myself. I always thought the answer was to draw closer to God, but I went to Him in confusion, believing I was a sinner who couldn't be loved. *No more!* Through the Scriptures and the way you presented them to me, I am no longer a defeated Christian. I now know I am alive in Christ, dead to sin, and a slave of righteousness. I now live by faith according to what God said is true. Sin has no power over me; Satan has lost his grip on me.

The True Nature of Sin

Growth in the Christian life is totally dependent upon God's graceful presence in our lives; therefore, to grow, we must be rightly related to Him. Prior to receiving Christ, sin separates us from the righteous and holy God. As the prophet Isaiah declares, "Your iniquities have separated you from your God" (59:2). Our natural state is described by the apostle Paul as "dead in . . . trespasses and sins" (Ephesians 2:1), and as a consequence "separated from the life of God" (Ephesians 4:18). Before a person can grow, then, he or she must have a relationship with God. This requires dealing with the reality of sin.

Scripture declares that all people are naturally sinners: "All have sinned and fall short of the glory of God" (Romans 3:23). All are "under sin" as an alien power that dominates their life and brings guilt and condemnation before God as well as self (Romans 3:9; Galatians 3:22). Horatius Bonar, in his study of God's way of holiness, rightly says, "He who would know holiness must understand sin."[1]

It is difficult for us to grasp the true nature of sin for several reasons. First, we have always been personally involved in sin and lived in an environment conditioned by sin. It is difficult—if not impossible—for us to fully grasp the difference between living in sin and living in righteousness because we have never experienced perfect righteousness and holiness. Our understanding is also limited by our finiteness; we simply cannot understand sin in its full depth.

Second, our understanding is skewed because of our own sinfulness. Most people tend to think less of their sin than they should in order to excuse themselves. Rather than confess wrongdoing, they do the opposite—they rationalize it: "Well everybody does it!" Or, "I'm not as bad as that guy over there." Those kind of comparisons are all relative as opposed to comparing ourselves to God, who is sinless. Self-righteous people don't seem to realize that to God their righteous deeds are like a filthy rag (Isaiah 64:6).

Third, our awareness of what is sinful can easily grow dull with tolerance and exposure to it. The profanity and explicit sex commonly accepted in today's television and movies would never have been tolerated 40 years ago. I don't know who wrote this poetic piece, but he said it well:

Sin is a monster of such awful mein;
That to be hated, need not to be seen.
But seen too oft, familiar with face;
We first endure, then pity, then embrace.

Fourth, no human has yet experienced the full weight of sin's consequences. If we all got at this moment what we deserved, we would immediately be cast into hell. If we only knew the damage caused by the sins we thought we got away with, we would cover our faces in shame. Secret sin on earth is open scandal in heaven. And despite God's occasional judgments upon sinful man throughout history, the full consequences of sin have not yet been poured out on anyone. For all of these reasons it is difficult for us to fully understand the nature of sin.

To better understand the true nature of sin, we must look at the cross of Christ. There, the power of sin was unleashed from hell through sinful men in an attempt to hate and kill the most righteous and loving person to ever walk on the face of the earth. The cross also demonstrates the power of sin and its full consequences, which is spiritual death, or separation from God.

Scripture not only shows the heinousness of sin, but also reveals it as a power superior over all human effort. It "reigns" as king over fallen mankind, leading to death (Romans 5:21). As such, the problem of sin and its power over our lives cannot be overcome by any natural means. Sin is not mere ignorance that can be overcome by education. Sin is more than bad habits that can be overcome by the practice of moral disciplines. It is more than a twisted personality that can be overcome by natural psychology. Sin is a power that enslaves us. Paul's cry represents the reality of all people under sin's domination: "What a wretched man I am! Who will rescue me from this body of death? Thanks be to God—through Jesus Christ our Lord!" (Romans 7:24,25). Only the superior power of God in Christ can redeem us from the reigning power of sin.

A Relationship Broken by Sin

At creation, Adam and Eve had a relationship with God. That is the intended "natural" state of humanity—living in fellowship with God. In this relationship, Adam and Eve were designed to grow in every way to full maturity as human beings. Sin, however, broke this relationship and assumed the place of God. The original sin of Adam and Eve reveals the essence of what sin is. The temptation (as is every temptation) was an attempt by Satan to get Adam and Eve to exercise their will independent of God. They disobeyed God by eating the forbidden fruit of the tree of "the knowledge of good and evil." The real essence of sin is seen in Satan's words, "Your eyes will be opened, and you will be like God, knowing good and evil" (Genesis 3:5).

To have knowledge of good and evil means to be the origin or determiner of what is good or evil, and what is true or untrue. Thus when Adam and Eve chose to eat of the forbidden tree, they were saying, "We reject God as the one who determines what is right or wrong. We will determine for ourselves what is good for us, and we think that eating this fruit is, in fact, for our good." They assumed for themselves the prerogative to determine what is right or wrong. They played right into the hands of the devil, who is a deceiver and the father of lies.

In a distorted way, Satan was right. Adam and Eve acted like gods in determining for themselves what was right. But what they determined *wasn't* right, and rather than embracing the truth that would preserve their freedom, they believed a lie that led to death and bondage to sin. All sin is the inevitable consequence of rebellion toward God; "everything that does not come from faith is sin" (Romans 14:23). Sin is the "unbendable bent of every person who does not possess life from God."[2]

Since God is the only source of life, living apart from God can only mean death. Being separated from God, Adam and Eve and all their descendants had to find their own means to survive. Ultimately, every act of sin stems from people's attempts to meet their own needs, establish their own identity, receive acceptance from others, seek personal security, and search for significance independent of God. Acting like gods, we struggle to gain acceptance, security, and significance through physical appearance, performance, and status. Any threat to our security becomes a source of anxiety or anger. Every manifestation of sin, from negative attitudes to hurtful actions, stems from the one root of all sin—namely, the desire to play god over our own lives.

A Change in Our Legal Relationship

God, who created the universe and all that is in it, has established moral laws—a divine moral order for the harmonious relationship of all created beings. Fellowship with God and others is experienced by living according to the laws of His moral order. Sin is the breaking of God's righteous laws, which brings a break in fellowship with God. We might say that sin is a breaking of our "legal relationship" with God. We are guilty of breaking His laws, and therefore no longer stand in a right relationship with Him.

As a result, the sinner stands under God's condemnation as a lawbreaker: "Cursed is everyone who does not continue to do everything written in the Book of the Law" (Galatians 3:10). Although Paul's statement has specific reference to the Old Testament Law of Moses, it applies to all people in relation to God's moral laws. In the Bible, all people are said to be "shut up," "imprisoned," or "under sin," which means that they are under the power and condemnation of sin (Galatians 3:22).

In Romans 3:19 Paul wrote, "We know that whatever the law says, it says to those who are under the law, so that every mouth may be silenced and the whole world held accountable to God." The word "accountable" in that verse "describes the state of an accused person who cannot reply at the trial initiated against him because he has exhausted all possibilities of refuting the charge against him and averting the condemnation and its consequences which [inevitably] follow."[3]

One effect of breaking God's moral laws is that we come under His judgment, or condemnation. This is not simply the result of some arbitrary decree made by God. A moral universe requires moral laws, and moral laws require that lawbreakers be punished. If lawkeeping and lawbreaking were treated the same, then there would be no difference between good and evil. Both would be the same.

Another effect of sin is that it not only brings guilt before God, it also brings pollution and corruption into the life of the sinner. It makes what is pure and holy become defiled and impure. It takes what is ordered and beautiful and makes it disfigured and ugly. The moral nature of a sinner, then, is the opposite of God's moral nature. And the Bible teaches that we cannot have fellowship with God unless we are pure and clean. Paul asks, "What fellowship has light with darkness?" (2 Corinthians 6:14).

Only people with "clean hands and a pure heart" can stand in God's holy presence (Psalm 24:3,4). David asked for a pure heart so that he could live in the presence of God and His Holy Spirit (Psalm 51:10,11). Isaiah's uncleanness needed the cleansing touch of an angel's burning coal (Isaiah 6:5-7). James commands, "Come near to God and he will come near to you." But then he goes on to add what is necessary: "Wash your hands . . . and purify your hearts . . ." (4:8). It is the "pure in heart" who will "see God" or experience intimate fellowship with Him (Matthew 5:8).

In summary, sin breaks our legal relationship with God, causing us to stand guilty and under the condemnation of God. Sin also breaks our personal moral relationship with Him, causing our nature to be impure and at odds with God's holiness and purity.

Restoring the Relationship

Let's suppose that an employee whom you personally trained to manage your estate suddenly decides to rebel against you. This happens because your most formidable competitor has been feeding him a pack of lies and wooing him over to his side. As a result, the relationship that you had very carefully cultivated and nourished for the employee's own good is broken. Your competitor then subjects your former employee to a subservient existence in a coal mine, which will eventually lead to black death. How many of us would be willing to do what is necessary to help save such a person? Our most natural response would be to say, "That self-seeking traitor got what he deserved. Let him rot in the coal mine." We most likely wouldn't be willing to take the initiative to win him back at any great cost—especially if we had to sacrifice the life of our own son!

No illustration can come close to capturing the incredible love that God demonstrates when He takes the initiative to restore a person's relationship with Himself—especially when the fault lies entirely with the sin of the person. "God so loved the world that he gave his one and only Son that whoever believes in him shall not perish but have eternal life" (John 3:16). It was *God* who sought Adam and Eve in the Garden of Eden after they sinned. He always takes the initiative. We, however, want to hide from God or pretend that He doesn't exist as we seek to cover up our guilt and shame.

Speaking of a Christian, Bonar says, "All that he can say for himself is, that he 'has known and believed the love that God hath to us' (1 John 4:16); and, in believing, has found that which makes him not merely a *happy*, but a *holy* man. He has discovered the fountain-head of a holy life."[4] A proper understanding of our restored relationship with God is absolutely essential to our growth, which is possible only in Christ. We cannot begin to grow unless the relationship is restored with the Author of life.

Our legal relationship is restored through what Scripture calls "justification." *Justification*, in this sense, is a judge's pronouncement of a person's right standing before the law.   The meaning of *justification* as a declaration of righteousness rather than the making of one righteous is clear from its use as the opposite of "condemnation" (Romans 8:33,34; *see also* Deuteronomy 25:1). When a judge condemns someone, he does not *make* the person a sinner, he simply *declares* that such is the case. So also in our "justification" God is not *making* us inherently righteous, He is *declaring* that we are in right standing before His law.

Our justification is thus God's declaration of our righteousness or right standing before Him as the moral Law-Giver of the universe. The condemnation due our sins has been removed. This change of legal relationship is totally a gift from God because of Christ's work for us. Romans 3:21-26 makes clear this truth:

> Now a righteousness from God, apart from law, has been made known, to which the Law and the Prophets testify. This righteousness from God comes through faith in Jesus Christ to all who believe. There is no difference, for all have sinned and fall short of the glory of God, and are justified freely by his grace through the redemption that came by Christ Jesus. God presented him as a sacrifice of atonement, through faith in his blood. He did this to demonstrate his justice, because in his forbearance he had left the sins committed beforehand unpunished—he did it to demonstrate his justice at the present time, so as to be just and the one who justifies those who have faith in Jesus.

Several truths in this passage are important to note. First, the righteousness which provides the basis for God to declare us right is His and not ours. It is a "righteousness from God, apart from law," or apart from our keeping His law. We are not going to be saved by how we behave, but by how we believe.

Second, the righteousness made available to us is the righteousness that is in Christ Jesus. This righteousness is based on Christ's work for us. Verse 24 says that our justification is "through the redemption that came by Christ Jesus." How it came by Christ in redemption is further explained: He was "a sacrifice of atonement," or more literally, a "propitiation" (NASB). He was a sacrifice that satisfied God's wrath and judgment against us as breakers of His moral law. Paul says in Galatians 3:13, "Christ redeemed us from the curse of the law by becoming a curse for us."

But the forgiveness of our sins through Christ's payment of the penalty is not all that's necessary for God to declare us righteous. Let us explain: Christ forgave us by taking the consequences of our sins upon Himself. Forgiveness erases the penalty of sin, but it does not provide us with a positive righteousness by which God can declare us righteous. Our need for a true righteousness is supplied by Christ's total obedience to God. We know this because Paul says, "Through the obedience of the one man the many will be made righteous" (Romans 5:19).[5] Because of God's work, we are "in Christ Jesus, who has become for us wisdom from God—that is, our righteousness, holiness and redemption" (1 Corinthians 1:30). This last statement helps to clarify the whole situation: Christ is "our righteousness" because we are "in him." We are, as Isaiah said, "clothed . . . with garments of salvation and arrayed . . . in a robe of righteousness" (61:10). This aspect of our justification, then, is supplied by the imputing or reckoning of Christ's righteousness to us so that "in him" we stand perfectly righteous before God.

Third, because the forgiveness and righteousness we receive is all from God, our justification is totally a matter of God's grace. We are "justified freely [as a gift] by his grace" (Romans 3:23).

Finally, our justification or right standing before God comes to us solely through faith in Jesus Christ. "This righteousness from God comes through faith in Jesus Christ to all who believe." God justifies "those who have faith in Jesus" (verse 22; see also verses 26,30). That justification is by faith alone follows logically and inevitably from all of the previous points. The person under sin cannot provide his own righteousness by which he might be justified. Forgiveness of sins and a positive righteousness in Christ are God's gracious gift to which the sinner can add nothing, and nothing more is needed. All that is "required" on the part of sinful man is to receive the free gift of eternal life, gratefully accept God's forgiveness, and believe that we are fully justified before God by virtue of the blood of the Lord Jesus Christ.

The Results of Our Restoration

The change of legal relationship brought about by God's gracious gift of justification provides results that are absolutely essential as a foundation for life with God, which is the only means to growth and sanctification. Paul writes, "Since *we have been justified* through faith, we have peace with God through our Lord Jesus Christ, through whom we have gained access by faith into this grace in which we now stand. And we rejoice in the hope of the glory of God" (Romans 5:1-3, emphasis added). These verses point to the fruits of justification, which provide the basis for growth in the Christian life.

It is important to notice in that passage Paul's use of the past tense: "We have been justified." Too many Christians live under a false condemnation. They walk on egg shells hoping that God won't find out what they are really like. When they make some little mistake in life they think, *I'm going to get it now!* They live in fearful anticipation that the hammer of God is going to fall any minute. Dear Christian, the hammer has already fallen. It fell on Christ. That is the good news. God loves you. "There is no fear in love; but perfect love casts out fear, because fear involves punishment, and the one who fears is not perfected in love" (1 John 4:18 NASB).

Peace with God. Because we have been justified, we have peace with God. Before justification we were enemies, alienated from God (*see* Romans 5:9,10). Now we stand in right relationship to Him. We are reconciled and therefore saved from His wrath. And now, no one can condemn us (Romans 8:33,34). Bonar writes:

> The adjustment of the relationship between us and God is an indispensable preliminary, both on God's part and on ours. There must be friendship between us, before *he* can bestow or *we* can receive his indwelling Spirit; for, on the one hand, the Spirit can not make his indwelling in the unforgiven; and on the other, the unforgiven must be so occupied with the one question of forgiveness, that they are not at leisure to attend to anything till this has been finally settled in their favor.[6]

It is significant that concepts of peace and righteousness are often linked together in Scripture (for example, Psalm 72:3; 85:10; Isaiah 9:6,7; 32:17; 48:18; 60:17). This fundamental principle is especially manifest in justification. God cannot make peace with sin. But through His gracious gift we stand justified in Christ, being clothed with His righteousness. Therefore we have peace with God.

If you were a sinner in the hands of an angry God, would you approach Him? Most people probably wouldn't. The Israelites were afraid when they saw God as a consuming fire on Mount Horeb. The occasion was the giving of the Mosaic Law, and we see their response in Exodus 20:18-21:

> When the people saw the thunder and lightning and heard the trumpet and saw the mountain in smoke, they trembled with fear. They stayed at a distance and said to Moses, "Speak to us yourself and we will listen. But do not have God speak to us or we will die."
>
> Moses said to the people, "Do not be afraid, God has come to test you, so that the fear of God will be with you to keep from sinning."
>
> The people remained at a distance, while Moses approached the thick darkness where God was.

The Israelites were afraid because they wanted to avoid punishment. They preferred a secondhand experience with God. That, unfortunately, is true of many Christians today. They go to church just often enough to get God off their backs.

Once they have their "fire insurance" against hell, that's enough. Some people feel totally inadequate to approach God, so they ask or expect their pastor or others to do it for them, just as the Israelites asked Moses to intercede for them. But we can't have a secondhand relationship with God. A pastor is not a mediator. There is only one mediator between God and man, and that is Jesus Christ (1 Timothy 2:5).

We as Christians do not need to live under any sense of condemnation, nor do we need to ask other people to intercede before God on our behalf. Although there is a place for possessing a proper fear of God's chastisement if we persist in sin, the greatest motivation to living a holy life should not be the threat of hurt. Rather, we should be compelled to draw near to Him out of love—a love borne out of gratitude for what He has done for us. We can run to Him knowing that He is our sanctuary. Let me (Neil) illustrate.

The school district in the farming community where I was raised used to have religious day instruction. Classes were shortened so students could go to the church of their choice. Those who didn't want to go to church went to study hall. One Tuesday afternoon, a friend of mine and I skipped religious day instruction and played in the city gravel pit. The next day the principal called me in and confronted me with the fact that I had skipped school. He concluded his remarks by saying that he had arranged for me to be home from school on Thursday and Friday of that week. I was in shock, thinking that I had been suspended from school for two days because I skipped religious day instruction.

I was terrified as I rode the bus home from school that afternoon. I was not looking forward to seeing my parents. . . . I slowly walked our long lane, fearing the prospect of having to face the wrath of mom and dad. I thought about faking an illness for two days, or maybe I could get dressed as though I were going to school, but instead hide in the woods until it was time to come home! No, I couldn't do that to my parents. Lying wasn't the answer.

There was no peace in my heart as I trudged up that lane, and there was no joy in my mind. Because I was suspended from school, there was no way that I could hide from my parents what I had done. When I told my mother, she was at first surprised, then she started to smile. "Oh Neil, I forgot to tell you that I called the principal earlier this week and asked permission for you to be released from school for two days to help us pick corn."

Incredible![7]

Had I known that staying home Thursday and Friday was already justified, would I have feared facing my parents? Would the ride home have been an agonizing experience? No, I would have raced up that lane and joyfully looked forward to seeing my mother and father!

Dear Christian, if we would just rest in the truth that we have been fully justified, we would go running to our heavenly Father. Because we have been fully justified, and through faith in Him we may approach God with freedom and confidence (Ephesians 3:12), then "let us draw near to God with a sincere heart in full assurance of faith, having our hearts sprinkled to cleanse us from a guilty conscience" (Hebrews 10:22).

Access to God. Justification through the gift of God's righteousness in Christ not only brings the cessation of enmity between the believer and God and a right standing before Him, it also brings the privilege of access into His presence. Before Christ made God's righteousness available to mankind through His work, only the Levitical high priest—on the basis of animal sacrifice—had access into the presence of God in the Holy of Holies. But now, because of Christ's sacrifice, all believers "in Him" can come directly into God's holy presence.

We will find unconditional love and acceptance when we come into His presence. Paul describes this as an access "into this grace in which we not stand" (Romans 5:2). The same thought is expressed in Hebrews 4:16: "Let us then approach the throne of grace with confidence, so that we may receive mercy and find grace to help us in our time of need."

What incredible good news! Bonar wrote,

> The gospel is the proclamation of free love; the revelation of the boundless charity of God. Nothing less than this will suit our world; nothing else is so likely to touch the heart, to go down to the lowest depths of depraved humanity, as the assurance that the sinner has been *loved*; loved by God; loved with a righteous love; loved with a free love that makes no bargain as to merit, or fitness, or goodness.[8]

Luther said, "Not to be under the law is to do good and abstain from evil, not through compulsion of law, but by free love and with gladness."[9] Tyndale said, "If any man asks me, seeing faith justifies me, why I work, I answer, love compelleth me; for as long as my soul feeleth what love God hath showed me in Christ, I can not but love God again, and his will and commands and of love work them; nor can they seem hard to me."[10]

A Change in Our Personal Moral Relationship

In addition to the change in *legal relationship* which takes place in justification, there is also another change that is foundational for Christian growth—a change in what might be called personal *moral relationship*. We have seen that God is holy and pure and only those who are likewise can enjoy fellowship and intimacy with Him. Because fallen humanity is by nature unclean and unholy, a change is required.

The change that allows us who are unholy and polluted by sin to have fellowship with a holy God is most often called positional sanctification. As we saw in chapter two, this refers to our holy position "in Christ." Even as the believer in Christ is clothed with His righteousness, so also he is clothed with His holiness. The believer is declared righteous not because of his own holiness but rather because of the holiness of Christ, to whom he has been joined through faith.

Positional sanctification is not fictional; a *real* change has taken place in relationship to our holiness. By the grace of God and His calling of us to Himself, we have been separated from sin and set apart for Him. As part of this *reality*, sin's power over us has been broken. We are to consider ourselves alive in Christ and dead to sin (Romans 6:11). Considering it doesn't make it so; we are to consider it so because it *is* so. Because we are alive in Christ, sin no longer has any rightful authority over us. We belong to a new master and are legally freed from the bondage of sin. For this reason some people have preferred to use the term *definitive* rather than *positional* sanctification to describe this foundational concept of sanctification.[11]

Definitive sanctification means that we are a new creation in Christ. We are no longer in Adam; we are in Christ. We can say with Paul, "I have been crucified with Christ and I no longer live, but Christ lives in me. The life I live in the body, I live by faith in the Son of God, who loved me and gave himself for me" (Galatians 2:20). This definite sanctification, which takes place at the point of our salvation in Christ, is the indispensable point from which we now grow in progressive or experiential sanctification. Progressive sanctification begins with the realization of our new position and the definitive change of relationship to God and sin in actual-life experiences.

This is not pie-in-the-sky theology or wishful thinking. Every child of God has been reconciled to God. Nor is this a peripheral issue in the process of sanctification. It is the core issue—our relationship with God, apart from which there can be no further growth. Consider these words from Paul:

> You are all sons of God through faith in Christ Jesus, for all of you who were baptized into Christ have clothed yourselves with Christ. There is nether Jew nor Greek, slave nor free, male nor female, for you are all one in Christ Jesus. If you belong to Christ, then you are Abraham's seed, and heirs according to the promise. . . . Because you are sons, God sent the Spirit of his Son into our hearts, the Spirit who calls out, "Abba, Father." So you

are no longer a slave, but a son; and since you are a son, God has made you also an heir (Galatians 3:26-29; 4:6,7).

Our justification through Christ's righteous obedience removes the condemnation from the guilt of sin, and our sanctification in Christ's holiness makes it possible to walk in fellowship with God. Prior to salvation, we could not fellowship with God, for light cannot have fellowship with darkness. Formerly we were "darkness," but now we are "light in the Lord" (Ephesians 5:8) and can have fellowship with a holy God who is light. We can draw near to Him and enter the "Most Holy Place" of His presence with confidence because of our sanctification in the holiness of Christ (Hebrews 10:19,22).

Recognizing Our New Identity

Peace and acceptance with God are what makes it possible for us to experience *practical* sanctification. True spiritual growth happens only when we have a personal relationship with God. Because we as Christians are no longer at enmity with God and are free from the fear of His condemning judgment, we can enjoy a relationship in which we are conformed more and more into His likeness.

This growth cannot take place, however, if we still see ourselves as slaves of sin and we live under fear of condemnation. Only as we see ourselves as sons and daughters of God can we really grow in holiness (*see* Romans 8:15). Only as we are free from the task of trying to gain a relationship to God by our own righteousness or cleanness will we be free to appropriate His righteousness and holiness for our growth.

Jesus chose His disciples that they might bear fruit (John 15:16). Notice that this challenge came to them as they were *already* attached to the vine. They were to grow from the position that they had in Christ, not to attain it. They were to grow from a position of "cleanness" ("you are already clean"—John

15:3). They did not have to work to become clean. Let's hear from Bonar again:

> Every plant must have both soil and root. . . . Holiness must have these. The root is "peace with God"; the soil in which that root strikes itself, and out of which it draws the vital sap, is the free love of God, in Christ Jesus our Lord. "Rooted in love" (Ephesians 3:17) is the apostle's description of a holy man.[12]

Jesus taught that the sum of our sanctification is love of God and our neighbor (Matthew 22:37-40). But we cannot love unless we recognize and receive God's love for us. "We love because he first loved us" (1 John 4:19), and "Christ's love compels us" (2 Corinthians 5:14).

Finally, Paul says that we are "transformed in his [Christ's] likeness" as our faces are turned toward the Lord and as we reflect His glory (2 Corinthians 3:18). But we will turn our faces toward Him only if we are friends. Bonar said, "Reconciliation is indispensable to resemblance; personal friendship must begin a holy life."[13] Through Christ, we are friends: "I no longer call you servants, because a servant does not know his master's business. Instead I have called you friends" (John 15:15).

As the beloved of God, we have the assurance that God will supply all our needs "according to His riches in glory in Christ Jesus" (Philippians 4:19 NASB). The most critical needs that all of us have, which are wonderfully met in Christ, are the "being" needs. They are life itself, identity, acceptance, security, and significance. Read through the scriptural list on the next page, which was taken from Neil's book *Living Free in Christ*.

In Christ

I am accepted:

John 1:12	I am God's child
John 15:15	I am Christ's friend
Romans 5:1	I have been justified
1 Corinthians 6:17	I am united with the Lord and one with Him in spirit
1 Corinthians 6:20	I have been bought with a price—I belong to God
1 Corinthians 12:27	I am a member of Christ's body
Ephesians 1:1	I am a saint
Ephesians 1:5	I have been adopted as God's child
Ephesians 2:18	I have direct access to God through the Holy Spirit
Colossians 1:14	I have been redeemed and forgiven of all my sins
Colossians 2:10	I am complete in Christ

I am secure:

Romans 8:1,2	I am free from condemnation
Romans 8:28	I am assured that all things work together for good
Romans 8:31ff.	I am free from any condemning charges against me
Romans 8:35ff.	I cannot be separated from the love of God
2 Corinthians 1:21	I have been established, anointed, and sealed by God
Colossians 3:3	I am hidden with Christ in God
Philippians 1:6	I am confident that the good work that God has begun in me will be perfected
Philippians 3:20	I am a citizen of heaven
2 Timothy 1:7	I have not been given a spirit of fear, but of power, love, and a sound mind
Hebrews 4:16	I can find grace and mercy in time of need
1 John 5:18	I am born of God and the evil one cannot touch me

I am significant:

Matthew 5:13	I am the salt and light of the earth
John 15:1,5	I am a branch of the true vine, a channel of His life
John 15:16	I have been chosen and appointed to bear fruit
Acts 1:8	I am a personal witness of Christ
1 Corinthians 3:16	I am God's temple
2 Corinthians 5:17ff.	I am a minister of reconciliation
2 Corinthians 6:1	I am God's co-worker
Ephesians 2:6	I am seated with Christ in the heavenly realm
Ephesians 2:10	I am God's workmanship
Ephesians 3:12	I may approach God with freedom and confidence
Philippians 4:13	I can do all things through Christ who strengthens me

5

A New Person with a
New Heart

In my inner being I delight in God's law.
—Romans 7:22

Every farmer understands cause and effect. If you don't feed the sheep they die. If you don't sow seeds in the spring, there will be nothing to harvest in the fall. I (Neil) lived on a farm in Minnesota, and after I finished eighth grade, my family moved to Arizona. I remember how excited I was to see palm and citrus trees. Fresh fruit was not readily available in most places those days, so the idea of picking an orange from a tree right in our own back yard was exciting. What I didn't know was that we had an ornamental orange tree, which was pretty to look at, but the fruit was not fit to eat. Ornamental oranges were a hardy stock, so the city used them in parks and to line boulevards.

Later I learned that these trees were used for root stock. The ornamental orange was allowed to grow to a certain height; then it was totally cut off, and a new life (such as a navel orange) was grafted in. Everything that grew above the graft took on the nature of the new, sweet orange, and everything below the graft retained the physical characteristics of the ornamental orange.

The end product was a single tree with hardy roots that went deep into the soil for water and nutrition, and branches that bore sweet oranges. What grew above the graft took on only the nature of that which was grafted in. Everything that grew from that seed bore fruit. Although the analogy given here is somewhat different than the picture Jesus gave of the vine in John 15:1-5, we're sure you'll see the similarities, which are significant:

> I am the true vine, and my Father is the gardener. He cuts off every branch in me that bears no fruit, while every branch that does bear fruit he prunes so that it will be even more fruitful. You are already clean because of the word I have spoken to you. Remain in me, and I will remain in you. No branch can bear fruit by itself; it must remain in the vine. Neither can you bear fruit unless you remain in me. I am the vine; you are the branches. If a man remains in me and I in him, he will bear much fruit.

Spiritual growth in the Christian life requires a relationship with God, who is the fountain of spiritual life. Only through this relationship can we bear new seed or tap into the root of life. As in nature, unless there is some seed or root of life within an organism, no growth can take place. So unless there is a root of life within the believer—that is, some core of spiritual life—growth is impossible. There is nothing to grow.

The New Birth

Adam and Eve were born both physically and spiritually alive. Because of sin, they died spiritually. They were separated from God. From that time on, everyone who has come into this world has been born physically alive but spiritually dead (Ephesians 2:1). In that state, man is completely unable to discern the things of God (1 Corinthians 2:14). Like an ornamental orange, he may look good, but the fruit he bears is bitter. All that it's good for is dropping to the ground and bringing forth more natural stock that will only look good for a season.

Every person is basically made up of body (or the physical nature) and the inner person (or the spiritual nature). According to Scripture, the center of the person is the heart, which has the capacities to think, feel, and choose because we are created in the image of God. In our natural state, "the heart is deceitful above all things and beyond cure" (Jeremiah 17:9). It is deceitful because it was born separated from God with an innate tendency to be its own god. It has been conditioned, from the time of birth, by the deceitfulness of a fallen world rather than by the truth of God's Word. According to Proverbs 4:23, the heart is the "wellspring of life," in which wickedness must not be allowed to take root. That is why we are to forgive from the heart and not allow a root of bitterness to spring up by which many will be defiled. Although no two-dimensional diagram is adequate to show who we are, the following is a functional depiction of the natural man:

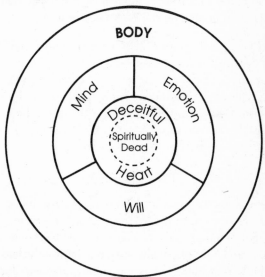

One of the greatest prophecies concerning our salvation is given in Ezekiel 36:26: "I will give you a new heart and put a new spirit in you; I will remove from you your heart of stone and give you a heart of flesh." In the new covenant (which every

Christian lives under), God says, "I will put my laws in their hearts" (Hebrews 10:16). Jesus came that we might have life, and the believer receives that spiritual life at the moment of salvation: "To all who received him, to those who believed in his name, he gave the right to become children of God" (John 1:12). In other words, "All the ornamental orange trees that choose to put their trust in God and believe His Word will become navel orange trees."

The moment you were grafted into the vine, you were sanctified or set apart as a child of God. "You are already clean" (John 15:3), and you will continue to be sanctified as He prunes you so that you may grow and bear fruit. You are now alive in Christ, who is the foundation and source for spiritual growth. In fact, you are described as a new creation with a new life that has new desires and a new direction. The following diagram depicts every born-again child of God:

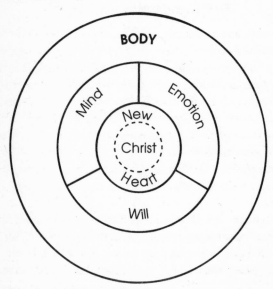

Our newness as believers in Christ is expressed in several meaningful ways in Scripture. The change from our old state of being spiritually dead as a result of sin is so great that salvation is described as a new birth. God has given us "new birth into a living hope through the resurrection of Jesus Christ from the dead" (1 Peter 1:3). We have been "born again . . . through the living and enduring word of God" (1 Peter 1:23; *see also* James 1:18). New Christians are called "newborn babies" and challenged to "crave pure spiritual milk, so that by it you may grow up" (1 Peter 2:2).

The best-known reference to the new birth of the believer is found in Jesus' teaching to Nicodemus: "I tell you the truth, no one can enter the kingdom of God unless he is born [again] . . . you must be born again" (John 3:5,7). The Greek terms that Jesus uses probably refer both to being born again and from above.[1] It is a birth from heaven by the Spirit (verse 8). This new birth of the believer is also described as a *regeneration*; we have been saved "by the washing of regeneration" (Titus 3:5, NASB). The idea in regeneration is "a new beginning."

Our Identification with Christ

Another way that Scripture describes our renewal at salvation is with concepts related to Christ's death and resurrection. Faith not only unites the believer with Christ, but also unites him with the death and resurrection of Christ. The apostle Paul said, "Don't you know that all of us who were baptized into Christ Jesus were baptized into his death? We were therefore buried with him through baptism into death in order that, just as Christ was raised from the dead . . . we too may live a new life" (Romans 6:3,4). Paul also wrote, "God . . . made us alive with Christ even when we were dead in transgressions" (Ephesians 2:5,6).

Paul, in his testimony, wrote, "I have been crucified with Christ and I no longer live, but Christ lives in me. The life I live in the body, I live by faith in the Son of God, who loved me, and gave himself for me" (Galatians 2:20). Paul was saying, "I died, but I live, obviously a new and different person" (*see also* Colossians 3:1-3). In other words, "My old ornamental tree has been cut off. I no longer live as an ornamental orange; I now live as a new navel orange. We as

Christians have a new identity, and it comes from who we are in Christ, not who we were in Adam. The apostle Paul consistently identified every believer with Christ:

- In His death   Romans 6:3,6; Galatians 2:20;
                          Colossians 3:1-3

- In His burial   Romans 6:4

- In His resurrection Romans 6:5,8,11

- In His ascension   Ephesians 2:6

- In His life   Romans 6:10,11

- In His power   Ephesians 1:19,20

- In His inheritance Romans 8:16,17;
                          Ephesians 1:11,12

A New Man

"If anyone is in Christ, he is a new creation; the old has gone, the new has come!" (2 Corinthians 5:17). It is possible to translate "he is a new creation" as "there is a new creation." Paul was teaching in this statement that through Christ's death and resurrection, a new creation has been effected, in which all things—including all of creation, the earth, and the heavens—will finally be made new (Revelation 21:1; *see also* Isaiah 65:17; 66:22; 2 Peter 3:13). The believer who has died and now lives in Christ is part of this new creation.

Parallel to the concept of being a new creation is the teaching that the believer has put on "the new self" (Colossians 3:9,10), or more literally, "the new man." The phrase "the new man" at times refers both to the new individual (or self) in Christ as well as the new humanity. Bible scholar F.F. Bruce says, "The new man who is created is the new personality that each believer becomes when he is reborn as a member of the new creation whose source of life is Christ."[2]

What does it mean to be a "new man"? Does it mean that every aspect of the believer becomes new? This may seem confusing because we still have the same physical appearance, and we still have many of the same thoughts, feelings, and experiences. Picture, for instance, an ornamental orange tree that has just had a tiny new branch grafted into it. The tree doesn't look all that different, but eventually we'll know there is a difference when we taste the navel orange.

Because so much appears to be the same when we become Christians, some people say that our newness refers only to our position in Christ. They say that our newness relates only to our being declared righteous (justification) and our positional sanctification. There is no real change in us until we are finally glorified. However, that would be like teaching justification without regeneration (we are forgiven, but there is no new life). If we are still ornamental orange trees even after salvation, then how is it that we can bear navel oranges? We *have* to believe that our new identity is in the life of Christ and commit ourselves to grow accordingly. A primary work of the Holy Spirit is to bear witness with our spirit that we are children of God (Romans 8:16).

Despite the fact that we at times live according to the old self, we are, in reality, new persons—new in relationship to God and new in ourselves. The change that takes place in us when we come to Christ involves two dimensions: First, we have a new master. As mortals, we have no choice but to live under a spiritual power—either our heavenly Father, or the god of this world. But at salvation we experience a change in the power that dominates life. Second, there is an actual change in the "nature" of the believer so that the propensities of his life or the deepest desires of his heart are now oriented toward God rather than toward self and sin. All of these changes amount to a new identity for the person "in Christ."

A New Master

At salvation, when you became identified with Christ in His death and resurrection, you became a new person and part of the new humanity. In this change you came under a new power that has dominion over your life. Nowhere is this expressed more clearly than in Romans 6:5-7:

> If we have been united with him . . . in his death, we
> will certainly also be united with him in his resurrection.
> For we know that our old self was crucified with him so
> that the body of sin might be done away with, that we
> should no longer be slaves to sin—because anyone who
> has died has been freed from sin.

The phrase "old self" in this passage is literally "old man."
The "old man" in relation to the believer has been crucified in
Christ, and he has put on the "new man" (Colossians 3:10).

The biblical concept of the new man also has a corporate
meaning, referring to a collective mankind—that is, the old humanity related to Adam, and the new humanity related to
Christ. The latter is the "new man" created in Christ (Ephesians 2:15). This corporate sense is evident when Paul speaks of
the "new man" as a *place*[3] or *sphere* "in which there is no distinction between Greek and Jew, circumcised and uncircumcised" (Colossians 3:11 NASB). The individual person or "self,"
however, is not excluded from this corporate sense, for all
people exist and have their identity in either the old humanity
and are dominated by its characteristics, or they are regenerate
and belong to the new humanity and are under its domination.

Again we need to understand that this is a reality that has
already taken place. Paul says in Romans 6:6, "Our old self was
crucified" (past tense). Some of us try and try to put the old man
to death and we can't do it. Why not? Because he is already
dead. We cannot do for ourselves what Christ has already done
for us. Because many Christians are not living the abundant life,
they incorrectly reason, "What has to happen in order for me to
experience the life of the new man?" The only thing that has to
happen already happened nearly 2,000 years ago, and the only
way you can enter into that experience is by faith.

A dear pastor who heard of our ministry asked for an appointment. He said, "I have struggled for 22 years in ministry
and I finally think I know what the answer is. I came across the
following passage, 'For you died, and your life is now hidden
with Christ in God' (Colossians 3:3). That's it, isn't it?" I

assured him that it was. Then he asked, "How do I do that?" I suggested that he read the passage just a little bit slower. For 22 years this dear man had been desperately trying to become somebody he already is, and many other believers have been doing likewise. It is not *what* we do that determines who we are, it is *who* we are that determines what we do. We don't labor in the vineyard hoping that God may someday love us. God already loves us, and that is why we labor in the vineyard. We don't serve God with the hope that someday He will accept us. We already are accepted in the Beloved; that is why we serve Him.

Too many Christians are trying to show that the Bible is true by the way they live. It will never work for them. We believe what God says is true and live accordingly by faith, and then it works out in our experience. If we try to make it true by our experience, we will never get there. Paul points out the futility of such thinking in Galatians 3:2: "I would like to learn just one thing from you: Did you receive the Spirit by observing the law, or by believing what you heard? Are you so foolish? After beginning with the Spirit, are you now trying to attain your goal by human effort?"

We are saved by faith, and we walk or live by faith. We have been sanctified by faith, and we are being sanctified by faith alone. We are neither saved nor sanctified by how we behave, but by how we believe.

Freedom from Sin and Death

When we become a new creation in Christ, there is a change of dominion over our lives. Both the old and new spheres of life—or the old man and new man—are spheres of existence which are determined by events and the powers associated with them. The old man is determined by the sin of Adam and is therefore dominated by the power of sin. The new man is determined by the righteous obedience of Christ and is ruled by the power of the new resurrection life of Christ. Dying to the old sphere means dying to the powers that dominated it and coming into a new life under a new power.

The change of power over our lives as believers is described by the apostle Paul in Romans 6:6,7. Our old self—that is, our unregenerate self as individuals existing in the old natural sphere of sinfulness—was crucified so that the "body of sin might be done away with, that we should no longer be slaves to sin." Before we became new creations in Christ, we were slaves to sin (*see also* 6:16,17; *see also* Romans 7:23,25, "the law of sin"), or to "impurity and to ever-increasing wickedness" (Romans 6:19). We had no choice because we were born physically alive but spiritually dead, and Scripture says that "sin reigned in death" (Romans 5:21) and thus death reigned over us (5:14,17). Living in the sphere of the old man included slavery to the law (*see* Romans 7:1-6; Galatians 4:9,10). This is not in the sense that the law is sin, but that living in the sphere of the old man and sin we were under the curse of the law (Galatians 3:13).

But our slavery to sin and death and the various servitudes that were involved have come to an end through our death and resurrection in Christ. The goal of our crucifixion with Christ was "so that the body of sin might be done away with, that we should no longer be slaves to sin" (Romans 6:6). The "body of sin" refers to the person or self (living in the present bodily form) under the rule of sin. This person was "done away with" by being crucified with Christ. The Greek term translated "done away with" can mean "rendered ineffective or powerless," "destroyed," "brought to an end," or "released from."[4] The *New Jerusalem Bible* translates Paul's words as follows: "so that the self that belonged to sin should be destroyed and we should be freed from the slavery of sin." In other words, the old self that was in bondage to sin and therefore utilized all of his bodily existence in servitude to sin and its mastery died with Christ. Now, a new self exists, which is no longer under the taskmaster of sin. This new self can now utilize his whole being as an instrument of righteousness in service to God (Romans 6:11-13).

Free to Live Abundantly

Note that the way to the goal of freedom from sin is through death (Romans 6:6). Sin reigns through death. But when a person dies, sin loses its mastery over that person. Because the believer has died *with Christ* (participated with Him in His death to sin), he is free from the mastery of sin and lives a new life of freedom. This new freedom from sin is powerfully expressed by Paul:

> Just as you used to offer the parts of your body in slavery to impurity and to ever-increasing wickedness, so now offer them in slavery to righteousness leading to holiness. When you were slaves to sin, you were free from the control of righteousness. . . . But now that you have been set free from sin and have become slaves to God, the benefit you reap leads to holiness, and the result is eternal life (Romans 6:19-22).

Because of our union with Christ in His death and resurrection, we too live spiritually and eternally in newness of life—a life over which death (including physical death) has no mastery. This truth is made clear by Paul in Romans 6:8,9: "Now if we died with Christ, we believe that we will also live with him. For we know that since Christ was raised from the dead, he cannot die again; death no longer has mastery over him." Paul is so confident of this truth that he writes, "For to me, to live is Christ, and to die is gain" (Philippians 1:21). Put anything else in the formula, and it doesn't work: For me to live is my career, then to die would be loss. Or, for me to live is my family, and again to die would be loss.

Because death no longer has mastery over you, all that will happen when you die physically is you'll receive a resurrected body and be ushered into the presence of God. The person who is free from the fear of death is really free to live the abundant life in Christ, "because through Christ Jesus the law of the Spirit of life set [him] free from the law of sin and death" (Romans 8:2).

Just as the proclamation of emancipation brought freedom to the slaves in America, so too has the Gospel brought freedom to us. Paul says, "Now that you have been set free from sin, and have become slaves to God, the benefit you reap leads to holiness, and the result is eternal life" (Romans 6:22). The god of this world is to us as the plantation owners were to the slaves. Both still want to be served, and neither want you to know of your freedom in Christ. They will try to keep you from the truth that sets you free.

But Why Do I Still Sin?

If we are now free in Christ and we are now a new man, then why do we still sin every now and then? Let's see if we can partially explain why we still at times serve the old slaveries of sin and death. Since we were born physically alive but spiritually dead, we had neither the presence of God in our lives nor the knowledge of His ways. So during those formative years of our lives, we learned how to live independent of God as a natural person. When we came to Christ, we were born again and became a brand new creation in Him. Unfortunately, everything that was previously programmed into our minds was still there. Nobody pushed the "delete" or "clear" button as is done when erasing information on a computer. That's why Romans 12:2 says, "Do not conform any longer to the pattern of this world, but be transformed by the renewing of your mind." Even as Christians we can still choose to conform to this world by reading the wrong literature, thinking the wrong thoughts, going to the wrong movies, and having the wrong friends.

When I served in the United States Navy, the captain of a ship was referred to as the Old Man. In my first tour of duty I was assigned to a ship that had a lousy Old Man. He really was. He drank every night with the enlisted chief petty officers and belittled his commissioned officers. He was a very difficult commanding officer to serve under. But if I was going to cope, succeed, or survive on board that ship, I had to do it under his authority while relating to him as my Old Man.

Then one day he got transferred off the ship. I no longer had any relationship to him, and I was no longer under his authority. We got a new captain, and he was a good one, but how do you think I continued to serve aboard that ship? The way I was trained under the *old* Old Man, until I got to know the *new* Old Man.

Paul wrote of the contrast between the old man and new man in his own life. He was trained under the law, a "Hebrew of Hebrews; in regard to the law, a Pharisee" (Philippians 3:5). After conversion the old man (self) was dead, and he wrote, "I consider everything a loss compared to the surpassing greatness of knowing Christ Jesus my Lord" (Philippians 3:8).

We have a new master who has come to set the captives free from sin and death. God has "rescued us from the dominion of darkness and brought us into the kingdom of the Son he loves" (Colossians 1:13). Bible commentator Peter O'Brien observes,

> Like a mighty king who was able to remove peoples from their ancestral homes and to transplant them . . . into another realm, God had taken the Colossians (Christians) from the tyranny of darkness . . . where evil powers rule (Luke 22:53) and where Satan's authority is exercised (Acts 26:18), transferring them to the kingdom in which His beloved Son held sway.[5]

Under the dominion of God and His Son, the grace and righteousness of God dominates our lives. In fact, we "have become slaves to righteousness," which leads to holiness, and finally our reigning in life (Romans 5:17; 6:18,19). This truth shows that we have not simply exchanged one dominion for another. In actuality, our new servitude to God leads to a fullness of life that can be spoken of as our reigning in life.

When speaking of our being under another dominion, keep in mind that we are not talking about eliminating our own responsibility or power to choose. Within the slavery on both sides, there is a certain freedom on the part of the human being to "present" himself or herself to the master (Romans 6:13,19; 12:1). Nevertheless, the person is so dominated that he or she cannot escape the mastery of the dominion under which he or she lives.

A New Person with New Desires

Identifying with Christ in His death and resurrection involves more than an external change of master. It also involves a transformation within ourselves. Our very being is changed at its deepest level so that we now have new desires and new prevailing dispositions of life. By describing this as a "change of nature" we are using the word *nature* in the sense of our prevailing characteristics or dispositions and not in the sense of our nature as human beings. All humans have the same human nature, but that nature can have different propensities and forces at work in it. So when we talk about a change in nature, we are referring to a change in the *fundamental* orientation, propensities, desires, or direction of our person, including our thoughts and actions.

The newness of our person or self is seen clearly in the fact that we have been given a new heart. According to Scripture, our heart is who we really are as a person.[6] "As water reflects a face, so a man's heart reflects the man" (Proverbs 27:19). Just as still water gives an accurate reflection of what we look like, so also does looking into the heart provide an accurate reflection of who we really are.

God knows who we really are because He looks at the heart. In the Old Testament, Samuel could not understand why God had passed up the older sons of Jesse in favor of David. But God replied, "The LORD does not look at the things man looks at. Man looks at the outward appearance, but the LORD looks at the heart" (1 Samuel 16:7). In the New Testament, Peter encourages godly women to make their beauty the qualities of the "hidden person of the heart" (1 Peter 3:4 NASB).

We have been given a new heart because we have been made a new creation in Christ. In fact, it is the new heart that makes a new person. Our new birth means "a new heart" (Ezekiel 11:19; 36:26; *see also* Deuteronomy 30:5,6). "A man is not a Jew if he is only one outwardly, nor is circumcision merely outward and physical. No, a man is a Jew if he is one inwardly; and circumcision is circumcision of the heart, by the Spirit, not by the written code. Such a man's praise is not from men, but from God" (Romans 2:28,29).

The need for a righteous heart is the basic message of the Sermon on the Mount. For instance, Jesus said, "I tell you that anyone who looks at a woman lustfully has already committed adultery with her in his heart" (Matthew 5:28). He wasn't saying that a person committed adultery by looking, but that looking lustfully at a woman is the evidence that a person has already committed adultery in his heart. What needs to be changed is the heart. The heart not only reflects who we are, it also directs our life. We live according to the condition of our heart. That's why Proverbs 4:23 tells us, "Above all else, guard your heart, for it is the wellspring of life."

The last part of Proverbs 4:23, in Hebrew, literally means "for out of it are the issues of life." The heart is not only the fountain of our life, it also controls the course of our life. The direction that our life takes is determined by the heart. This is seen in Ecclesiastes 10:2, where we read, "A wise man's heart *directs him* toward the right, but the foolish man's heart *directs him* toward the left" (NASB, emphasis added).

Jesus taught that what we do comes from our heart: "Out of the overflow of the heart the mouth speaks. The good man brings good things out of the good stored up in him, and the evil man brings evil things out of the evil stored up in him" (Matthew 12:34,35).

Our whole life thus stems from our heart. Our thoughts, motives, words, feelings, attitudes, and actions all originate from our heart. As one person said, the heart is the "mission control center of human life."[7] The believer in Christ, through death and resurrection with Him, has received a new heart and thus has a new control center of life.

The Propensity of the Heart

It is the nature of the human heart to be controlled by an outside master. As Robert Jewett explains, "A characteristic of the heart as the center of man is its inherent openness to outside impulses, its directionality, its propensity to give itself to a master and to live towards some desired goal."[8] This, of course, is due to the fact that we are not the source of our life. We do not have the fountain of life in ourselves. The heart and soul of man were never designed by God to function as master. We are dependent creatures and therefore by nature we look outside of ourselves for life. Self-seeking, self-serving, self-justifying, self-glorifying, self-centered, and self-confident living is in reality serving the god of this world.

The heart is not only open to receive from the outside, but as Jewett's statement suggests, what the heart takes in also becomes its master, stamping the heart with its character. Jesus instructed His disciples to store up treasures that could not be destroyed, concluding with the statement, "Where your treasure is, there your heart will be also" (Matthew 6:21). Bible teacher D.A. Carson captures the significance of this teaching when he says, "The point is that the things most highly treasured occupy the 'heart,' the center of the personality. . . . and thus the most cherished treasure subtly but infallibly controls the whole person's directions and values."[9]

The change of masters from the dominion of sin to the rule of Christ and His Son, which happened when we became Christians, has thus effected a real change in us and our lives. Commenting on the apostle Paul's teaching of our transfer from under the dominion of darkness to that of the kingdom of Christ, Peter O'Brien says, "This change of dominion so vividly described under the categories of 'light' and 'darkness' and which had taken place in the lives of the Colossians (together with other Christians including Paul—'us') at their conversion was 'absolutely determinative for the life of the believer.' . . . They are now 'children of light' . . . (1 Thessalonians 5:5) and are to behave accordingly."[10]

Desiring Change

The Old Testament revealed that the heart is deceitful above all things and beyond cure (Jeremiah 17:9). While the heart of the new person still carries remnants of the old, Jeremiah's picture of the heart is not the dominant picture of the new heart of the believer. According to Scripture, the deepest desire of the believer has been changed. This truth is seen in Paul's words to the Galatians: "Because you are sons, God sent the Spirit of His Son into our hearts, the Spirit who calls out, 'Abba, Father'" (4:6). The cry, "Abba, Father!" is typical of a son speaking intimately with his Father and represents the believer's most basic relationship with God. This cry is determined by the presence of the Spirit, who brings Christ the Son into the center of our personality to live within our hearts. As Jewett explains, "The center of man is thus his heart; the heart's intentionality (or desire) is determined by the power which rules it. In the case of Christian man, the direction of the heart's intentionality is determined by Christ's Spirit."[11]

The desire or intentionality of the human heart is, in reality, its love. And it is our love that finally determines our identity. The identity of the believer is thus a person who, at his core, loves God rather than sin.

Someone once said that if we could see the very center of the Christian's heart, we would find it always at prayer. This corresponds with the biblical truth that under the new covenant, God would write His law on the heart of the believer, and that is the law of love: "God is love. Whoever lives in love lives in God, and God in him. In this way, love is made complete among us so that we will have confidence on the day of judgment, because in this world we are like him" (1 John 4:16,17).

The presence of sin in the life of the believer indicates that remnants of the old, disordered love of self remains. But those remnants now stand at the periphery of the real core of the person, who is God-oriented and thus bent toward righteousness in his nature. As Calvin says, "God begins His good work in us, therefore, by arousing love and desire and zeal for righteousness in our hearts; or, to speak more correctly, by bending, forming, and directing, our hearts to righteousness."[12]

This core of the new person is often not evident in conscious life, but still it is the dominating aspect of his being. As Bible commentator Franz Delitzsch notes:

There is a kind of will of nature that is basically self-consciously unreflected. This deep will of nature precedes the conscious actions of the person, and, in the believer, has been changed through regeneration despite the fact that residual effects of the old person still remain and continue to express themselves in the practice of life.

We might say with Delitzsch that the action of regeneration is directed not so much to "our occasional will, as to the substance of our will, *i.e.* to the nature and essence of our spiritual being."[13]

Thus the real Christian, in the depth of his heart, has a nature that is oriented toward God. Although he can still sin, this sin is related to a more surface level of his being, which can still act contrary to the real person of the heart. But these surface actions are temporary and do not change the real nature of the heart and thus the person's identity. In fact, this very issue may be the surest way to determine whether or not a person is a Christian. If someone did something that is contrary to the nature of God and he sensed no remorse or conviction, then we could legitimately question his salvation. On the other hand, I have talked to hundreds of people who are questioning their own salvation because they are struggling in their Christian walk. In almost every case, after hearing these people's testimonies, I do what I can to assure them of their salvation because what they are struggling with wouldn't even bother them if they weren't a Christian.

Our Hearts Affect Our Actions

The relationship of the real core nature of the human heart to its more surface activities is seen in Pedersen's discussion of "the soul" or what is perhaps better termed "the heart":

It [the soul] is partly an entirety in itself and partly forms an entirety with others. What entireties it is merged in depends upon the constant interchange of life. [We would suggest that what entireties merge into our heart is based on what we love, since love seeks to unite with its object.]

Every time the soul merges into a new entirety, new centers of action are formed in it; but they are created by temporary situations, which only lie on the surface and quickly disappear. There are other entireties to which the soul belongs, and which live in it with quite a different depth and firmness, because they make the very nucleus of the soul. Thus there may be a difference between the momentary and the stable points of gravity in the soul. But none of the momentary centers of action can ever annul or counteract those which lie deeper. The deepest-lying contents of the soul are, it is true, always there, but they do not always make themselves equally felt.[14]

This understanding of the human heart helps to explain the practice of sin in the believer's life as well as the "good" in the life of the unbelieving sinner: The true nature of a person does not always express itself fully in his or her life. But the basic identity of that person is still there, and in the case of the believer, it is positive toward God. This is clearly evident in Paul's description of a believer in Romans 7:14-25, which we'll look at now.

Love for God, Hatred for Sin

The identity of the person described in that passage has been much debated. Is he referring to himself as an unbeliever or a believer? And if a believer, is the description that of an Old Testament believer living under the Mosaic Law before Christ? Or is this a description of the "wretched man" who struggles to know the new life of a believer yet does so apart from the available power of the Holy Spirit?

> We know that the law is spiritual; but I am unspiritual, sold as a slave to sin. I do not understand what I do. For what I want to do I do not do, but what I hate I do. And if I do what I do not want to do, I agree that the law is good.

As it is, it is no longer I myself who do it, but it is sin living in me. I know that nothing good lives in me, that is, in my sinful nature. For I have the desire to do what is good, but I cannot carry it out. For what I do is not the good I want to do; no, the evil I do not want to do—this I keep on doing.

Now if I do what I do not want to do, it is no longer I who do it, but it is sin living in me that does it. So I find this law at work: When I want to do good, evil is right there with me. For in my inner being I delight in God's law; but I see another law at work in the members of my body, waging war against the law of my mind and making me a prisoner of the law of sin at work within my members. What a wretched man I am! Who will rescue me from this body of death? Thanks be to God—through Jesus Christ our Lord! So then, I myself in my mind am a slave to God's law, but in the sinful nature a slave to the law of sin (Romans 7:14-25).

It seems, in our opinion, that this passage is describing someone who has experienced the renewing grace of God. But it also appears to show this person in relation to the law of God apart from the enabling work of the Spirit of God. The passage certainly shows the powerlessness of the law to set him free. Thus it could have reference to the experience of a Christian who is living according to the flesh or in his own strength,[15] or to the experience of the pious Jew living under the law, viewed from a Christian perspective.[16]

We can be certain this person is not an unbeliever because of his likes and dislikes or his propensities of life. When we consider the actions of the person speaking in the passage, we find that all three dimensions normally seen as constituting personhood—that is, thought, emotion, and will—are oriented toward God and His righteous law. For example, he says, "I do not understand what I do" (verse 15), or perhaps better, "I do not approve what I do."[17] In other words, his thinking is opposed to his action of sin. This is seen again when he says, "I myself in my mind am a slave to God's law, but in the sinful nature [literally, 'flesh'] a slave to the law of sin" (verse 25).

His emotion is likewise seen to be on God's side in opposition to sin when he says, "What I hate I do" (verse 15). As Bible commentator James Dunn says, "He wholly detests and abhors what he does."[18] If hatred is the emotional opposite of love, then we can conclude that the speaker's love is directed toward righteousness. A further expression of emotion is seen when he says, "In my inner being I delight in God's law" (verse 22). And finally, his will or volition is also for God: "What I want [or, 'will,'] to do," he says, "I do not do. . . . I have the desire [or, 'will'] to do what is good" (verses 15,18; *see also* verse 21).

Only a believer, as a rule, desires to do what is good. Does the natural man delight in God's law? When we as Christians make public stands for the sake of justice and righteousness according to the Word of God, do unbelievers around us "agree that the law is good" (verse 16)?

Those descriptions of the personal attributes of the speaker clearly define him as one with a positive nature. But more than this, Paul goes so far as to finally absolve the speaker from sinning: ". . . if I do what I do not want to do . . . it is no longer I myself who do it, but it is sin living in me" (verses 16,17; *see also* the same thought in verse 20).

Within the same passage we clearly see the "I" or the speaker as the subject of sinful actions as well as being opposed to sin, so Paul is not trying to evade the speaker's personal responsibility in sin. Remember, it is our responsibility to not allow sin to reign in our mortal bodies (Romans 6:12). But notice that when the "I" or the speaker is related to sin, it is never described in terms of the functions of personhood. There are no equal statements of thought, emotion, and will on the side of sin. The speaker does not say, "I want to do the will of God, but I also want to sin." Nor does he say, "I love the law of God, but I also love sin." The true Christian hates the sin that enslaves him. Thus the "I" who is positively oriented toward God is the person in the deepest sense of his personhood or identity. He is the "I" of the "inner man" (Romans 7:22 NASB), the "I" who is the subject of the "mind" in Romans 7:25.

The assertion that it is no longer "I" but sin that actually does the sinning is similar to other apparently contradictory statements of the apostle, in which he points to the dominating power that masters him: "It is no longer I who live, but Christ lives in me" (Galatians 2:20 NASB); "I worked harder than all of them—yet not I, but the grace of God that was with me" (1 Corinthians 15:10). In these statements, Paul is not intending to disavow responsibility of free agency, but to affirm the existence in himself of a power that exercises a dominating influence upon him. The heart of the believer willingly assents to this dominating power. In the case of sin, as in the Romans 7 passage, the real "I" opposes it and can thus be set against it. Here, the ego or real "I" in the believer is viewed as so opposed to sin that they can be isolated from each other. And the actual commission of sin, instead of being the action of the ego, can be regarded as the action of the sin that enslaves the ego contrary to its will. As Delitzsch says, "The Ego is no longer one with sin—it is free from it; sin resides in such a man still, only as a foreign power. . . ."[19]

Romans 7:14-25 thus presents the real person of the believer as having positive propensities toward God. Though at times he commits sin both in thought and act, sin and righteousness do not in any way characterize the real person of the believer in the same way. The believer is capable of experiencing a double servitude, as indicated by Paul's words: "On the one hand I myself with my mind am serving the law of God, but on the other, with my flesh the law of sin" (verse 25).[20] This statement, along with the entire passage, confirms that the real person of the believer willingly serves God.

Every believer's nature has positive propensities; this is true of the most defeated Christian. He may still have remnants of his old desires, but they are not dominant anymore. His heart has been changed so that his deepest desire is now toward God and His way. The new prevailing disposition is a love for God and a love for that which is God—that is, His Son, His people, and His righteous ways. Charles Hodge shares the nature of this love for God:

The Scriptures give special prominence to the love of God as the most comprehensive and important of all the manifestations of this inward spiritual life. We are so constituted as to take delight in objects suited to our nature; and the perception of qualities adapted to our constitution, in external objects, produces complacency [complacence— "calm or secure satisfaction with one's self or lot"] and desire. The soul rests in them as a good to be loved for its own sake; and the higher these qualities, the more pure and elevated are the affections which they excite. It is the effect of regeneration to enable us to perceive and love the infinite and absolute perfection of God, as comprehending all kinds of excellence, and as suited to the highest powers and most enlarged capacities of our nature. As soon, therefore, as the heart is renewed it turns to God, and rests in His excellence as the supreme object of complacency and desire.

Love to God, however, is not mere complacency in moral excellence. It is the love of a personal being, who stands in the most intimate relations to ourselves, as the author of our existence, as our preserver and ruler, as our father, who with conscious love watches over us, protects us, supplies all our wants, holds communion with us, manifesting Himself unto us as He does not unto the world. The feelings of dependence, obligation and relationship, enter largely into that comprehensive affection called the love of God.[21]

A Vital Understanding

The believer "in Christ" is a new person with a new nature. This means that his deepest desires and the propensity of his life is directed toward God. Through death and resurrection with Christ, the real "inner person of the heart" has been born again. A new seed of life has been planted in the heart whose natural tendency, as is the case in all seeds, is to grow. It is absolutely vital that the believer understand this reality as a foundation for growth. Otherwise, growth in the Christian life and victory over sin is impossible.

Not understanding who we are in Christ can truly hinder our walk with God. The following testimony by one of our former students illustrates this truth. He was one of the most gifted, personable, and intelligent students that we have had the privilege of teaching. He attended one of Neil's seminars and later wrote him the following letter:

> I've always figured I was a rotten, no-good, dirty, stinking sinner, saved by grace yet failing God miserably every day. And all I could look forward to was a lifetime of apologizing every night for not being the man I know He wants me to be, "But I'll try harder tomorrow, Lord." As a firstborn, trying so hard to earn the approval of highly expectant parents, I've related to God the same way. He just couldn't possibly love me as much as He does other, "better" believers. Oh sure, I'm saved by grace through faith, but really I'm just hanging on until He gets tired of putting up with me here and brings me home to finally stop the failure in progress. Whew, what a treadmill!
>
> When you said, "You're not a sinner, you're a saint" in reference to our new, primary identification, you totally blew me away! Isn't that strange that a guy could go clear through a good seminary and never latch onto the truth that he is, indeed, a new creation in Christ?! I'm convinced that old tapes, laid down in early childhood, can truly hinder our progress in understanding who we are in Christ.
>
> Thank you for your clear teaching in this area. It has been so helpful and liberating to me. I'm beginning to grow out of my old negative thoughts about myself and God. I don't constantly picture Him as disappointed in me any more. I have been so deeply touched by what I've learned that I'm taking some people through a study of Ephesians so we can see who we are *in Christ* and what we have as believers *in Christ*. My preaching is different, and our people are profiting greatly, being built up in strength and confidence. Each day of service is a direct gift from God, and I bank each one carefully in heaven's vault for all eternity, to the honor and glory of my Savior!

6

Making the New
Person Real

*I urge you to live a life worthy of the calling you have
received.*

—Ephesians 4:1

The Christian life is full of what appear to be paradoxes to
the natural person. The path to glorification is death (John
12:23-26), and the path to exaltation is humiliation (Philippians 2:8,9). The first shall be last (Luke 13:30), and the one
who wishes to save his life must lose it. Understanding the truth
of this last seemingly paradoxical statement is the foundation
for Christian growth and living. Consider Jesus' words to His
disciples in Matthew 16:24-26:

> If anyone would come after me, he must deny himself
> and take up his cross and follow me. For whoever wants to
> save his life will lose it, but whoever loses his life for me
> will find it. What good will it be for a man if he gains the
> whole world, yet forfeits his soul? Or what can a man give
> in exchange for his soul?

The lack of understanding this central teaching of all four
Gospels might be called "the great omission." If what the Lord

is saying is not understood and personally appropriated, then fulfilling the great commission (going into all the world and making disciples) and the great commandment (loving God and your neighbor as yourself) will not be possible.

The occasion of Jesus' words in Matthew 16 was immediately after Peter's great confession that Jesus was the Christ, the Son of the living God (Matthew 16:16). Jesus assured Peter that flesh and blood had not revealed that truth to him, but rather His Father in heaven.

Then Jesus foretold of His death and resurrection in Jerusalem. Peter couldn't believe what he was hearing and rebuked Jesus. "'Never, Lord!' he said, 'This shall never happen to you!'" (Matthew 16:22). Jesus responded by saying, "Get behind me, Satan! You are a stumbling block to me; you do not have in mind the things of God, but the things of men" (verse 23). Peter, the noble confessor of the fundamental truth that Jesus is the Christ (Messiah), the Son of the living God, suddenly finds himself in league with the powers of darkness—the mouthpiece of Satan, the deceiver.

This memorable rebuke seems mercilessly severe, yet Christ's crediting of Satan as the source describes exactly and appropriately the character of the advice given by Peter, which is essentially this: "Save yourself at any rate, sacrifice duty to self-interest and the cause of Christ to personal convenience." This advice is truly satanic in principle, for the whole aim of Satan is to get self-interest recognized as the chief end of man. Satan is called the "ruler of this world" (Ephesians 6:12) because self-interest rules this world. He is called the "accuser of the brethren" (Revelation 12:10) because he does not believe that even the sons of God have any higher motive:

> Does Job or even Jesus serve God for nothing? Self-sacrifice, suffering for righteousness' sake, commitment to truth even unto death: it is pure romance and youthful sentimentalism or at best, hypocritical. There is no such thing as a surrender of the lower life for the higher life; all men are selfish at heart and have their price. Some may

hold out longer than others, but in the end every man will prefer his own thing to the things of God.

Such is Satan's creed, while man unwittingly serves Satan, being deceived into thinking that he is serving himself. Jesus counters by sharing the way of the cross: "If anyone would come after me, he must deny himself and take up his cross and follow me" (Matthew 16:24). Such a statement seems so austere—as though the Lord is asking for everything and promising very little. Nothing could be further from the truth, however, because he who wants to save his life will eventually lose it. Anyone who looks for his or her identity, fulfillment, or purpose for living in the natural world will lose everything. You cannot take your earthly gain with you. Whatever treasures you are able to store up on planet earth will remain here after you die physically.

By contrast, if you crucify the flesh and find your life in Christ, you will have the benefit of knowing Him now and for all eternity. If you shoot for this world you will miss the next, but if you shoot for the next world you will actually receive the benefits of living in Christ right now (as well as in eternity). Paul says, "Discipline yourself for the purpose of godliness; for bodily discipline is only of little profit, but godliness is profitable for all things, since it holds promise for the present life and also for the life to come" (1 Timothy 4:7,8 NASB). He's not saying that we shouldn't take care of ourselves physically, but he is saying that it has little value compared to disciplining ourselves spiritually.

Denying ourselves is the only way to put Christ back into the center of our lives. Some people perceive lordship as a negative doctrine, but it's not. Making Him the Lord of our lives is our only hope for now and for all eternity. If we make Him the Lord of our lives, then He is the Lord of our past, present, and future. He is also the Lord of all our problems, and we can "cast all [our] anxiety on him because he cares for [us]" (1 Peter 5:7). God is not out to get us; He is out to redeem us and restore us back to the state in which Adam was originally created.

For some unknown reason, it is the great ambition of mankind to be happy as animals instead of being blessed as children of God. The rewards of the latter option are much greater. When you deny yourself, identify with Christ, and follow Him daily, you sacrifice the pleasure of things, but you gain the pleasure of life. You sacrifice the temporal to gain the eternal. Some sacrifice! Only a fool would sacrifice his soul to gain in this world that which he cannot take with him. Jim Elliot, the missionary martyred in Ecuador, said, "He is no fool who would give up what he cannot keep in order to gain what he cannot lose."

So what do we who are liberated slaves do to live like free people? We don't begin by denying the reality of sin. We start by growing through the realization of who we are in Christ. In various ways, Scripture teaches that progressive sanctification is making our position in Christ and the newness of our person through regeneration increasingly real in life. It involves the process of turning from the attitude and practice of sin with all of their negative effects in life to that of the attitude and practice of righteousness with all of their positive effects.

Sin's Presence in the Believer's Life

John makes it clear in 1 John 1:7-10 that believers are still involved with sin:

> If we walk in the light, as he is in the light, we have fellowship with one another, and the blood of Jesus, his Son, purifies us from all sin. If we claim to be without sin, we deceive ourselves and the truth is not in us. If we confess our sins, he is faithful and just and will forgive us our sins and purify us from all unrighteousness. If we claim we have not sinned, we make him out to be a liar and his word has no place in our lives.

We are continually being cleansed from sin as we walk in the light. Walking in the light cannot mean sinless perfection, because verse 8 says we deceive ourselves if we say we have no sin.

It is absolutely vital to recognize at this point that "having sin" and "being sin" are two different issues. Walking in the light is living in continuous and conscious moral agreement with our heavenly Father. It is essentially the same as *confessing*, which means "to agree with God." This passage gives no instruction to ask God for forgiveness because we are already forgiven, but we do need to live honestly and openly before God. If it's necessary for believers to continually be cleansed from sin, then they must somehow have sin. Saying that we are without sin indicates that we do not have the truth in us.[1] Theologian John Calvin said that "there remains in a regenerate man a smoldering cinder of evil, from which desires continually leap forth to allure and spur him to commit sin."[2]

That sin is present in the new person is also affirmed in Paul's description of a continual battle going on in the believer: "I say, walk by the Spirit, and you will not carry out the desire of the flesh. For the flesh sets it desire against the Spirit, and the Spirit against the flesh; for these are in opposition to one another" (Galatians 5:16,17 NASB). The verb translated "sets its desire" is in the present tense indicating a continual ongoing antagonism between the "flesh" (or the old tendency to live life independently of God) and the Spirit (who lives in us and seeks to lead us in holiness). The battlefield of this war is the life of every believer; this combat with sin is seen when Paul talks about us continually "putting to death [present tense] the deeds of the body" (Romans 8:13 NASB).

To help us grow away from sin, our heavenly Father disciplines us as His children so that we may share in His Holiness and reap a harvest of righteousness and peace (Hebrews 12:5-11). Frequently we are told to stop various sins (for example, Ephesians 4:25-32; Colossians 3:5-9) and pursue holiness and purity (2 Corinthians 7:1). Even the apostle Paul, as great as he was, acknowledged that he was still pressing on toward the goal of knowing Christ more completely and that he had not "already been made perfect" (Philippians 3:12).

All of these Bible passages show that even though we are new persons in Christ with new dominant desires toward God and His holiness, we still sin. Sin no longer reigns over us, but it still dwells within us. Calvin is correct when he says that "sin ceases only to reign; it does not also cease to dwell in them [believers]. Accordingly, we say that the old man was so crucified (Romans 6:6), and the law of sin (*see also* Romans 8:2) so abolished in the children of God, that some vestiges remain; not to rule over them, but to humble them by the consciousness of their own weakness."[3] Growth in holiness means increasingly putting off the sinful desires and their actions by the increasing daily realization of our newness and the truth that we really are in Christ.

You've Already Been Changed

We saw in Romans 6:6 that our old self was crucified with Christ when we were united with Him by faith. This was a decisive and definite act in the believer's past. Colossians 3:9,10 reiterates that truth; there, Paul exhorts believers to stop living in the old sins of their past life "since you have taken off your old self [man] with its practices and have put on the new self [man]."[4] Growth in holiness takes place when we claim the reality of these past events and act on them.

That is Paul's point in Ephesians 4:22-24 when he says,

> You were taught, with regard to your former way of life, to put off your old self, which is being corrupted by its deceitful desires; to be new in the attitude of your minds; and to put on the new self, created to be like God in true righteousness and holiness.[5]

As Bible commentator Andrew Lincoln explains, this passage is challenging believers to make the past acts a reality in the present:

> Whereas both Romans 6:6 and Colossians 3:9 (cf. O'Brien, *Colossians*, 188-89) assert that the definitive break with the old person has been made in the past, Ephesians extends the tension between the indicative and

the imperative to the notion of putting off the old person. Putting off the old person has already taken place through baptism which transferred believers to the new order. *This injunction is not an exhortation to believers to repeat that event but to continue to live out its significance by giving up on that old person that they no longer are. They are new people who must become in practice what God has already made them, and that involves the resolve to put off the old way of life as it attempts to impinge. This is made clear by the qualifying phrase which precedes the mention of the old person—"as regards your former way of life"* (emphasis added).[6]

We need to renew our minds to the truth that a change *has* taken place in us and then live accordingly by faith, with the confidence that it will work out in our experience. Although Romans 6:6 and Colossians 3:9 look at the definative past act, the exhortations in the surrounding context urge us in a present sense to put away sin and live according to this past act. Accepting the tension between the past act (the indicative) and the present life (the imperative) enables us to better understand the change from the old man in Adam to the new man in Christ.

Putting on Christ

Just as putting on the new man is both a past act and a present challenge, so also is the putting on of Christ a past and present matter. Paul says in Galatians 3:27, "All of you who were baptized into Christ have clothed yourselves with Christ" (the Greek word translated "clothed yourselves" is the same word translated "put on" in relation to the new man in Galatians 3:27, Ephesians 4:24, and Colossians 3:10 and can be translated "put on Christ").

To clothe oneself with or to put on a person "means to take on the characteristics, virtues, and/or intentions of the one referred to, and so to become like that person."[7] Paul, then, is saying that when we came to Christ, we were joined to Him— we were made alive in Him. We became a partaker of the divine nature (2 Peter 1:4) and began the process of becoming like Him. God didn't simply give us the power to imitate Him; He actually reconciled us to Himself so that our soul is in union with His!

The implications of this past act are stated even more forcefully when Paul exhorts believers to "put on the Lord Jesus Christ" in Romans 13:14 (NASB). Bible commentator James Dunn explains that this is

> . . . a way of describing the spiritual transformation which has a decisive beginning in conversion-initiation, but which is hardly completed or final. The indicative needs to be held in tension with the imperative (hence Colossians 3:3-5; 3:10-12; and Ephesians 4:24). It is because the primary reference of the metaphor is to a spiritual transformation effected by the Spirit rather than to a once-forall act . . . that Paul must balance indicative (Galatians 3:27) with imperative (here).[8]

The following quote by New Testament scholar F.F. Bruce on Galatians 3:27 summarizes how putting off the old man in Adam and putting on the new man in Christ is the sanctifying process which makes real that decisive change that happened at salvation:

> To "put on Christ" is for Paul another way of expressing incorporation into Him. The closest parallel to Χριστὸν ἐνδύσασθε [have clothed yourselves with Christ] here is Romans 13:14 ἐνδύσασθε τὸν κύριον Ἰησοῦν [clothe yourselves with the Lord Jesus], but there believers are exhorted to do what they are here said to have done already. This indicative/imperative oscillation is not unparalleled in Paul. "Be what you are," he says in effect, meaning "Be in ordinary practice what God's grace has made you."[9]

In summary, we are to assume responsibility for becoming what we already are in Christ by the grace of God.

Spiritual Metamorphosis

God has given us many analogies in nature to show us the wonderful transformation that salvation brings. Consider the plight of the caterpillar. It crawls on the surface of the earth with tiny suction cup-like legs. Four times during its life, the caterpillar grows out of its own skin, which is a forecast for what is to come. This fuzzy little worm also happens to eat what it has shed because it is rich in protein. What it was plays a part in what it will be.

One day, as though led by instinct, it climbs as high as it can by its own strength—usually on the limb of a tree or on a small branch. There it sows a little button that forms an attachment for the cocoon that it spins around itself as it hangs upside down. The caterpillar then ceases to exist, and a miraculous transformation takes place. In the caterpillar's place is a butterfly that eventually fights its way out and learns to fly. The caterpillar "crucified" itself in order to be "resurrected" a butterfly. It gave up the security of its own limited resources and earthbound existence in order to fly in the heavenlies. Though a caterpillar would appear to be much stronger than a butterfly, it cannot escape the law of gravity. The butterfly is the more fragile creature, but it can gracefully soar in freedom. The caterpillar gave up all that it was in order to become all that the Creator designed for it to become. It gave up its short stubby legs for beautiful wings.

Now, imagine what would happen to the growth of the new butterfly if it chose to believe that it was still a caterpillar and walked instead of flying. He would come nowhere near to reaching his potential. Likewise, when we who are new in Christ perceive that we are still the old self, we won't experience the fullness of the Christian life as God intended us to.

By the way, just as the caterpillar cannot take credit for becoming a butterfly, we cannot take credit for the work of Christ which is imputed to us by the grace of God. We can only receive Christ's work by faith, and we must continuously choose to believe who we already are in Christ in order to become what we were created to be. If we think and act like caterpillars, the Lord will receive no glory for what He did on our behalf.

So that you might have a better understanding of who you are in Christ, we've included this following list of Scriptures from Neil's book *Victory Over the Darkness*:[10]

WHO AM I?

Matthew 5:13	I am the salt of the earth.
Matthew 5:14	I am the light of the world.
John 1:12	I am a child of God (part of His family—*see* Romans 8:16).
John 15:1,5	I am part of the *true* vine, a channel (branch) of His (Christ's) life.
John 15:15	I am Christ's friend.
John 15:16	I am chosen and appointed by Christ to bear *His* fruit.
Romans 6:18	I am a slave of righteousness.
Romans 6:22	I am enslaved to God.
Romans 8:14,15	I am a son of God (God is spiritually my Father—*see* Galatians 3:26 and 4:6).
Romans 8:17	I am a joint-heir with Christ, sharing His inheritance with Him.
1 Corinthians 3:16 and 6:19	I am a temple (home) of God. His Spirit (His life) dwells in me.
1 Corinthians 6:17	I am joined (united) to the Lord and am one spirit with Him.
1 Corinthians 12:27	I am a member (part) of Christ's body (*see* Ephesians 5:30).
2 Corinthians 5:17	I am a new creation (new person).
2 Corinthians 5:18,19	I am reconciled to God and am a minister of reconciliation.
Galatians 3:26,28	I am a son of God and one in Christ.
Galatians 4:6,7	I am an heir of God since I am a son of God.
Ephesians 1:1	I am a saint (see 1 Corinthians 1:2; Philippians 1:1; and Colossians 1:2).

Ephesians 2:10	I am God's workmanship (handiwork) created (born anew) in Christ to do His work that He planned beforehand that I should do.
Ephesians 2:19	I am a fellow citizen with the rest of God's people in His family.
Ephesians 3:1 and 4:1	I am a prisoner of Christ.
Ephesians 4:24	I am righteous and holy.
Philippians 3:20	I am a citizen of heaven and seated in heaven right now (see Ephesians 2:6).
Colossians 3:3	I am hidden with Christ in God.
Colossians 3:4	I am an expression of the life of Christ because He is my life.
Colossians 3:12	I am chosen of God, holy, and dearly loved.
1 Thessalonians 1:4	I am chosen and dearly loved by God.
1 Thessalonians 5:5	I am a son of light and not of darkness.
Hebrews 3:1	I am a holy brother, partaker of a heavenly calling.
Hebrews 3:14	I am a partaker of Christ . . . I share in His life.
1 Peter 2:5	I am one of God's living stones and am being built up (in Christ) as a spiritual house.
1 Peter 2:9,10	I am a chosen race, a royal priesthood, a holy nation, a people for God's own possession to proclaim the excellencies of Him.
1 Peter 2:11	I am an alien and stranger to this world I temporarily live in.
1 Peter 5:8	I am an enemy of the devil.
1 John 3:1,2	I am now a child of God. I will resemble Christ when He returns.
1 John 5:18	I am born of God, and the evil one (the devil) cannot touch me.

I am not the great "I AM" (Exodus 3:14; John 8:24,28,58), "but by the grace of God I am what I am" (1 Corinthians 15:10).

Living Out What You Really Are

The idea of Christian growth being the process of living out what happened to us at salvation is also seen in several exhortations to live according to what God has already done for us and in us. Paul says, "As a prisoner for the Lord, then, I urge you to live a life worthy of the calling you have received" (Ephesians 4:1). The Greek word for "worthy" has the idea of "bringing up the other beam of the scales," and therefore "equivalent."[11] The word is used to indicate the motive and goal of Christian action, which are in response to the preceding action of God, and thus distinguishes them from legalistic works.

Andrew Lincoln says, "The call of God is the actualization in history of his electing purpose and involves God's initiative in bringing a person into relationship with himself."[12] Left to our own, we would be nothing more than caterpillars with no other purpose in life than to "eat and drink, for tomorrow we die" (1 Corinthians 15:32). But God has called us out of darkness into light. Lincoln comments:

> The high privileges of the call have been delineated in the first part of the (Ephesians) letter. Believers have been called into all the blessings of salvation and into the experience of the power of the God who raised Christ from the dead and who brought them from death to life and to a share in Christ's reign in the heavenly realm. They have been called into the new humanity out of Jews and Gentiles, into the new temple, the one body (cf. Colossians 3:15, "called in the one body") of the church, and thus called to be part of God's purposes for cosmic unity. In exhorting to a way of life that corresponds to such a calling, this first verse (4:1) provides a framework designed to ensure that what follows will not be seen as mere moral advice but as an appeal to the readers' experience of the theological heart of the gospel.[13]

The point we are trying to make is that believers, in sanctification, are actualizing their new position in Christ and their relationship with God by living out their "calling." Peter says:

> You are a chosen people, a royal priesthood, a holy nation, a people belonging to God, that you may declare the praises of him who called you out of darkness into his wonderful light. Once you were not a people, but now you are the people of God; once you had not received mercy, but now you have received mercy (1 Peter 2:9,10).

Can you imagine the exhilaration of emerging from the darkness of a cocoon into the light? I have seen that same exhilaration on the faces of thousands of people when they found their freedom in Christ and realized who they were as children of God.

Being a chosen people and a royal priesthood is both a privilege and a responsibility. Markus Barth says this about our calling:

> Both [election and calling] involve the appointment to, and the equipment for, a task to be fulfilled among other peoples or persons. . . . God's call entrusts man with a high status and a correspondingly high responsibility and task. . . . The nature and effect of calling may be compared with the bestowal of a title or a patent of nobility.[14]

The following passages exhort us to live a life worthy of our calling: "Conduct yourselves in a manner worthy of the gospel of Christ" (Philippians 1:27); "live a life worthy of the Lord" (Colossians 1:10); and "live lives worthy of God, who calls you into his kingdom and glory" (1 Thessalonians 2:12).

Understanding Transformation

A clear evidence that sanctification is the realization of what we already are as new people is seen in the biblical teaching of transformation. Paul writes, "Now the Lord is the Spirit, and where the Spirit of the Lord is, there is freedom.

And we, who with unveiled faces all reflect the Lord's glory, are being transformed into his likeness with ever-increasing glory, which comes from the Lord, who is the Spirit" (2 Corinthians 3:17,18). Elsewhere Paul writes, "Be transformed by the renewing of your mind" (Romans 12:2). We are in the process of transformation (the verbs in both passages are present tense).

The word "transform" refers to a change in which a person's true inner condition is shown outwardly. One commentator says that Paul's command to "be transformed" is concerned with "the new moral life in the Spirit as an obligation: 'Become what you are.'"[15] On the comparison of "conform" and "transform" in Romans 12:2, Harrisville says, "'Conform' refers to a posture or attitude that may be changed at will, whereas 'form' at the heart of 'transformed' refers to what grows out of necessity from an inward condition."[16]

Transformation is illustrated for us in the transfiguration of Jesus (Matthew 17:1-3). The Greek word for *transfiguration* ($\mu\epsilon\tau\alpha\mu\rho\phi\acute{o}\omega$) in relation to Jesus is the same as that used for "transformed" in Romans 12:2 and 2 Corinthians 3:18. That word is the origin of our English word *metamorphose*, which means "to change or be changed in form or character." In the transfiguration of Jesus, there was not a change in His nature. He was still God and man. Rather, Jesus was letting His true nature of deity shine through or become seen. He was seen for who He really was. His divine nature was manifest. Similarly, when Paul wrote about being transformed, he was not talking about a change in our real nature, or who we really are. Rather, he was referring to becoming outwardly (in our behavior and walk) what we really are in the depth of our being, a new inner person.

Dying and Rising with Christ

The same concept of sanctification—that is, experiencing the change or newness that is a reality for the person in his inner being—is seen in the believer's continual application of his death and resurrection with Christ. Every Christian has died with Christ and has been raised with Him. But we have not totally realized in our growing experience the full reality of these events. Thus the pattern of Christ's death and resurrection is presented in Scripture as the essence of transformation. These events through which we have passed in our inner person now determine our life and behavior. To be transformed into the image of Christ or have Christ formed in us (Galatians 4:19) means that Christ effects in us what took place in Him.

The essence of sanctification is dying in order that we might live. This was the pathway of Christ; it is also the pathway to glory for the believer. We find an analogy of this in nature during the winters in the north country. As a child I (Neil) would walk in the woods and observe the frozen trees, which seemed to be dead. I would snap a small branch in half and wonder if there was any life in it. Then in the spring, new life would burst forth from that which had appeared to be dead. (Christ's resurrection from the dead, which we celebrate every Easter, had to have happened in the spring!)

Another analogy is the new life that comes from every seed that is sown. If you wanted to grow a giant oak tree, what would you do? Plant an oak tree? No, you would plant an acorn. If you could watch the process, you would see that tiny acorn would die to itself so that out of it can grow a majestic oak tree. The acorn could sit alone and exist for itself, but it would never become what it was intended to be. Similarly, the seed to become what God intends us to be is sown in every child of God.

Jesus said, "The hour has come for the Son of Man to be glorified. Truly, truly, I say to you, unless a grain of wheat falls into the earth and dies, it remains by itself alone; but if it dies, it bears much fruit" (John 12:23,24). Like the caterpillar who voluntarily attaches itself to the tree in order to hang upside down, we too must realize that the path upward is first downward. In order to be glorified, Jesus had to first die. We too have to die to who we were in Adam and give up all our dreams for self-glorification in the flesh and joyfully choose to glorify God in our bodies.

No Pain, No Gain

If we all knew the truth perfectly, none of us would choose to live our life independent of God. None of us would rob ourselves of the blessings of God in order to temporarily satisfy the flesh. We would all gladly deny ourselves, pick up our cross daily, and follow Him. Under the inspiration of God, Paul knew that we wouldn't fully understand all that we have in Christ, "who has blessed us in the heavenly realms with every spiritual blessing in Christ" (Ephesians 1:3). So after listing all these blessings, Paul says, "I pray . . . that the eyes of your heart may be enlightened in order that you may know the hope to which he has called you, the riches of his glorious inheritance in the saints" (Ephesians 1:18).

The problem is that "self" will never cast out "self." We have to be led to do that by the Holy Spirit. That's what Paul meant when he said, "We who are alive are always being given over to death for Jesus' sake, so that his life may be revealed in our mortal body" (2 Corinthians 4:11). That is, we often have to struggle to overcome sin even though we have already died to it. Such struggling may appear to be a negative thing, but it's actually to our benefit. Let me illustrate with another analogy. If you saw a butterfly struggling to emerge from its cocoon, would you try to help it? That may seem to be the loving thing to do, but it isn't because that struggle, in part, is what gives the butterfly the strength to fly. You would actually be interfering with the butterfly's potential to fly. The same is true of a baby eagle emerging from its egg.

Whether we walk among the turkeys or soar with the eagles in the heavenlies has much to do with our willingness to overcome the residual effects of our past. John writes, "He who overcomes will inherit all this, and I will be his God and he will be my son" (Revelation 21:7). No pain, no gain seems to be a principle of life. Therefore, "endure hardship as discipline; God is treating you as sons" (Hebrews 12:7).

If we didn't have a part to play in overcoming the power of sin, then we would all probably wallow in it. That our spiritual growth is connected with our endeavors to overcome sin is evident in 1 John 2:12-14, where we read that "children" have overcome the penalty of sin, but the "young men" in the faith have overcome the evil one and the power of sin. We must always remember that the god of this world and the prince of power of the air is always roaring around like a hungry lion seeking someone to devour. Learning how to resist the devil and crucify the flesh is a critical part of growing in Christ. The flesh desires to sin, but our new nature in Christ desires to live righteously. John Calvin wrote:[17]

> The life of a Christian man is a continual effort and exercise in the mortification of the flesh, till it is utterly slain, and God's Spirit reigns in us. Therefore, I think he has profited greatly who has learned to be very much displeased with himself, not so as to stick fast in this mire and progress no farther, but rather to hasten to God and yearn for him in order that, having been engrafted into the life and death of Christ, he may give attention to continual repentance. Truly, they who are held by a real loathing of sin cannot do otherwise. For no one ever hates sin unless he has previously been seized with a love of righteousness.

As Christians we are no longer in Adam because we are in Christ. "For as *in Adam* all die, so *in Christ* all will *be made alive*" (1 Corinthians 15:22, emphasis added). Because of our position in Christ we are no longer "in the flesh," but since the flesh remains after salvation, we can still choose to walk according to it (that is, we can choose to live as a natural man—the way we did before we were born again). Paul said, "So it is written, 'The first man Adam became a living being;' the last Adam, a life-giving spirit" (1 Corinthians 15:45). We could summarize who we are by looking at the chart on page 118.

Love's Key Role in Sanctification

If a person were a fully sanctified child of God, he would be free from his past and be like Christ in His character, which is love. Paul says, "The goal of our instruction is love from a pure

Who We Are

In Adam (1 Corinthians 15:22a)		In Christ (1 Corinthians 15:22b)
old man	*by ancestry*	new man
sinful (Ephesians 2:1-3)	*by nature*	partaker of divine nature (2 Peter 1:4)
in the flesh (Romans 8:8)	*by birth*	in the Spirit (Romans 8:9)
walk after the flesh (Galatians 5:19-21)	*by choice*	walk after the Spirit (Galatians 5:22,23) *or* after the flesh

heart and a good conscience and a sincere faith" (1 Timothy 1:5 NASB). Sanctification is nothing less than God living in us to perfect His nature in us. The fact that God is love makes love the focus of our Christian life. Knowledge of God and union with Him through Christ means a life of love. Glenn Hinson comments:

> What can we do to attain purity of heart? The answer to this is: surrender, abandon ourselves, submit, yield, humble ourselves, give ourselves over to God. However apt we may be at education, self-understanding or formation, we cannot transform the impure into the pure, the sinful into the saintly, the unlovely into the lovely. God alone can do that. God's love alone can perform the miracle required. If we surrender, love will come in and cleanse and purify and transform.[18]

Jesus said, "A new command I give you: Love one another. As I have loved you, so you must love one another" (John 13:34). Why would that be a new command? Hasn't it always been a command to love one another? Actually, apart from Christ, we couldn't. What makes Christ's love so different than our natural love is that His love is not dependent upon its object. God loves us not because we are lovable, but because it is His nature to love us—"God is love" (1 John 4:8). That is the only explanation for the assurance that the love of God is unconditional. Human love, in contrast, is selective: "If you love those who love you, what credit is that to you? Even 'sinners' love those who love them" (Luke 6:32). God's love, when it comes into us, enables us to love as He does. "We love because He first loved us" (1 John 4:19). In other words, because we have become a partaker of the divine nature, which is love, we can by the grace of God love the unlovely.

We can gain a better understanding of the meaning of the word *agape* (love) in Scripture when we realize that it can be used both as a verb and a noun. When used as a noun (*agape*), it refers to the character of God because God is love. For instance, "Love is patient, love is kind" (1 Corinthians 13:4) because God is patient and kind. When used as a verb (*agapeo*), then it describes the sacrificial actions taken by one who seeks to meet the needs of another: "God so loved the world that he gave his one and only Son . . ." (John 3:16). Jesus' sole purpose was to do the will of God (John 4:34), to the point of suffering as He did in Gethesemane: "Father . . . not my will, but yours be done" (Luke 22:42).

It could be said that the evidence of John 3:16 being fulfilled in our lives is described in 1 John 3:16-18:

> This is how we know what love is: Jesus Christ laid down his life for us. And we ought to lay down our lives for our brothers. If anyone has material possessions and sees his brother in need but has no pity on him, how can the love of God be in him? Dear children, let us not love with words or tongue but with actions and in truth.

This passage underscores an important point: The capacity to do loving things for other people springs from the nature and character of God within us. We are not first called to do what appears to be loving things for others; we are first called to be like Christ. Loving deeds flow out of our new nature in Christ.

Jesus said the greatest commandment is to "love the Lord your God with all your heart and with all your soul and with all your mind. This is the first and greatest commandment. And the second is like it: Love your neighbor as yourself. All the Law and the Prophets hang on these two commandments" (Matthew 22:37-40). The last verse implies that the end purpose for the entire prophetic word of God is to fall in love with Him and mankind. A love for God is what ought to drive all our actions. Henry Scougal comments:

> Love is that powerful and prevalent passion by which all the faculties and inclinations of the soul are determined and on which both its perfection and happiness depend. The worth and excellency of a soul is to be measured by the object of its love. He who loveth mean and sordid things doth thereby become base and vile, but a noble and well-placed affection doth advance and improve the spirit into a conformity with the perfections which it loves. The image of these do frequently present themselves unto the mind, and, by a secret force and energy, insinuate into the very constitution of the soul and mold and fashion it into their own likeness. . . . The true way to improve and ennoble our souls is by fixing our love on the divine perfections that we may have them always before us and derive an impression of them on ourselves. . . .[19]

Love is fundamentally what moves us. "Augustine says all evil comes from disordered love, for it is love that moves me where I go. Love is my gravity: *Amor meus, pondus meum,* 'My love is my weight.' I go where my love moves me. That is why all persons are either going toward God and heaven or away from God and toward hell."[20] Peter Kreeft says, "My identity and my eternal destiny are determined by my love. For what I love

becomes my end, and my end is my destiny. . . ." He further states
that the story of life is

> the drama of two loves, the old story of "the eternal tri-
> angle": whom will I marry? God, my true beloved? Or
> some idol, and thus ultimately myself? That is the funda-
> mental option, the fundamental question of every human
> life. That is what decides heaven or hell. Compared with
> this even clarity of thought and feeling happy is trivial.[21]

In Ephesians 5:22-33 we read that the sanctified church is the
bride of Christ. The Lord Jesus wants "to present her to himself as a
radiant church, without stain or wrinkle or any other blemish, but
holy and blameless" (verse 27). The language here and in the Song
of Solomon is one of unbridled affection between two lovers, between God and His people. This intimacy and uninhibited expression of love comes with righteous commitment. Henry Scougal says:

> The *love* of God is a delightful and affectionate sense
> of the divine perfection's which makes the soul resign and
> sacrifice itself wholly unto him, desiring above all things
> to please him, and delighting in nothing so much as in fel-
> lowship and communion with him, and being ready to do
> or suffer anything for his sake or at his pleasure.[22]

Love Is the Starting Point

Scripture portrays love as the fulfillment of all of the commandments and righteous acts we show toward other people. If
such is the case, then it is crucial for us to focus on the character
of God, which is love. When we focus on the source of life we
will bear fruit, and the fruit of the Spirit is love (Galatians
5:22). Notice that the fruit of the Spirit is *singular* (that is, the
verse does not say fruits), which is love. The other traits listed
in Galatians 5:22,23—joy, peace, patience, and so on—are
characteristics of love. The characteristic of the new person (or
the primary characteristic of sanctification) is love.

Love is the fulfillment of all ethical commands. It is not
doing this or that, but loving so that the doing will flow. Paul

says, "He who loves his fellowman has fulfilled the law" (Romans 13:8). Peter Kreeft makes this observation:

> One of the things we mean when we say that love is the fulfillment of the law is that when we do not love a person, it is difficult or impossible to fulfill the moral law with respect to that person; but when we love someone, it is possible, even easy, even inevitable and positively delightful to do what the moral law commands us to do to him or her. It is hard to do good deeds to one you despise, but joy to do the same deeds to one you love.[23]

To contrast between the acts of the old nature (the flesh) and the fruit of the Spirit is the difference between death and life. Deeds done in the flesh without life are dead acts; fruit can only be produced by something that is alive. The flesh can perform certain acts, but the fruit of the Spirit produces character.

To be perfected in love is the ultimate goal of being sanctified in Christ. St. John of the Cross said, "In the twilight of our lives, we will be judged on how we have loved."[24] The power and centrality of love in sanctification is seen in the hymn "My Jesus, I Love Thee":

> My Jesus, I love Thee, I know Thou art mine; For Thee all the follies of sin I resign . . .

Once we have fallen in love with God and all that is true and good, we will naturally (or better, supernaturally) fall in love with all others created in the image of God. "Whoever loves God must also love his brother" (1 John 4:21). The love of God simply compels us to do so. Henry Scougal wrote, "A soul thus possessed with divine love must needs be enlarged towards all mankind in a sincere and unbounded affection, because of the relation they have to God, being his creatures and having something of his image stamped upon them."[25]

The nature of godly love corresponds with dying to the old self and becoming a new self. We move from a fleshly type of love that loves others because of what they do for us. Such "love" seeks to satisfy its own lusts. It is in reality a love of self, which seeks to meet its own needs. It is conditional because it says, "I will love you if you will love me." And it is very much dependent upon its object. Sanctified love, in contrast, is sacrificial and not dependent upon its object. Henry Scougal captured that truth well in the following words:

> Perfect love is a kind of self-dereliction, a wandering out of ourselves; it is a kind of voluntary death, wherein the lover dies to himself and all his own interest, not thinking of them nor caring for them any more, and minding nothing but how he may please and gratify the party whom he loves. Thus he is quite undone unless he meet with reciprocal affection; he neglects himself, and the other hath no regard to him; but if he be beloved, he is revived, as it were, and liveth in the soul and care of the person whom he loves; and now he begins to mind his own concernments, not so much because they are his as because the beloved is pleased to own an interest in them. He becomes dear unto himself, because he is so unto the other.[26]

7

The Agents of Sanctification

His divine power has given us everything we need for life and godliness through our knowledge of him who called us by his own glory and goodness.

—2 Peter 1:3

When I (Neil) was growing up on a farm in Minnesota, spring was a busy season of preparing the ground and sowing our seeds. One method of sowing was called *broadcasting*. You simply cast the seeds upon the surface of the earth. Of course, some of the seeds never took root, but most did if it rained. To spread the seed, we used an end-gate seeder that we mounted on the tailgate of a wagon. A tractor pulled the wagon that did the broadcasting. This job required at least two people—one to drive the tractor, and one to sit in the wagon and keep the seeder filled.

Although the seeder did the actual broadcasting, the power to sow the seed was in the tractor, not the seeder. If the tractor stopped, so did the sowing. But the sowing also stopped if the seeder got clogged or failed to work. Should the latter happen, the tractor was still able to continue supplying all the power and maintain a straight but narrow path toward the end of the row.

We as Christians are like the seeder. We have the privilege of sowing the seed, cultivating it, and watering the plants, but God causes the growth. Notice that both we and God are involved in this process: If we don't plant and water nothing grows, but if God doesn't make it grow there will be no harvest. He also supplies the seed that we are called to sow: "He who supplies seed to the sower and bread for food will also supply and increase your store of seed and will enlarge the harvest of your righteousness" (2 Corinthians 9:10). In his first letter to the Corinthians, Paul says:

> I planted the seed, Apollos watered it, but God made it grow. So neither he who plants nor he who waters is anything, but only God, who makes things grow. The man who plants and the man who waters have one purpose, and each will be rewarded according to his own labor. For we are God's fellow workers; you are God's field, God's building (1 Corinthians 3:6-9).

From germination to harvest, our sanctification is first and foremost the work of God. He is the One who drives the tractor that supplies all the power, and He furnishes all the seed. He is the source of the divine life that is necessary for our growth. We have no resources in ourselves to overcome the power of sin still present in our lives. Scripture makes it very clear that sanctification is the work of God. At the same time, Scripture also teaches the need for us to assume our responsibility for the continuing process of sanctification. That is only logical, since sanctification involves the change of our own self, which includes our thinking, our emotions, and our will.

There is a real distinction between what God has done and will do, and what our responsibility is. In the space below, a line is drawn. Everything on the left side is God's responsibility and everything on the right is our responsibility:

God's sovereign grace	Man's responsibility

We cannot do for ourselves what God has already done and will do for us. We can try to save ourselves, but it would do us no good. We shouldn't try to be another person's conscience or make promises that only God can deliver on. We can and should rest in the finished work of Christ, trust in the sovereign grace of God to be faithful to His Word, and have confidence that He will continue to be and do all that He said He would be and do.

On the right side of the line is our responsibility, which has been clearly revealed in God's Word. He will not do for us what He has called us to do. In a very real sense He can't. He can only do that which is consistent with His holy nature, and He cannot deviate from His Word. He has to stay true to His Word. There can be nothing but defeat and disappointment for Christians who expect God to do for them what He has commanded them to do. They will be just as defeated if they try to do for themselves what God and only God can do. For instance, suppose there is a very difficult "Christian" in your church. Several people get together in prayer and ask God to remove him. Nothing seems to happen. So they ask, "Why not, God? This is Your church; why don't You do something?"

Why *doesn't* God do something? Because the Lord has clearly told us that it is *our* responsibility to go to the person first in private. If he or she will not repent, then we are to bring two other witnesses and continue onward in the discipline process outlined for us by Jesus in Matthew 18:15-17. Church discipline is our responsibility, and inner conviction of sin is God's responsibility.

If you yourself become involved in attempting to resolve a spiritual conflict, then the need to know your responsibility in spiritual matters becomes even more critical. Suppose someone has a frightening demonic attack in his room at night. Nearly paralyzed in his fear, he cries out to God and asks Him to do something. But God doesn't seem to do anything. So the person asks, "Why not, God? You are all-powerful and You know what I'm going through right now. Why won't You help me? You can make it stop!" When the attack continues, the person begins to question God's love and concern for him and perhaps even wonder about his salvation. After all, if he really is a child of God, then wouldn't his loving heavenly Father take care of him?

Of course God would, but whose responsibility is it to submit to God and resist the devil? God has done all He needs to do in order for us to live a victorious Christian life. He has defeated the devil, forgiven our sins, and given us eternal life. He has equipped us with His Holy Spirit, and we are now seated with Christ in the heavenlies. From that position of authority we are to continue the work of Christ on planet Earth. Does the devil have to flee from us if we don't resist him? Probably not! You cannot be passive about taking your place in Christ. You must "put on the full armor of God, so that when the day of evil comes, you may be able to stand your ground, and after you have done everything, to stand" (Ephesians 6:13).

When we fail to recognize the spiritual matters we are responsible for, then we set ourselves up for disappointment because we will think that either God isn't at work in our lives or we are spiritual failures because things didn't go the way we expected.

God the Father's Role in Our Sanctification

God is the primary agent of our sanctification because He is the only source of life, righteousness, holiness, love, truth, and so on. In fact, sanctification is the process of God sharing His life with and through us. Paul prayed, "May God himself, the God of peace, sanctify you through and through. May your whole spirit, soul and body be kept blameless at the coming of our Lord Jesus Christ. The one who calls you is faithful and he will do it" (1 Thessalonians 5:23,24). The truth that God is the primary agent of sanctification is also shown in 2 Peter 1:3-9, which goes into specific detail about God's role and our responsibility.

What God Has Done

His divine power has given us everything we need for
life and godliness through our knowledge of him who

called us by his own glory and goodness. Through these he has given us his very great and precious promises, so that through them you may participate in the divine nature and escape the corruption in the world caused by evil desires (verses 3,4).

What We Must Do

For this very reason, make every effort to add to your faith goodness; and to goodness, knowledge; and to knowledge, self-control; and to self-control, perseverance; and to perseverance, godliness; and to godliness, brotherly kindness; and to brotherly kindness, love. For if you possess these qualities in increasing measure, they will keep you from being ineffective and unproductive in your knowledge of our Lord Jesus Christ. But if anyone does not have them, he is nearsighted and blind, and has forgotten that he has been cleansed from his past sins (verses 5-9).

God has given us everything we need for life and godliness; He has equally distributed Himself to all His children because every Christian has been made a partaker of His divine nature. Our responsibility is to make every effort to add on to our faith the character qualities of goodness, knowledge, self-control, perseverance, godliness, brotherly kindness, and love. If we do so, we will live effective and productive lives. The people who don't do this have forgotten that they are alive in Christ and dead to sin. What should they do then? Try harder? No! They should affirm again their faith foundation of who they are in Christ and commit themselves to their growth in character: "Brethren, be all the more diligent to make certain about His calling and choosing you; for as long as you practice these things, you will never stumble" (2 Peter 1:10 NASB).

One question some people ask is, "God may have given us everything we need, but what about the fact that God does not equally distribute spiritual gifts or talents?"

We don't need to be concerned about the amount of spiritual giftedness we have because God is fair to all His children and will not make our effectiveness and productivity dependent upon that which He has not equally distributed. Second Peter 1:3-9 doesn't mention spiritual gifts, so we can know that our effectiveness is not measured on that basis.

Returning to our earlier discussion, all that we have received from God has eternal value. "We are God's workmanship" (Ephesians 2:10), and "his incomparably great power" (Ephesians 1:19) is at work in us to produce a new creation. The Greek word translated "workmanship" is frequently used in the Septuagint (a Greek translation of the Old Testament produced before Christ's time on earth) to refer to creation as God's work. Paul says in Romans 14:20 that believers are "the work of God."

The biblical teaching that various aspects of God's nature are given to the believer is strong evidence that sanctification is truly the work of God. God comes into the believer and transforms him by His very presence. Sanctification is the increasing experience of "life" or "eternal life," of which God is the only source (see Psalm 36:9; John 17:3; Ephesians 4:18). Our sanctification, therefore, must be a work of God.

God disciplines us so that we may share in His holiness. In the book of Hebrews we are exhorted, "Endure hardship as discipline; God is treating you as sons. For what son is not disciplined by his father? . . . Our fathers disciplined us for a little while as they thought best; but God disciplines us for our good, that we may share in his holiness" (Hebrews 12:7,10). God does not punish us for doing something wrong; He disciplines us for our good in order to share in His holiness. Our holiness comes from sharing in His holiness. Man has no source of holiness in himself apart from Christ.

Becoming a partaker of God's holiness does not mean that we have become deified. In other words, we don't become God or a god. Rather, we receive a holiness that is like God's—a holiness that will produce righteousness and peace. In Scripture we are told to "make every effort to live in peace with all men and to be holy; without holiness no one will see the Lord" (Hebrews 12:14).

While God the Father is the primary agent in our sanctification, Christ and the Holy Spirit also play roles in our sanctification. All three members of the Trinity have a part in making us holy.

Christ's Role in Our Sanctification

Jesus came that we might have life (John 10:10). To make that possible, He had to first die for our sins. At the moment of salvation, believers are joined to Christ so that He is their life. The often-repeated prepositional phrases "in Christ," "in Him," and "in the beloved" all mean that our soul is in union with God. They indicate that we are right now "alive in Christ." Every aspect of Christian ministry is dependent upon this glorious truth because apart from Christ we can doing nothing. Paul wrote, "For this reason I have sent to you Timothy, who is my beloved and faithful child in the Lord, and he will remind you of *my ways which are in Christ, just as I teach everywhere in every church*" (1 Corinthians 4:17 NASB, emphasis added). Richard Longenecker comments:

> In Pauline parlance, that reality of personal communion between Christians and God is expressed from the one side of the equation as being "in Christ," "in Christ Jesus/Jesus Christ," "in him," or "in the Lord" . . . [some 172 times including the pastoral epistles]. Viewed from the other side of the equation, the usual way for Paul to express that relation between God and his own is by some such phrase as "Christ by his Spirit" or "the Spirit of God" or simply "the Spirit" dwelling "in us" or "in you," though a few times he says directly "Christ in me" (as here in 2:20; cf. Colossians 1:27,29; see also Ephesians 3:16,17) or "Christ in you" (cf. the interchange of expressions in Romans 8:9-11).[1]

For every verse that says Christ is in you, there are approximately ten verses that say you are in Christ. According to Robert Tannehill, the phrase "in Christ" refers to "action or existence as it is characterized by a particular power, the power of Christ and his saving acts."[2] That is consistent with the fact that there are no verses in the Bible that instruct us to pursue power because we already have it in Christ. Paul said in Ephesians 1:18,19, "I pray also that the eyes of your heart may be enlightened in order that you may know the hope to which he has called you, the riches of his glorious inheritance in the saints, and his incomparably great power for us who believe."

Pursuing something you already have can only lead you down the wrong road. Power for the Christian is found in the truth, and the power of the devil is in the lie. If you expose Satan's lies, you will destroy his power because he truly is a defeated foe. Satan has deceived the whole world (Revelation 12:9); consequently, the world lies in the power of the evil one. However, Satan cannot do anything about your position in Christ. But if he can get you to think that your position in Christ isn't for real, then you will live as though it isn't. "Our struggle is not against flesh and blood, but against the rulers, against the authorities, against the powers of this dark world and against the spiritual forces of evil in the heavenly realms" (Ephesians 6:12). It cannot be overstated how important it is to know who we are in Christ. The apostle John makes that point in 1 John 5:18-20 (NASB):

> We know that no one who is born of God sins; but He who was born of God keeps him and the evil one does not touch him. We know that we are of God, and the whole world lies in the power of the evil one. And we know that the Son of God has come, and has given us understanding, in order that we might know Him who is true, and we are in Him who is true, in His Son Jesus Christ. This is the true God and eternal life. Little children, guard yourselves from idols.

We could say, then, that Christ is the mediator of God's sanctifying work. He is the mediator of the new creation just as much as He was the original one (*see* Colossians 1:16;

Hebrews 1:2). "For we are God's workmanship, created in Christ Jesus to do good works, which God prepared in advance for us to do" (Ephesians 2:10). The new creation "in Christ" is also seen as effected in the solidarity of union with Him as the head or representative of the new humanity. James Dunn comments:

> So far as Paul is concerned, his religious experience as a whole is characterized by a dependency on Jesus as Lord: it is not merely the experience of sonship, but the experience of Jesus' sonship, made possible by the Spirit of the Son; it is not merely the experience of grace, it is the experience of the grace of Christ; it is not merely the experience of Spirit, of life and death, it is the experience of the Spirit of Christ, the experience of that death which Jesus died, of that life which Jesus lives. In short, it is experience of Jesus, consciousness of Christ, that is, the recognition of the impress of Christ's character in Paul's experience and its outworking—a shaping of life and death which reproduces Jesus' death and life, not just in an accidental way, but as the purposeful action of divine power. Consequently, Jesus is not merely the first Christian, he is the Christ; he is not merely the typical man caught in the overlap of the ages, he is the archetypal man, the Last Adam. In the end of the day the religious experience of the Christian is not merely experience like that of Jesus, it is experience which at all characteristic and distinctive points is derived from Jesus the Lord, and which only makes sense when this derivative and dependent character is recognized.[3]

The continuing process of sanctification is a walk with God "in Christ." Notice what Jesus said in the greatest invitation ever extended to mankind: "Come to me, all you who are weary and burdened, and I will give you rest. Take my yoke upon you and learn from me, for I am gentle and humble in heart, and you will find rest for your souls. For my yoke is easy and my burden is light" (Matthew 11:28-30). Jesus didn't say come to the synagogue or submit to some program. He said, "Come to Me"—come to My presence and I will give you rest. There is a "Sabbath-rest for the people of God; for anyone who enters God's rest also rests from his own work" (Hebrews 4:9,10). This much-needed rest in the Lord is not an abdication of our responsibility nor a cessation of labor. Rather, it is practicing the presence of God and living by faith in the power of the Holy Spirit. If we try to serve the Lord by walking according to the flesh, we will burn out.

When Jesus taught spiritual principles, He often used illustrations that the people of His day could relate to. He was especially familiar with illustrations and metaphors related to carpentry, for He was raised in the home of a carpenter. Carpenters in those days fashioned yokes and doors, both of which the Lord used to speak of Himself. The yoke in Matthew 11:28-30 was a heavy wooden beam that fit over the shoulders of two oxen. The only way the yoke could work was if both oxen were in it and pulling together. If only one tried to use the yoke, it would be a chaffing and binding affair. When a farmer had to break in a new ox, he would place it in a yoke with an older, seasoned ox who had learned obedience from the things he suffered (see Hebrews 5:8). The older ox knew it had a whole day of work ahead and knew better than to run when he should be walking. He knew better than to stray off to the left or to the right, since such sidetracks only led to more work later on down the path.

A young ox often becomes restless because he thinks the pace is a little slow, so he may try to run ahead, only to burn out before noon. And if he is tempted to stray off to the left or the right, he will get a sore neck. It doesn't take too long for a young ox to realize that maybe the older ox knows what he is doing, so it's best to settle down and learn from the one who knows where he is going and how to get there.

What do we learn from all this? To take one day at a time. To learn the priority of relationships. And to learn the graceful ways of God.

Do you not know? Have you not heard? The LORD is the everlasting God, the Creator of the ends of the earth. He will not grow tired or weary, and his understanding no one can fathom. He gives strength to the weary and increases the power of the weak. Even youths grow tired and weary, and young men stumble and fall; but those who hope in the LORD will renew their strength. They will soar on wings like eagles; they will run and not grow weary, they will walk and not be faint (Isaiah 40:28-31).

The Holy Spirit's Role in Our Sanctification

There do not seem to be many references in the Bible that explicitly teach that progressive sanctification is done by the Holy Spirit. Some of these references to the Spirit's sanctifying work seem to emphasize only the positional aspect—that is, the person is set apart unto God by the work of the Spirit. For example, Paul says in 2 Thessalonians 2:13, "From the beginning God chose you to be saved through the sanctifying work of the Spirit and through belief in the truth." There are, however, some scholars, such as F.F. Bruce, who believe 2 Thessalonians 2:13 refers to the present aspect of our holiness. Commenting on this verse, Bruce says, "Sanctification is the Spirit's present work in believers; it will be completed at the *Parousia*, when Christ is 'glorified in his holy ones' (1:10)."[4]

Yet, it's clear that Paul *does* directly attribute the continuing process of sanctification to the Holy Spirit (1 Thessalonians 4:3-8). In verse 3 it is stated that God has called us to "be sanctified." In verses 7,8 we read that God has called us not to be impure "but to live a holy life." Verse 8 then goes on to connect the presence of the Holy Spirit to Paul's discussion about our sanctification: "Therefore, he who rejects this instruction does not reject man but God, who gives you his Holy Spirit."

While the word "sanctification" in the present progressive sense is not frequently tied directly to the Spirit, such a connection *is* implied in many references. For example, the actual fruit of sanctification is said to be produced by the Spirit in

Galatians 5:22,23, the love of God is poured into our lives through the Spirit (Romans 5:5), the requirements of the law are worked through the Spirit (Romans 8:4), it is by the Spirit that we put to death the misdeeds of the body (Romans 8:13,14), and we are renewed by the Spirit (Titus 3:5).

Jesus, in His concern that we still live in a fallen world, prayed this to the Father: "My prayer is not that you take them out of the world but that you protect them from the evil one. They are not of the world, even as I am not of it. Sanctify them by the truth; your word is truth" (John 17:15-17). It is the Holy Spirit who leads us into all truth (John 16:13). This may be the greatest ministry of the Holy Spirit, who is first and foremost "the Spirit of truth" (John 14:17). As we will see in the next chapter, truth is the means by which we are sanctified.

The work of our sanctification, then, has all of its source in God. It involves the Father, the Son, and the Spirit in their usual working relationship as the Trinity. We could say that 1) the Father is the initiator of sanctification; 2) Christ is the mediator whose saving work in death and resurrection provides the basis for our sanctification; and 3) it is the Holy Spirit who actually comes into all creation to sustain and enliven it. He is the one who indwells the believer to apply the sanctifying work of Christ and bring personal union with all the members of the Trinity.

Our Role in Our Sanctification

Since we are what we are by the grace of God, and He is the primary agent of our sanctification, should we simply "let go and let God" take care of making us holy? Is the role we play in our sanctification only passive? Scripture clearly teaches that is not the case. Both the human and divine dimensions are seen in the Old Testament passage Leviticus 20:7,8: "Consecrate [sanctify] yourselves and be holy, because I am the LORD your God. Keep my decrees and follow them. I am the LORD, who makes you holy [sanctifies you]." The same truth is taught in the New Testament in Philippians 2:12,13: "Continue to work out *your* salvation with fear and trembling, for it is God who works in you to will and to act according to his good purpose" (emphasis added). While it's true that we are saved when we are born again and placed in Christ, still, we are exhorted to be actively involved in our restoration to wholeness or holiness.

The Greek word for "work out" (*katergazomai*) means "to bring about, produce, create."[5] Bible commentator Moses Silva says, "It is impossible to tone down the force with which Paul here points to our conscious activity in sanctification. . . . our salvation, which we confess to be God's from beginning to end, is here described as something that we must bring about."[6]

Later in Philippians, Paul describes his own activity in his growth in terms of a runner: "Brothers, I do not consider myself yet to have taken hold of it. But one thing I do: Forgetting what is behind and straining toward what is ahead, I press on toward the goal to win the prize for which God has called me heavenward in Christ Jesus" (Philippians 3:13,14). The prize to which he and all believers are called is "the culmination of the whole work of salvation."[7] This goal or prize is the completion of our sanctification, or our conformity to Christ.

Doing Our Part

There's a story about a pastor who found great joy in gardening. On a rare day off, one of his deacons found him working in his garden. "My, the Lord sure gave you a beautiful garden," he said to the pastor. The pastor responded, "Well, thank you very much, but you should have seen it when God had it to Himself!" In a similar way, when it comes to sowing and harvesting for God's kingdom, the Lord has sovereignly chosen to allow us to participate in His work.

The church, which is comprised of all believers, has something in common with an electrical appliance store. Every appliance is created for a specific purpose, but none can accomplish anything without electricity. They come in all shapes and colors, but they will never fulfill their purpose unless they receive power from a generating station. By themselves they don't even make good furniture or decoration for the house. But with the flip of a switch they are all energized in order to fulfill their purpose. The toaster makes toast, the coffeemaker brews coffee, and the refrigerator preserves our food. It would be foolish to say one appliance is better than the other, for they were all designed with a different purpose in mind.

That's true for all Christians as well, and we are not supposed to keep our work hidden. The Lord will receive no glory if we don't do good deeds or let our light shine. Neither will He receive any glory if we draw attention to ourselves by trying to find some meaningful existence without being plugged in to Him. Jesus said, "You are the light of the world. A city on a hill cannot be hidden. Neither do people light a lamp and put it under a bowl. Instead they put it on its stand, and it gives light to everyone in the house. In the same way, let your light shine before men, that they may see your good deeds and praise your Father in heaven" (Matthew 5:14-16).

A Combined Effort

How much will be accomplished to the glory of God in this present church age if we try to do everything by ourselves? Nothing! How much will be accomplished if we sit back in some "holy piety" and expect God to do it all? Apparently nothing, because God has committed Himself to work through the church. Paul wrote:

> His intent was that now, *through the church*, the manifold wisdom of God should be made known to the rulers and authorities in the heavenly realms, according to his eternal purpose which he accomplished in Christ Jesus our Lord. In him and through faith in him we may approach God with freedom and confidence (Ephesians 3:10-13, emphasis added).

We cannot passively take our place in Christ, nor can we passively stand against the evil one. We are told to "put on the Lord Jesus Christ, and make no provision for the flesh in regard to its lusts" (Romans 13:14). What if we don't actively take our place in Christ? What if we do make provision for the flesh? We are told to put on the armor of God; what if we don't? We are told not to use our bodies as instruments of unrighteousness (Romans

6:12,13). What if we do? We are told to take every thought captive to the obedience of Christ (2 Corinthians 10:5); what if we don't? At best we will surely stop bearing fruit, and at worst we will be utterly defeated.

Because God Works, We Work

We are saved by faith and sanctified by faith, but faith without works is dead, according to James:

> What good is it, my brothers, if a man claims to have faith but has no deeds? Can such faith save him? . . . faith by itself, if it is not accompanied by action, is dead. But someone will say, 'You have faith; I have deeds.' Show me your faith without deeds, and I will show you my faith by what I do (2:14,17,18).

If a person is truly a Christian, then it will be demonstrated by how he or she lives. What a person does is a reflection of what he or she has chosen to believe.

In Scripture, the works of sanctification are termed as "our" or "your" righteousness and works—that is, the works are those of the believer and not just God. For example, Deuteronomy 6:25 says, "It shall be *our* righteousness, if we observe to do all these commandments" (KJV, emphasis added). Paul says that the One who supplies you with the seeds to sow will "enlarge the harvest of *your* righteousness" (2 Corinthians 9:10, emphasis added), and he also talks about "*your* work produced by faith" (1 Thessalonians 1:3, emphasis added). John says, "He who does what is right is righteous" (1 John 3:7).

In the process of sanctification, we are yoked together with Christ, and we must pull together under His direction and by His power. It is inappropriate to speak of synergism—that is, God does part and man does part. God's work is always initiatory and primary, and our work is dependent upon Him. Even then, Scripture clearly shows the necessity of our work. The relation between God's work and our work is well stated by John Murray:

God's working in us is not suspended because we work, nor our working suspended because God works. Neither is the relation strictly one of cooperation as if God did his part and we did ours so that the conjunction or coordination of both produced the required result. God works and we also work. But the relation is that because God works, we work. All working out of salvation on our part is the effect of God's working in us. . . . We have here not only the explanation of all acceptable activity on our part, but we also have the incentive to our willing and working. . . . The more persistently active we are in working, the more persuaded we may be that all the energizing grace and power is of God.[8]

According to Ephesians 2:10, our good works are already prepared, but we must walk in them. Commenting on this passage, Karl Barth said, "The distinctive thing about Christian or theological ethics is that we do not have to do any carrying without remembering that we are carried."[9] The fact that God's work is prior and primary means that sanctification is ultimately a matter of faith, just as justification is. We are not departing from the sphere of faith when we move from justification to sanctification. We are not justified by faith and then sanctified by works. If we took that route, Paul would rise out of his grave and say again, "You foolish Galatians! Who has bewitched you? . . . I would like to learn just one thing from you: Did you receive the Spirit by observing the law, or by believing what you heard? Are you so foolish? After beginning with the Spirit, are you now trying to attain your goal by human effort?" (Galatians 3:1-3).

What Christ Does, and What We Do

The biblical teaching about sanctification includes the wonderful truth that Christ's work in salvation is substitutionary. His sinless life and His death were *for* us as a substitute. But the Spirit's work in applying the fruit of Christ's substitution is not done as a substitute. Rather, God works *in* us to will and to do, but He does not will and do *for* us (*see* Philippians 2:13). We must actively exercise our will and do good works.

Why? Substitutionary sanctification would destroy the individual, separate human person. For the Spirit to actually perform the work of sanctification without the human person's active involvement would entail the mystical absorption of the human person into God and destroy the individual. If it is Christ or the Spirit doing everything, then there is no human person left.

The truth of what Paul says in Galatians 2:20 ("I no longer live, but Christ lives in me") cannot be interpreted as substitutionary in the sense that Christ lives my life *instead* of me. Somehow Christ lives in me and yet I also actively live. Paul continues, "The life I live in the body, I live by faith in the Son of God, who loved me and gave himself for me" (Galatians 2:20). The "I" that continues to live is still intact but is now complete in Christ. Sanctification, then, is actually the restoration of true selfhood. As such, it calls the human faculties of personhood (mind, emotion, and will) into action so that they may be exercised and grow in holiness. God does not trample on our humanness; He sets us free in Christ to be fully human.

What we are saying is that our thinking, our feeling, and our active willing are part of us. These capacities must be renewed in sanctification. And God cannot renew them without working through them, which means that they must be active. Thus we must believe and obey by thinking, choosing, and feeling. These cannot be carried along passively, for then part of us is not functioning and thus left out of our total renewal. For example, there is no other way to renew a will than through the exercise of that will. It's at that point that God somehow renews a person by challenging him and providing the power for him to actively exercise his will and other capacities.

The Heart's Place in Sanctification

The prophet Ezekiel challenged his listeners to "get a new heart and a new spirit" (Ezekiel 18:31), yet he knew that people are dependent on God for this to happen. God Himself said in Ezekiel 11:19, "I will give them an undivided heart and put a new spirit in them; I will remove from them their heart of stone and give them a heart of flesh." Later, and in Ezekiel 36:26, He said, "I will give you a new heart and put a new spirit in you."

From these passages we can clearly see that the new heart and spirit are gifts from God, and yet we are called to have a part in receiving these gifts.

Jeremiah prophetically brings together our relationship with God, and the gift of a new heart in Jeremiah 24:7: "I will give them a heart to know me, that I am the LORD. They will be my people, and I will be their God, for they will return to me with all their heart." This is a heart to know or experience God. In the new covenant, which every child of God is privileged to be under, the Lord says, "I will put My law within them, and on their heart I will write it; and I will be their God, and they shall be My people. And they shall not teach again, each man his neighbor and each man his brother, saying, 'Know the LORD,' for they shall all know Me, from the least of them to the greatest of them" (Jeremiah 31:33,34 NASB).

The heart is the real person (Proverbs 27:19) and the place from which all life comes (Proverbs 4:23). The heart is thus the place of personhood, intellect, emotion, and will. And God's covenant promise is a changed heart: "I will make an ever-lasting covenant with them: I will never stop doing good to them, and I will inspire them to fear me [literally, put the fear of me in their hearts], so that they will never turn away from me" (Jeremiah 32:40). We also see this reflected in Paul's prayerful words, "May the Lord direct your hearts into God's love and Christ's perserverance" (2 Thessalonians 3:5).

Sanctification is the process of changing the heart, which is actually a change of the total person (that is, the mind, emotion, and will or actions). The Bible portrays the heart as the center where all these elements of personhood come together. Not only do these elements come together in the heart, they also cannot be separated within the heart. We will explore how truth must penetrate the heart in order to touch the emotions and our behavior, but first we must understand that sanctification is *total*—that is, the whole person is involved.

The Heart and Our Intellect

Contrary to popular thinking, the dominant function of the heart is not emotional. The heart, according to Scripture, is first the place where the human being thinks, secondly where he wills, and only thirdly where he feels. This was confirmed by H. Wheeler Robinson, who counted 822 uses of the word *heart* for some aspect of human personality. According to his categorization, 204 of the 822 uses refer to intellectual activity, 195 to the volitional aspect, and 166 to an emotional state.[10] Bible scholar Hans Wolff, in his discussion about references to the heart in the Old Testament wrote, "In by far the greatest number of cases, it is intellectual, rational functions that are ascribed to the heart—that is precisely what we ascribe to the head and, more exactly, to the brain. . . ."[11]

A good illustration of this kind of usage for the word "heart" is seen when Moses says to the Israelites, "To this day the LORD has not given you a heart to know, nor eyes to see, nor ears to hear" (Deuteronomy 29:4 NASB). Just as the eyes are for seeing and the ears are for hearing, so also is the heart for knowing. When Job wants to tell his so-called friends that he is not inferior to them in understanding, he literally says, "I have a heart as well as you." The NASB translates this, "I have intelligence as well as you" (Job 12:3). The "man of heart" in Scripture is not a man of deep feeling, but a man "of understanding" (Job 34:10,34). Insanity is a problem of the heart (Ecclesiastes 9:3), and to lack reason is to have the "heart" of a beast (Daniel 5:21 NASB).[12] While we have commonly understood the heart to be the seat of emotion, the verses we just looked at show it's more accurate to understand the heart as the seat of reflection.

The essential business of the heart is stated in Proverbs 15:14: "The mind [literally, heart] of the intelligent seeks knowledge" (NASB). In this regard it is interesting that the word for "heart" occurs by far most frequently in the portions of the Bible known as the wisdom literature (for example, 99 times in Proverbs and 42 times in Ecclesiastes), as well as in the "strongly didactic book of Deuteronomy"[13] (51 times). These portions of Scripture instruct us in the ways of God's wisdom, which we are to know and understand with our hearts. Thus the goal of life is a heart of wisdom (Psalm 90:12).[14]

Many mental functions are related to the heart. We believe with the heart (Romans 10:10; Hebrews 3:12); we meditate with the heart (Psalm 19:14; 49:3); we consider and worry in our hearts (Psalm 14:1; 15:2; Luke 12:45; Romans 10:6); and that which we memorize is kept in the heart (Psalm 119:11; Proverbs 6:21; Luke 2:51).

The Old Testament consistently uses the word "heart" for the place of thinking because the Hebrew vocabulary had no other word for "mind." The New Testament does have another word for mind, which is related to knowing and reasoning. That does not mean, however, that the New Testament changed the meaning of "heart" by separating the functions of the mind from the heart. The usage of mind is quite limited in the New Testament, being used primarily by the apostle Paul for discourse in the Hellenistic environment.[15] And more importantly, in contrast to Greek philosophy, which tended to separate the human capacity for reason from other dimensions of the soul, the New Testament use of mind retained the Old Testament meaning—in which the intellectual sphere was anchored firmly in the whole person, especially the will.[16]

The new Testament connects the concept of the mind with the heart in several places; this suggests that the mind is, in reality, the thinking function of the heart. People are said to "understand" (*voeo*) with their heart (John 12:40). In Romans 1:21, futile speculations lead to a darkened heart, and in Ephesians 4:17,18 the same problem of a futile mind (*nous*) involves a darkened understanding (*dianoia*). The similarity of heart and mind is even more apparent in Hebrews 10:16, which quotes the new covenant promise given in Jeremiah 31:33: "I will put My laws upon their heart, and upon their mind I will write them" (NASB). The relationship of heart and mind is also seen in Robert Jewett's comment on Paul's words about the peace of God guarding both heart and mind. He says, "Retaining the assumption of a unified personal center in the heart, Paul assumes that the thoughts flow from the heart and conceives of the mind as a constellation of thoughts and knowledge."[17]

Thus, despite the use of a different word for "mind" in the New Testament, it is obvious that the mind still represents the intellectual function of the heart.

The Heart and Our Will

In addition to being the place where we think, the heart is also the place where we will or purpose. We desire and choose in our heart. David rejoiced in God because he said God had given him the desire of his heart (Psalm 21:1,2). When God

THE AGENTS OF SANCTIFICATION   145

tested his people in the wilderness, Moses says it was "to know what was in your heart, whether or not you would keep his commands" (Deuteronomy 8:2). God looked at their hearts to see whether they would choose to obey or not. That's because the heart is the place of all purposes and plans, all motives and intentions, and all resolutions.[18]

Other than the presence of God in our lives, the capacity to choose is the greatest power that we possess. We can choose to believe or not believe. We can choose to walk by the Spirit or walk by the flesh. That's why we can say that successful Christian living lies in the exercise of the will.

The Heart and Our Emotions

The heart is also the place where we experience emotion. Love and hate, joy and sorrow, courage and fear, and all other emotions are viewed as being in the heart. For example, we are to love God with all our heart (Deuteronomy 6:5); shout joyfully to him with a glad heart (Isaiah 65:14); and, keep our heart from being troubled by believing in Christ (John 14:1).[19]

It is especially in connection with the emotions that Scripture demonstrates the holistic nature of the human person. Emotions are not simply experiences of the psyche or the inner person. They are felt physically, especially in the heart. The Old Testament in particular vividly expresses emotions as movements of the heart. If a person loses courage, his heart quivers like leaves in the wind (Isaiah 7:2); it is faint (Deuteronomy 20:8); it melts like wax (Psalm 22:14); or it turns to water (Joshua 7:5). Fear is described in terms of a person's heart going out (Genesis 42:28), leaving him (Psalm 40:12), or dropping down (1 Samuel 17:32). By contrast, courage is the strengthening of the heart (Psalm 27:14).

This relationship between the emotions and the physical body is the reason Scripture teaches that even physical health is affected by our emotional states. For example, in Proverbs 14:30 we read, "A heart at peace gives life to the body, but envy rots the bones." Nehemiah affirmed that positive emotions are truly healing to the body when he said, "The joy of the LORD is your strength" (8:10).

The heart, then, is the place of knowing, willing, and feeling. It is the center of our personality. It is the place where God addresses us and from which we respond as whole persons. That is why its function of knowing stands first—for the ultimate function of the heart is to seek wisdom and knowledge by paying attention to God's Word.

It's All in the Heart

We often conceive of thinking, feeling, and willing as separate functions. For instance, we may characterize someone as rational, left-brained, or cerebral, suggesting that he or she is heavy on reason and light on emotion. Or, perhaps we say someone has a tendency to live primarily from his or her emotions without thinking. But these kinds of separation are contrary to biblical thought. Thinking, feeling, and willing all come together in the heart in holistic unity.

That these different functions are all closely related can be seen biblically. In the Bible, to "know" something is to grasp it such that it affects the total personality. Pedersen explains this biblical concept of knowing when he says:

> For the Israelite, *thinking* was not the solving of abstract problems. He does not add link to link, nor does he set up major and minor premises from which conclusions are drawn. To him thinking is to grasp a totality. He directs his soul [Pedersen uses "soul" to include the heart; in fact, for him, "heart" is the center of the soul or "the soul in its inner value"] towards the principal matter, that which determines the totality, and receives it into his soul (heart), the soul thus being immediately stirred and led in a certain direction.[20]

For the soul or heart to be stirred and led, as Pedersen says, indicates that such thinking is not just an intellectual affair; it also involves the emotions and the will. An interesting example of knowledge involving the will or actual behavior is seen in Isaiah's statement, "An ox knows its owner, and a donkey its master's manger, but Israel does not know, My people do not understand" (Isaiah 1:3). Even though donkeys and oxen are not very intelligent, they know who cares for them and respond accordingly. But Israel did not know her Master. Her lack of knowledge, as one Bible expert says, is "not theoretical ignorance, but rather failure to practice the filial relationship in which they stand with God."[21]

Another place where we see thoughts connected with emotion and will is in Genesis 4:1: "Adam knew Eve his wife; and she conceived, and bare Cain" (KJV). We can be certain that Adam's knowledge of Eve involved feeling and actual behavior.

Acknowledging that thought, emotion, and will are united within the heart is critically important for understanding Bible passages that talk about our knowledge of God and His knowledge of us (Matthew 7:22,23; John 10:27; Galatians 4:9). That is why eternal life can be described as knowing God through His Son Jesus Christ (John 17:3). It is this understanding of "know" that also makes sense of our Lord's promise that "you will know the truth, and the truth will set you free" (John 8:32). So often believers know the truth, but they are not free. That's because they do not know the truth in their *hearts*—they do not know it emotionally and behaviorly as well as intellectually.

Other biblical examples of the unity found in knowing, feeling, and willing are seen in the concepts of hearing, purposing, and loving. To "hear" something in Scripture, such as the voice of God, is not simply to listen thoughtfully. It is to listen and obey with the will. A person does not really hear something until it touches his thoughts, feelings, and will. With regard to "purposing," we could say that all of the Hebrew words most commonly used in reference to the function of thinking include the movement of the heart toward activity.[22] And finally, the concept of love clearly involves our thoughts, emotions, and activities. Unless all are involved, we are not experiencing biblical love.

Sanctification in Summary

God is the primary agent of our sanctification because He gave us a new heart so that we would turn toward Him. When we do, we become an agent in our own sanctification, and our heart is conformed to the image of God. It is in the heart that our mind, emotions, and will are united in Christ-centered living. When we turn our hearts toward God, we begin to love Him and others. Henri Nouwen said it well:

> Somehow during the centuries we have come to believe that what makes us human is our mind. Many people who do not know any Latin still seem to know the definition of a human being as a reasoning animal: *rationale animal est hommo* (Seneca). But Adam [a severely mentally handicapped person] keeps telling me over and over again that what makes us human is not our mind but our heart, not our ability to think but our ability to love. Whoever speaks about Adam as a vegetable or an animal-like creature misses the sacred mystery that Adam is fully capable of receiving and giving love. He is fully human, not a little bit human, not half human, not nearly human, but fully, completely human because he is all heart. And it is our heart that is made in the image and likeness of God.[23]

8

Transformed by the Renewing of the Mind

Do not conform any longer to the pattern of this world, but be transformed by the renewing of your mind. Then you will be able to test and approve what God's will is—his good, pleasing and perfect will.

—Romans 12:2

An undergraduate student at a Christian university was referred to me (Neil) for counseling by the chairman of her department. I was told she wasn't going to make it through the semester if she didn't get some help. She couldn't concentrate on her work, and her countenance revealed total defeat. She came from a Mormon family that was split down the middle when her mother realized, after much searching and diligent study, that Joseph Smith was a false prophet. After following her mother's lead in making a decision for Christ, she enrolled in a good Christian college. The first year went well, but now she found herself in a spiritual battle for her mind.

After hearing her story, I realized that she had not fully come to terms with her past. So I led her through a comprehensive process of repentance using the Steps to Freedom in

Christ.[1] Her greatest struggle was having to face the false beliefs and religious practices of her Mormon family. Finally she chose the truth and renounced all the religious ceremonies that she had participated in such as baptizing and marrying for the dead. The dramatic change in her countenance revealed that the truth had set her free. I encourged her to visit the restroom to freshen up and take a good look at herself in the mirror. "Why? Do I look that bad?" She asked. "No," I responded, "you look that good!" My secretary accompanied her and told me later that when she looked in the mirror, she said in astonishment, "Why, I'm pretty!"

Reprogramming Our Minds

The truth will indeed set us free and transform our character. To understand how, we need to start by realizing that a greater transformation took place when we were born again spiritually than will take place when we die physically. Salvation isn't addition; it is transformation. As Christians, we are both physically and spiritually alive as long as we reside on planet Earth. When we die physically, we will be absent from the body and present with the Lord. Our tired old physical bodies will return to dust and we will receive resurrected bodies, for flesh and blood cannot inherit the kingdom of God (1 Corinthians 15:50-54). Until then, Paul urges us not to use our bodies as instruments of unrighteousness (Romans 6:12-14), because if we do we will allow sin to reign there. We are urged by the mercies of God to present our bodies to Him as living sacrifices (Romans 12:1). Paul then admonishes us to be transformed by the renewing of our minds (12:2) because, before we came to Christ, our minds were programmed to live independent of God. In progressive sanctification, we have to assume our responsibility to reprogram our minds to the truth of God's Word.

Like a computer, our brains record the experiences we have in life. Newborn babies come into this world with a clean slate. The only world they know is what they can see, hear, feel, taste, and smell. Nothing has been programmed into their computer. They have no vocabulary and therefore no way to communicate with those who are charged to take care of them. They have neither the presence of God in their lives nor the knowledge of His ways. So during their early and formative years, they learn to live independent of God.[2] In later years, when these individuals come to Christ, their minds are still programmed to live independent of God. There is no "delete" or "clear" button, that can be pushed to get rid of old thinking patterns; hence, the need to renew (reprogram) their minds.

Some children are fortunate enough to have godly parents who raised them according to His principles, and when they come to Christ, we don't see as drastic a difference between the old man and the new man. But make no mistake about it, these children needed salvation as much as the children who were raised by unbelieving parents. Both types of children will pass from spiritual death to life in Christ when they experience salvation. And both will still have times when they exhibit fleshly behavior that stands in opposition to the Spirit of God.

It takes time to renew our minds and replace the lies we have believed with the truth of God's Word. Yet that should not discourage us, for we have all the resources we need to make that happen. The Lord has given us the Holy Spirit, who is the Spirit of Truth (John 14:17), and He will guide us into all truth (John 16:13). Also, because we are one with God, "we have the mind of Christ" (1 Corinthians 2:16). And finally, Paul tells us we have superior weaponry available to us for winning the battle for our minds:

> Though we live in the world, we do not wage war as the world does. The weapons we fight with are not the weapons of the world. On the contrary, they have divine power to demolish strongholds. We demolish arguments and every pretension that sets itself up against the knowledge of God, and we take captive every thought to make it obedient to Christ (2 Corinthians 10:3-5).

Paul is not talking about defensive armor; he's talking about battering-ram weaponry that tears down strongholds that have been raised up against the knowledge of God. A stronghold is a negative pattern of thinking that has been burned into our minds either by habitual reinforcement or because of certain traumas we have experienced.

The Problem of Strongholds

How are these strongholds erected in our minds? There is basic agreement among developmental theorists that our vocabulary, worldview, and attitudes about life are assimilated primarily from the environment in which we are raised. Our temperaments and personalities are basically established by the time we are six years old.

This programming of our minds is said to take place in two ways. The first is through prevailing experiences that we had in early childhood—such as the family we were raised in, the churches that we went to or didn't go to, the neighborhoods where we grew up, the communities we belonged to, the friends that we had or didn't have, and so on. These external factors all had an effect upon our development.

It isn't just the environment, however, that determines how we develop. Two children can be raised in the same home, have the same parents, eat the same food, have the same friends, go to the same church, and respond differently. Our environment isn't all that shapes us because every one of us has a different way of interpreting the world we live in. In addition, God has created each of us uniquely in a way that He planned even before the foundation of the world (Ephesians 1:4; 2:10). Jacob and Esau came from the same womb, but they were very different in their temperament and personality.

Along with the prevailing experiences that we have had, the second greatest contributor to the development of strongholds are traumatic experiences. For instance, you may have been raped when you were a child; you may have had parents who didn't get along and are divorced; or perhaps someone close to you died unexpectedly. These kinds of experiences are not assimilated into our minds over time; rather, they are burned into our minds because of their intensity.

All of these experiences have been stored in our memory like a file in our computer. Consequently, all kinds of mental strongholds have been raised up against the knowledge of God. And at the moment of salvation, there is no "clear" button to delete all the information that has been programmed into our minds.

As we struggle to reprogram our minds, we are also confronted daily with a world system that is not godly. Remember, Paul warned us, "Do not conform any longer to the pattern of this world" (Romans 12:2). Obviously we can continue, even as Christians, to allow the world we live in to affect our minds. That is why Paul also warned, "See to it that no one takes you captive through hollow and deceptive philosophy, which depends on human tradition and the basic principles of this world rather than on Christ" (Colossians 2:8).

Even though we have the Spirit of truth to lead us, we can still choose to follow the ways of the world. The right and the responsibility to choose is the greatest power we possess other than the presence of God in our lives. We can choose to pray or not pray, to read our Bible or read books that aren't edifying. Every child of God can choose to walk by the Spirit or walk by the flesh.

Dealing with Temptation

Because we live in this world, we are always going to face the reality of temptation. Keep in mind, however, that it's not a sin to be tempted. If that were so, then the worst sinner who ever lived would be Christ because He "has been tempted in every way, just as we are—yet was without sin" (Hebrews 4:15).

When Satan wants to tempt you, he knows exactly which button to push! He knows your weaknesses as well as ours. The things that may tempt you may not tempt us at all. And Satan's goal with temptation is to get all of us to live our lives independent of God—that is, to walk according to the flesh rather than the Spirit (*see* Galatians 5:16-23).

Some Christians seem to think a good way to deal with temptation is to simply shut themselves off from the world. But that's not a realistic option, nor is that Christ's calling for us. Besides, even if we did try to shut out the world, we would still face temptation because there is so much junk already programmed into our memory banks that we could be tempted for years without having to leave our homes. This is especially true in the area of sexual temptation. Once sexual strongholds are formulated in the mind, the mental impressions are there for instant recall.

If we are going to take the "way of escape" that God has provided for us, we must take our thoughts captive to the obedience of Christ. If we allow tempting thoughts to ruminate in our minds, we will eventually take a path that leads to destruction.

The apostle James tells us this about temptation:

> When tempted, no one should say, "God is tempting me." For God cannot be tempted by evil, nor does he tempt anyone; but each one is tempted when, by his own evil desire, he is dragged away and enticed. Then, after desire has conceived, it gives birth to sin; and sin, when it is full-grown, gives birth to death (1:13-15).

Understanding the New Man

The Mind and the New Man

To better understand how temptation affects us, please refer to the following diagram featuring the new man. Scripture says we have an outer man and an inner man (2 Corinthians 4:16). The outer man is our physical body, which relates to the world. Our physical brain is a part of the outer man. Our mind, on the other hand, is a part of the inner man. There is a fundamental difference between our brain and our mind: Our brain is organic matter. When we die physically, our brain will return to dust.

We will be absent from the body and present with the Lord, but we will not be mindless.

The New Man

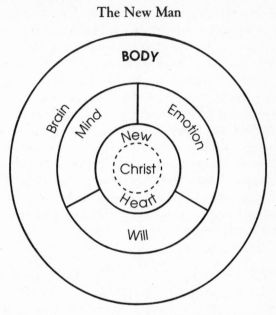

It would only make sense that God would create the outer man to correlate with the inner man. The obvious correspondence between the mind and the brain makes up a very sophisticated computer operation. The brain functions much like a digital computer that has millions of switching transistors that code all the information in a binary numbering system of 0's and 1's. In a similar fashion, every neuron operates like a little switch that turns on and off. Each neuron has many inputs (dendrites) and only one output that channels the neurotransmitters to other dendrites.

Millions upon millions of these make up the computer hardware, or the brain. Our minds, on the other hand, represent the software. The brain receives data from the external world through the five senses of the body. The mind is the compiler and chooses to interpret the data by whatever means it has been programmed. Until we come to Christ, it has been programmed by external sources and internal choices made without the knowledge of God or the benefit of His presence.

The tendency of our Western world is to assume that mental problems are primarily caused by faulty hardware (the brain). There is no question that organic brain syndrome, Alzheimer's disease, or lesser organic problems such as chemical or hormonal imbalances can impede our ability to function. And little can be done to correct faulty hardware (or brains). The best software program won't work if the computer is turned off or in disrepair. However, our primary problem is not the hardware, it is the software. Other than submitting our bodies to God as a living sacrifice and taking care of ourselves physically, we can do little to fix the hardware, but we *can* change the software. Now that we are alive in Christ, we have been given the mind of Christ, a new heart, and the Holy Spirit will lead us into all truth.

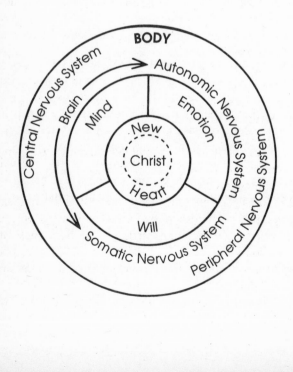

The Nervous System and the New Man

The brain and the spinal cord make up the central nervous system, which splits off into a peripheral nervous system (as shown on the previous page). The peripheral nervous system has two channels: the autonomic and the somatic nervous systems. The somatic nervous system regulates our muscular and skeletal movements, such as speech, gestures, and so on. In other words, that which we have volitional control over. This system correlates to our will.

How Our Thoughts Affect Us

Our autonomic nervous system regulates our glands. We have no volitional control over our glands. We don't say to our heart, "Beat, beat, beat," or to our adrenal glands, "Adren, adren, adren," or to our thyroid, "Thy, thy, thy." They function automatically. In a general sense, we don't have volitional control over our emotions either. You cannot will yourself to like someone you find emotionally unattractive. We do, however, have control over what we think, and we *can* decide to believe that what God says is true. Just as our glands are regulated by our central nervous system, so also are our emotions a product of our thoughts. It is not the circumstances of life that determine how we feel. Rather, how we feel is basically determined by how we interpret the events of life. Between the external stimulus (the event) and our emotional response is our brain (the receiver) and our mind (the interpreter). That is, our brain and mind assess the world around us, and our emotions respond to that information. In chapter 9 we will explain further this interaction between the mind, will, and emotions.

Let's apply all this to the problem of stress. When external pressures put demands on our physical system, our adrenal glands respond by secreting cortisone-like hormones into our physical body. This is the natural "fight or flight" response to the pressures of life. If the pressures persist too long and our adrenal glands can't keep up, then our stress becomes distress. The result can be physical illness, or we may become irritable about things that wouldn't bother us physically or emotionally in less stressful times.

This raises a key question: Why is it that two people can respond differently to the same stressful situation? Some people actually thrive under pressure, while others fall apart. What is the difference between them? Do some people have superior adrenal glands? We don't think so. Although every person may differ considerably in his or her physical makeup, the major difference isn't in the external factors. We all face the pressures of deadlines, schedules, trauma, and temptations. The major difference is in the software—that is, how we mentally interpret the external world and process the data our brain is receiving.

When we encounter a difficulty, our mind can choose to respond by trusting God with the assurance of victory or by viewing ourselves as the helpless victim of circumstances. The Israelite soldiers saw Goliath in reference to themselves and became stressed out. Young David saw the same giant in reference to God and triumphed in the same situation that had left experienced soldiers in defeat.

Faith in God greatly affects how we interpret and respond to the pressures of this world. And no matter what happens in life, we can always rest in the assurance that "in all things God works for the good of those who love him, who have been called according to his purpose" (Romans 8:28).

The Power of Choice

Our sex glands are also part of our autonomic nervous system. They function apart from our will and regulate normal sexual functioning according to our sexual identities. For instance, adult women don't control their menstrual cycle, but most record it. Our God-given sexual functioning and identity are not the cause of a lack of sexual self-control. That is, our sex glands are not the cause of sexual immorality. But if we load up our minds with pornographic images and use our bodies as instruments of unrighteousness, we will drive our sex glands into overload. Indeed, we do have control over what we choose to think, believe, and consequently do.

When we allow our minds to be stimulated externally or by recalling experiences that we have had, an autonomic signal causes a hormone called *epinephrine* to be secreted into the bloodstream, which locks into our memory whatever stimulus is present at the time of the emotional excitement. This reaction causes us to involuntarily remember emotionally charged events—negative and traumatic ones as well as positive ones. That is why pornographic images and experiences can remain in our memories for months and even years, whereas boring academic facts that we've had to study can fade from our minds before the final exam is given. The positive benefit of this is that thinking of good memories can help result in a positive mood elevation. (For more complete explanation on understanding and resolving chemical addictions and sexual bondages in Christ, see Neil's books *Freedom from Addiction* and *A Way of Escape*.)

In every tempting situation we have a choice. We can respond according to the flesh (the way we learned to respond before we came to Christ), or we can respond according to the Spirit. Galatians 5:17 tells us the two are in opposition to each other because the flesh is programmed to live independent of God and the Holy Spirit is dependent upon God the Father. How do you know which one you have chosen? "The deeds of the flesh are evident" (Galatians 5:19-21), and so is "the fruit of the Spirit" (Galatians 5:22,23). Our countenance and behavior reveal the choices that we have made.

Suppose you choose to walk "according to the elementary principles of the world, rather than according to Christ" (Colossians 2:8 NASB). If you continue to do that for about six weeks, you will establish a habit that leads to the formation of a stronghold. As we said earlier, mental strongholds are negative patterns of thinking that have been burned into our minds by habitual reinforcement of external stimulus or because of certain traumas that we have experienced. The result is something less than a

Christlike temperament. For instance, feelings of inferiority is a stronghold that most Christians struggle with. How did they develop an inferiority complex? Were they born with it? No, it was developed over time because of the pressures foisted upon them by the performance-based world they live in. Not everybody got perfect grades or made the football team or won the beauty contest. Does that mean they are inferior? The world gives the message that they are, but God doesn't do that. He loves *all* His children the same even though He has not equally distributed spiritual gifts, talents, or intelligence.

There are a countless number of strongholds that have been raised up against the knowledge of God. The philosophies of this world have affected the way we think, which affects the way we feel, which results in less-than-godly character. Sanctification works the opposite way. It begins by receiving forgiveness, the life of Christ, and a new heart. It continues as we renew our minds by choosing the truth, which affects our emotions and transforms our character.

Positional sanctification assures us that we are a new creation in Christ, and we need to daily appropriate that truth by faith. Progressive sanctification is based upon the foundation that we are already children of God, and that the "inner man is being renewed day by day" (2 Corinthians 4:16 NASB). At the same time, we are still contending with the world, the flesh, and the devil. Because we were created in God's image, we have the capacity to choose whom we will serve—the god of this world, or the one and only Creator of all things. Much of progressive sanctification is a struggle to choose between external influences coupled with internal mental strongholds raised up against the knowledge of God, and the internal presence of God coupled with the external help of the body of Christ. Wholeness and true mental health comes when we choose the truth, appropriate it by faith, and walk by the Spirit.

9

Truth: The Means
of Sanctification

Then you will know the truth, and the truth will set you free.

—John 8:32

My prayer is not that you take them out of the world but that you protect them from the evil one. . . . Sanctify them by the truth; your word is truth.

—John 17:15,17

I (Neil) was asked by a desperate husband if I would visit his wife, who was committed by law to a psychiatric hospital. This young mother of two had graduated from a fine Christian college, but now she was considered mentally ill because of irrational fears and condemning voices that she heard in her head. I had the privilege of helping this young woman find her freedom in Christ. No manipulation of drugs in kind or quantity can cure a mentally sick person if the problem is in the software and not the hardware. Taking medication to cure the body is commendable, but taking drugs to cure the soul is deplorable.

This brings up a very important question: What is mental health? Secular mental health experts define mental health as being in touch with reality and relatively free of anxiety. Those are reasonable standards, but anyone caught in a spiritual battle for his or her mind would fail on both counts.

We believe that mentally healthy people are those who have a true knowledge of God, know who they are as children of God, and have a balanced biblical worldview that includes the reality of the spiritual world. If you knew that God loved you, that you were forgiven, that He had gone before you to prepare a place for you for all eternity, that you have no need to fear death, and you had the peace of God guarding your heart and mind, would you be a mentally healthy person? Of course you would! But let us quickly add that mentally sick people usually have a distorted concept of God and a terrible perception of themselves. If you don't believe that is true, then visit a psychiatric ward, and you'll find some of the most religious people you have ever met, but their concept of God and themselves is very distorted.

The reality presented in Scripture is defined more fully than the reality of the world. Actually, the Bible presents the unseen spiritual and eternal world as more real than the temporal world we now see and exist in: "We fix our eyes not on what is seen, but on what is unseen. For what is seen is temporary, but what is unseen is eternal" (2 Corinthians 4:18).

What is reality is truth, and God is the Truth and the revealer of truth. Truth in Scripture is that which is genuine, real, and trustworthy. In some Bible verses the concept of being faithful or trustworthy is more significant, and in other verses the idea of being genuine or real is more prevalent. But the total concept includes both what is real and trustworthy. Anything that is opposed to God and His revelation, then, is unreality, or a lie. True life, according to Scripture, can come only through living in harmony with God and His will, which is truth.

The natural man is spiritually dead; he is separated from God. His mind has been programmed by the world, and consequently his heart is deceitful. Paul says, "The man without the Spirit does not accept the things that come from the Spirit of God, for they are foolishness to him, and he cannot understand them, because they are spiritually discerned" (1 Corinthians 2:14). On the other hand, "we know that we are children of God, and that the whole world is under the control of the evil one. We know also that the Son of God has come and given us understanding, so that we may know him who is true. And we are in him who is true—even in his Son Jesus Christ. He is the true God and eternal life" (1 John 5:19,20).

The Trinity and Truth

In the previous chapter we saw that every member of the Godhead is the source of our sanctification and life. Every one of these primary agents is also described as *true* or *truth*. (In the verses that follow, we have italicized these key words for emphasis.)

The prophet Jeremiah tells us, "The LORD is the *true* God; he is the living God" (10:10). Jesus prays, "This is eternal life: that they may know you, the only *true* God" (John 17:3—notice the connection Jesus makes between truth and life). The psalmist says God is the "God of *truth*" (Psalm 31:5). John says, "God is *truthful*" (John 3:33).

God is true, and what He says is true whether fallen humanity believes Him or not. Paul raises the question, "What if some did not have faith? Will their lack of faith nullify God's faithfulness? Not at all! Let God be *true*, and every man a liar" (Romans 3:3,4). God is truth and what He says is true no matter whether we believe it or not.

Christ, the ultimate revelation of God, is the truth incarnate. "The Word became flesh and made his dwelling among us. We have seen his glory, the glory of the One and Only, who came from the Father, full of grace and *truth*" (John 1:14). Jesus said, "I am the way and the *truth* and the life" (John 14:6). He is the way to God because He is the truth, and the truth is life. Paul says, "Surely you heard of him and were taught in him in accordance with the *truth* that is in Jesus" (Ephesians 4:21). When Jesus completed His work, He said, "I will ask the Father, and he will give you another Counselor to be with you forever—the Spirit of truth" (John 14:16,17). Later, He added, "When he, the Spirit of *truth*, comes, he will guide you into all *truth*" (John 16:13, emphasis added). The Holy Spirit is God dwelling in believers to actually carry on the work of sanctification and holiness in their lives.

In summary, then the Trinitarian God is the source of sanctification. He is the ultimate reality (truth), and therefore the source of all truth. He sanctifies people by making Himself and His truth known to mankind—objectively before the world in the person of His Son, and then within the human heart by the Spirit, who indwells the believer. Because God is truth and life, to know God's life in sanctification is to know the truth in one's innermost being. When David offered a prayer of repentance in Psalm 51, he said, "Surely you desire *truth* in the inner parts; you teach me wisdom in the inmost place" (verse 6). This work is accomplished by God Himself through Christ and His Holy Spirit. The person whose walk is blameless and who lives righteously is a person "who speaks the *truth* from his heart" (Psalm 15:2).

The Truth Is What Changes Us

Over and over Scripture teaches that we are changed or sanctified by the truth. It is the truth that brings people to God and then bears fruit in them: "The word of *truth*, the gospel that has come to you. . . . this gospel is bearing fruit and growing, just as it has been doing among you since the day you heard it and understood God's grace in all its *truth*" (Colossians 1:5,6). "From the beginning God chose you to be saved through the sanctifying work of the Spirit and through belief in the *truth*" (2 Thessalonians 2:13). Paul also tells of those who refuse "to love the *truth* and so be saved" (2 Thessalonians 2:10).

As believers we are to "live by the *truth*" (1 John 1:6) or "practice the truth" (NASB). Paul says, "You were taught, with regard to your former way of life, to put off your old self, which is being corrupted by its deceitful desires; to be made new in the attitude of your minds; and to put on the new self, created to be like God in *true* righteousness and holiness" (Ephesians 4:22-24). The latter part of verse 24 is more literally "in righteousness and holiness of the *truth*" (NASB). Many commentators say that truth should be seen as the source of the righteousness and holiness that is being created in the new person. Andrew Lincoln writes,

> The evil desires which characterized the old person sprang from deceit (verse 22). Now by contrast, the virtues which characterize the new person can be said to come from the truth. This truth is ultimately divine reality which has been disclosed in the gospel and the apostolic tradition (cf. 1:13; 4:21).[1]

Commentator John Eadie agrees and then adds that "this truth in Jesus [verse 21] has a living influence upon the heart, producing, fostering, and sustaining such rectitude and piety."[2]

As Christians, then, we have the truth and the life within us, we can recapture lost ground as we are being renewed in the inner man. Let's add to the diagram we saw on page 156 and see how progressive sanctification gradually renews the mind and heals damaged emotions as the will is led by the Spirit (see page 166).

Overcoming the effects of the world, the flesh, and the devil is possible only because of our co-crucifixion with Christ. First, we are *crucified to the law*: "Through the law I died to the law so that I might live for God. I have been crucified with Christ and I no longer live, but Christ lives in me. The life I live in the body, I live by faith in the Son of God, who loved me and gave himself for me" (Galatians 2:19,20).

Second, because of the great work of Christ, we have been *crucified to the world*. Paul said, "May I never boast except in the cross of our Lord Jesus Christ, through which the world has been crucified to me, and I to the world" (Galatians 6:14). We still live *in* this fallen world, but we are no longer *of* it. Our citizenship is in heaven.

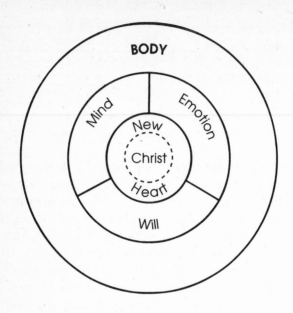

Third, we have been *crucified to sin*: "We know that our old self was crucified with Him so that the body of sin might be done away with, that we should no longer be slaves to sin—because anyone who has died has been freed from sin" (Romans 6:6,7). All this has been accomplished for us by Christ.

Fourth, by our own conscious choice, we have *crucified the flesh*: "Those who belong to Christ Jesus have crucified the sinful nature [flesh] with its passions and desires. Since we live by the Spirit, let us keep in step with the Spirit" (Galatians 5:24,25). Romans 8:13,14 tells us, "If you live according to the sinful nature [flesh], you will die; but if by the Spirit you put to death the misdeeds of the body, you will live, because those who are led by the Spirit of God are sons of God." Death is the ending of a relationship, not an existence. The world, the devil, and the flesh still exist, but we have a new relationship in Christ, who has overcome all the adversaries that would keep us in bondage.

Putting Off the Old Man

Renewing our mind begins with genuine repentance. John the Baptist preached, "Repent and believe the good news!" (Mark 1:15). Luke 24:45-47 says of Jesus, "Then he opened their minds so they could understand the Scriptures. He told them, 'This is what is written: The Christ will suffer and rise from the dead on the third day, and repentance and forgiveness of sins will be preached in his name to all nations, beginning at Jerusalem.'"

The New Testament word "repentance" (Gk. *metanoeo*) is a conjunction of *meta*, which means "after," implying change, and *noeo*, which means "to perceive." *Noeo* comes from the root word *nous*, which is usually translated "mind." Repentance, then, literally means a change of mind, but in Scripture this means more than just a change of intellectual thought. It is a change of disposition or attitude. Thus repentance implies a change that affects the whole person. This is confirmed in Matthew 3:7,8, which mentions some Pharisees and Saduccees who came to be baptized by John. "He said to them: 'You brood of vipers! Who warned you to flee from the coming wrath? Produce fruit in keeping with repentance.'" John discerned that their repentance was not genuine. They wanted the blessings of God without giving up their habits, traditions, customs, worldly positions, and religious practices.

When giving a profession of faith, the early church converts would stand, face the west, and make the following public declaration: "I renounce you, Satan, and all your works and all your ways." Every work of Satan had to be renounced for repentance to be complete. These converts understood the necessity to renounce all the evil practices and beliefs that had been going on in their synagogues, families, and personal lives. The early church preached, "Repent, then, and turn to God, so that your sins may be wiped out, that times of refreshing may come from the Lord" (Acts 3:19). Paul said to Agrippa, "I preached that they should repent and turn to God and prove their repentance by their deeds" (Acts 26:20). Peter said the Lord doesn't want "anyone to perish, but everyone to come to repentance" (2 Peter 3:9).

Repentance is the first step in renewing our minds. Without repentance, the effects of the old self are still in our minds. Progressive santification is then stalled because we are still believing the lies of this world while at the same time professing to believe the truth. People who are expressing faith in God but manifest no substantial change in their lives are caught between two kingdoms. They are actually in the kingdom of light, but they are still believing the father of lies. Satan cannot do anything about our position in Christ, but if he can get us to believe that it isn't for real, we will live as though it isn't.

The Lie Kills

The most fundamental teaching that the lie kills and is associated with unrighteousness is seen in the paradigm of sin in the Fall. Here the truth of God is at stake. Satan blatantly opposed the truth of God when he said, "You will not surely die" (Genesis 3:4). Adam and Eve believed the lie. The result is that mankind dies. This first sin is the real picture of all sin. It stems from the lie and leads to the destruction of true life. The effects are seen in guilt, fear, shame, alienation, misery, and death (3:7-24).

Jesus affirms all that in His teaching in John 8. He clearly shows that murder stems from the lie. Thus, lying is not simply a sin among other sins, such as murder. It is the *root* of all other sins; thus, it is the root of murder. The devil "was a murderer from the beginning, not holding to the truth, for there is no truth in him" (verse 44). It's also interesting to note that Jesus' enemies sought to kill Him because they would not receive the truth (verses 40,45).

The connection between the lie and unrighteousness and its consequence (death) is also emphasized in the book of Romans: "The wrath of God is being revealed from heaven against all the godlessness and wickedness of men who suppress the truth [divine reality] by their wickedness" (Romans 1:18). This passage demonstrates that truth is a power that can have life-transforming effects. But many people restrain the truth or hold it back, and the result is that they are affected by the opposite of truth—the lie. This, in turn, results in godlessness and wickedness, which brings the wrath of God, and finally, death.

Sin's Deceitfulness

The real disease of the heart is its deceitfulness (Jeremiah 17:9). The basic connection between sin and the lie is also seen in the relation between sin and deceit. Notice how Paul brings this out in the following verses: "Sin . . . deceived me" (Romans 7:11); "every sort of evil . . . deceives those who are perishing" (2 Thessalonians 2:10); "encourage one another . . . so that none of you may be hardened by sin's deceitfulness" (Hebrews 3:13). The outcome of sin's connection with the lie and deceitfulness is that mankind is killed and destroyed. Sin cheats man of life, which is found in truth. Consequently, the real battle is between Christ and the Antichrist, good and evil, the truth and the lie, divine revelation and satanic deception, the father of lies and the True One.

The Battle for the Mind

This battle is going on for the hearts and minds of every person created in the image of God—both believers and unbelievers. Satan has blinded the minds of unbelievers (2 Corinthians 4:4), and Paul says to believers, "I am afraid, lest as the serpent deceived Eve by his craftiness, your minds should be led astray from the simplicity and purity of devotion to Christ" (2 Corinthians 11:3 NASB). Elsewhere, Paul says, "The Spirit clearly says that in later times some will abandon the faith and follow deceiving spirits and things taught by demons" (1 Timothy 4:1). Is that happening? It is—all over the world. I (Neil) have counseled hundreds of people in many cultures who were struggling with their thought lives and having difficulty concentrating and reading their Bibles. In the more extreme cases, people were actually hearing voices. With few exceptions, these people were in a spiritual battle for their minds—a battle that can be resolved with complete repentance. (This discipleship/counseling process is outlined in Neil's book *Helping Others Find Freedom in Christ*.)

What is being passed off as mental illness oftentimes is nothing more than a battle for the mind. "You have a chemical imbalance," is the common medical explanation given to those who are hearing voices, plagued with negative thoughts, having panic attacks, or struggling with chronic depression. The assumption is that the problem is organic (that is, a hardware problem), and a prescription is usually given in an attempt to correct the problem. While it's true that our body chemistry *can* get out of balance and hormonal problems *can* cause sickness and disorientation, still, we have to ask questions that consider other possibilities. Possibilities such as, how can a chemical in the brain produce a personal thought? And how can our neurotransmitters involuntarily and randomly fire in such a way as to create a thought that we are opposed to thinking? Is there a *natural* explanation for that? Can the natural sciences be so certain about their answers when they have not taken into account all reality, including the spiritual realm?

When troubled people hear "voices," what are they actually hearing? The only way we can hear a sound with our ears is if there is a physical source of that sound. A sound wave is a rhythmic compression of air molecules. Sound moves physically through the air and is picked up by our eardrums, which in turn send signals to our brains. But the "voices" or disturbing thoughts that many people "hear" do not come from any kind of physical source. These people are often deemed mentally ill because, from a natural science perspective, they appear to be out of touch with reality—with the physical world around them.

What about people who say they are "seeing things"? What are they actually seeing? The only way we can see something with our physical eyes is when light reflects off a material object. The spiritual world, however, doesn't have material substance, so we cannot see a spiritual being with our natural eyes nor hear it with our ears. Remember, Paul says that "our struggle is not against flesh and blood, but against the rulers, against the authorities, against the powers of this dark world and against spiritual forces of evil in the heavenly realms" (Ephesians 6:12).

Girding Ourselves with the Truth

Our first line of defense against spiritual attacks upon our minds is to gird our loins with the truth. The armor of God, like any other armor, stops penetration, yet it cannot be appropriated passively. We have to actively take our place in Christ: "Put on the full armor of God, so that when the day of evil comes, you may be able to stand your ground, and after you have done everything, to stand. Stand firm" (Ephesians 6:13,14).

Paul then admonishes believers to gird their loins with truth so they can do battle and stand victorious in spiritual warfare (Ephesians 6:14). Commenting on this verse, Jerome Murphy-O'Connor says,

> The meaning, then, is that divine truth must become the existential environment in which the Christian lives, moves and has his being. He girds himself with "truth" in becoming aware of the change that has been effected in him through his contact with Truth. This is not a speculative recognition of his reception of the "word of truth" (Ephesians 1:13), or of his subsequent ever deeper immersion in it (Ephesians 4:20). It is achieved only by "living the truth in love" (4:15).[3]

As Jesus was preparing to depart after finishing His work here on earth, He met with His disciples. Following this last supper, Jesus prayed to the Father:

> My prayer is not that you take them out of the world but that you protect them from the evil one. They are not of the world, even as I am not of it. Sanctify them by the *truth*; your word is *truth*. As you sent me into the world, I

have sent them into the world. For them I sanctify myself, that they too may be truly sanctified (John 17:15-19, emphasis added).

The only way we can overcome the father of lies is not by human reasoning, nor by scientific research, but by God's revelation—His truth. That's why Paul tells us, "From the beginning God chose you to be saved through the sanctifying work of the Spirit and through belief in the *truth*" (2 Thessalonians 2:13, emphasis added).

The Word Is the Source of Truth

The Word Brings Life

Peter admonishes us, "like newborn babies, crave pure spiritual milk, so that by it you may grow up in your salvation, now that you have tasted that the Lord is good" (1 Peter 2:2). The Word of God is for us what milk is to babies. Without milk, babies don't grow, and without the Word of God, neither do we. In addition, "The word of God is living and active. Sharper than any double-edged sword, it penetrates even to dividing soul and spirit, joints and marrow; it judges the thoughts and attitudes of the heart" (Hebrews 4:12). God's Word has living power because the written Word of God cannot be separated from His person. As John tells us, Jesus is the Word incarnate (1:1,14).

God's Word is the expression of His mind, and the expression of His mind is the expression of His person. Thus His Word is the expression of His omnipotent self. Earlier we learned that it was by His word (or the expression of His mind) that creation came into being: "By the word of the LORD were the heavens made" (Psalm 33:6).

In the Old Testament, God assured His chosen people of success if they meditated on His Word (Joshua 1:8). And in Psalm 119, we find many references to the life-changing quality of the Word:

Verse 9—"How can a young man keep his way pure? By living according to your word."

Verse 11—"I have hidden your word in my heart that I might not sin against you."

Verse 16—"I delight in your decrees; I will not neglect your word."

Verses 25,37—"Preserve my life according to your word."

Verse 45—"I will walk about in freedom, for I have sought out your precepts."

Verse 133—"Direct my footsteps according to your word."

Psalm 19:7 says, "The law of the LORD is perfect, reviving the soul." The concept of "reviving" in the Hebrew language means "cause me to live." Psalm 107:19,20 says, "They cried to the LORD in their trouble, and he saved them from their distress. He sent forth his word and healed them; he rescued them from the grave." The Lord said through the prophet Isaiah, "My word . . . goes out from my mouth: It will not return to me empty, but will accomplish what I desire and achieve the purpose for which I sent it" (55:11). There is life, power, and direction in the Word of God; Jesus said, "The Spirit gives life; the flesh counts for nothing. The words I have spoken to you are spirit and they are life" (John 6:63).

The Word Has Power

If it's truth that sanctifies us, and God's Word is truth, then there is tremendous power in the Word. This can be illustrated on a much smaller scale in the power of human words. Scripture declares that, "Death and life are in the power of the tongue" (Proverbs 18:21 NASB), and "A soothing tongue is a tree of life, but perversion in it crushes the spirit" (Proverbs 15:4 NASB). James also reveals the destructive power of words; "The tongue also is a fire, a world of evil among the parts of the body. It corrupts the whole person, sets the whole course of his life on fire, and is itself set on fire by hell" (James 3:6). That's why Paul ex-horts, "Do not let any unwholesome talk come out of your mouths, but only what is helpful for building others up according to their needs, that it may benefit those who listen" (Ephesians 4:29). The next two verses say that we grieve the Holy Spirit when we use our words to tear down rather then build up. If every person could put into practice Ephesians 4:29, I'm sure that many of the problems in our churches and homes would disappear overnight.

Frederick Dale Bruner says,

> Our culture tends to underplay words, to say that "words aren't so important; it is our deeds that count." And yet in much of life words are our main deeds. Every married partner knows this. At a testimonial dinner one gracious word weighs more than a hundred gifts. Words are what people live by, and if words are real and good, then life and relationships are real and good. But if words are unreal and cutting, then life is hard. People do not live by bread alone, but by every word that other people say. "Sticks and stones may hurt my bones, but names really hurt me"[4]

Dallas Willard says, "The word . . . is therefore to be under-stood as a spiritual power, whether of man or of God or of other personal agency, whether for evil or for good. It is the power of the person who speaks."[5]

Finding God's Truth

Sanctification takes place when we appropriate the truth. But where is the truth found? First, God's truth can be revealed to us through nature. This can be seen in rainbows (Genesis 9:12-17), in creation itself (Psalm 19:1-4; Romans 1:20), and in the beneficient provisions for life (Acts 14:17). In Romans 1:19-21, Paul shows that all people know something of the truth of God: "What may be known about God is plain to them, because God has made it plain to them. . . . God's invisible qualities . . .

have been clearly seen, being understood from what has been made, so that men are without excuse. For although they knew God, they neither glorified him as God nor gave thanks to him." The sinfulness within the hearts of unsaved men caused them to suppress God's truth (verse 18), but they could not totally suppress it.

God's truth is also revealed in our moral nature (Romans 2:14,15). He has written His truth in the hearts of all people—even the hearts of unbelievers. Thus all people do have some knowledge of God's truth. Though an unbeliever's heart will try to resist this truth, he cannot totally silence it. God's moral truth speaks constantly even to unbelievers because it is what compels us to create some semblance of moral order through human government and laws.

For the believer, truth is revealed via the Spirit's presence as a witness within the heart (Jeremiah 31:33). Our conscience, which is a function of the mind, is not yet perfect, and thus not a source of infallible truth. The conviction of the Holy Spirit, however, *is* infallible, and works in the believer's heart to move him or her to God's truth. In addition, Paul says we can know something of God by looking at our own nature: "Since we are God's offspring, we should not think that the divine being is like gold or silver or stone—an image made by man's design and skill" (Acts 17:29). We are persons, and if we are God's offspring, then He must be a person. That rules out ultimate reality or truth as being some kind of nonpersonal spirit or reality, as some people think.

Truth is also revealed through other believers' lives. Every Christian displays God's truth in his or her life (2 Corinthians 3:1-3; 1 Thessalonians 1:6,7). This is especially true of mature Christians (1 Corinthians 11:1; Hebrews 13:7; 1 Peter 5:3). Their example of a changed life is an important witness of truth.

The most important place we can find truth, of course, is in God's Word—in His special revelation, which is the only normative record describing God and His works, and thus the place of canonical truth (Psalm 119:43; 142; 151; 160; John 17:17; 2 Timothy 2:15; James 1:18).

The Central Truths of Sanctification

Within the Bible are central truths that are essential to a believer's understanding and growth. These include 1) the truths related to our salvation, including what God has already done for us and what He will do; and 2) the imperatives or commands that reveal how we as Christians should live. These commands for living are based on what is already true about our salvation and the absolute assurance of what is yet to come because of our salvation. The beginning point of sanctification is belief in the gospel—that is, believing what God has done for us in salvation. This entails what He has done in the past and what He will yet do for us in the future. Bonar says,

> The gospel does not command us to do anything in order to obtain life, but it bids us live by that which another has done; and the knowledge of its life-giving truth is not labor but rest—rest of soul, which is the root of all true labor; for in receiving Christ we do not work in order to rest, but we rest in order to work.[6]

By faith, we rest in the finished work of Christ. Faith is a choice to trust in Christ, to believe that He did for us what we couldn't do for ourselves. Faith is the operating principle of life:

> Faith has the same place in the divine life which sense hath in the natural, being indeed nothing else but a kind of sense or feeling persuasion of spiritual things. It extends itself unto all divine truths; but, in our lapsed estate, it hath a peculiar relation to the declarations of God's mercy and reconcilableness to sinners through a Mediator, and therefore, receiving its denomination from that principal object, is ordinarily termed faith in Jesus Christ.[7]

Our sanctification is dependent upon believing the truth of who we are in Christ, resting in His finished work, and then living out the implications of this new perspective. According to Romans 6:11, we are to choose to believe that we are alive in Christ and dead to sin. Commenting on this passage, Sinclair Ferguson said:

> In actual practice, it is the dawning of this perspective which is the foundation for all practical sanctification. Hence Paul's emphasis on "knowing" that this is the case (verses 3,6,9), and his summons to believers to "count" themselves dead to sin and alive to God in Christ Jesus (verse 11). . . . Sanctification is therefore the consistent practical outworking of what it means to belong to the new creation in Christ. That is why so much of the New Testament's response to pastoral and personal problems in the early church was: "Do you not know what is true of you in Christ?" (Romans 6:3,16; 7:1; 1 Corinthians 3:16; 5:6; 6:2-3,9,14,19; 9:13,24). Live by the Spirit's power in a manner that is consistent with that![8]

Growing in Truths That Apply Today

We believe that God's desire for us in the ongoing process of sanctification is for us to experience in real life who we really are in Christ. This necessitates choosing to believe who we are as children of God on a daily basis. To help you in this process, here is a helpful list from Scripture:

SINCE I AM IN CHRIST, BY THE GRACE OF GOD . . .

Romans 5:1—I have been justified (completely forgiven).

Romans 6:1-6—I died with Christ and died to the power of sin's rule over my life.

Romans 8:1—I am free from condemnation.

1 Corinthians 1:30—I have been placed into Christ by God's doing.

1 Corinthians 2:12—I have received the Spirit of God into my life that I might know the things freely given to me by God.

1 Corinthians 2:16—I have been given the mind of Christ.

1 Corinthians 6:19,20—I have been bought with a price. I am not my own; I belong to God.

2 Corinthians 1:21—I have been established, anointed, and sealed by God in Christ.

2 Corinthians 5:14,15—I have died, I no longer live for myself, but for Him.

2 Corinthians 5:21—I have been made righteous.

Galatians 2:20—I have been crucified with Christ and it is no longer I who live, but Christ lives in me (the life I am now living is Christ's life).

Ephesians 1:3—I have been blessed with every spiritual blessing.

Ephesians 1:4—I have been chosen in Christ before the foundation of the world to be holy and without blame before Him.

Ephesians 1:5—I was predestined (determined by God) to be adopted as a son.

Ephesians 1:7,8—I have been redeemed, forgiven, and am a recipient of His lavish grace.

Ephesians 1:13,14—I have been given the Holy Spirit as a pledge (a deposit/down payment) guaranteeing my inheritance to come.

Ephesians 2:5—I have been made alive together with Christ.

Ephesians 2:6—I have been raised up and seated with Christ in heaven.

Ephesians 2:18—I have direct access to God through the Spirit.

Ephesians 3:12—I may approach God with boldness, freedom, and confidence.

Colossians 1:13—I have been delivered (rescued) from the domain of darkness (Satan's rule) and transferred to the kingdom of Christ.

Colossians 1:14—I have been redeemed and forgiven of all my sins (the debt against me has been cancelled—see Colossians 2:13,14).

Colossians 1:27—Christ Himself is in me.

Colossians 2:7—I have been firmly rooted in Christ and am now being built up in Him.

Colossians 2:10—I have been made complete in Christ.

Colossians 2:11—I have been spiritually circumcised (my old, unregenerate nature has been removed).

Colossians 2:12,13—I have been buried, raised, and made alive with Christ.

Colossians 3:1-4—I have been raised up with Christ. I died with Christ; my life is now hidden with Christ in God. Christ is now my life.

2 Timothy 1:7—I have been given a spirit of power, love, and self-discipline.

2 Timothy 1:9—I have been saved and called (set apart) according to God's doing.

Titus 3:5—I have been reborn and renewed by the Holy Spirit.

Hebrews 2:11—I am sanctified and am one with the Sanctifier (Christ), and He is not ashamed to call me His brother.

Hebrews 4:16—I have a right to come boldly before the throne of God (the throne of grace) to find mercy and grace in time of need.

2 Peter 1:4—I have been given exceedingly great and precious promises by God, by which I am a partaker of the divine nature (God's nature).[9]

Growing in Truths for the Future

Making real who we are in Christ is enlivened not only by looking at the realities of the past and present in Christ, but also by exercising faith in the promises of the future. As life grows out of the seed in which it started and the soil in which it is planted, so it is drawn to the sun beyond it. Because God's promises are grounded on what He has already done in Christ, they are gospel indicatives as sure as the realities of the past. Our effort to be holy as God is holy is fueled by the "living hope" (1 Peter 1:3) that one day we will be like our Lord (1 John 3:2,3) and we will live in a new creation that Peter describes as "the home of righteousness" (2 Peter 3:13).

Believing in the realities of our future is a powerful means to change. Peter Kreeft wrote:

> Now suppose both death and hell were utterly defeated. Suppose the fight was fixed. Suppose God took you on a crystal-ball trip into your future and you saw with indubitable certainty that despite everything— your sin, your smallness, your stupidity—you could have free for the asking your whole crazy heart's deepest desire: heaven, eternal joy. Would you not return fearless and singing? What can earth do to you if you are guaranteed heaven? To fear the worst earthly loss would be like a millionaire fearing the loss of a penny—less, a scratch on a penny.
>
> But this *is* our true state, according to God's own Word. This is the gospel, the scandalously good news: that we are guaranteed heaven by sheer gift.[10]

In addition to thinking about and believing the truths of God's grace—what God has done for us, who we are in Christ, and our future hope—we must also hear and believe the commands given to us in Scripture. It is important to understand how these instructions relate to our sanctification. This requires us to understand exactly what the commands or imperatives really are in relation to God's gracious work in salvation and the truth that sanctifies us. Later, in chapter 10, we will look at the place those commands have in our growth. But for now, we're going to learn how we can establish the truth in our hearts by faith so that we can live and walk like saints.

10

Making God's Life-Changing Truth Personal

And let the peace of Christ rule in your hearts, to which indeed you were called in one body; and be thankful. Let the word of Christ richly dwell within you, with all wisdom teaching and admonishing one another with psalms and hymns and spiritual songs, singing u :th thankfulness in your hearts to God.

—Colossians 3:15,16 (NASB)

Have you ever sat with another person on the opposite ends of a teeter-totter and tried to balance it? It's easy to ride up and down, but it is much harder to balance the board. To do so requires cooperation from both people. Each person needs to make minor adjustments in order to maintain a balance. In a similar way, if we want to live a stable Christian life, we need to find the biblical balance between God's sovereignty and man's responsibility when both are clearly taught in Scripture. The board would remain level if we all stood in the middle where Christ is, but there will always be some individuals who tip the board one way or another. Unfortunately, if either end gets too far from the center (Christ), then the church as a whole will lose its balance and suffer.

Balancing the sanctification teeter-totter requires some delicate maneuvering. It is easy to see how the board can be tipped one way or the other if you look at the two extreme views of sanctification. Adopting either extreme will cause us to experience negative results in the process of conforming to the image of God; that's why balance is so important.

One end of the teeter-totter emphasizes the past tense or positional aspects of sanctification and overlooks the progressive, present-tense instructions. The tendency is to claim holiness and overlook the reality of sin in our own personal lives and the necessity to assume responsibility for our growth. This can lead to a denial of our own imperfections, and we end up having to pretend that we have it all together.

The other end of the teeter-totter emphasizes the progressive aspects of sanctification and overlooks Scripture's more numerous references to the past-tense realities of sanctification. There are some people who don't overlook these verses, but they treat them as if they were irrelevant to our present position in Christ—as though being alive in Christ has no practical, present-day benefit. This orientation usually leads to a negative view of Christians and fails to see them as new creations in Christ. The result is believers who struggle all life long to become somebody they already are.

Humility in Christ is always found in the center of the board. Go to either end, however, and we'll find pride. At one end of the board are those who think more highly of themselves then they ought (Romans 12:3). They say, "We're already holy in Christ. We don't need to concern ourselves with sin or growing toward holiness."

Going to the other end of the board can lead to false humility. By insisting they are just sinners with desperately sick hearts, these people can claim their "humility" while at the same time have an excuse to continue in sin or have an explanation for why we still sin. But this professed humility is false. "Look how humble I am" is a subtle form of pride.

True humility is confidence properly placed. We are to "glory in Christ Jesus, and . . . put no confidence in the flesh" (Philippians 3:3). Paul says, "Let no one keep defrauding you of your prize by delighting in self-abasement" (Colossians 2:18 NASB). God is not trying to put us down; He is trying to restore a fallen humanity and build us up, and we should be building up each other as well.

Ironically, the people at both extremes have a tendency toward legalism. One group has to behave as though they are completely sanctified, which they believe they are. The other group emphasizes obedience to the commandments of Scripture. Nobody wants to be identified as a legalist, but in many cases all we have done is gone from negative legalism (don't do this and don't do that) to positive legalism (do this, do that, do this, and do that). To avoid the Galatian heresy (Galatians 3:1-5), we must understand that we are both saved by faith *and* perfected by faith.

Paul said, "I am confident of this very thing, that He who began a good work in you will perfect it until the day of Christ Jesus" (Philippians 1:6 NASB). We ought to have the same confidence that the seed which was sown in our hearts will bear fruit, and that we can present every person complete in Christ (Colossians 1:28). If *truth* is the means by which we are sanctified, then *faith* is the means by which truth is appropriated through thought and action. In this chapter we will look at the appropriation through thought (or belief). In the next chapter, we'll examine the appropriation through action (or obedience).

Appropriating God's Truth Through Faith

There is no operating principle of life that has greater significance in our daily walk than the concept of faith. The writer to the Hebrews says, "Without faith it is impossible to please God" (11:6). Every aspect of life is shaped or determined by what we believe. First, we are saved by faith: "It is by grace that you have been saved, through faith" (Ephesians 2:8). And second, we walk or "live by faith, not by sight" (2 Corinthians 5:7). Faith is the only means by which we relate to God.

There are three principles of faith that need to be understood and appropriated if we hope to be led of the Lord, stay in His will, and conform to His image.

1. Faith is dependent upon its object.

The question is not whether you believe or how much you believe. The real question is *what* you believe, or *whom* you believe in, because everybody walks by faith. The only difference between Christian faith and non-Christian faith is the *object* of the faith. For example, we drive our cars by faith. Consider the simple action of driving through a green light at an intersection. You believed that the cross-traffic had a red light even though you couldn't see it, and you believed those who were driving on that cross-street would obey the law by stopping at the red light. When you drove through that intersection, then, you exercised faith in mankind, the laws of our country, and the electric circuitry of the traffic lights. If you didn't have such faith, how would you approach that intersection?

"Now faith is the assurance [substance, KJV] of things hoped for, the conviction [evidence, KJV] of things not seen" (Hebrews 11:1 NASB). Approaching a green light at an intersection without slowing down requires an inner assurance that there will be no collision. Boldly driving through that intersection without checking the cross-traffic is evidence of your faith in science, mankind, and traffic laws. That is a lot of faith to put in mankind, especially since you were staking your physical well-being on it. If you have that much faith in fallen humanity, how much more faith should you have in Jesus Christ, who is the way, the truth, and the life (John 14:6)?

What makes Jesus Christ the only legitimate object of our faith? We find the answer in Hebrews 13:7,8: "Remember your leaders, who spoke the word of God to you. Consider the outcome of their way of life and imitate their faith. Jesus Christ is the same yesterday and today and forever." Notice that the writer of Hebrews didn't tell his audience to imitate their leaders' actions, but rather, their leaders' *faith*. That's because their actions were just a product of what they believed, or better, whom they believed in—God. The fact that God cannot change nor lie is what makes Him and His Word the only legitimate object for our faith. Have you ever noticed that our faith in an object grows when it has demonstrated consistency over time? God's unwavering consistency proves He is worthy of our faith.

By the way, encouraging people to "just walk by faith" can actually destroy their walk with God. You can't have faith in faith, because faith has no validity without an object. The "Faith Hall of Fame" members listed in Hebrews chapter 11 had great faith because they had a great God . . . and so do we!

2. *How much faith we have is determined by how well we know the object of our faith.*

If we know seven promises from God's Word, the best we can have is a seven-promise faith. If we know 7,000 promises from God's Word, we can potentially have a faith based on 7,000 promises. In Romans 10:17, Paul said, "Faith comes from hearing the message, and the message is heard through the word of Christ."

That is why faith can't be pumped up. Any attempt to step out on faith beyond that which is known to be true can only lead to disaster. That isn't faith; it's presumption. If we make unsubstantiated assumptions about God or a person, we are setting ourselves up for disappointment and undermining our future confidence in them. We can't merely assume anything to be true; we have to *know* it to be true. A similar problem occurs when people respond to the gospel message by saying, "Oh, I could never believe that!" Of course they can believe it. If one person can believe the truth, then can't any other person do likewise? Of course. Belief is a choice. Faith is something you *decide* to do, not something you *feel* like doing.

Every person has to decide who or what they will believe. Joshua said, "If serving the LORD seems undesirable to you, then choose for yourselves this day whom you will serve. . . . But as for me and my household, we will serve the LORD" (Joshua 24:15). "Elijah went before the people and said, 'How long will you waver between two opinions? If the LORD is God, follow him; but if Baal is God, follow him'" (1 Kings 18:21).

Our sanctification is totally dependent upon what we choose to believe. Every great saint has chosen to trust in God and believe that His Word is absolute truth and the only authoritative and infallible source for life and living. The only other choice is to believe in one or more of God's created and fallen beings, including Satan and ourselves. That would be an unfortunate choice, because "the foolishness of God is wiser than man's wisdom, and the weakness of God is stronger than man's strength" (1 Corinthians 1:25).

3. Scripture presents faith as an action word.

This principle is what James is trying to get across when he says, "What good is it, my brothers, if a man claims to have faith but has no deeds? Can such faith save him? . . . But someone will say, 'You have faith; I have deeds.' Show me your faith without deeds, and I will show you my faith by what I do" (James 2:14,18). He makes an even stronger statement later: "You see that a person is justified by what he does and not by faith alone" (2:24). Does this threaten the Protestant assertion of "justification by faith and faith alone"? Not if we understand what James is trying to say.

In most Bible translations, the majority renderings of "faith," "trust," and "believe" are the same Greek noun, *pistis* or verb, *pisteuo*. In common English usage, however, to believe in something has less personal commitment than to trust in something. It is easy to give mental assent by saying, "I believe that" and totally miss the biblical meaning of belief. To believe something biblically is not just giving mental assent to something, but showing full reliance upon it. That is why James said, "You believe that there is one God. Good! Even the demons believe that—and shudder" (James 2:19). In other words, the demons believed there is one God, but that belief didn't translate into trust. If we truly believe in God and choose to believe that what He says is the only absolute truth, then it should affect the way we live. For example, Jesus said, "Blessed are those who hunger and thirst for righteousness, for they shall be satisfied" (Matthew 5:6 NASB). Do you believe that? If you do, then what would you be doing? You would be hungering after righteousness. If you aren't doing that, then you don't really believe. Such "belief" is only mental assent or wishful thinking which will neither save you nor sanctify you.

In recent years, the concept of biblical faith has been twisted by the "name it and claim it" or "positive confession" movement. The people within this movement advocate that we can use faith to fulfill our every whim. They base their teaching on passages such as Matthew 21:21,22:

> Truly I say to you, if you have faith, and do not doubt, you shall not only do what was done to the fig tree, but even if you say to this mountain, "Be taken up and cast into the sea," it shall happen. And all things you ask in prayer, believing, you shall receive.

Proponents of the positive confession movement rightly point out that the mountain is removed only when faith is put into operation when we say, "Be taken up." That is, what you believe needs to be acted upon, which is in keeping with what James says about belief. You step over the line of orthodox Christianity, however, when you begin to think something has to happen simply because you said it. Only God can speak and bring something into existence, and we are not God. We simply cannot create reality with our mind, as New Age proponents would have us believe. To be able to do so would make us gods, and that is precisely what they are teaching. But as created beings, we can only respond to reality in a responsible way.

Also, we don't have the privilege or the right to determine for ourselves what it is that we are to believe. The teaching that if we believe something hard enough it will become true is not biblical. Christianity says, "It is true; therefore, I believe it." Just because we believe something doesn't make it true, and our unbelief doesn't make something false. We as Christians choose to believe the truth, we don't choose what truth is.

Jesus said He is the way, the *truth*, and the life (John 14:6, emphasis added). Through prayer and reading God's Word, God reveals *His* truth to us. He can reveal the truth, show us the way, and give us the life that we need in order to follow Him. Truth originates in heaven, and our responsibility is to believe it.

Storing the Truth in Our Hearts

The faith that will actually change our character and consequently our behavior involves appropriating the truth in our hearts so that our faith is not just mental assent. Paul admonishes, "Let the peace of Christ rule in your hearts" (Colossians 3:15). The word "rule" (Greek, *brabeuo*) means "to act as an umpire." We are to let the peace of Christ decide all the matters of our heart. The question is, how do we get that truth into our heart? The next verse says, "Let the word of Christ dwell in you richly as you teach and admonish one another with all wisdom" (Colossians 3:16). Although separated in our English translations, the words "let" and "dwell" are one word in the original Greek text, and it means "to live in, to take up one's residence in, or to make one's home among." *What* or *who* is he saying should take up residence in our hearts? "The word [Greek, *logos*] of Christ." The truth that centers on Christ—which He embodies—is to be at the very core of our being. We are to let His peace arbitrate the matters of our heart. Arbitration is necessary because the voices of the world, the flesh, and the devil are contending for control.

I (Neil) had a very innocent childhood and a good moral upbringing, but I wasn't a Christian. During my four years of service in the navy, my mind was exposed to some material I wished afterward that I had never seen. When I first became a Christian, I desired to clean up my mind. The moment I decided to do that, the battle for my mind became intense. That's because I was now making a choice to not give in to tempting thoughts.

If ever we find that the battle for our mind is not very intense, it's probably because we are forfeiting without a fight. The need to submit to God and resist the devil (James 4:7) can't be overstated because "the weapons we fight with are not the weapons of the world. On the contrary, they have divine power to demolish strongholds" (2 Corinthians 10:4). We need the peace of God to guard our hearts and minds (Philippians 4:7).

Imagine that your mind is like a pitcher that was intended to be filled with crystal-clear water, but it got contaminated with coffee over the years. One day you decide you want the water in the pitcher to be pure, but are saddened upon discovering that there is no way to get the coffee out. Then you discover nearby a bowl of crystal-clear ice cubes, which is labeled, "Word of God." There is no way you can pour the whole bowl of ice cubes into the pitcher at once, so you drop in one ice cube a day. At first the task seems hopeless, because the coffee is so pervasive. Slowly, however, the daily infusion of truth eventually nullifies the effects of the coffee. Then finally comes the day when the coffee can no longer be seen, smelled, or tasted, even though a remnant of it is still there. Likewise, that process of renewing our minds *will* work, provided that we don't pour in a tablespoon of coffee for every ice cube.

That illustration reinforces what we learned earlier about the part we have in our own sanctification. The apostle Paul says, "Do your best to present yourself to God as one approved, a workman who does not need to be ashamed and who correctly handles the word of truth" (2 Timothy 2:15). There is no substitute for that in this present church age; God will not study for us. He has revealed Himself and His ways in His Word, and it is our responsibility to know the truth. And according to Scripture, meditation is a sure way to let the Word of God richly dwell within us. Let's see what we can learn about the discipline of meditation in biblical history.

Meditation and Holiness

The Great Value of Meditation

According to Joshua 1:8, meditating on God's Word is the key to successful living: "Do not let this Book of the Law depart from your mouth; meditate on it day and night, so that you may be careful to do everything written in it. Then you will be prosperous and successful." The root meaning of the word "prosperous" is "to accomplish satisfactorily what is intended." The Hebrew word for "success" refers to having wisdom that leads to wise behavior, and in the Bible, wise behavior means a life which conforms to the character of God. Bible commentator Trent Butler translates these phrases, " . . . then you shall make your paths successful, and then you will be prudently prosperous."[1] To be successful or live wisely involves two things: 1) doing according to the truth of the Word of God, and 2) continual meditation on the Word, which produces that doing.

The psalmist began the book of Psalms by saying also that meditation is the key to life:

> Blessed is the man who does not walk in the counsel
> of the wicked or stand in the way of sinners or sit in the
> seat of mockers. But his delight is in the law of the LORD,
> and on his law he meditates day and night (Psalm 1:1,2).

There are certain things that the blessed or happy man does not do. He doesn't take advice from the unrighteous: "What partnership have righteousness and lawlessness, or what fellowship has light with darkness?" (2 Corinthians 6:14 NASB). Neither does the blessed man identify or party with sinners: "Do not be misled: Bad company corrupts good character" (1 Corinthians 15:33). Nor does the blessed man mock God or His Word. Instead, he delights in the truth and meditates on it continuously. Consequently, "he is like a tree planted by streams of water, which yields its fruit in season and whose leaf does not wither. Whatever he does prospers" (Psalm 1:3).

Meditation in the Bible

The words "meditate" or "meditation" are found at least 21 times in the Old Testament, and eight of those times are in Psalm 119 alone. But the concept of meditation is mentioned in other ways throughout the Bible. For example, in Deuteronomy 6:6-9 we read,

> These words, which I am commanding you today, shall be on your heart; and you shall teach them diligently to your sons and shall talk of them when you sit in your house and when you walk by the way and when you lie down and when you rise up. And you shall bind them as a sign on your hand and they shall be as frontals on your forehead. And you shall write them on the doorposts of your house and on your gates.

One of the most "natural" things we do is think and talk what is on our hearts. If God's Word is hidden in our hearts, we will speak of it from sunup to sunset. It will affect all that we do (your hands), all that we think (frontals on your forehead), all that happens in our homes (the doorposts of your house), and all that we do publicly (the gates).

Psalm 63 reveals King David in a very depressing situation. He is on the western shore of the Dead Sea, which is described as "a dry and weary land where there is no water" (verse 1). This wilderness area is the same place where the devil confronted our Savior. Throughout Scripture we find that the wilderness is a place of trial and temptation. The bleak surroundings alone are depressing, but far worse is the reason for David's presence there. He is fleeing from Jerusalem for his life. His own son Absalom had formed a conspiracy against him and was attempting to wrest the kingship of Israel from him.

But David's heart is strong toward God even in the midst of this circumstance. How was that possible? The answer is the same as it is in all the other places that Scripture talks about successful living—meditation on God's truth.

O God, you are my God, earnestly I seek you; my soul thirsts for you, my body longs for you, in a dry and weary land where there is no water. . . . Because your love is better than life, my lips will glorify you. I will praise you as long as I live, and in your name I will lift up my hands. My soul will be satisfied as with the richest of foods; with singing lips my mouth will praise you. On my bed I remember you; I think of you [or meditate on you] through the watches of the night (verses 1-6).

The next time you can't sleep at night because of oppressing circumstances, try what David did. Focus your mind on God by recalling great moments that you have had with Him. Then mentally ascribe to Him His attributes. Finally, involve your whole body by raising your hands or laying prostrate before Him and singing. Fixing your eyes on Jesus, the author and finisher of your faith (Hebrew 12:2), will refocus your troubled mind, and singing will give greater expression and harmony to your troubled soul. Like the psalmist, you will be able to say, "Why are you in despair, O my soul? And why are you disturbed within me? Hope in God, for I shall again praise him, the help of my countenance, and my God" (Psalm 43:5).

The Meaning of Meditation

There are two basic words for meditation in the Old Testament. The first is *haghah* (as in Psalm 63:6). The basic verb means "to moan, growl, utter, speak, or muse." It is used for the growling of a lion (Isaiah 31:4) and the cooing of doves (Isaiah 59:11). It is also used in reference to resounding music or music that continues to sound—as if it were echoing.[2] Although it can be used to speak of silent musing, it seems that the basic idea of the word involves some kind of utterance—such as murmuring, or whispering, or talking to yourself. Regarding its use for "meditate" in Joshua 1:8, Ringgren says, "This could have reference to softly spoken oral recitation in connection with the study of the law. . . ."[3] At times, *haghah* expresses the feelings of the soul of a person "'lost in his religion' . . . filled with thoughts of God's deeds or his will."[4]

The second word for meditation, *siach*, is found in Psalm 77:6: "I remembered my songs in the night. My heart mused [*siach*] and my spirit inquired." Rehearsing something over in one's mind is the basic idea of this word. It may be done outwardly (talking) or inwardly (meditation).

Meditating on God's Word helps us go beyond superficial obedience to His commands. It helps us absorb their rich meaning of what He has to say. For instance, Psalm 119:129 says, "Thy testimonies are wonderful; therefore my soul observes them" (NASB). Franz Delitzsch says:

> In this connection of thoughts . . . ["observes them"] is not intended of careful observance, but of attentive contemplation that is prolonged until a clear penetrating understanding of the matter is attained. . . . God's word giveth light, inasmuch as it makes the simple (as in Proverbs 22:3) wise or sagacious; in connection with which it is assumed that it is God Himself who unfolds the mysteries of His Word to those who are anxious to learn.[5]

Let's take the well-known twenty-third Psalm and meditate on the first verse: "The LORD is my shepherd, I shall not be in want." Notice the psalmist doesn't say "*a* LORD," he says "*the* LORD." The article is definite because there is only one Lord. He is *the* LORD, and the word "LORD" is the English rendering of the divine name for God, which is YHWH (Yahweh). This sacred name for God, commonly referred to as the Tetragrammaton, wasn't spoken by the Hebrews. His name was considered too holy. Clearly, the psalmist was being reverent. He was saying in a sense, "God is not my lord in the sense of being my boss; He is the almighty, everlasting God of all creation."

What's amazing is that this Lord "is" my shepherd—right now. The verse doesn't say He will be my shepherd sometime in the future, nor was He my shepherd sometime in the past. He "is," at this present moment, "my" shepherd. What an overwhelming thought that the God of Abraham, Isaac, and Jacob is *my* personal shepherd!

And what is He to me? He is my "shepherd." He watches over me, and leads me by quiet waters. While other sheep win mankind's awards for beauty or performance, I have the assurance that He is always my shepherd and cares for me just as much as He does any other sheep. If I should lose my way, He will leave the others to find me. What a wonderful shepherd! He will protect me from the wolves even if it costs Him His life. What more can I want?

Can you see now the value of meditating upon God's Word? Psalm 23:1 is just one example of how God's powerful words and truths can bring blessing, comfort, and reassurance to us if we would just let them permeate our hearts.

Wrong Uses of Meditation

Just like faith, the object of our meditation is the critical issue. Encouraging people to meditate without telling them what to meditate on can be destructive to their spiritual health. They could end up paying attention to a deceiving spirit such as those described in 1 Timothy 4:1: "The Spirit clearly says that in later times some will abandon the faith and follow deceiving spirits and things taught by demons." A dear lady who attended one of Neil's conferences shared this following testimony:

> I have been a committed Christian for many years, but I was still struggling with some painful childhood memories. Several years ago I attended an inner-healing seminar in my church, hoping to get some help. Wanting all the Lord had for me, I fully participated in a guided imagery. The leader had the entire group close their eyes, quiet their minds with music, and imagine that we climbed onto a magic carpet that took us to a beautiful meadow with a lake. She then led us through several imaginary events. To think about them makes my skin crawl. I now know they were from the Adversary.
>
> Because of great turmoil in my life, and desperately needing help, I flew to my sister in another state. Her pastor

and his wife led me though the Steps to Freedom in Christ. It was an encounter with the awesome love of my heavenly Father like I've never experienced before. With the help of a loving, gentle pastor, the Lord revealed a spirit guide that had gained entrance during the inner-healing guided imagery. I had learned to look forward to its presence in my prayer life in the form of a purple light that guided me in many situations. I had often shared with my pastor about "my color purple" and he didn't recognize it as demonic either. Believing it was from the Lord, we were both deceived.

As a result of this demonic guide, my marriage ended, my son is alienated from me, and I am alienated from my church. Now as a result of an encounter with truth I am free in Christ. I truly know the peace that passes all understanding and my heart and mind are guarded in Christ Jesus.

God never bypasses our mind; He works *through* it. Scripture instructs us to direct our thoughts outwardly, never inwardly, and actively, never passively. To let your mind go passive is the most dangerous thing you can do spiritually: "Brothers, stop thinking like children. In regard to evil be infants, but in your thinking be adults" (1 Corinthians 14:20). "Be transformed by the renewing of your mind . . . think so as to have sound judgment" (Romans 12:2,3 NASB).

Directing our thoughts inward leads to nothing but a morbid introspection. We're to invite God to examine us: "Search me, O God, and know my heart; test me and know my anxious thoughts. See if there is any offensive way in me, and lead me in the way everlasting" (Psalm 139:23,24).

The intended purpose of the meditative practices of Eastern religions is to induce a passive state of mind. In transcendental meditation, for example, you close your eyes and repeat your mantra over and over again for 20 minutes. They want you to achieve a trancelike state where the mind is neutralized. Their theory is to get the mind out of the way so you can perceive truth directly. But your mind would turn to mush if you did that, and Jesus warned us about praying in vain repetitions (Matthew 6:7).

How Meditation Can Change Us

Thinking the wrong thoughts can lead to despair, which some of God's choicest saints have confirmed. David cried out, "How long, O LORD? Will you forget me forever?" (Psalm 13:1). Can an omniscient God forget anything or anyone, much less forever? But that is what David thinks and therefore believes at that moment. "How long must I wrestle with my thoughts ['take counsel in my soul' in the NASB], and every day have sorrow in my heart?" (Psalm 13:2). David was depressed because he was entertaining thoughts about God that were not true. After complaining about his enemies and his circumstances, he finally petitioned God. Then his thoughts became singular and focused on Him: "But I trust in your unfailing love; my heart rejoices in your salvation. I will sing to the LORD, for he has been good to me" (13:5,6).

Jeremiah became depressed when he reflected on all his hardships. "I remember my affliction and my wandering, the bitterness and the gall. I well remember them, and my soul is downcast within me" (Lamentations 3:19,20). He had lost hope in God (verse 18). Anybody would be depressed if they took time to "well remember" all the negative things that have happened to them and think about all the evil in this world. But then Jeremiah turns everything around: "Yet this I call to mind and therefore I have hope: Because of the LORD'S great love we are not consumed, for his compassions never fail. They are new every morning; great is your faithfulness" (Lamentations 3:21-23). Notice that nothing changed in Jeremiah's circumstances, and God never changed. All that changed was what Jeremiah chose to believe about God, and it was *in his mind* that he recalled what he must have already known about God.

The apostle Paul also suffered great hardship, but he didn't lose heart. He was imprisoned, beaten numerous times, shipwrecked, and persecuted from within and without the Christian ranks, and was on the run from continuous danger (2 Corinthians 11:23-27). You could knock Paul down, but he would always get up:

> We are hard pressed on every side, but not crushed; perplexed, but not in despair; persecuted, but not abandoned; struck down, but not destroyed. We always carry around in our body the death of Jesus, so that the life of Jesus may also be revealed in our body. . . . Therefore we do not lose heart. Though outwardly we are wasting away, yet inwardly we are being renewed day by day. For our light and momentary troubles are achieving for us an eternal glory that far outweighs them all (2 Corinthians 4:8-10,16,17).

Paul must have believed his own message, which is why he could live with such hardship. He testified, "I know what it is to be in need, and I know what it is to have plenty. I have learned the secret of being content in any and every situation, whether well fed or hungry, whether living in plenty or in want. I can do everything through him who gives me strength" (Philippians 4:12,13). He knew that our countenance is not shaped by the circumstances of life, but by how we perceive them. If we interpret the trials and tribulations of life correctly, they will produce character, and that is where our hope lies because the love of God has been poured into our hearts (Romans 5:3-5). Paul shares the mental focus that we must have in Philippians 4:8,9:

> Finally, brothers, whatever is true, whatever is noble, whatever is right, whatever is pure, whatever is lovely, whatever is admirable—if anything is excellent or praiseworthy—think about such things. Whatever you have learned or received or heard from me, or seen in me—put it into practice. And the God of peace will be with you.

The word "think" in the phrase "think about such things" is the Greek word *logidzomai*, which means "to consider, or calculate." The NASB translates this phrase, "let your mind dwell on these things." Paul is not talking about superficial thinking, he is referring to the process of disciplining our minds to think truthfully, carefully, and comprehensively. This is not merely trying to remember a Bible verse when we're tempted or in trouble as though it were some magic formula, this is learning to think scripturally about all matters of life.

How Mediation Can Affect Our Actions

The New Testament doesn't use the term "meditate" very often, but the concept of meditation appears frequently. For example, Colossians 3:1,2 says, "Since, then, you have been raised with Christ, set your heart on things above, where Christ is seated at the right hand of God. Set your minds on things above, not on earthly things." The Greek word for "set your minds" in this passage is *phroneo*, which means "to be minded in a certain way. It implies moral interest or reflection, not mere unreasoning opinion."[6] This is the same word that Paul chose to use in Romans 8:5 when he wanted to show that what we choose to set our mind on is what determines how we live: "Those who live according to the sinful nature [flesh] have their minds set on what that nature desires; but those who live in accordance with the Spirit have their minds set on what the Spirit desires."

Whatever we meditate on in our minds goes into our hearts and affects our actions. I remember listening to a sports program covering the winter Olympics when East Germany was still its own country. The commentators were talking about the East German luge racers, who would stop at the top of the run, close their eyes, and seem to go into some kind of meditative state. A sports psychologist explained that they were going over the whole run in their minds, every grade and turn. The first time down the run would be a learning experience, but every successive run would leave more and more of an imprint on the mind. After enough runs, the luge racers could mentally picture the entire course, and then they could prepare themselves for trying to win the gold medal on the final run.

The same phenomenon takes place when we learn to ride a bike or drive a car, especially a car with a stick shift mechanism. After many practice attempts, the process eventually becomes more a part of you so that you can ride the bike or drive the car almost without any conscious thought at all.

Similarly, when we continually think upon God's truth, it enters into the depth of our hearts. Whatever is borne into the depth of our being will come out in our words and actions. "The good man brings good things out of the good stored up in his heart, and the evil man brings evil things out of the evil stored up in his heart. For out of the overflow of his heart his mouth speaks" (Luke 6:45).

Solomon's request to God for a "discerning heart" (1 Kings 3:9) was literally for "a hearing heart"—a heart that hears God's Word so he could judge the people rightly. We all have "hearing hearts" that continually take in whatever we focus our minds on. Meditating on God's Word is simply talking to our hearts so that the Word of God is instilled there and comes out in our actions.

One of the more colorful means of getting God's thoughts into our hearts is the soliloquy, which is simply talking to ourselves. Telling yourself to "Get a grip on yourself," or "Stay cool" are common soliloquies. Notice the psalmist's soliloquies: "Find rest, O my soul, in God alone; my hope comes from him" (Psalm 62:5) or, "Praise the LORD, O my soul; all my inmost being, praise his holy name" (Psalm 103:1). The soliloquy functions as a good teacher if the truth that is spoken to the soul is from God's Word, or at least consistent with it.

The Objects of Our Meditation

The first object of our thoughts should be God Himself. He is the Creator, the King of kings, and Sovereign Lord of the universe. We need to think about Him until we stand in awe of His greatness. Don't get the impression, however, that we worship God because He is an egomaniac who needs His ego stroked every Sunday morning. The idea of appeasing God so that He won't do bad things to us is rooted in paganism.

To worship God is to ascribe to Him His divine attributes. We do this so that our minds are programmed to know Him and His ways. Meditation on God inevitably leads us to think also of His Word, His will, and His wonderful acts. Look at what the psalmist meditated upon:

Psalm 1:2—"On his law he meditates day and night"

Psalm 48:9—"We meditate on your unfailing love"

Psalm 77:12—"I will meditate on all your works"

Psalm 119:15—"I meditate on your precepts"

Psalm 119:27—"I will meditate on your wonders"

Psalm 119:48—"I meditate on your decrees"

Psalm 119:97—"I meditate on [your law] all day long"

Psalm 119:99—"I meditate on your statutes"

Psalm 119:148—"I may meditate on your promises"

Psalm 143:5—"I meditate on all your works"

Beyond God and His ways, we should meditate on whatever is good. Recall Paul's words in Philippians 4:8: "Brothers, whatever is true, whatever is noble, whatever is right, whatever is pure, whatever is lovely, whatever is admirable—if anything is excellent or praiseworthy—think about such things."

We're not saying you should deny your negative circumstances; of course we need to stay in touch with reality. But God tells us that our minds should not *dwell* on negative things. Yes, we need to face our problems, but we also need to focus on the answer, who is Christ and the truth that will set us free. When we are spiritually fatigued, we need to respond to the invitation, "Come unto me, all you who are weary and burdened, and I will give you rest" (Matthew 11:28). When we are fearful, we need to remember that God is present: "Do not fear, for I am with you; do not be dismayed, for I am your God. I will strengthen you and help you; I will uphold you with my righteous right hand" (Isaiah 41:10). And in the times when we feel guilty, we need to know that "there is now no condemnation for those who are in Christ Jesus" (Romans 8:1).

When you're preparing to teach a Sunday school class or preach a message, have you ever visualized yourself doing the task in the power of the Holy Spirit? That can positively enhance your presentations, but such visualization needs to be tempered by the truth taught in 1 Peter 1:13: "Prepare your minds for action; be self-controlled; set your hope fully on the grace to be given you when Jesus Christ is revealed." What we prepare our minds for is action. Is there a place for sanctified imagination, or is there such a thing as Christian visualization? There is nothing wrong with visualizing yourself doing something in the power of the Holy Spirit, provided that your thoughts are consistent with God's Word. But you will depart from reality and enter a world of fantasy if you imagine things that are not consistent with God's Word or you never do what you visualize. You will actually lose self-control.

The New Age practice of visualization has no basis in truth. The intention of this practice is to *create* truth or reality with the mind, but those who engage in such a practice are being deceived and are deceiving others. Hope is not wishful thinking, nor does our hope lie in our own strength and attributes. Hope is the present assurance of some future good, which is based solely on the grace of God—not on people acting as their own gods.

Truth, Christ, and Ourselves

When John said that "the word became flesh and made his dwelling among us" (John 1:14), he was saying the Word of God had become man. Jesus was the embodiment of the written Word, the personification of truth. You can't separate Jesus from His Word because He is the Word. Everything He thought, felt, and did was true because He is the truth. If we were fully sanctified in the truth we would think, feel, and do what Jesus did. Because we have the life and mind of Christ (1 Corinthians

2:16), the truth is within us and causes us to fall in love with God and mankind. It is less than Christian for us to say we know the Word of God when it has not touched our hearts nor transformed our character to Christlikeness.

When truth is appropriated, it touches every aspect of the heart. We are emotionally transformed and our wills are moved to action. The psalmist says, "May my meditation be pleasing to him, as I rejoice in the LORD" (Psalm 104:34). Meditation on the Word should produce thoughts that reach our emotions. If thought and feeling are joined in the heart, then any thought that reaches the heart will touch the emotions. God's Word, then, will not change our lives unless it changes our emotions. As the great church Father Augustine explained, "On our journey to God, the affects are the feet that either lead us closer to God or carry us farther from him, but without them we cannot travel the way at all."[7]

Thinking Upon the Truth

We stated earlier that our emotions are the product of our thought life. We are not shaped so much by the external events in life as we are by how we perceive them. Every experience is picked up by one or more of our five senses and sent to the brain (computer) and processed by the mind (central processing unit). It would logically follow, then, that if what we think does not reflect truth, then what we feel does not reflect reality. For example, suppose you are waiting to hear the outcome of an important job interview. You are one of two final candidates for a position that you want very much. While you are waiting, a false rumor circulates, saying that the other person got the job. Let's say you hear the rumor and believe it. How would you feel? Probably very disappointed.

In reality, however, you got the job, but your interviewers haven't had a chance to tell you yet. Suppose a friend inside the company hears the good news and calls you. When you answer the phone he says, "Hey, congratulations!" You respond angrily, "Why are you being so rude? You know I wanted the job!"

Unaware of the rumor, your friend wonders why you are upset. It's because you *think* you didn't get the job. Your feelings are a product of a lie—a false rumor. Why are you feeling angry, upset, and disappointed? You are feeling that way because what you believed wasn't true. But when you find out the truth that you did indeed get the job, will your feelings change? Yes!

There are countless thousands of Christians who have let Satan's lies affect the way they feel about themselves and God. They don't feel saved, or they think that God doesn't love them. Why? Because wrong thoughts have been raised up against the knowledge of God. Unfortunately, just telling such people the truth will not necessarily resolve their problems. For example, several years ago a pastor's wife who had some serious problems was referred to me (Neil). Condemning thoughts were plaguing her continuously. After listening to her for 30 minutes, I said, "You really love Jesus, don't you?" She nodded in agreement. "And you really love the Holy Spirit, don't you?" Again she agreed. "But you don't even like God the Father, do you?" She broke down and cried. Because her beliefs about her heavenly Father were distorted, I gave her a set of tapes on God's attributes by A.W. Tozer.

She listened to those tapes three times with no impact on her life. I was disappointed and confused. I had given her the best teaching that I knew of on the character and nature of God, and the impact was zero! Since then I have wondered how many great biblical truths are being missed by Christians today. Could it be that they just don't want to know or learn? I'm sure that is true in some cases, but after years of helping people, I have discovered that the primary problem is a lack of genuine repentance as well as unresolved personal and spiritual conflicts. Bitterness due to unforgiveness is the biggest hurdle for most people to overcome.

The Steps to Freedom in Christ were developed by Freedom in Christ Ministries to help people resolve the conflicts that were keeping them from having an intimate relationship with their heavenly Father. Repenting from sin, pride, rebellion, bitterness, and deception resulted in a freedom that many had never experienced before. In the vast majority of cases the people involved were able to joyfully connect with their heavenly Father—as did the pastor's wife mentioned a moment ago. Those who are free in Christ have a peace guarding their hearts and their minds, and they know who they are as children of God because the Holy Spirit is bearing witness with their spirit. The emotional impact of all this can be seen on their faces. Before they resolved their conflicts, the Holy Spirit was being quenched, but now the Spirit of truth was bearing witness in a repentant heart.

The Place of Emotions

One of the most common results of finding freedom in Christ is an affection for God and His Word. Latent feelings are released from the subconscious to the conscious, which moves people to act in accordance with the truth that transformed their emotions. Jonathan Edwards, whose ministry was committed to true religion, believed that in his day the proper place of emotion was often overlooked. Speaking of people hearing the truths of the gospel and the commands of God, he said:

> . . . they often hear these things, and yet remain as they were before, with no sensible alteration on them, either in heart or practice, because they are not affected with what they hear; and ever will be so till they are affected. I am bold to assert, that there never was any considerable change wrought in the mind of conversation [conduct or behavior] of any person, by anything of a religious nature, that ever he read, heard or saw, that had not his affections moved.[8]

Jonathan Edwards further pointed to emotions as the driving force of human actions, including religious actions. He said, "The will never is in any exercise any further than it is affected."[9] Evelyn Underhill shared a similar thought:

> Now, when we do anything consciously and with purpose, the transition from inaction to action unfolds itself in

a certain order. First we form a concept of that which we shall do; the idea of it looms up, dimly or distinctly, in the mind. Then, we feel that we want to do it, or must do it. Then we determine that we *will* do it. These phases may follow one another so swiftly that they seem to us to be fused into one; but when we analyze the process which lies behind each conscious act, we find that this is the formal sequence of development. First we think, then we feel, then we will.[10]

The coming together of thought, feeling, and action in the heart can be seen in the life of Christ. First, because He was "moved with compassion" He fed the multitude in Matthew 15:32, healed two blind men in Matthew 20:34, cleansed the leper in Mark 1:41, and He forgave us all (Matthew 18:27). Second, because the Lord was moved by anger, He overturned the tables of the moneychangers. They had turned God's house of prayer into a robbers' den (Matthew 21:12). It is important to note that He turned over the tables, not the moneychangers. If we are moved by anger and wish not to sin, then we should be angry as Christ was—be angry at *sin*. Anger that is rooted in righteous indignation is not wrong; it moves us to take action against what is unrighteous.

Writing on the emotions of Jesus, Robert Law commented:

> Anger, to speak broadly, is the combative emotion. While compassion springs from the love by which we identify ourselves with others, anger is naturally aroused by our antagonism, of whatsoever sort. And as the purpose of compassion is to enable us to do, and to do spontaneously or graciously, kind and self-sacrificing actions which otherwise we might not do, or might do coldly and ineffectively, so the natural use of anger is to enable us to perform actions. . . . and which without its stimulus we might be prevented from doing by fear, or by the sympathetic sensibility which makes the infliction of pain on others painful to ourselves; or which, again, we might do

only in half-hearted and unimpressive fashion. . . . [Anger] is . . . a force, an explosive liberation of psychical force, which for the moment raises a man above his normal self. It gives physical courage, overcoming the paralyzing effects of fear, so that with blood boiling and swollen muscles a man in anger will hurl himself furiously upon an antagonist whom in cold blood he scarcely durst encounter. It reinforces moral courage.[11]

God works through the emotional core of our hearts to move us to repentance. We see this in 2 Corinthians 7:9,10, where Paul said,

I now rejoice, not that you were made sorrowful, but that you were made sorrowful to the point of repentance; for you were made sorrowful according to the will of God, in order that you might not suffer loss in anything through us. For the sorrow that is according to the will of God produces a repentance without regret (NASB).

I have seen people feel sorry about their past or sorry that they shared about their past with others. But I have never seen anyone feel sorry after he or she repented. The conviction of sin produces the sorrow that leads to repentance without regret. True inner peace is the result of complete repentance.

David became physically sick when he kept quiet about his sin with Bathsheba. The hand of God pressed heavily upon him until he finally repented. Then he was able to say, "Blessed is he whose transgressions are forgiven, whose sins are covered. Blessed is the man whose sin the LORD does not count against him and in whose spirit is no deceit" (Psalm 32:1,2). That tells us that sorrow which leads to repentance is never divorced from the truth that is within us. In another Psalm in which David expressed repentance over his sin with Bathsheba, he said, "Surely you desire truth in the inner parts; you teach me wisdom in the inmost place" (Psalm 51:6).

Meditation Increases Our Faith

When we meditate on God's greatness and His love for us, and when we see all that He has done for us, we are led to place our confidence in Him. David's meditation on all that God had done for him led him to declare, "My soul clings to you; your right hand upholds me" (Psalm 63:8). David didn't give up on God even though the Lord allowed him to be driven into the wilderness. His soul clung to God even in the midst of difficult circumstances. The truth of God's love for him, which had been confirmed in the past, was engraved on his heart. He didn't let outward circumstances in the present erase that truth, and neither should we. David, through meditation, realized that God was upholding him. He knew he was being sustained by God's strong right hand. That's the kind of faith that allows God to work in our lives.

When we realize that God is always present and at work in our lives, life becomes different. We have the power we need to live, no matter what the circumstances. We're not talking about a power that merely makes us happy, but rather gives us an inward joy that becomes our strength. Meditating on the truth prepares us for all of life's circumstances, according to Proverbs 6:20-22:

> My son, keep your father's commands and do not forsake your mother's teaching. Bind them upon your heart forever; fasten them around your neck. When you walk, they will guide you; when you sleep, they will watch over you; when you awake, they will speak to you.

A lady who was critically injured from an auto accident was semiconscious for several weeks, during which time she heard careless hospital personnel refer to her as having only a short time to live. During the same time she heard other words speak to her from her inner being—words such as those in Psalm 34:4: "I sought the LORD, and he answered me; he delivered me from all my fears." She had memorized these words years before. In her dim awareness, she found comfort and strength. Eventually she recovered, and says that the truths she meditated on were her source of hope during her battle to stay alive. A soldier who spent eight years in a North Vietnam prison received similar hope from some hymns that he had sung as a child. He reconstructed 120 hymns, which gave him strength through that ordeal.

Not only can we receive comfort and strength from words we've meditated upon, we can receive correction as well. The psalmist declared, "How can a young man keep his way pure? By living according to your word. I seek you with all my heart; do not let me stray from your commands. I have hidden your word in my heart that I might not sin against you" (Psalm 119:9-11).

Practical Methods of Meditation

Meditation is basically thinking on the Word of God, going over its truth in our minds repeatedly so that God's truth finally reaches our hearts, affecting our emotions and will. But *how* should we practice meditation? Dietrich Bonhoeffer was a Christian leader in Germany during the Second World War. He was executed by Hitler just a few days before the prison camp in which he resided was freed by the allies. He was noted for his habit of meditating on Scripture, especially the Psalms. People always wanted to know his method. His response was simply, "Accept the Word of Scripture and ponder it in your heart as Mary did. That is all. That is meditation."[12]

We have found the following process to be helpful for hiding God's Word in our hearts:

1. *Personalize the truth.* Place yourself or your name in the verse. For instance, Romans 5:5 says, "The love of God has been poured out within our hearts" (NASB). Say to yourself, "The love of God has been poured into *my* heart." You could also try this with Paul's prayer in Ephesians 3:14-19:

> For this reason *I* kneel before the Father, from whom his whole family in heaven and on earth derives its name. *I* pray that out of his glorious riches he may strengthen *me*

with power through his Spirit in my inner being, so that
Christ may dwell in my heart through faith. And I pray
that I, being rooted and established in love, may have
power, together with all the saints, to grasp how wide and
long and high and deep is the love of Christ, and to know
this love that surpasses knowledge—that I may be filled to
the measure of all the fullness of God.

It is too easy for us to sit outside the experiences of life
and critique them without applying them to ourselves. Oftentimes when we go to church, we critique the message and
the choir. But we aren't supposed to sit in judgment of the
message; the message is to sit in judgment of us! We're not
supposed to criticize the music; we are to join together with the
corporate body of Christ and worship God. We aren't supposed
to study Scripture just so we can indict others; we are to first appropriate Scripture into our own lives and then share from our
heart the truth of God's Word. Anything less is dead orthodoxy
which falls on deaf ears.

2. *Visualize the truth.* The Bible gives us many word pictures.
What kind of mental picture could come to your mind after
reading Romans 5:5: "The love of God has been poured out
within our hearts"? (NASB). Try to picture what Jesus said about
the person who believes in Him in John 7:38: "From his innermost being shall flow rivers of living water" (NASB).

3. *Respond to the truth.* If God's Word calls for praise, then
stop and praise Him. If you really want to establish truth and
praise in your heart, then learn to sing in your heart. Those who
are filled with the Holy Spirit and the Word of God will sing
and make melody in their hearts to the Lord (Ephesians 5:16-
20; Colossian 3:15-17). If Scripture calls for repentance and
confession, then stop and fulfill the exhortation. If it calls for
obedience, then by all means decide that you will obey. James
1:22-25 gives us excellent words about obedience:

Do not merely listen to the word, and so deceive yourselves. Do what it says. Anyone who listens to the word
but does not do what it says is like a man who looks at his
face in a mirror and, after looking at himself, goes away
and immediately forgets what he looks like. But the man
who looks intently into the perfect law that gives freedom,
and continues to do this, not forgetting what he has heard
but doing it—he will be blessed in what he does.

4. *Let God's Word transform you.* Meditating on Scripture
involves reading the Bible not for information only, but for
transformation. It is not simply a question of getting into the
Word, it is a question of the Word getting into us. It is not
merely getting through the Bible in a year, it is letting the Bible
get through us and lodge in our hearts. It means staying in the
Word until it reaches our emotions and our wills.

Meditation takes time. It is not simply repetition, it is more
like the type of reflections we engage in when we read a love
letter over and over. And that is what God's Word is: a letter to
the bride from the Groom, who loves us more than we could
ever fathom. "We must put ourselves in the presence of God
and pause over each verse while we say it."[13]

5. *Meditate on the Word to strengthen your relationship with the
Author.* You are hearing from God. George Müller wrote these
words in his autobiography:

I saw more clearly than ever, that the first great and
primary business to which I ought to attend every day was,
to have my soul happy in the Lord. The first thing to be
concerned about was not, how much I might serve the
Lord, how I might glorify the Lord; but how I might get my
soul into a happy state, and how my inner man might be
nourished. . . . I saw that the most important thing I had
to do was, to give myself to the reading of the Word of
God and to meditate on it, that thus my heart might be
comforted, encouraged, warned, reproved, instructed; and
that thus, whilst meditating, my heart might be brought
into experimental communion with the Lord."[14]

It is a fundamental truth of Scripture that we as Christians live by the Word of God. We are born again by the Word, and we grow by the Word. The Word is the food of our soul. In order to grow by that food, we must take it in and digest it. Meditation is the digestive process by which we incorporate the Word into our lives by taking it into our hearts, the wellspring of our lives.

Psychiatrist Paul Meier tells of the power meditation has to change lives in his account of a study that he did on seminary students. In brief, he attempted to see if he could find a correlation between a person's psychological state and spiritual life. To do so, he had each student complete a standard psychological test and a spiritual life questionnaire.

At first, Meier was surprised and disappointed. The students who had been Christians for many years were only slightly healthier and happier than those who had recently become Christians. The difference was not statistically significant. His disappointment, however, turned to joy when he found the crucial factor that made the difference: daily or almost daily meditation in the Scriptures.

While Meier acknowledges that mind renewal can be encouraged by a number of influences, a variety of sources, especially Christian friends, he concludes, "Daily meditation on Scripture, with personal application, is the most effective means of obtaining personal joy, peace, and emotional maturity. . . . On average, it takes about three years of daily Scripture meditation to bring about enough change in a person's thought patterns and behavior to produce statistically superior mental health and happiness."[15]

We close this chapter with these words from the nineteenth-century saint, Horatius Bonar:

> He that would be like Christ, moreover, must *study* him. We cannot make ourselves holy by merely *trying* to be so, any more than we can make ourselves believe and love by simple energy of endeavor. No force can effect this. Men *try* to be holy, and they fail. They cannot by direct

effort work themselves into holiness. They must gaze upon a holy object; and so be changed into its likeness "from glory to glory" (1 Corinthians 3:18). They must have a holy being for their bosom friend. Companionship with Jesus, like that of John, can alone make us to resemble either the disciple or the Master. He that would be holy must steep himself in the word, must bask in the sunshine which radiates from each page of revelation. It is through THE TRUTH that we are sanctified (John 17:17). Exposing ourselves constantly to this light, we become more thoroughly "children of the light."[16]

11

The Power of Our Actions

For this reason, since the day we heard about you, we have not stopped praying for you and asking God to fill you with the knowledge of his will through all spiritual wisdom and understanding. And we pray this in order that you may live a life worthy of the Lord and may please him in every way: bearing fruit in every good work, growing in the knowledge of God, being strengthened with all power according to his glorious might so that you may have great endurance and patience, and joyfully giving thanks to the Father, who has qualified you to share in the inheritance of the saints in the kingdom of light.

—Colossians 1:9-12

One of the more popular toys that children enjoy receiving for a birthday or Christmas present is a Slinky. Even adults find it fascinating to watch the spiraling cylinder of wire snake itself down a stairway. But the fun doesn't stop there. Children (and some adults) will play with it time and again, watching it slink from one hand to the other, playing with it like a yo-yo.

Understanding Christian Growth

Christian growth is somewhat like a Slinky that is being stretched to its limits. We cycle from one experience to another as we ascend upward in Christian maturity. Paul revealed this

215

cycle of growth in Colossians 3:9-12, which is quoted above. The fact that you can even begin to grow is based on the truth that God "has qualified you to share in the inheritance of the saints in the kingdom of light." And Paul shares how we can grow by giving us the foundational elements, which are listed in the following diagram:

THE CYCLE OF GROWTH

spiritual wisdom
and understanding

②

①

living a worthy life
bearing fruit

knowledge of
His will

③

④

growing in the
knowledge of God

strengthened in power
great endurance
patience
joyfully giving thanks

The growth process begins with a knowledge of God's will, which we find in God's Word. His truth must enter our hearts for us to spiritually understand how it applies to life in all wisdom. The cycle isn't complete, however, until we choose to live according to what we understand. Living by faith requires us to exercise our will by being submissive through humble obedience. When we do, we grow in the knowledge of God, and the cycle comes full circle, back to where we started. In other words, we will receive greater knowledge as we act out the knowledge we already have.[1] The spin-offs of this growth cycle are increasing spiritual strength, endurance, patience, joy, and thankfulness, which become increasingly evident in our character.

The cycle can be blocked at any one of the four points in the diagram. We can block it at the first stage by reading the Bible as an academic exercise and never seeking to apply it to our lives. We would have knowledge, but no wisdom nor any understanding of how the Word of God applies to life. At stage two, God's Word could penetrate our hearts and consequently convict us of sin and give us discernment and direction for life. But the growth process would again be stymied if we never actually repented, acted on our discernment, or stepped out in faith. The usual culprit here is fear, such as fear of failure or fear of rejection. Fear of anything other than God is mutually exclusive of faith in God. That is why we are to encourage one another, "for God did not give us a spirit of timidity, but a spirit of power, of love and of self-discipline" (2 Timothy 1:7).

At the third stage, we grow and bear fruit when we decide to live by faith. We actually gain knowledge from our experiences. Our faith can have only one object and that is God (and His Word), but maturity gained through living causes us to understand the Word of God in a way that we didn't before. If we fail to live by faith, however, we won't bear much fruit.

Finally, we can stop the process of growth at stage four by failing to come back to the Word of God. One of the great dangers of successfully bearing fruit or experiencing victory is that we might decide to rest on our laurels. We are tempted to think that we have arrived. That's why Paul's encouragement in Philippians 3:12-14 is so helpful:

> Not that I have already obtained all this, or have already been made perfect, but I press on to take hold of that for which Christ Jesus took hold of me. Brothers, I do not consider myself yet to have taken hold of it. But one thing I do: Forgetting what is behind and straining toward what is ahead, I press on toward the goal to win the prize for which God has called me heavenward in Christ Jesus.

Let me (Neil) illustrate this process of growth from my own experience with a look at Colossians 3:22-24:

> Slaves, obey your earthly masters in everything; and do it, not only when their eye is on you and to win their favor, but with sincerity of heart and reverence for the Lord. Whatever you do, work at it with all your heart, as working for the Lord, not for men, since you know that

you will receive an inheritance from the Lord as a reward.
It is the Lord Christ you are serving.

I was convicted by this passage when I was still working as an electronic engineer. I was somewhat reluctant to bring my Christianity into the aerospace firm that I worked for. My witness consisted of trying to be a nice person who did his work well, was submissive to his boss, and got along with fellow workers.

How did the truth of Colossians 3:22-24 transform me? First, I began to realize that I was far more than an employee who was making a living to support my family. It was the first time that I understood who I was really serving. I was working for God at the company. That caused me to be a better engineer—not for the purpose of winning points with the boss, but because I was really serving God, who sees me all the time. I now knew that my work ethic shouldn't change based on whether or not my employer was present.

Second, I realized that I was called to be a witness—an ambassador for Christ. So I made a point of identifying myself as a Christian without being obnoxious, and I started a Bible study. Work became far more challenging and exciting. Other Christians came forward and we saw several people come to Christ as a result of the Bible study.

All this happened because I had a new perspective: I was working for God at the office. As a result, I was bearing fruit. I grew tremendously from that experience, and two years later, the Lord called me into full-time ministry.

I saw this same process of growth take place in the lives of other people when I started a school of evangelism at our church. Previously we had encouraged people to share their faith from the pulpit, but few wanted to. Most of them had no heart for the lost, and teaching them how to share their faith only made them feel guilty about not evangelizing. Then I started using some of the insights taught by Dr. James Kennedy in his Evangelism Explosion program. We began to follow-up visitors who came to our church. Trainers took trainees to visitors' homes so each trainee could get on-the-job training. The trainees merely observed for the first few weeks, which helped them get over their fear, which is a major obstacle in evangelism.

Every night was an adventure, and many trainees came back from the visits with glowing testimonies or questions they couldn't answer. This drove them back to the Bible and helped them put their faith in action. No preaching or teaching that I had ever done before had produced the growth in others that this program did. Those who participated developed a burden for the lost, and they learned the truth recorded in 1 Peter 3:13-16:

> Who is going to harm you if you are eager to do good? But even if you should suffer for what is right, you are blessed. Do not fear what they fear; do not be frightened. But in your hearts set apart Christ as Lord. Always be prepared to give an answer to everyone who asks you to give the reason for the hope that you have. But do this with gentleness and respect, keeping a clear conscience, so that those who speak maliciously against your good behavior in Christ may be ashamed of their slander.

The Paths to Change

In previous chapters we learned that changing the heart begins with a change of thought or belief. When truth penetrates the heart, it touches our emotional core, which motivates us to action (as illustrated below).

THE PRIMARY FLOW

Thoughts ⟶ Emotion ⟶ Action

In this chapter, we want to show that our actions or behavior also influence both our thoughts and emotions. This is able to happen because these three elements are united in the heart.

Our Actions Can Affect Our Feelings

That an action can change how we feel was revealed early in biblical history. Cain and Abel brought their offerings to God, who was pleased with Abel's offering but for some reason was not pleased with Cain's. So Cain became angry. "Then the LORD said to Cain, 'Why are you angry? And why has your countenance fallen? If you do well, will not your countenance be lifted up? And if you do not do well, sin is crouching at the door; and its desire is for you, but you must master it'" (Genesis 4:6,7 NASB).

God was saying that we don't always feel our way into good behavior; rather, we behave our way into good feeling. If we wait until we feel like doing something we may wait forever. Jesus revealed the same truth in the New Testament: "Now that you know these things, you will be blessed if you do them" (John 13:17).

The effect of actions on feelings is plainly evident in everyday life. When we are feeling downcast, if we stop and deliberately put a smile on our face, we find that it softens and lifts our spirits. Similarly, we have all heard of "whistling in the dark" as an expression for keeping up our courage in the face of fear. We do it because it works. It actually affects our countenance and lifts our spirits.

We can actually "will" ourselves out of certain moods as David did when he was depressed, "I have trusted in Thy lovingkindness; my heart shall rejoice in Thy salvation. I will sing to the LORD, because He has dealt bountifully with me" (Psalm 13:5,6 NASB). Notice that the process began with recalling the greatness of God, and then David expresses confidence that his heart will rejoice. The rejoicing might not happen immediately, but David anticipated that rejoicing would come, even if it weren't until sometime in the future. But he did make the choice to sing as he recalled God's goodness to him.

You can do the same. When you feel down, start singing or playing a musical instrument. That will go a long way toward changing your feelings. You can even change your feelings by simply changing your posture. If you find yourself walking around in a stooped-over slouch, chances are you will feel like a slouch. Instead, try standing up straight, pull your shoulders back, take a deep breath, and decide to walk with confidence while holding your head up high—and see what happens to your countenance.

When we read what Scripture has to say about our emotional life, we find that it seems to command us to feel a certain way. Many times we are commanded to rejoice and be joyful—

commands that, unfortunately, are often disobeyed. There are other commandments, about showing love, having peace, and not giving in to fear.

All that raises a question: How are we to obey those biblical commands? If we cannot change our emotions directly, what *can* we do to change them?

Keeping in mind what we have already said about the relationship of emotions to thoughts, we believe that Scripture teaches we can change our emotions by changing our thoughts. The Bible also teaches that we change our emotions by changing our actions. In other words, by acting or behaving in a certain way, we can change our emotions correspondingly:

ACTIONS AFFECT EMOTIONS

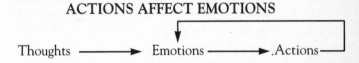

Thoughts ⟶ Emotions ⟶ Actions

In his study of the expression of grief and joy in the religion of Israel, Gary Anderson observes that certain emotions are legally commanded in the law. These commands concerning emotions must therefore include "specific implications for behavioral enactment."[2]

Such is clearly the case with the commands to love one another. We are not commanded to "like" people or feel good about them, which in some cases would be impossible for us to do. We often hear people say, "I love you in the Lord," which could imply, "I detest you in the flesh!" But a love for someone or something, according to Scripture, cannot be devoid of any emotion. Because the emotion of love cannot be directly evoked, these commands are therefore not directed toward the *emotive aspect* of love, but toward the *actions* that are also part of genuine love. If our emotions and wills are truly connected in the depths of our hearts, then a sincere act must effect a change in our emotions. To put it simply, the doing of a loving act from our hearts also incites the emotion of love.

In the case of marriage, a husband is to love his wife as Christ loved the church (Ephesians 5:25), and older women are to teach younger women to love their husbands (Titus 2:3,4). Any married couple can tell you that the emotional aspect of loving our spouses can come and go like the wind. What makes a marriage relationship unique is the commitment, and what holds it together is the gracious act of loving each other whether or not you feel like it. And the essence of such love is meeting one another's needs. When one spouse says he or she doesn't feel any love for the other person, we advise that person to honor their marriage vows and faithfully love the other person by meeting his or her needs. In doing so, the feelings toward the other person will follow in time. Doing the loving thing, based on God's Word, will eventually connect emotionally in our hearts. That will be true if there are no unresolved conflicts caused by failing to speak the truth in love or to forgive from the heart. Then we need to kiss and make up—and not necessarily in that order. (For more about how marital conflicts can be resolved as a couple, see Neil and Charles Mylander's book *The Christ-Centered Marriage*.)

The idea of behavior changing how we feel is clearly seen in what Scripture says about joy. In the Old Testament we find the interesting biblical idiom "to do a joy." Along with telling the Israelites, "The joy of the LORD is your strength," Nehemiah commanded the people not to grieve. In response to this command, "all the people went away to eat, to drink, to send portions and to celebrate a great festival" (Nehemiah 8:12 NASB). The words "celebrate a great festival," in the original Hebrew text, are literally, "to make a great joy." A similar expression is found in relation to mourning when Joseph and those with him are said to have "made a mourning" at the burial of Jacob (Genesis 50:10).

In Scripture, the concepts of joy and sorrow are associated with specific actions. Frequently joy is connected with eating and drinking, which is still true in most church socials. Nine out of the eleven Pentateuchal texts commanding joy occur in Deuteronomy, and in almost all of these Deuteronomic passages, the command to rejoice is connected with offering sacrifices.[3] An example of this is seen in Deuteronomy 12:11,12:

> The place which the LORD your God shall choose for
> His name to dwell, there you shall bring all that I command you: your burnt offerings and your sacrifices, your

tithes and the contribution of your hand, and all your choice votive offerings which you will vow to the LORD. And you shall rejoice before the LORD your God, you and your sons and daughters, your male and female servants, and the Levite who is within your gates.

In that passage, the command to rejoice is inseparably linked to sacrificial obligations and, according to Anderson, "finds concrete expression in the sacrificial feast." The link between eating sacrificial food and rejoicing before the Lord is unmistakable in other passages as well.[4] For example, when the Israelites crossed the Jordan and entered the Promised Land, Moses instructed them to build an altar on Mount Ebal. Then he said, "You shall sacrifice peace offerings and eat there, and you shall rejoice before the LORD your God" (Deuteronomy 27:7).[5]

The actions of singing, dancing, and praising God are also associated with joy.[6] When Nehemiah dedicated Jerusalem's rebuilt walls, the joy of Jerusalem was "heard far away" (Nehemiah 12:43). For that to be true, there had to be a lot of noise. Verse 27 tells us that people were singing to the accompaniment of musical instruments.

The connection between joy and praising God is particularly prominent in the Psalms. David declared, "I will be glad and exult in Thee; I will sing praise to Thy name, O Most High" (9:2); "let them shout for joy and rejoice, who favor my vindication; and let them say continually, 'The LORD be magnified'" (35:27); "I will also praise Thee with a harp . . . to Thee I will sing praises with the lyre. . . . My lips will shout for joy when I sing praises to Thee" (71:22,23).

The experience of joy was also connected to the action of anointing with oil. The Messiah was to anoint His people with the "oil of gladness," bringing an end to their period of mourning (Isaiah 61:3). The phrase "oil of gladness" is more than a metaphor. In Bible times, a regular feature at the conclusion of mourning was the act of anointing oneself with scented oils (see 2 Samuel 12:20,21; Daniel 10:3).

The donning of certain clothing was also associated with joy. The psalmist wrote, "You turned my wailing into dancing; you removed my sackcloth and clothed me with joy" (30:11). In the NASB, the word "joy" is the noun "gladness," which includes the special clothing related to this emotion.[7]

In contrast to the actions related to joy, Scripture mentions corresponding opposite actions connected with mourning. Fasting was often associated with mourning, rather than eating and drinking. Mourning called for lamentation rather than praise to God. Gladness called for anointing the head with oil, and mourning called for ashes or dust upon the head. Sackcloth was worn in mourning instead of festal clothing. Finally sexual relations between spouses was associated with joy, while continence was practiced in mourning.[8]

In Scripture, then, emotion was not simply an inner feeling; it was related to action. And the fact that the emotions were often commanded and obligatory—as in the case of joy—suggests that the relationship was not always from the feeling to the action. It could also go from the action to the feeling. That is, the action related to the emotion could precede and influence the subjective experience of that emotion.

Our Actions Can Affect Our Thoughts

If our actions can affect our emotions, it is equally evident that our actions can affect our thoughts and beliefs:

ACTIONS AFFECT THOUGHTS

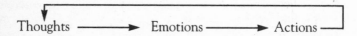

Thoughts   ⟶   Emotions   ⟶   Actions

Again this is seen both in human experience and in Scripture. For example, a woman told me (Neil) that she wanted to believe that there was a God, but she just couldn't get herself to do it. No amount of proof that I could offer seemed to help, so I advised her to live as though there was a God. Because she wanted to believe, she took my advice. I saw her again a year later, and I could hardly believe the change. Her decision to live like a Christian helped serve as a catalyst to actually becoming one.

Psychologists Martin Bolt and David Myers, writing in 1984, asserted that if the last 20 years have taught us anything, they have taught us that "we are as likely to act ourselves into a way of thinking as to think ourselves into action."[9] While we might not want to go quite that far, there is much evidence to show that behavior affects our beliefs and attitudes.[10] If a person lives out a certain role, that role will become internalized and can bring about change to the person, including in his or her thinking. For example, young women smokers who played the emotional role of a lung cancer victim cut back their smoking more than those who were simply given information about the hazards of smoking. The Marines' promise to "make a man out of you" is not done by intellectual study, but "by active practice of the new role requirements.[11] You have a better chance of becoming a mature man if you act like one.

A well-known experiment demonstrated that when people willingly bind themselves to a public action, they come to believe more strongly in that action. For example, California housewives were more apt to allow a large, ugly "Drive Carefully" sign to be placed in their front yard if they had first been asked to sign a safe driving petition.

This principle is also evident in relation to morality. Acts in relation to good or evil influence a person's moral beliefs and attitudes. Older children who are actively engaged in teaching or enforcing moral behavior in younger children follow that behavior themselves more than those who are simply taught the moral behavior. The harsh actions required of soldiers during wartime have often led them to finally do things that, at first, their beliefs would never allow them to do. These behavioral research findings tell us that our actions not only reflect the thoughts and emotions of our hearts, they also shape our hearts.

A Principle Affirmed in Scripture

The idea that our actions affect our thoughts is affirmed repeatedly in Scripture. Many biblical terms include in themselves both thought and action. The word "know" in Scripture includes actions as well as thoughts. As Bible scholar O.A. Piper points out, this biblical meaning is contrary to the Greek meaning of "knowledge," which has so influenced our Western way of thinking. "This feature, more than any other, brings out the wide gulf which separates the Hebraic from the Greek view of knowledge. In the latter, knowledge itself is purely theoretical

. . . whereas in the Old Testament the person who does not act in accordance with what God has done or plans to do has but a fragmentary knowledge.[12]

Similarly, biblical faith involves obedience. According to Calvin, faith "is born of obedience."[13] The inherent link between actions and faith is even more evident in Bonhoeffer's words: "Only he who believes is obedient, and only he who is obedient believes. . . . You can only know and think about it by actually doing it."[14]

Other biblical words, which we might be inclined to take as involving only the intellect, incorporate some expression of the will. According to Goetzmann, the Greek term *phroneo*, translated in Colossians 3:2 as "set your minds on" (*see also* Philippians 2:2; 4:2), "expresses not merely an activity of the intellect, but also a movement of the will; it is both interest and decision at the same time."[15] Similarly, the term *logizesthe* used in the exhortation "let your mind dwell on these things" (Philippians 4:8 NASB) does not suggest only "thoughtful contemplation." "It is an admonition to action," to make that which the mind thinks about a part of one's life.[16] Wisdom in biblical thinking is not a "deeper knowledge in the theoretical mastery of the questions of life and the universe." It is the practical knowledge or skill to live life, thus involving both thought and act.[17]

You can see how all this comes together in the cycle of growth. "The knowledge of his will" (Colossians 1:9) cannot mean mere intellectual ascent or the growth process will be stopped. You really don't *know* God's will until it is appropriated and finally applied. Pedersen says, "Thus thinking is not theoretical, but of a pronouncedly practical character. He who understands how to think well is wise. Wisdom is a property of the soul, or rather a faculty, an ability to produce, a skill in shaping the very thought which yields the right result."[18]

A Principle Taught in Scripture

Not only are thought and action connected in certain biblical terms, they are also connected in the teaching of Scripture. After assuring us that God's divine power has granted us everything pertaining to life and godliness (2 Peter 1:3), and that we have been made a partaker of the divine nature (verse 4), Peter then shares our responsibility:

> For this very reason also, applying all diligence, in your faith supply moral excellence, and in your moral excellence, knowledge; and in your knowledge, self-control, and in your self-control, perseverance, and in your perseverance, godliness; and in your godliness, brotherly kindness, and in your brotherly kindness, love (2 Peter 1:5-7 NASB).

Faith is the foundation in this linear progression toward the ultimate character of love. In fact, faith is the basis for all that we are and do. If what we believe is wrong, then all that comes from us will be skewed. We can't do anything without first thinking it. Every action is preceded by a thought. That is how the central nervous system operates. We choose to believe the truth and act accordingly, which should result in moral excellence. Why, then, does knowledge follow moral excellence in Peter's progression toward love? Perhaps that is best illustrated by the relationship between a child and a parent.

Suppose a father tells his son to do something, and the child says, "I don't know why I have to do that." The father may say, "Trust me, I know what is best." The rebellious son may respond, "I'm not going to do it until you tell me why." At that point he doesn't need an explanation, he needs to be disciplined in love. The father would be wise to say, "Son, you need to do it because I told you to do it, and when you have done it we will sit down and talk." The songwriter was right when he wrote, "Trust and obey for there is no other way to be happy in Jesus, than to trust and obey." The point is, the only appropriate response to faith in God is to do it—and then you will know why. You don't have to know why in order to trust and obey, but there is a good chance that you will know why if you have been faithful. The knowledge gained from the experience of trusting and obeying leads to greater self-control, which eventually perfects us in love.

The understanding of love is borne out in our actions:

> This is how we know what love is: Jesus Christ laid down his life for us. And we ought to lay down our lives for our brothers. If anyone has material possessions and sees his brother in need but has no pity on him, how can the love of God be in him? Dear children, let us not love with words or tongue but with actions and in truth (1 John 3:16-18).

In a similar fashion, the Old Testament teaches that the one who loves someone or something cleaves to him (Deuteronomy 11:22; 30:20; Proverbs 18:24), runs or goes after him (Isaiah 1:23; Jeremiah 2:2), seeks him (Psalm 4:2; 40:16; Proverbs 8:17), and produces benevolent actions toward the object of love (Jeremiah 31:3; Hosea 11:4). This evidence leads to the conclusion expressed by Wallis in *The Theological Dictionary of the Old Testament:* that the Hebrew word for love and its derivatives "have a strongly pragmatic character," which includes conscious actions.[19] God writes His law on our hearts, which surely entails thought, but that law is summed up in love.

The fact that love of God can be commanded also speaks of action (Deuteronomy 6:5). This is especially seen in loving God with all your "strength." "The question has been raised as to how such love as this can be commanded. However, if love is not merely an emotional feeling for a person or a thing, but also involves a behavior that is becoming to love, then it is possible for Deuteronomy to elevate this behavior to the level of a commandment.[20]

Scripture also makes it clear that to know love, we must actually experience love. We must be loving people. The apostle John says:

> We have come to know and have believed the love which God has for us. God is love, and the one who abides in love abides in God. . . . If someone says, "I love God," and hates his brother, he is a liar; for the one who does not love his brother, whom he has seen, cannot love God whom he has not seen (1 John 4:16,20 NASB).

Our experiential actions of love lead us to the real knowledge of love.

I (Neil) have counseled hundreds of people who said they loved the Lord and yet their lives were all messed up, and many were living in sin. Something was wrong with their faith foundation because Jesus said, "Whoever has my commands and obeys them, he is the one who loves me" (John 14:21). On the other hand, I have worked with hundreds of people who weren't very lovely. In some cases I had to work at loving them. Yet I'm always amazed at the miracle of love that takes place in my own heart after I have done everything I can to help them. An emotional bond will develop—a bond that comes by actively loving them by the grace of God. In a similar fashion, I have found it difficult at times to go to convalescent hospitals. Usually the depressing sights and strong odors make me want to turn around and leave. But after doing the loving thing, I have always left with a sense of peace. And every successive visit purifies my heart, producing an emotional love for people in need.

The truth that actions affect our beliefs and thoughts is also shown in Matthew 6:20,21: "Store up for yourselves treasures in heaven. . . . For where your treasure is, there your heart will be also." Jesus was saying that where we store up our treasures (surely an action) determines the place of our heart. And of course, our heart includes our thoughts and emotions. As we learned earlier, it's in the heart that thought and action are inseparably tied together. You cannot affect one without having an effect on the other. Not only does a thought lead to action, but the action also strengthens the thought behind it.

The Need to Be Willing

The intertwining of thought and action is further evident in the biblical teaching that truth is what a person *does*, not simply what he knows. John said, "Whoever lives by the truth comes into the light, so that it may be seen plainly that what he has done has been done through God" (John 3:21). Living by the truth brings it into the light. The more we choose to live the truth, the more we come to know the truth. "If we claim to have fellowship with him yet walk in the darkness, we lie and do not live by the truth" (1 John 1:6). John also said he receives great joy from knowing that his friends are "walking in the truth" (2 John 4; 3 John 3,4).

Jesus said, "If any man is willing to do His will, he shall *know*" (John 7:17 NASB, emphasis added). You probably won't understand the will of God if you are not willing to do it. But if you are willing to do His will, then you will likely know what it is. That is especially true in divine guidance because God guides a moving ship. The rudder has no effect unless the ship is under way. God can't make mid-course corrections if the ship has never set sail.

Suppose the direction that God is taking you is on the other side of a closed door. You won't know what's on the other side of the door unless you are willing to *do* His will—even before you *know* what it is. Why do you need to know what's on the other side of the door before you go through it? So you can decide beforehand whether or not you want to go? If God is God, He has the right to decide what is on the other side. If He doesn't have that right, then He isn't God.

We have to decide whether to trust God with our lives on this side of the closed door before He will let us see what is on the other side. Do we believe that the will of God is "good, pleasing and perfect," as Romans 12:2 tells us? According to that verse, the renewing of our minds will result in testing and proving that the will of God is indeed good, pleasing, and perfect for us.

One reason God doesn't unfold His plan for our lives all at once is because there may be some significant trials and tribulations on the other side of that door. Had I (Neil) known beforehand what my family would have to go through for me to be where I'm at today, I don't think I would have chosen to come this way. On the other hand, looking back, I'm glad I came. The will of God is good and pleasing, and it was perfect for me and my family.

Proverbs 4:23-27 tells us that guarding the heart involves practical action. The issues of life come from the heart, but apparently the actions of the mouth, eyes, and walk can affect the heart. Commenting on verse 24, Bible commentator Derek Kidner says, "Superficial habits of talk react on the mind; so that cynical chatter, fashionable grumbles, flippancy, half-truths, barely meant in the first place, harden into well-established habits of thought."[21]

Our Actions Can Affect Our Knowledge

When the Bible talks about how our actions affect our thoughts, we find that there is an interesting interplay between knowledge and action. We rightly think of the "fear of the LORD" as being the beginning or first principle of wisdom (Psalm 111:10; Proverbs 9:10). Thus we conclude that wise living begins with knowing God and being in awe of Him. But the "fear of the LORD" is more than knowledge and awe, it also includes a practical life of piety and, therefore, is much the same as "wisdom." In fact, Job made this connection: "The fear of the LORD—that is wisdom" (28:28).

Both the fear of God and wisdom involve thought and act, but it is action that leads to an increase in both. Someone wisely said, "Do the thing you fear the most, and the death of fear is certain." Likewise, Psalm 111:10 begins, "The fear of the LORD is the beginning of wisdom," but then goes on to say, "a good understanding have all those who do His commandments" (NASB). Fohrer explains the relationship of these two elements when he says, "He who practices the fear of Yahweh as practical piety (*hokma* [wisdom]) has valuable insight (Psalm 111:10), so that the most important knowledge of life is attained in the sphere of right action rather than in that of the cultus [formal worship] or of thought."[22]

Our Actions Can Affect Our Faith

We should also observe what James said about how works affect our faith. After declaring that Abraham's faith was at work in the act of offering Isaac, James then added, "As a result of the works, faith was perfected" (2:22 NASB). Scripture clearly teaches that faith and works are related, but we often think of that relationship as flowing only one way—that is, faith produces works. But James says the flow goes both ways. Works also affect faith. The idea is not that work adds something to an incomplete or defective faith, but rather that work fulfills, strengthens, and matures faith.[23] Because faith involves an intellectual component, we can say that when we actually exercise faith in an action, this action thus effects a change in the intellectual aspect of our faith. So our actions perfect our faith.

Our actions may add new dimensions to our understanding of God and His work or simply strengthen the understanding we already have.

Showing Ourselves Faithful

If we want to grow in our spiritual life, we must *actualize* the truth of God as well as know it. Having biblical knowledge by itself does not necessarily change our life, but when we practice God's truth, we actually gain in our knowledge and insight into His truth. A change of heart includes both change of mind and change of action. We cannot directly command our emotions, but we *can* command the input of truth and the practice of it. Both are essential if we want to change our hearts and have change take place in us.

Karl Menninger was once asked, "If one feels on the verge of a nervous breakdown, what should they do?" He answered, "Lock your house, go across the railroad tracks, find someone in need, and do something for him"[24] That was good advice. It was the same advice given to me when I (Neil) was a young pastor. A dear old saint handed me a note on the way out of church which said, "It is one of life's great compensations that you cannot sincerely help another without helping yourself in the process."

The Christian life is more than a set of beliefs; it is a skill. It is the skill of a wise person who knows how to live practically in the ways of God. Learning a skill involves both theoretical knowledge and the practice of that knowledge. Similarly, growing in the Christian life involves both right belief or theoretical knowledge about life *and* the knowledge that comes only through the practice of living that life.

So much of the Christian life is accepting and doing our duty. We don't need any special guidance to love our neighbor as ourselves or to be a witness of the resurrected life within us. We dignify our calling and honor God when we show ourselves faithful in what He has entrusted to us. Our duty is not to see what lies dimly in the distance, but to do what clearly lies at hand. Solomon said, "Here is the conclusion of the matter: Fear God and keep his commandments, for this is the whole duty of man" (Ecclesiastes 12:13). Bob Benson wrote about "Duty's Dignity":

> Her name was Cissy. She was solid black, and even though there was some question as to her family tree, she was a fine dog. As a pup she had destroyed the required number of newspapers, shoes, and flower beds to reach her maturity.
>
> She had a fine litter of pups, seven to be exact, and it was something to watch her care for them. Who taught that little dog, so recently a pup herself, to care and feed, clean and protect those seven wiggling, squirming, yapping appetites rolled in fur? Who placed that look of intense pride, beaming happiness? Who gave that air of dignity? God did. God made that little dog. And in His world He gave her a share, a place to fill, a task to perform—a duty that dignified.
>
> All of God's creatures have dignity, but it is only reached through the doorway of duty. He made you to stand tall, walk straight, play fairly, love wholeheartedly—and every time you think the mean thought, do the "small" thing you stoop beneath your dignity.
>
> Oh God, make us to be too tall to be stooped, too straight to be crooked, too big to be small. Help us to do the tasks that ennoble, the duties that dignify.[25]

12

Does God's Law Apply Today?

Such confidence as this is ours through Christ before God.
Not that we are competent in ourselves to claim anything for
ourselves, but our competence comes from God. He has
made us competent as ministers of a new covenant—not
of the letter but of the Spirit; for the letter kills, but the
spirit gives life. . . . Now the Lord is the Spirit, and where
the spirit of the Lord is, there is freedom. And we, who with
unveiled faces all reflect the Lord's glory, are being trans-
formed into his likeness with ever-increasing glory, which
comes from the Lord, who is the Spirit.

—2 Corinthians 3:4-6,17,18

Remember the teeter-totter? The same delicate balance exists with the concept of freedom. Legalism and license sit on opposite ends of the board, and our freedom in Christ is the fulcrum. In Romans 6:1-11, Paul identifies us with Christ in His death, burial, and resurrection. He says in verse 7, "Anyone who has died has been freed from sin." Every Christian has died with Christ and is, therefore, free from sin. However, Paul adds in Galatians 5:1,2, "It is for freedom that Christ has set us free. Stand firm, then, and do not let yourselves be burdened again by a yoke of slavery. Mark my words! I, Paul, tell you that if you let yourselves be circumcised, Christ will be of no value to you at all." In other words, don't go back to the law. If you claim

235

you are already free in Christ but are steeped in legalism or have failed to maintain your freedom by living a responsible Christian life, you are at one end of the teeter-totter. One pastor who obviously espoused this position said, "There is no such thing as bondage for a Christian!" His associate muttered under his breath, "There is only denial!"

If you deny or seriously question that there is such a thing as freedom from sin and our past, then you are at the other end of the teeter-totter. The people at this end have never learned how to resolve their conflicts nor appropriate the truth that we are indeed new creations in Christ. They emphasize hard work and personal discipline as a means of surviving. I (Neil) once asked a leading proponent of this view what his cure rate was in helping people. He said, "Cure? We don't really cure anybody; we help them cope with life!" Is that all the gospel is—a new and better way to cope? Are we supposed to muddle through life with little hope for any victory on this side of eternity?

Living Free in Christ

Christians are indeed positionally free in Christ, but how many are living like they are? We estimate that approximately 15 percent of Bible-believing Christians are living free, productive lives. What a tragedy! Being alive and free in Christ is the birthright of every child of God. Those who are liberated know who they are in Christ, bear fruit, and have a satisfying prayer and devotional life. Sure they have problems, but they resolve them in Christ. There is a major difference between the issues that constitute freedom and those that constitute growth. We don't believe in instant maturity; we know it will take us the rest of our lives to renew our minds and conform to God's image. We know we will never achieve perfection in our relatively short lifespan, but that should still be our focus—to be like Christ.

If a person isn't experiencing freedom in Christ, then he is stymied in his growth. People like this go from book to book, pastor to pastor, and counselor to counselor, but can't seem to get unstuck. But when they have had their eyes opened to the truth about who they are in Christ and have resolved their personal and spiritual conflicts, watch them grow!

An undergraduate student stopped by my (Neil's) office one day and said that she was researching satanism, and wanted to ask me some questions. After talking with her for a few minutes, I suggested that she probably shouldn't be studying that subject. "Why not?" she asked. "Because you aren't living a free life in Christ yourself," I responded. "What do you mean by that?" she asked. I told her, "You are probably struggling in your Bible classes just trying to pay attention. I would suspect that your devotional and prayer life is virtually nonexistent. I would guess that your self-esteem is probably down in the mud somewhere, and you probably entertain a lot of thoughts about suicide."

She almost came out of her chair. "How did you know that?" she asked. After years of helping people find their freedom in Christ, I can frequently discern whether a person is living free in Christ. She got permission as an undergraduate student to take my graduate-level class that covered the material in my books *Victory Over the Darkness* and *The Bondage Breaker*. After the class, and with no further counseling, she wrote me this letter:

> What I have discovered this last week is this feeling of control. Like my mind is my own. I haven't sat and had these strung out periods of thought and contemplation; that is, conversations with myself. My mind just simply feels quieted. It is really a strange feeling.
>
> My emotions have been stable. I haven't felt depressed once this week. My will is mine. I feel like I have been able to choose to live my life abiding in Christ. Scripture seems different. I have a totally different perspective. I actually understand what it is saying. I feel left alone. Not in a bad way. I'm not lonely, just a single person. For the first time in my life, I believe I actually understand what it means to be a Christian, know who Christ is, and who I am in Him.
>
> I've already had an idea to develop a Bible study from your material and use it next year on my floor for a Bible study. I feel capable of helping people and capable of handling myself. I've been a codependent for years, but this last week I haven't had the slightest need for someone else.
>
> I guess I am describing what it is like to be at peace. I feel this quiet, soft joy in my heart. I have been more

friendly with strangers and comfortable. There hasn't been this struggle to get through the day. And then there is the fact that I have been participating actively in life and not passively, critically watching it. Thank you for lending me your hope. I believe I have my own now in Christ.

Making the Right Choice

Paul says, "Sin shall not be your master, because you are not under law, but under grace" (Romans 6:14). We can choose to live as though we are still under the law and rob ourselves of the freedom Christ purchased for us on the cross. We can also go to the other extreme, license, which Paul warns against in Galatians 5:13: "You, my brothers, were called to be free. But do not use your freedom to indulge the sinful nature [flesh]; rather, serve one another in love." Both legalism and license lead to bondage that can be resolved only through repentance and faith in God.

Imagine walking down a narrow mountain road. On one side is a steep cliff. It is too steep to climb down, and too far up from the bottom for you to jump. On the other side of the road is an intense forest fire. Behind you is a roaring lion seeking someone to devour, and ahead of you is a church. Which way would you go? One option would be to jump off the cliff. You would experience an initial sense of "freedom" and perhaps exhilaration from the free-fall. But there are serious consequences to that choice—like the sudden stop at the end. That is the nature of license or being licentious, which is a total disregard for rules and regulations. License is counterfeit freedom. The "free" sex that was so popular in the sixties came with a staggering price tag. Instead of sexual freedom, people got sexual bondage, which has torn up many homes and given many people serious diseases. Choices have consequences.

True freedom doesn't just lie in a person's right to make choices. It comes by making responsible choices based on the truth of God's Word so that the freedom that Christ purchased for us on the cross can be a living reality. The tempter has a field day with those who choose the license end of the teeter-totter. He whispers in their ear, "Go ahead and do it. You know you want to. Everybody else does it." Temptations always look good, or nobody would ever give in. When was the last time you were tempted to eat spinach?

Another option on the narrow mountain road is to turn into the forest fire, which represents legalism. The result is just as disastrous, which is "Burn, baby, burn." The accuser has a field day with those who choose the legalism end of the teeter-totter; he tells them they'll never measure up and that God is disappointed in them.

Temptation and accusation are two sides of the same coin that Satan flips in his relentless pursuit of our defeat. We are truly liberated in Christ when we walk the tightrope between legalism and license. All the sanctuary we need is right in front of us, but it isn't a church building. The only sanctuary we have in this present time is our position in Christ. In Him, we are safe and secure: "Now the Lord is the Spirit, and where the Spirit of the Lord is, there is freedom" (2 Corinthians 3:17).

The Curse of Legalism

Paul wrote, "All who rely on observing the law are under a curse, for it is written: 'Cursed is everyone who does not continue to do everything written in the Book of the Law.' Clearly no one is justified before God by the law, because, 'The righteous will live by faith'" (Galatians 3:10,11). With such clear statements from Scripture, why are we still struggling with legalism after 2,000 years of church history? It's not God's law that is a curse, but legalism. Those who choose to relate to God purely on the basis of law will indeed be cursed. These are the perfectionists who can never be good enough or do enough. And they can't because "whoever keeps the whole law and yet stumbles at just one point is guilty of breaking all of it" (James 2:10).

Paul said, "If a law had been given that could impart life, then righteousness would certainly have come by the law" (Galatians 3:21). But the law is powerless to give life. Telling someone that what he is doing is wrong does not give him the power to stop doing it. Thankfully we are not saved by how we behave, but by how we believe, or nobody would have any hope. Jesus came to give us life (John 10:10) because it is His life that saves us, not the law. Bonar said, "The demand of the law is perfection. Between everything and nothing the Bible gives us our choice. If we are to be saved by the law, it must be wholly by the law; if not wholly by the law, it must be wholly without the law."[1]

Even more devastating for the legalist is the truth taught in Romans 7:5: "When we were controlled by the sinful nature, the sinful passions aroused by the law were at work in our bodies, so that we bore fruit for death." The law actually has the capacity to stimulate our desire to do what it prohibits. Paul continues, "But sin, seizing the opportunity afforded by the commandment, produced in me every kind of covetous desire" (Romans 7:8). If you don't think that is true, then tell your son that he can go here, but he can't go there. The moment you say where he *can't* go, where will he want to go? There! He probably didn't even want to go there until you told him he couldn't. A similar response was seen at a Christian school that distributed a list of movies that the students could not see. Guess what happened? The forbidden movies became the ones that everybody wanted to see! Why is the forbidden fruit seemingly the most desirable? Such a question caused Paul to ask, "What shall we say, then? Is the law sin? Certainly not!" (Romans 7:7).

What Is God's Law?

Now that we are in Christ and no longer under the law, how then does the Christian relate to the law? To answer that, we need first to understand what the law of God is. The term "law" in Scripture is often associated with specific commands, especially the commands of the Old Testament Mosaic Law (for example, Romans 2:20-27). But the concept of God's law is much broader. The Hebrew word *torah*, which is the basic term for "law" in the Old Testament, is related to the Hebrew verb *hora*, meaning "to direct, to teach, to instruct in."[2] It is similar in meaning to the New Testament Greek word for law, which is *nomos*. Its fundamental meaning is not "command," but "instruction." Thus the word came to be used not only for specific laws, but for the entire Word of God and its record of God's dealings with His people.

The essential element in the biblical concept of the law is seen in the explanation of *torah* as "that which points the way for the faithful Israelite and for the community of Israel. Not merely the laws of the Pentateuch provide guidance; the entire story of God's dealings with mankind and with Israel points the way."[3] Thus the term "law" can refer to entire sections of Scripture and to Scripture as a whole, including both God's commandments and His gracious promises. Such is the case in Matthew 5:17, where Jesus said He came not to abolish the law, but to fulfill it (*see also* Luke 24:44 and John 15:25).

The law of God may be said to be the expression of His will, which stems from His holy character. Even as there are physical laws by which the physical world is structured, so also there are the personal and moral spheres of God's creation governed by His moral and spiritual laws, which are the expression of His holy nature. With that in mind, it is interesting that the apostle Paul never spoke of God's law in the plural (that is, "laws"), but only in the singular ("law"). For in the final analysis, all laws are expressions of the unified moral character of God. For Israel, God's law took the form of the written Scriptures; for the Gentiles, it was the law "written on their hearts" (Romans 2:15). But there is "only one Lawgiver" for all people (James 4:12).

To encounter God's law is to come in contact with God. Scripture says that all people are in some way aware of that law, which expresses His divine nature: "Since the creation of the world God's invisible qualities—his eternal power and divine nature—have been clearly seen, being understood from what has been made, so that men are without excuse" (Romans 1:20). Many people don't acknowledge God, however. They see the created order of the universe but they depersonalize God because an impersonal god doesn't have to be served. So they worship the creation rather than the Creator. Thus "the sinful mind" is said to be "hostile to God. It does not submit to God's law, nor can it do so. Those controlled by the sinful nature cannot please God" (Romans 8:7,8).

As the expression of the moral structure of the universe, God's law is designed for the good of His creatures. Just as the laws of physics permit our world and universe to run smoothly, so also is the law of God designed for the well-being of His moral creatures. His commandments are not restrictive; rather, they are protective and have our best interests at heart. It is God's revelation that brings true life, peace, well-being, and fullness of joy. In short, God's moral laws are designed for the blessing of His people. The Christian life is termed "the Way," and God's laws are the rules of the way.

As we have seen, God's law is seen in all of His dealings with His people—in His historical actions as well as His words, and in His gracious promises as well as His commandments. The imperatives as well as the gracious promises of salvation are therefore God's truth—truth that He uses to sanctify and transform His people. Thus Paul describes the Mosaic Law as "the embodiment of knowledge and truth" (Romans 2:20). The psalmist delighted in God's law, declaring, "Your law is true" (Psalm 119:142—or, "Thy law is truth" NASB). The meaning of calling God's law truth in that verse is explained by Murphy-O'Connor:

> What does the psalmist mean by "truth" here? The whole psalm is a hymn in praise of the divine Law. The center of his universe, it polarizes his entire existence. He prays for greater knowledge (verses 27,29,33, etc.) that he may ever conform himself more perfectly to it (verse 44). In a world where evil ever attempts to suck him down into its mire (verses 61,78,85,95, etc.) it is the one thing on which he can rely with absolute confidence (verse 133). Opposed to unreality (verse 37), it is the supremely real. To sum up in one word all that the Law meant to him he could hardly have chosen better than 'mt [truth], whose basic idea is solidity, firmness; it is the quality that makes a being dependable, deserving of confidence.[4]

The commands of Scripture are thus part of the truth that sanctifies. They are part of the truth that brings life—as opposed to the lies that express unreality and thus lead to suffering and death. The commands in Scripture, then, are expressions of God's holy love for us. Commenting on God's instructions to the Israelites that they impress His commands on their hearts and teach them to their children (Deuteronomy 6:6-9), Craige says:

The commandments, which provide the framework within which the Israelites could express their love of God, were to be upon your heart—that is, the people were to think on them and meditate about them, so that obedience would not be a matter of formal legalism, but a response based upon understanding. By reflecting on the commandments, they were reflecting on God's words . . . and by understanding the path of life set down by the commandments, they would at the same time be discovering the way in which God's love for them was given expression.[5]

Not only are God's commands an expression of His love for us, they are also the sum of what it means for us to live in love toward God and our neighbor: "Love is the fulfillment of the law" (Romans 13:10); "the entire law is summed up in a single command: 'Love your neighbor as yourself'" (Galatians 5:14). Thus God's laws are nothing less then the moral law of the universe that rightly relates and binds man to God and his fellow man in the perfect way of truth and life. His laws, then, are an essential aspect of the truth that we must focus on to know a transformed life.

Our Relationship to God's Law

Because Gods' laws are the moral principles of the universe, we can rightly conclude that all moral creatures are related to these laws. In the Old Testament, believers as well as unbelievers were subject to the overarching principle that following God's laws led to life, and disobeying them led to misery and death. The believer "in Christ," however, is related to that law principle in a radically different way than the person without Christ. The latter stands before the law in himself—that is, as a sinner and consequently a lawbreaker. He thus lives under the condemnation of the law and the penalty of death. But the believer "in Christ" has the same relationship to the law that Christ has.

We Are Free

What is Christ's relationship to the law? Scripture says that the law has reached its "fulfillment" in Christ (Matthew 5:17), meaning that God's righteous principles for life all point to Christ and are fully realized in Him.[6] Paul's statement that "Christ is the end of the law" (Romans 10:4) expresses a similar thought. The word "end" (Greek, *telos*), which can mean "fulfillment," "goal," or "termination," is best understood in that verse as a combination of all these meanings. Christ as the fulfillment of the law is also its goal; that is, the law looked forward to Him. And as we will see shortly, Christ also brought an "end" to the time when God's people lived under the law like children under a tutor (Galatians 3:24).

To speak of Christ as the fulfillment or goal of the law simply means that the total significance of law has been attained in Him. This significance may be summed up in two primary points: 1) The law as the instrument of the just condemnation of lawbreakers is perfectly realized in Christ's sacrifice for sins at the cross. Christ took the penalty of lawbreaking, or "the curse of the law by becoming a curse for us" (Galatians 3:13). Christ satisfied the just requirements of the law. But more than that, 2) the law as the expression of God's will was perfectly realized in Christ, who always acted in obedience to His Father's will. All of the righteousness expressed in commands and ceremonial ordinances pointed to their goal in Christ. He was the righteousness of God incarnate.

Christ as the fulfillment or end of the law, therefore, clearly brings the believer "in Him" into a radically new relationship to the law. As believers "in Christ," Scripture describes us as no longer living "under law" (Romans 6:14,15; Galatians 3:23-25; 5:18), and being free from the law (Romans 7:6; Galatians 4:8-10; 5:1-3; Colossians 2:20).

These descriptions of the believer and the law do not mean that we no longer have any relationship with God's law. They do, however, describe a freedom from the law that is absolutely vital to understand for living and growing as God intends. "In Christ" we are free from the law in two significant ways.

Free from Legal Bondage

First, we are free from what might be termed the legal bondage of the law. Under the law, violators of the law are rightly deserving of punishment. Because everyone has broken the law, we all were under the judgment of death. "In Christ," however, we are viewed as having died to the law through His sacrificial death for us and are thus "released from law" (Romans 7:6). "Christ redeemed us from the curse of the law by becoming a curse for us" (Galatians 3:13). As believers in Christ, we have fully met the requirements of the law in terms of our law-breaking because we have been identified with Christ in His death (Romans 6:5).

In addition, because we have been identified with Christ's resurrection, we stand in His righteousness—His perfect obedience—so that the law can no longer condemn us in the future. We have "become the righteousness of God" in Christ; He is our "righteousness" (1 Corinthians 1:30). That's why Paul could say, "There is now no condemnation for those who are in Christ Jesus, because through Christ Jesus the law of the Spirit of life set me free from the law of sin and death" (Romans 8:1,2). In Christ we are totally free from living under the law as a legal principle in which we either keep the law or pay the penalty. We exist in Christ, in whom this principle has been fully fulfilled by His life and death on our behalf.

Free from the Legal Requirement

Not only are we as believers in Christ free from the law as a legal requirement, we are also free from the law as a "supervisory custodian" of our lives. Paul wrote, "The Law has become our tutor to lead us to Christ, that we may be justified by faith. But now that faith has come, we are no longer under a tutor" (Galatians 3:24,25 NASB). The word "tutor," which suggests a teaching function, is perhaps not the best translation of the Greek word *paidagogos*. The *paidagogos* was usually a slave who was "charged with the supervision and conduct of one or more sons" in the ancient patrician household. He did no formal teaching, but "administered the directives of the father in a custodial manner." His supervision and discipline, of course, did contribute indirectly to the instruction.[7]

Paul's point in using the Greek word *paidagogos* is that the law served this supervisory control over God's people for a limited time—until Christ came. Paul goes on to explain this truth in Galatians 4:1-5:

> What I am saying is that as long as the heir is a child . . . he is subject to guardians and trustees until the time set by his father. So also, when we were children, we were in slavery under the basic principles of the world. But when the time had fully come, God sent his Son, born of a woman, born under law, to redeem those under law, that we might receive the full rights of sons.

Prior to Christ's coming, God's people were like children under a tutor. But with Christ's work on the cross completed and the sending of the Holy Spirit, believers are now "adult sons" and no longer under the "tutor" of the law.

Although most families do not have a slave performing the function of the *paidagogos*, our experience of growing up from childhood into adulthood is very illustrative of Paul's words about the change in our relationship to the law. When we were children our parents set down rules under which we lived. Those rules may have had rewards (or blessings) when we obeyed; and most certainly discipline was applied when we disobeyed. Eventually, however, when we became adults, our relationship to our parents' rules changed. We no longer lived directly under their laws with the rewards and penalties attached. Hopefully by that time, the principles of right living, established by our parents' rules, had been instilled into our own mind and heart through living under them.

As adults we are still related to our parents' principles, but now they control our life from within our own mind and heart rather than from the outside through parental laws. That is exactly what Paul was talking about in Galatians 4:1-5. Through the finished work of Christ, we have become adult sons and daughters of God. The Holy Spirit has come to indwell our hearts and effect the new covenant relationship with the law—

a relationship described by the prophet Jeremiah: "I will put my law in their minds and write it on their hearts" (31:33).

The change in our relationship to the law does not, however, mean that the law itself has changed, for the moral nature of God has not changed. Rather, the law is simply no longer an external code written on clay tablets as in the Old Testament. It is now written on our hearts—the very fountain of our lives (Proverbs 4:23)—by the presence of the Spirit, who works from there to live it out in our life.

Thus the believer before Christ lived "under the law" as the regulation according to which he was blessed or punished. The problem was that he could never fulfill the law; he could never keep all the commandments. Therefore the promised blessings could never be fully realized. This brings us to the fullest meaning of what it meant for the believer before Christ to live in bondage "under the law": Under the Old Testament arrangement before Christ, the law functioned somewhat as a contractual agreement between God and His people.[8]

It is vitally important to clarify that the law was *not* a way to earn God's grace. It was not given as a way to become God's people. God had already, by pure grace, redeemed the people of Israel from the bondage of Egypt when He gave them the law (*see* Exodus 19:4-6). The believer under the Mosaic Law was thus related to God by faith through God's gracious redemption even as we are in the New Testament after Christ. The law was never designed to serve as the basis for being rightly related to God.

In the law, God was simply asking His people to live in accordance with the principle of righteousness that would bring to them the experience of the promised blessing. He graciously provided the sacrificial system by which they could receive forgiveness for their failures and so maintain their relation to Him. He even provided a certain measure of His power to them through the Holy Spirit. But the record of the people under the old covenant is that none could ever keep the law. Sin and sacrifice, over and over again, was their experience—to the point of God's declaration, "You have burdened me with your sins and wearied me with your offenses" (Isaiah 43:24).

Scripture says that under the old covenant, the people could never be perfected (*see* Hebrews 7:11,19). The believer living under the law could never have final peace in relation to sins. Eugene Peterson's paraphrase of Hebrews 10:1-4 (in *The Message*) captures well their situation:

> The old plan was only a hint of the good things in the new plan. Since that old "law plan" wasn't complete in itself, it couldn't complete those who followed it. No matter how many sacrifices were offered year after year, they never added up to a complete solution. If they had, the worshipers would have gone merrily on their way, no longer dragged down by their sins. But instead of removing awareness of sin, when those animal sacrifices were repeated over and over they actually heightened awareness and guilt. The plain fact is that bull and goat blood can't get rid of sin.

In that situation, the saints could only look forward to God's final redemption: "O Israel, put your hope in the LORD, for with the LORD is unfailing love and with him is full redemption. He himself will redeem Israel from all their sins" (Psalm 130:7). They looked forward to the day when God would "tread our sins underfoot [they recognized that sin was a power that only God could subdue] and hurl all our iniquities into the depths of the sea" (Micah 7:19).

Before Christ, God's people were held under the bondage of the law. They lived their lives under the obligation of the law as a contract with God as His people. But they could never fulfill the contract in perfect righteousness. It stood over them as a supervisory custodian that constantly held them in bondage to the rules and regulations and their accompanying rewards and punishments.

But the believer "in Christ" is no longer contractually obliged to the law because Christ has fulfilled that contract perfectly. Paul said that Christ was "born under law" (Galatians 4:4), meaning that He took upon Himself the full requirements of the law. He took on not only the condemnation that was due for our sin (Galatians 3:13), but also the obligations that regulated the believer's life. In His perfect life, He perfectly fulfilled all of the righteous commands of the law—something no one had ever been able to do.

We who are identified with Christ in His death and resurrection thus have paid the price the law demands for our sin and have fully met the law's obligations for life. Our new life in Christ is no longer a life controlled by laws and regulations that could never be kept; it is a life lived in the realm of Christ by the power of the Spirit: "By dying to what once bound us, we have been released from the law so that we serve in the new way of the Spirit, and not in the old way of the written code" (Romans 7:6).

The believer "in Christ" bears the same relationship to the law that Christ does. Christ, as the end or goal of the law, has fulfilled the law by satisfying its demands both negatively (paying the penalty) and positively (with perfect righteousness). Because the believer is in Christ, these two directions are both complete positionally. That is, the believer is free from *all* condemnation (Romans 8:1) and is *completely* holy, clothed with Christ's righteousness. What is positionally true, of course, is still being worked out in progressive sanctification. Even in this process, however, the believer's relationship to the law must be understood by his position in Christ. He should not strive to meet the righteous demands of the law. That has already been done in the obedience of Christ. Rather, the believer strives to *allow* Christ's righteousness—which has already met all of the law's demands—to be worked out in his life so that he might be conformed to the image of his Savior, who is the full realization of God's law in every respect. "For we are God's workmanship, created in Christ Jesus to do good works, which God prepared in advance for us to do" (Ephesians 2:10).

We Are Responsible

The fact that the believer in Christ is free from the law's condemnation and custodial control does not mean that he has no relation whatsoever to law. Our liberty as Christians doesn't mean we are autonomous. That would be *antinomianism*, which means "against (*anti*) law (*nomos*)." The grace of God is not a license to sin, it is a dynamic enabling us to live a righteous life.

It makes us free to be what we were created to be—free to do what we know in our hearts that we should do. But this kind of freedom is known only in relation to God, and relation to God cannot be in exclusion of His righteous law. Bonar said:

> Our new relationship to the law is that of Christ Himself to it. It is that of men who have met all its claims, exhausted its penalties, satisfied its demands, magnified it, and made it honorable. For our faith in God's testimony to Christ's surety-obedience has made us one with Him. . . . His feelings towards the law ought to be our feeling. . . . And does not he say, "I delight to do Thy will, O my God; Thy Law is within my heart" (Psalm 40:8).[9]

Keeping the law before coming to Christ would be unnatural because we were dead in our trespasses and sins and were by nature children of wrath (Ephesians 2:1-3). We simply could not do it. But now that we are in Christ, living according to the righteous standards of the law by the Holy Spirit's power is the natural—or better, supernatural—thing to do. God's desire for His people is true life, and that life is lived according to His moral and spiritual laws. Thus sanctification and growth in holiness is, in reality, growth in conformity with God's laws. In the sanctification process, then, God sets before us His norms and calls us to use our minds to see them, our emotions to love them, and our wills to live them. The expressions of God's laws are thus God's aid in helping us toward conformity to His pattern for holiness and true life.

Christ as the fulfillment of the law means that the law's righteousness is now capsulized in Him and His teaching. As one writer said, "He bids men come to Him, learn of Him, listen to Him, obey Him as if all other authority was at an end."[10] Instead of exhorting people to live under the "yoke of the law" or the Old Testament Mosaic Law, Jesus invited them to "take my yoke upon you and learn from me" (Matthew 11:29). "The Gospel does not command us to do anything in order to obtain life, but it bids us live by that which another has done; and the knowledge of its life-giving truth is not labor but rest—rest of soul—rest which is the root of all true labor; for in receiving Christ we do not work in order to rest, but we rest in order to work."[11] The law for the believer in Christ is no longer the Mosaic Law, but Christ's law (1 Corinthians 9:21; Galatians 6:2), which is described by James as the "perfect law" and "royal law" (2:8).

The righteous standards of the law of Christ are expressed both in the example of His life here on earth as well as in His teachings. We are to walk as He walked (1 John 2:6), following His example (Romans 15:2-5; 1 Corinthians 11:1; 1 Peter 2:21). We are also to obey everything that He commanded (Matthew 28:20; see John 14:15,21; 1 John 2:3-5; 3:22,24; 5:3). His teachings were not limited to the timespan of His earthly ministry, they were also the teachings of the apostles who followed Him. In fact, the apostles' teachings were really those of our ascended Lord (see John 14:26; 16:13; Revelation 3:8).

While the teachings of Jesus and His disciples may be the most direct expression of Christ's law, in reality, all of Scripture is involved. Though we are no longer directly under the old Mosaic Law, the righteousness of that law is taken up in the law of Christ. As Bible scholar Douglas Moo explains, in Christ's fulfillment of that law, "some of the Mosaic commandments are taken up and reapplied to the New Covenant people of God. Thus, while the Mosaic Law does not stand as an undifferentiated authority for the Christian, some of its individual commandments remain authoritative as integrated into the law of Christ."[12]

Ultimately all Scripture is the revelation of Christ and His righteousness—sometimes directly, sometimes indirectly, and sometimes in the form of temporary institutions and ceremonies or shadows. Living in Christ as the fulfillment of the law, then, must encompass the careful study of the entire Bible. "All Scripture . . . is useful for teaching, rebuking, correcting and training in righteousness, so that the man of God may be thoroughly equipped for every good work" (2 Timothy 3:16,17).

To determine if commands given to believers *before* Christ apply to believers *in* Christ, we must consider the plain commands of Jesus and His apostles along with the fundamental moral principles found throughout Scripture. Today's believer also has the help of the indwelling Spirit, who leads and guides him in applying the objective commands of Scripture.

As Christians, we are free from the law and yet obligated to keep the commandments of the "law of Christ." Christ's fulfillment of the law has brought a new kind of obedience for the person who is "in Him." Lawkeeping is the *result* of a relationship with Christ, and not the means to gain such a relationship. Our total relation to the law is now "in Christ." A rule without a relationship will lead to rebellion, but those who are rightly related to God will gladly live out His will. As theologian Herman Ridderbos says, "The church no longer has to do with the law in any other way than in Christ and thus is *ennomos Christos* [that is, within law in relation to Christ]." [13] This means that our lawkeeping is done from our position in Christ. Sanctification is working out the righteousness that is ours because of who we are in Christ.

A Divine Empowerment

The law itself has no power to sanctify. Thus lawkeeping itself is not the means of our santification. We cannot sanctify ourselves simply by keeping the law. Remember, it is not *what we do* that determines who we are, it is *who we are* that determines what we do. Sanctification is applying the finished work of Christ in our lives through the power of the Holy Spirit. We stand against the unrighteousness of this world by clothing ourselves with Christ (Romans 13:14; Galatians 3:27).

The power to overcome sin and live out the righteousness of Christ's law comes from the Holy Spirit. "Live by the Spirit," Paul said, "and you will not gratify the desires of the sinful nature" (Galatians 5:16). The "righteous requirements of the law" are met by those who live "according to the Spirit" (Romans 8:4). And the "fruit of the Spirit" (Galatians 5:22,23) is the righteous fulfillment of the law. Again, the power to live according to Christ's law comes only through the Spirit as He lives Christ's life (which was victorious over all sin) in and through us.

An Obedience Compelled by Love

I was once asked on a national radio program, "If you could tell our audience only one truth, what would you tell them? What one thing would you want them to know most?" I paused for about a microsecond and then said, "Your heavenly Father loves you, and He loves you far more than you could ever humanly hope for." John 3:16 gives us some idea of the extent of that love: "God so loved the world that he gave his one and only Son, that whoever believes in him shall not perish but have eternal life." The love of God is the single most powerful motivation in life, not fear: "There is no fear in love. But perfect love drives out fear, because fear has to do with punishment. The one who fears is not made perfect in love" (1 John 4:18).

Motivating God's people by fear or laying down the law without grace is a blatant denial of the Gospel. It is Pharisaic to respond to immorality by saying, "We just have to lay down the law." Even in the Old Testament, God's love was a motivating factor for the people who attempted to keep the law, which stood over them as a *paidagogos*. But love becomes even a greater motive for the New Testament believer, who can look back at Christ's complete fulfillment of the law on his behalf, and his consequent adoption as a free child in the family of God. It was Christ's death and resurrection and all that it meant which made Paul a new creature who no longer lived "under law" but was adopted into God's family as an adult son—with God's Spirit living in him. That's what led Paul to say, "Christ's love compels us" (2 Corinthians 5:14).

During the peak of the war in what was formerly Yugoslavia, I (Neil) was training Croatian pastors in a Christian refugee center. Listening in was a Bosnian refugee named Mohammed, who was raised in the Islamic tradition with all its fatalistic legalism. After listening to me teach for four days about the gracious love of God and how we could be free in Christ, he asked through an interpreter to see me. That night I had the privilege of leading him to Christ. He asked to be baptized, and the next day he was baptized in the Adriatic Sea.

Mohammed had arrived at the refugee center just a week earlier with his two daughters, who appeared to be deaf, either physically or psychologically. They had seen their mother blown up before their eyes by a mortar attack. They also had always been told that Christians were their enemy. The day after their father was baptized, these two little innocent girls, ravaged by war, said with wonder in their eyes, "Jesus loves me!" I will never hear those words uttered again by anyone without realizing the power of that truth to transform lives.

A few years ago, the state of Oregon had a hotly contested proposition on the ballot—a matter related to homosexuality. A pastor's wife, who was familiar with Freedom in Christ Ministries, sensed the Lord leading her to work with a group that was trying to help homosexuals. The problem was, it was a closed group. You had to be "one of them" to attend. Suddenly she became very self-conscious of the fact that her hair was quite short and she often wore slacks. She thought, *Maybe I ought to wait until my hair grows out and wear a dress, or they may think that I am one of them.* Then the Lord grabbed her heart: "Dear child, that is what I did." When Jesus reached out to the lost, never did He say, "Let's get one thing straight before we go on: I'm not one of you, and you better shape up because I'm God!" On the contrary, He took upon Himself the form of a man, dwelt among us, and identified with us.

The pastor's wife went to that group and identified with them. Three months later she was their spokesperson. Then her husband became the chairman of their board, and they are now setting captives free. If we want to reach the lost, we can't preach the good news and be the bad news. Laying down the law will not set people free; only Christ can do that. Overbearing authoritarianism leaves people in bondage to legalism. If we want to help people find their freedom in Christ, the love of God must compel us.

He First Loved Us

Love has its source only in God (1 Timothy 1:14), and it is God's love that enables the believer to love: "We love because he first loved us" (1 John 4:19). It is God's love that moves us to obey the law of Christ. We are reminded in John 14:15, "If you love me, you will obey what I command." Love is the essence of lawkeeping (John 13:34,35), as Jesus demonstrated when He washed the feet of His disciples. Then He said "My command is this: Love each other as I have loved you" (John 15:12). Paul said, "The entire law is summed up in a single command: 'love your neighbor as yourself'" (Galatians 5:14).

The Benefits of God's Law

In addition to all the blessings that are ours because of His love and grace, God has made possible a way for us to make the great truths of salvation real in our lives. He has given us His moral laws of life so that we might have abundant life and grow toward fullness of life. The commands of the law of Christ are thus part of the truth that God uses to transform our lives and bring increasing sanctification or holiness. We must never look at these commands as restrictions on our freedom and joy, but as aspects of truth designed to help us have true freedom and joy.

13

Abiding in Christ:
The Source of Holiness

Abide in Me, and I in you. As the branch cannot bear fruit of itself, unless it abides in the vine, so neither can you, unless you abide in Me. I am the vine, you are the branches; he who abides in Me, and I in him, he bears much fruit; for apart from Me you can do nothing.

—John 15:4,5

While speaking to adult Christian groups in evangelical churches, several years ago, I (Neil) would make the following statement: "Christian maturity is understanding the principles of the Bible and trying as best we can to live them." I then asked how many people agreed with that statement. Nearly everybody did. Then I told them I disagreed with almost every aspect of that statement! It's true that it's understanding the principles of Scripture that is essential for Christian maturity, but that in *itself* is not Christian maturity. Christian maturity is Christlike character. If you know all the principles but don't have the character, then you are only a "resounding gong or a clanging cymbal" that is without love (1 Corinthians 13:1). Also, trying as best you can to live the Christian life will probably bear no fruit because apart from Christ you can do nothing. Only by God's grace can you live the Christian life.

Progressive sanctification is a supernatural work. Clearly the victory over sin and death through Christ's crucifixion and resurrection was God's victory and not ours. Only God can redeem us from the power of sin, set us free from our past, and make us new creations "in Christ." Even though we have become a partaker of the divine nature due to Christ's presence in our lives, we still need to be dependent upon God to supply the power to conform us to His image. Becoming a Christian does not mean that we have more power in and of ourselves. It means that we are inwardly connected to the only source of power that is able to overcome the laws of sin and death, which is the law of the Spirit of life in Christ Jesus (Romans 8:2). That we are tempted to misunderstand this truth or perhaps unconsciously forget it in our attempt to grow as believers is seen in Paul's sharp question to the Galatians: "Are you so foolish? After beginning with the Spirit, are you now trying to attain your goal by human effort?" (Galatians 3:3).

Christ's Strength or Yours?

One of the greatest temptations that we face is to stop being dependent upon God and relying on our own intellect and resources. As long as we think we can live the Christian life by ourselves, we will fail miserably. Wisdom says, "Trust in the LORD with all your heart and lean not on your own understanding; in all your ways acknowledge him, and he will make your paths straight" (Proverbs 3:5,6).

Luke 2:52 gives us an idea of what true Christian growth looks like: "Jesus grew in wisdom and stature, and in favor with God and men." Jesus' growth was perfectly balanced spiritually, mentally, physically, and socially. Many Christian authors have endeavored to help us know that kind of growth by writing about marriage, parenting, rest, prayer, and other personal disciplines. But even with all these resources available, many Christians aren't seeing much fruit in their lives. Why?

PERSONAL DISCIPLINES

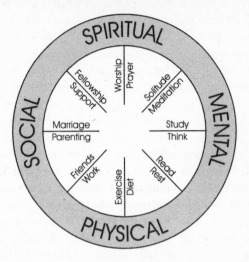

Each discipline named in the chart is like a spoke in a large Christian wheel. Even though the spokes are related to the hub of the wheel, they may not be connected in a living, dynamic, and dependent way. The result is a subtle form of Christian behavioralism, which sounds something like this: "You shouldn't do that; you should do this. That is not the best way to do that; here is a better way to do it." And we dutifully respond, "Okay, I'll try my best." The result is a "try harder" methodology: "You're not trying hard enough. If only you will try harder, maybe your Christianity will work!"

The result? Guilt. Condemnation. Defeat. Instead of being called, we are being driven into burnout or disillusionment. The further we are from the hub, the harder we try, until something snaps. We are trying to fulfill the Bible's commands in our own strength.

Those who are the closest to the hub are sweet-spirited and gentle people. They seem to bear fruit with little effort. They are living testimonies of the beatitudes (Matthew 5:3-12). Those furthest from the hub become judgmental and legalistic. They can tell you with biblical accuracy how a Christian should behave. They know what is right and what is wrong. They have captured the letter of the law which kills, but not the Spirit which gives life (2 Corinthians 3:6). They have no deep and meaningful relationships. Everything remains on the surface. Any effort to break through the barriers to get at their inner man will be resisted. Their insecurity results in complete withdrawal and passivity or they become controllers. They are threatened by the idea of being transparent and are terrified that someone may find out what is really going on inside.

Most of these legalistic people have never had any bonding relationships. None of them are experiencing freedom in Christ. They have made themselves victims, and unless they are set free in Christ, they will perpetuate their cycle of abuse. Many books have been written to help such people, yet some of them neglect to explain the right order in which to solve a person's problems. To better understand what we mean, let's look at an illustration.

Prior to the sixties, certain authorities claimed that if families had devotions and prayed together, only one in a thousand would separate. But today, that figure is much worse.

The rebellious sixties wreaked havoc with the family. Since then, much has been done in an effort to save our marriages and families. Seminaries developed programs and offered degrees in marriage, child, and family counseling. In these programs, the old ministerial faculty in pastoral care were slowly replaced by clinical psychologists. Most of these psychologists came from secular schools because, in those days, there were no Christian schools offering doctoral degrees. Evangelism and discipleship ended up getting overlooked because getting help for the personal needs within families became overwhelming. Today, some of the largest parachurch ministries and most-listened-to radio programs are geared to the family. Christian books on the family sell better than books on any other topic because getting help for the family is the number-one felt need in America. Never in the history of Christianity has there ever been such a concerted effort to save the family. How are we doing? Have our families gotten any stronger? Are our children doing any better? The answer seems to be no. What's wrong?

Where Changed Behavior Begins

To find out what the Bible says about marriage and the family, we consulted our concordances and discovered that most of the Bible's practical instructions are in the second half of Paul's epistles. The reason is because the second half of each epistle is the applicational portion of Paul's teaching. If you were only concerned about the family, then you would probably address only those passages.

Yet we cannot approach the Christian life merely by looking at the practical applications. The first half of Paul's epistles form for us a necessary foundation—they establish us in Christ. Not until we establish ourselves in the truths about being complete in Christ can we begin to apply what we find in the second half of Paul's epistles. People who try to behave as children of God will produce little fruit when they have no understanding of who they are in Christ or how to live by the Spirit's power.

I (Neil) have told many struggling couples to temporarily forget about trying to fix their marriage. They were so torn up on the inside that they couldn't get along with their dog, much less each other! The problem for such couples is not primarily external and resolved by learning to behave better. The problem is internal, and is resolved by learning to believe and speak the truth in love. I have seen marital conflicts resolved and stay resolved when couples focus first on who they are in Christ, and then deal with their other problems. I've never seen marriage resolution work when that order is turned around. People today are spending too much time trying to change behavior, and not enough time trying to change what they believe about God and themselves.

In the book of Proverbs we read, "As [a man] thinks in his heart, so is he" (23:7 NKJV). What people are on the outside starts on the inside. If their beliefs are wrong, so also will their behavior be wrong. Before people can change, they must first become established in their freedom in Christ (become connected to the hub) so they know who they are as children of God. *Then* all those good instructional books on how to change behavior will be effective. Then all those studies on family systems and role relationships will work. People can't live out the law of Christ without the life of Christ. The personal disciplines diagram should look like this:

CHRIST-CENTERED
PERSONAL DISCIPLINES

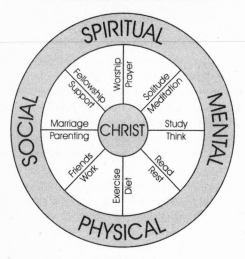

The following letter, which was sent to Neil, illustrates well the necessity of making Christ first in our lives:

> In August I met with my ex-husband for the first time in several months. He was now a Christian and had learned to overcome pressure and trials. He was attending an evangelical church and the people there recommended that I read two of your books, *Victory Over the Darkness* and *The Bondage Breaker*. I was intrigued by my husband's peace and contentment, and wanted very much to feel the same way.
>
> I had been attending a Catholic church; however, after meeting my husband again, I decided to attend his church, and I have never looked back. In reading *Victory Over the Darkness*, my identity was affirmed. I learned that I could find true peace, fulfillment, and satisfaction in only one relationship—with God through Jesus Christ. *The Bondage Breaker* took me through the Steps to Freedom in Christ. Before, confusion and anxiety had plagued my days and

nights. Now, I feel order and peace, and my life is whole and meaningful.

God's timing is perfect, and your books were exactly what I needed to recognize my sin and give me the strength and hope I needed. It was evident I needed to change from the self-centered person I was and start walking in obedience to God and Christ. As a result, my marriage has been reconciled—praise and glory to God!

There is nothing wrong with programs that are designed to help Christians change their behavior, improve their marriage, or make their family stronger as long as Christ is at the center. The spiritual erosion comes when our confidence and dependence upon God gets shifted to confidence and dependence upon the program itself. Instead of searching for God, we search for better programs or techniques. As a result, we burn ourselves out trying to bear fruit.

Jesus tells us how our heavenly Father is glorified: "This is to my Father's glory, that you bear much fruit, showing yourselves to be my disciples" (John 15:8). Many people ignore the context and incorrectly reason, "I have to bear fruit!" No, Jesus said we have to abide in Him (verses 4-7). If we abide in Him, we will bear fruit. Bearing fruit is the evidence that we are abiding in Christ. If we are abiding in Christ, then any program will work. If we try to live the Christian life in our own strength, no program will work. Of course, when we abide in Christ, a good program will bear more fruit than a bad program; dedicated incompetency is still incompetency.

No matter how long you are a Christian, your need to remain dependent on Christ stays constant. Only with Him at the center of your life can you bear fruit. Is He the center of your life, marriage, and ministry?[1]

Ask yourself this question: How much of what I do in my own personal life, marriage, and ministry is based on laws or principles that call for obedience? Then ask yourself, How much of what I do is based on my spiritual life in Christ, which causes me to walk by faith according to what God said is true and then live by the power of the Holy Spirit so I don't carry out the desires of the flesh? The first is a law principle, and the second is grace. Someone once said that if the Holy Spirit were taken away from us, 95 percent of what we do in our churches would still go on as scheduled.

God, Our Power Source

Scripture repeatedly teaches us that sanctification in our daily lives is possible only through the power of God. We are to abide in Christ, for without Him we can do nothing (John 15:4-9). It is no longer we who live, but Christ who lives in us (Galatians 2:20). The Christian life is one of walking by the Spirit (Galatians 5:16) and being filled or controlled by Him (Ephesians 5:18). We are what we are and do what we do for God only by the grace of God working in us (1 Corinthians 15:10).

Yet what do these statements really *mean*? How do they become real in our daily lives? What does it mean to "abide in Christ" or "walk by faith" in the "power of the Holy Spirit" so that true growth in holiness takes place?

The Trinity's Involvement

In the Scripture passages we just mentioned, we see that Christ, the Spirit, and the Father are all involved in our daily growth. Before we examine what happens in day-by-day sanctification, we'll find it helpful to understand the roles that the Father, Son, and Spirit have in our growth.

In Our Salvation

Our *salvation* involves the activity of each person of the Trinity—Father, Son, and Holy Spirit. Their place and relationship in the saving process is seen in Titus 3:4-6: "When the kindness and love of God our Savior appeared . . . he saved us through the washing of rebirth and renewal by the Holy Spirit, whom he poured out on us generously through Jesus Christ our Savior." The love of the Father is the source of salvation; the Holy Spirit applies that salvation to us; and the salvation that the Holy Spirit brings was made possible by Christ's work and therefore comes "through" Him. This pattern is seen again in Romans 8:2-4: God sent His Son to do what the law could not do (set us free from the law of sin and death), so that the righteousness of the law might be met in those who live according to the Spirit.

In Our Sanctification

Our *sanctification* also depends on the work of the entire Godhead. The Father is the fountain of all salvation, but that salvation is worked out through Christ by the Spirit. Scripture places our focus on all three when it talks about sanctification. Christ, by His perfect life and sacrificial death, conquered sin and death. He made it possible for us to become restored to our proper relationship with God and thus alive with God's life and righteousness. And it is the Spirit's work to bring Christ into us so that His salvation might become operative in our experience. John Calvin summed up this ministry of the Spirit in relation to Christ when he said, "The Holy Spirit is the bond by which Christ effectually unites us to himself.[2]

What Christ Does, the Spirit Does

Indeed, Scripture frequently mentions that Christ and the Spirit have identical places in the work of salvation, especially in relation to our sanctification. We are "sanctified in Christ Jesus" (1 Corinthians 1:2); we are "sanctified by the Holy Spirit" (Romans 15:16). We are to "walk in Him [Christ Jesus]" (Colossians 2:6 NASB); we are to "walk by the Spirit" (Galatians 5:16 NASB). We are called "into fellowship with his Son Jesus Christ" (1 Corinthians 1:9); we are blessed with "the fellowship of the Holy Spirit" (2 Corinthians 13:14). We have received the Spirit that "we may understand what God has freely given us," and therefore "we have the mind of Christ" (1 Corinthians 2:12,16). In all those passages, the same reality given to us in Christ through His saving work is applied to us by the Spirit. The Spirit comes to bring into our lives the presence of the risen Lord and all that He is. What Christ does, the Spirit does.

We see this connection again in Christ's letters to the seven churches found in Revelation chapters 2 and 3. Each letter closes with the words: "He who has an ear, let him hear what the Spirit says to the churches" (Revelation 2:7,11,17,29; 3:6,13,22). Notice that the key is not whether Christ will speak to His church, the key is whether or not the church is listening to the Spirit. In the Old Testament, the Spirit came as the Spirit of God, powerfully effecting God's work in the world. He was God at work on earth. Similarly, in the New Testament, the Spirit was sent by Christ and came as the Spirit of Christ (Romans 8:9; Galatians 4:6; Philippians 1:19). He is the powerful presence of Christ on earth, effecting His saving work in the lives of people.

Paul's prayer for the Ephesian believers (3:14-17) helps us to better understand the relationship between the Spirit and Christ in the Christian life:

> I pray that . . . [the Father] may strengthen you with power through his Spirit in your inner being, so that Christ may dwell in your hearts through faith. And I pray that you . . . may have power, together with all the saints, to grasp how wide and long and high and deep is the love of Christ, and to know this love . . . that you may be filled to the measure of all the fullness of God.

According to Paul's prayer, God's power is at work in our "inner being" (that is, the real essential self) through the Spirit so that Christ may dwell in our hearts by faith with the goal that we might be filled with the fullness of God. It is the Spirit who empowers us to lay hold of Christ by faith (*see also* 2 Corinthians 4:13 and Galatians 5:5, where faith is related to the Spirit's work). The result of the Spirit's work is that "the character of Christ increasingly becomes the hallmark of believers' lives."[3]

Jesus taught this same truth when He said that the Spirit "will bring glory to me by taking from what is mine and making it known to you" (John 16:14). The Spirit works in us to cause us to see Jesus for who He really is. We confess Christ as Lord only by the Spirit (1 Corinthians 12:3). The Spirit ministers to us not only in our initial salvation, but He also causes us to continue focusing on Christ in faith so that He becomes more and more at home in our hearts—the center of our personality, the place where our thoughts, emotions, and actions originate, and thus "the wellspring of life" (Proverbs 4:23).

In summary, the Spirit empowers us to lay hold of Christ, grasp His incomprehensible love for us, and focus on His way of life so that it might be lived in us. Our walk by the Spirit is one of focusing on Christ with faith so that we "abide" in Him and His life is "formed" in us.

Bible commentator Frederick Godet said,

> Jesus is the object to be assimilated, the Spirit is the assimilating power. Without the objective revelation given in Jesus, the Spirit would have nothing to fertilize in us; without the Spirit, the revelation granted in Jesus remains outside of us . . . from one without us, Jesus becomes one within us.[4]

The basic principle of our growth, then, is to remain focused on Christ our Savior through every means by which He is revealed, and to do so in openness to the Spirit of God, who works in us to make Christ's victorious life dynamic in our lives.

With that in mind, we are now ready to look at some of the key statements about how the salvation of Christ is effected in our daily lives by the work of the Spirit.

Abiding in Christ

Progress in the Christian life is attained through living in union with Christ through faith. This thought is expressed in a variety of ways:

Colossians 2:6,7 (NASB)—"As you therefore have received Christ Jesus the Lord, so walk *in Him*, having been firmly rooted and now being built up *in Him* and established in your faith, just as you were instructed."

Galatians 2:20—"I no longer live, but Christ lives in me. The life I live in the body, I live by faith *in the Son of God*."

Ephesians 6:10—"Be strong *in the Lord* and in his mighty power."

Colossians 2:19 (NASB)—We grow by "*holding fast to the head*," which is Christ.

Romans 13:14—"*Clothe yourselves with the Lord Jesus Christ*, and do not think about how to gratify the desires of the sinful nature."

Colossians 3:17—"Whatever you do, whether in word or deed, *do it all in the name of the Lord Jesus*." (*See* 1 Peter 3:16, our behavior is to be *in Christ*.)

It is clear from these verses that our life, strength, and all our activities as believers are to be related to Christ (connected to the hub). They are to flow out of our being in union with Christ. This truth could not be made clearer than it is in Jesus' statement about the necessity of abiding in Him: "Abide in Me, and I in you. As the branch cannot bear fruit of itself, unless it abides in the vine, so neither can you unless you abide in Me. . . . For apart from Me you can do nothing" (John 15:4,5 NASB).

The Greek word translated "abide"[5] also means "remain, or continue." But in the Gospel of John, in the context of a relationship with Christ, it denotes more than a static relationship. Paul's statements about being "in Christ" and having "Christ in us" are expanded upon in John's concept of "abiding in," which expresses a dynamic, intimate union with that person.[6]

What this all-embracing concept means in our relationship to Christ is seen in the relationship between the Father and Christ. Even as we abide in Christ and He in us, so do the Son and the Father abide in each other. The result of Christ abiding in His Father is that everything He says and does manifests the character of the Father. Jesus said, "If I do not do the works of My Father, do not believe Me; but if I do them . . . believe the works, that you may know and understand that the Father is in Me, and I in the Father" (John 10:37,38 NASB). In John 14:10, He added, "The words that I say to you I do not speak on My own initiative, but the Father abiding in Me does His works" (NASB). Christ expressed the words and deeds of the Father because He lived in obedience to Him (John 5:19,20; 14:31).

We have the same kind of relationship with Christ that Christ has with the Father. We abide in Christ, and Christ abides in us. Through this mutual abiding, Christ conveys His life to us so that our lives display His character as we trust and obey Him.

The Practice of Abiding in Christ

Scripture reveals that abiding in Christ involves two basic practices: First, it means that we nourish ourselves through faith in all that Christ is to us; and second, it means that we follow Him in obedience to His commands. In a very real sense we are back to the simple concepts of trust and obey.

Receiving Christ by Faith

Abiding in Christ means first to receive His life and saving work into our own life through faith. In a vivid statement depicting appropriation and assimilation, Jesus said, "He who eats My flesh and drinks My blood abides in Me, and I in him" (John 6:56 NASB). Jesus is not talking about literal eating and drinking, but as is clear from an earlier statement, He is talking about receiving Him and His work through faith. In this context, eating is synonymous with believing: "I am the bread of life; he who comes to Me shall not hunger, and he who believes in Me shall never thirst" (verse 35 NASB). In the spiritual life, hunger and thirst are satisfied by coming to Christ or believing in Him.

Abiding in Christ, then, means first to receive by faith all that Christ is for us. In Him we are rightly related to God as His beloved children. We are alive with His victorious eternal life. We are, in Paul's words, "blessed . . . with every spiritual blessing in the heavenly places in Christ" (Ephesians 1:3 NASB).

To abide in Christ means to consider all of these blessings, meditate on them, and appropriate them to our lives through faith. Abiding in Christ, then, is the equivalent of letting His words abide in us: "If you abide in Me, and My words abide in you . . ." (John 15:7; see also John 8:31 and 1 John 2:24, where we abide in His words). And as we think about abiding in Christ's words, we must remember that He Himself is the Word incarnate. Abiding in Christ's words doesn't simply mean that we consider propositional truths about Jesus. Rather, it means we let His truths help us to more fully come to know and treasure Him as our personal Truth and Life.

Obeying Christ's Commands

When Jesus said He abided in His Father, He was saying that He lived in total obedience to Him. Likewise, for us to abide in Christ means that we live in obedience to our Lord's commands. This second aspect of abiding in Christ was suggested by Jesus Himself when He said that His words were to abide in us (John 15:7). They are to so lodge in our minds and hearts that they will naturally direct our actions in a life of conformity to Christ. In the illustration of the vine and the branches (John 15:1-8), this is represented by the fruit that inevitably results when a person is abiding in the vine.

Christ makes it clear that obedience is an aspect of abiding when He says, "Abide in My love. If you keep My commandments, you will abide in My love; just as I have kept My Father's commandments, and abide in His love" (John 15:9,10). Keeping Jesus' commands includes walking after His pattern of life. This means showing the same kind of love He showed. Jesus said, "A new commandment I give to you, that you love one another, even as I have loved you" (John 13:34). We are to look to Jesus' example as a pattern for our own lives: "A pupil [or, disciple] is not above his teacher; but everyone, after he has been fully trained, will be like his teacher" (Luke 6:40 NASB). First John 2:6 adds, "The one who says he abides in Him ought himself to walk in the same manner as He walked" (NASB).

Living in union with Christ, which is essential for growth in holiness, involves *both* our constant receiving of supernatural life from the vine *and* a determination to follow Christ in our daily walk. Jesus' illustration of the vine and the branches makes this absolutely clear. Reading this passage about fruit-bearing, we subtly hear and focus on an imperative to bear fruit. Elsewhere in Scripture, we see this fruit described in terms of our moral and ethical behavior. But before we can bear fruit, Jesus tells us first to "abide in Me . . . abide in My love" (John 15:4,9). Just as a branch bears fruit by abiding in the vine, so we are able to live out Scripture's commands by nourishing ourselves on Christ's life. As one scholar explains, the loyalty demanded in abiding in Christ is "not primarily a continued being *for*, but a being *from*; it is not the holding of a position, but an allowing oneself to be held." The relationship is reciprocal, but the action of the branch is totally dependent on the life from the vine.[7]

The Priority in Abiding in Christ

That our nourishment from Christ precedes our ability to obey is seen in Jesus' command to love one another (John 15:12,17). But we cannot show this love unless we are abiding in God's love (verse 9) or continuing in the love that we have received: "We love because he first loved us" (1 John 4:19). It is futile to attempt to love other people unless we first nourish ourselves daily by receiving afresh God's love for us. Only as we receive God's love for us and respond in love can we obey His commandments. Our obedience is possible only as a result of the love we have for Christ: "If you love me, you will obey what I command" (John 14:15; *see also* verse 21).

Conforming to the image of God is a long, steady process of internal change as we abide in Christ. People simply do not change overnight, nor can they be forced to do so. Abiding in Christ is being yoked to the gentle Jesus (Matthew 11:29). Servants of Christ who minister to others know that and, like Christ, show great patience and gentleness.

The End Result

A few years ago I (Neil) received a large box for Christmas from a lady who had experienced terrible abuse as a child. The gift was a handmade wreath with the following poem decoupaged in the middle:

THE WREATH

A friend of mine whose grapevine died, had put it out
    for trash.
  I said to her, "I'll take that vine and make something
    of that."
At home the bag of dead, dry vines looked nothing but a mess,
    but as I gently bent one vine, entwining 'round and
    'round.
A rustic wreath began to form, potential did abound.
    One vine would not go where it should, and anxious
    as I was,
  I forced it so to change its shape, it broke—and what the cause?
    If I had taken precious time to slowly change its form,
It would have made a lovely wreath, not a dead vine, broken,
    torn.
As I finished bending, adding blooms, applying trim, I realized
    how the rustic wreath is like my life within.

You see, so many in my life have tried to make me change.
  They've forced my spirit anxiously, I tried to rearrange.
But when the pain was far too great, they forced my fragile
    form, I plunged far deeper in despair, my spirit broken,
    torn.
Then God allowed a gentle one that knew of dying vines, to
    kindly, patiently allow the Lord to take His time.
And though the vine has not yet formed a decorative wreath,
    I know that with God's servants help one day when
    Christ I meet,
He'll see a finished circle, a perfect gift to Him.
It will be a final product, a wreath with all the trim.
So as you look upon this gift, the vine round and complete,
    Remember God is using you to gently shape His wreath.

We grow as believers by focusing on Christ and abiding in Him by faith so that His life is lived in us. We lay hold of Him as our total salvation—past, present, and future. He not only rescued us from sin and death, but He continues to save us, conforming us to His righteousness as we follow His pattern of life in obedience.

14

Filled with the Spirit: The Power for Holiness

So I say, live by the Spirit, and you will not gratify the desires of the sinful nature.

—Galatians 5:16

A young pilot who was flying in bad weather found himself in a difficult predicament when the weather changed for the worse. Visibility dropped to a matter of feet as foggy conditions descended to the earth. Putting total trust in his airplane's instruments was a new experience to him. The ink was still wet on the certificate verifying that he was qualified for instrument flying.

He wasn't worried about the flying, however. Rather, he was concerned about being able to land. His destination was a crowded metropolitan airport that he wasn't familiar with. He would be within radio contact within minutes. Until then, he was alone with his thoughts. Flying alone with no visibility, he was aware how easy it would be to panic. Twice he reached for the radio to broadcast, "Mayday!" Instead, he forced himself to go over the words of his instructor again and again. His instructor had practically forced him to memorize the rule book. He didn't care for it at the time, but now he was thankful.

Finally the voice of the air-traffic controller was heard. Trying not to sound apprehensive, the young pilot asked for landing instructions. "I'm going to put you in a holding pattern," the controller responded. *Great!* thought the pilot. However, he knew that his safe landing was in the hands of a person he couldn't see. He had to draw upon his previous instruction and training, and trust the guidance of the air-traffic controller. The words of an old hymn, "Trust and obey for there's no other way," took on new meaning. Aware that this was no time for pride, he informed the controller, "This is not a seasoned pro up here. I would appreciate any help you can give me." "You got it!" he heard back.

For the next 45 minutes, the controller gently guided the pilot through the blinding fog. Course and altitude corrections came periodically. The young pilot realized the controller was guiding him around obstacles and away from potential collisions. With the words of the rule book firmly placed in his mind and the instructions from the controller, he finally landed safely. During the ordeal, the controller assumed that the instructions of the flight manual were understood by the young pilot. His guidance could only be based on that. Such is the case with the Holy Spirit, who guides us through the maze of life with the knowledge of God's will established in our minds.[1]

We were given the assurance of divine guidance when Jesus said, "When He, the Spirit of truth comes, He will guide you into all the truth" (John 16:13 NASB). Jesus is the truth, and the Holy Spirit is the agent of truth that sanctifies us. *It is the Holy Spirit* who empowers us to lay hold of all that Christ is *for us* and work it *in us*. In one of his letters, Paul said that the Corinthian believers were a "letter from Christ [that is, authored by Christ] . . . written not with ink but with the Spirit of the living God . . . on tablets of human hearts" (2 Corinthians 3:3). It is by the Spirit that Christ lives and demonstrates His life in us. The Spirit dwells in our hearts and comes as the "Spirit of life" (Romans 8:2)—the one who "gives life" (2 Corinthians 3:6; *see also* Galatians 5:25). He also is the power that enables us to live righteously in our new life. The fullness of the Spirit's ministry is well summed up in Ezekiel's promise of His coming: "I will give you a new heart and put a new spirit [living power] in you . . . I will put my Spirit in you and move you to follow my decrees and be careful to keep my laws" (Ezekiel 36:26,27).

We are to focus on Christ, but live by the dynamic of the Spirit. The first is empowered and directed by the second. Every aspect of our Christian life is performed by the Spirit. In addition to living by the Spirit, we love by the Spirit (Romans 15:30; Colossians 1:8); are sanctified by the Spirit (Romans 15:16; 1 Corinthians 6:11; 2 Thessalonians 2:13); pray by the Spirit (Ephesians 6:18; see also Romans 8:26); hope by the power of the Spirit (Romans 15:13); by the Spirit put to death the deeds of the body (Romans 8:13); are led by the Spirit (Romans 8:14; Galatians 5:18); worship in the Spirit (Philippians 3:3); are strengthened by the Spirit (Ephesians 3:16); walk by and according to the Spirit (Romans 8:4; Galatians 5:17); are taught by the Spirit (1 Corinthians 2:13; 1 John 2:20,27); and produce good fruit by the Spirit (Galatians 5:22,23). Many more of the Spirit's activities in the life of the believer could be listed. But these are sufficient to show that Christian growth is accomplished only by the Spirit, and that it is absolutely necessary for us to be rightly related to Him and sensitive to His leading.

Scripture gives us four commands about our relationship with the Spirit. Two are positive: "walk by the Spirit" (Galatians 5:16 NASB); "be filled with the Spirit" (Ephesians 5:18). And two are negative: "do not grieve the Holy Spirit" (Ephesians 4:30); "do not quench the Spirit" (1 Thessalonians 5:19). These commands are related and are all instructive about how we can enjoy a right relationship with the Spirit.

Walking by the Spirit

In Galatians 5:16, Paul exhorts us to "walk by the Spirit." The Greek word translated "walk" literally means "to go about, to walk around." Life is pictured as a "way" on which a person journeys. How a person lives or conducts his life is considered to be the way he walks. This word picture appears frequently in the Old Testament—probably because the nomadic lifestyle was so common in the ancient world. Life for those people meant being on the move.[2] Thus, "to walk" meant to live or conduct life.

According to Scripture, a godly man walks as if he were always before God. God told Abraham, "I am God Almighty; walk before me and be blameless" (Genesis 17:1; *see also* Genesis 5:22; 6:9). Bible commentator Claus Westermann observed that "God orders Abraham . . . to live his life before God in such a way that every single step is made with reference to God and every day experiences him close at hand."[3] Walking before God means devotion to Him that is expressed in obedience—as seen in God's exhortation for Abraham to be blameless. Walking before God also results in blessings; God turns His face in grace toward the person who walks before Him. The psalmist rejoiced that he was granted the privilege to "walk before God in the light of life" (Psalm 56:13; *see also* Genesis 48:15).

Scripture calls the believer to walk in a certain way of life—so much so that in the New Testament era, Christians were known as "followers of the Way" (*see* Acts 9:2; 22:4). We are called to a supernatural walk. Formerly we "walked according to the course of this world, according to the prince of the power of the air" (Ephesians 2:2 NASB); "according to the flesh" (Romans 8:4 NASB); "like mere men" (1 Corinthians 3:3); "in the darkness" (1 John 1:6; 2:11). Now we are to walk in Christ (Colossians 2:6); "in the light" (1 John 1:7); "as children of light" (Ephesians 5:8); "according to love" (Romans 14:15 NASB); "in the same manner as [Jesus] walked" (1 John 2:6); "according to the Spirit" (Romans 8:4).

This walk is possible only as we obey the command to "walk by the Spirit." That's because only the Spirit can overcome the tendencies of the flesh (or the characteristics of the old walk): "Walk by the Spirit, and you will not carry out the desire of the flesh. For the flesh sets its desire against the Spirit, and the Spirit against the flesh" (Galatians 5:16,17). We cannot reject the tendencies of the flesh by our wisdom or willpower. Only the Spirit of God is capable of doing that. Our task is to walk continually, every moment, by the power and direction of the Spirit. (In Galatians 5:16, the word "walk," in the original Greek text, is present tense.)

Just as in physical walking, spiritual walking must have power and direction. We are to walk by means of the Spirit's power and direction. The Spirit enables our spiritual walk because He makes us alive with the victorious life of Christ. And He also provides the direction of that life: "Since we live by the Spirit, let us keep in step with the Spirit" (Galatians 5:25). By the life given through the indwelling Spirit, we are called to walk in harmony with the Spirit, who is continually at work leading and directing our lives (Galatians 5:18; *see also* Romans 8:14). The result of this new walk is that we bear the fruit of the Spirit, which is nothing less than the manifestation of the life of Christ in us.

Inhibiting the Work of the Spirit

Living or walking by the Spirit suggests living in intimate fellowship with the Spirit. That we are able to grieve the Spirit indicates that sin can hinder our fellowship with Him (Ephesians 4:30).

As we saw earlier, Paul's first negative command about our relationship with the Spirit is that we "not grieve the Holy Spirit of God" (Ephesians 4:30). In that verse, the Greek word for "grieve" has the general meaning of physical and emotional pain. What causes grief or pain to the Spirit? The context reveals that we grieve the Holy Spirit when we say things that tear down another believer rather than build him or her up. In a general sense, Isaiah 63:9,10 tells us that the answer is *sin*: "In his love and mercy he redeemed them; he lifted them up and carried them all the days of old. Yet they rebelled and grieved his Holy Spirit." Sin is not only the breaking of God's law, it is also the wounding of His heart. It places a barrier between us and the Spirit of God, who not only indwells us but is also God's seal, the stamp of His holy character on us (Ephesians 1:13,14; 4:30).

Sin also stifles the Spirit's ministry in our lives and through us to others. This is clear in Paul's second negative command: "Do not quench the Spirit" (1 Thessalonians 5:19 NASB). In the Bible, the Spirit's dynamic activity in us is sometimes symbolized by fire; thus the NIV translates 1 Thessalonians 5:19, "Do not put out the Spirit's fire." Just as fire can be extinguished either by withholding fuel or dousing it with water, so also can we stifle the Spirit's ministry in our lives by refusing to heed His direction or rejecting His ministry from others.

The immediate context of 1 Thessalonians 5:19 suggests that the Thessalonian believers were in some way quenching the Spirit by limiting or denigrating the exercise of the spiritual gift of prophecy, and perhaps other gifts as well. But the exhortation certainly has broader application to any sin that disallows the Spirit's dynamic activity to be manifest in us. "The Spirit's fire is quenched whenever His presence is ignored and His promptings are suppressed and rejected, or the fervor which He kindles in the heart is dampened by unspiritual attitudes, criticisms, or actions."[4]

Walking by the Spirit, then, requires that we be sensitive to sin in our lives. We need to walk in the light so our sins can become exposed—not only our wrong actions, but also our selfish desires and all fleshly thoughts.

Scripture says, "Everything that does not come from faith is sin" (Romans 14:23). In other words, whatever we cannot do in consciousness of our relationship to Christ is sin and hinders the Spirit's ministry in our lives. Similarly, John says, "Everything in the world—the cravings of sinful man, the lust of his eyes and the boasting of what he has and does—comes not from the Father but from the world" (1 John 2:16). The thoughts and actions of our lives are either related to the Father, or they have their source in our fallen world.

Walking by the Spirit means renouncing all forms of worldliness, including all human wisdom (1 Corinthians 1:20–2:1-5), all human standards (1 Corinthians 2:14,15), and all human righteousness (Philippians 3:9). Walking by the Spirit entails a growing awareness of sin and even asking God to search our hearts and let us know if there is any "hurtful way in [us]" (Psalm 139:23,24 NASB).

Whenever we find that sin is hindering the Spirit's ministry in us, we must deal with that sin in a biblical way. This involves:

1. Repentance and confession (1 John 1:9). We need to openly agree with God that we have sinned and turn from our error.

2. Recognizing and receiving God's gracious forgiveness on the basis that Christ's work on the cross satisfied the penalty for our sins. The apostle John said that God is "faithful and just and will forgive us our sins and purify us from all unrighteousness" (1 John 1:9). This is possible on the basis of the good news, the Gospel. Christ has already made perfect satisfaction (or propiti-

ation) for our sins, and we are to simply apply what He has already done (1 John 2:1,2). If we fail to appropriate that truth, we will be left feeling defeated by sin and unmotivated to pursue walking by the Spirit. That's not how God wants us to feel. He still cares for us and is for us (Romans 8:31), even though He demands that we acknowledge our sin.

Being Filled with the Spirit

The Meaning of Being Filled

Obeying the negative commands that call us to avoid that which hinders the Spirit's ministry is vital for walking or living by the Spirit. But equally important—if not more—is Paul's positive command, "Be filled with the Spirit" (Ephesians 5:18).

To be filled with something means to be "completely controlled and stamped"[5] by its power and act in accordance with it. For example, some people who tried to throw Jesus off a cliff were "filled with rage" (Luke 4:28,29 NASB). A person can be "filled with jealousy" (Acts 5:17), "filled with comfort" (2 Corinthians 7:4 NASB), or filled with wisdom and understanding (Colossians 1:9).

To be "filled with the Spirit," then, means to let the Spirit who lives in us manifest Himself so that His presence fills us and controls all of our thoughts and actions. This fullness of the Spirit sometimes refers to special endowments for particular situations; for example, the disciples were "filled with the Holy Spirit" and spoke in tongues at Pentecost (Acts 2:4). Later, in the face of persecution, the disciples were emboldened to witness when they were filled with the Spirit (Acts 4:8,31; 13:9).

In Ephesians 5:18, however, Paul is talking about a filling of the Spirit that is an abiding characteristic of a person's life (see Acts 6:3). Stephen and Barnabas were such people; both were full of faith and the Holy Spirit (Acts 6:5; 11:24). When Paul said we are to be "filled with the Spirit," he wrote in the present tense, indicating that we are to let our lives be continually controlled by the Spirit. Instead of being under the influence of wine and other things that lead to debauchery (Ephesians 5:8-18), we are to let the Spirit have His way in us so that our lives will manifest the character of Christ.

We make room for the Spirit's filling by emptying ourselves of self-interest and self-sufficiency. Notice that when the disciples were caught in a storm in the middle of the night, Jesus "came to them, walking on the sea; and He intended to pass by them" (Mark 6:48 NASB). Jesus will pass by the self-sufficient. If we want to row by ourselves against the storms of life, He will let us do so until our arms fall off. Only those who are dependent upon the Lord will be helped. The Spirit can fill only what is empty.

Using the maxim from nature that we reap what we sow, Paul said, "The one who sows to his own flesh shall from the flesh reap corruption, but the one who sows to the Spirit shall from the Spirit reap eternal life" (Galatians 6:8). We have a choice of living for our own selfish satisfaction with all of its "works" (Galatians 5:19-21), or giving our lives over to the control of the Spirit.

Paul expressed that very thought in Romans 8:5: "Those who are according to the flesh set their minds on the things of the flesh, but those who are according to the Spirit, the things of the Spirit" (NASB). Paul was simply describing two people— the unbeliever, whose whole existence is lived in the flesh (that is, independent from God and consequently in bondage to sin), and the believer, who exists in the realm of the Spirit. But his description also teaches us what it means to live by the Spirit. For a person to set his mind on something means more than simply thinking a certain way; it means to make something an absorbing interest that involves our mind, affections, and purposes. It means to have our total existence bent toward something. If we want to grow in the Spirit, then, we must continually have our minds set on "the things of the Spirit," or, as the Jerusalem Bible says, "spiritual things." That's what Paul was talking about when he said we are to set our minds "on things above, not on earthly things" (Colossians 3:2).

The Means to Being Filled

Three disciplines of the Christian walk are especially related to our life in the Spirit: prayer, the Word, and our interaction with others in the corporate body of believers. If we want to be filled with the Spirit, then we must be people of prayer, students of the Word, and active in the church. Let's see how all that works.

One ministry of the Holy Spirit is that He testifies that we are children of God (Romans 8:16). It is the Spirit who leads us, as children, to cry, "Abba Father" to God (Romans 8:15; Galatians 4:6). He helps pray for us so that our prayers may be more effective (Romans 8:26,27). In fact, life in the Spirit is a life of unceasing prayer (1 Thessalonians 5:17). When the apostle Paul tells us to be "strong in the Lord and his mighty power" by putting on the full armor of God, notice that his final exhortation is that we pray: "*Pray* in the Spirit on all occasions with all kinds of *prayers* and requests. With this in mind, be alert and always keep on *praying* for all the saints. *Pray* also for me" (Ephesians 6:18,19, emphasis added). Prayer, then, has an important part in minding the things of the Spirit.

Being filled with the Spirit is also the same as being filled with God's Word. The command "be filled with the Spirit" in Ephesians 5:18 is parallel to Paul's command in Colossians 3:16, "Let the word of Christ dwell in you richly" (*see* the similarity of effects in the verses that follow). Notice that after both commands, Paul lists the results of obeying the command. Both lists are basically identical, which tells us that receiving the Word into our lives is the same as being filled with the Spirit. Also, keep in mind that the Spirit inspired God's Word (2 Peter 1:21; *see also* 2 Timothy 3:16). He also illumines it so that we can understand and appropriate it (1 Corinthians 2:12-14; 1 John 2:20,27).

Finally, it is the Spirit who creates and builds up the community of God's people. He empowers witness (Acts 1:8), forms the body of Christ (1 Corinthians 12:13), and equips every believer with spiritual gifts that help the body to grow (1 Corinthians 12–14).

The Yearning to Be Filled

Augustine, in his writings, tells us that in his early years his attitude was, "Lord, save me from my sins—but not yet." If we want to be filled with the Spirit, we must have a genuine desire to live a holy life. Speaking of the promised Holy Spirit and the transformation of life that He would bring, Jesus said, "'If anyone is thirsty, let him come to me and drink. Whoever believes in me, as the Scripture has said, streams of living water will flow from within him.' By this he meant the Spirit, whom those who believed in him were later to receive" (John 7:37-39). The requirement for experiencing the flow of "living water" within us is "thirst," which is one of the strongest natural yearnings that humans have. If we want to experience the Spirit's filling, we must have a genuine thirst for holiness. A.W. Tozer rightly said, "Every man is as holy as he really wants to be. But the want must be all compelling. . . . Every man is as full of the Spirit as he want to be. . . ."[6]

Jesus said, "When he, the Spirit of truth, comes, he will guide you into all truth" (John 16:13). This may be the Holy Spirit's greatest work on our behalf because Jesus said, "You will know the truth, and the truth will set you *free*" (John 8:32, emphasis added). The truth is not an enemy seeking to expose us, it is a liberating friend! Jesus also said, "Men loved darkness instead of light because their deeds were evil" (John 3:19). The Lord loves us too much to allow us to hide, cover up, and walk in darkness. We may fear exposure, but that fear is not from God. Demons fear exposure. They are like cockroaches. They come out at night, and run for the shadows when you turn on the light. In contrast, "God is light; in him there is no darkness at all" (1 John 1:5). The Holy Spirit will guide you out of darkness and into the light, where we can enjoy fellowship with God and other believers. He is first and foremost the Spirit of truth, and He will lead us into all truth. Our responsibility is to respond to that truth by faith.

Faith Is Where It All Begins

Scripture says, "In the gospel a righteousness from God is revealed, a righteousness that is by faith from first to last, just as it is written: 'The righteous will live by faith'" (Romans 1:17). The process of salvation, from beginning to end, is a matter of living by faith. Growth in sanctification, therefore, may be summed up as growing in the exercise of faith. We live by faith (Habakkuk 2:4; Galatians 2:20; Hebrews 10:38). We walk by faith (2 Corinthians 5:7 NASB). "The only thing that counts is faith expressing itself through love" (Galatians 5:6). We overcome the world by faith (1 John 5:4). The flaming arrows of the evil one are extinguished by the shield of faith (Ephesians 6:16). Living victoriously in Christ is the "good fight of the faith" (1 Timothy 6:12). We are kept for the final salvation by the power of God through faith (1 Peter 1:5). Bible teacher Walter Marshall observed that "all spiritual life and holiness continue, grow, or decay in us according as faith continueth, groweth, or decayeth in vigour; but, when this faith beginneth to sink by fears and doubtings, the man himself beginneth to sink together with it (Matthew 14:29-31). Faith is like the hand of Moses; while it is held up, Israel prevails; when it is let down, Amalek prevails (Exodus 17:11)."[7]

Faith is the lifeline that connects us to God. Faith is the avenue through which God invades our lives. Faith in God, then, is manifest by actions that are in harmony with our relationship with Him. By faith we pray and seek to hear His voice through the Word and the Spirit. By faith we are obedient to the law of Christ. If we say that we have faith but fail to practice those things, we are deceiving ourselves.

Faith Calls for Our Participation

Faith is simply responding to God—responding to what He does or says. When Mary learned that she was pregnant with Jesus, her response, "Let it be the way God has said" was a response of faith. She was simply responding to God's revealed Word. When we hear God tell us something and we respond, we are exercising faith. The practicality of this is explained by John White: "To realize that faith is your response to something God does or says will take pressure off you and enable you to adopt a more constructive attitude to it. Do not look inside yourself and ask, 'How much faith do I have?' Look to God and ask, 'What is he saying to me? What would he have me do?'"[8]

Living by faith means acting in faith. Some people say that our response should be passive, since the Christian life is in reality Christ living His life in us through the empowerment of the Spirit. They say we should just wait for God's power to act. But faith is an active concept, and living by faith requires us to live in obedience to God. The life of Christ is appropriated in us only through our activity of faith. One of the greatest illustrations of this truth appears in Mark 3:1-6, where Christ heals the man with the shriveled hand. Jesus commanded the man, "Stretch out your hand." The man could have looked at his hand and responded, "No, I can't move it until I feel strength in it." Instead, we are told that "he stretched it out, and his hand was completely restored." Clearly the power to move the hand was supplied by Christ, but the avenue by which Christ's power invaded the man's body was the faith which the man exercised.

Philippians 2:12,13 is another place in Scripture where we see the connection between our activity in faith and God's enabling power: "Continue to work out your salvation . . . for it is God who works in you to will and to act according to his good purpose." Even though it is God who moves us to will and to act, we are called to work out that which He does in us. Paul prays for God to perfect the believers at Corinth, yet he also exhorts them to "aim for perfection" (2 Corinthians 13:9,11). We are commanded to be blameless (Philippians 2:15), yet it is God who makes us blameless (1 Thessalonians 3:13). It is our responsibility to have faith, hope, and love, and yet all of these are gifts of God (faith: 2 Thessalonians 1:11; Ephesians 3:17; hope: Romans 15:13; love: John 13:34; Philippians 1:9).

Living by faith thus means obeying God's commands even when they seem contrary to reason. For example, you may have a sin habit that seems unconquerable, but if you believe that the power of Christ is greater than the power of sin, you will take steps in obedience to holiness. In faith you will say, "What God asks for, He will empower to accomplish through my obedience." When you exercise faith, you are looking past your human weakness and depending fully on the power of Christ's life in you.

Faith Calls for Total Dependence

It is by faith that we live and grow in holiness. To make sure you know exactly what that means, there are two important principles you must remember. First, exercising our faith is not the same as exercising our willpower. Living the Christian life and growing in holiness is not accomplished by resolving to conquer the sinful tendencies of the flesh or by the performance of rigid disciplines. The purpose of the spiritual disciplines—prayer, studying God's Word, fellowship, loving acts of service, and so on—is to stimulate us to go to Christ for the strength to become holy. They are of no use—in fact, they can be hindrances—if they are done with the thought of overcoming sin by our own power.

Living by faith means that everything in our lives is accomplished by God's grace. We're not saying that God simply helps us to be holy. The Pharisee in Luke 18:9-14 recognized that it was God who helped him to "not be like other men." Living by genuine faith, however, is different. As Marshall says, ". . . we must trust on Christ to enable us above the strength of our own natural power, by virtue of the new nature which we have in Christ, and by his Spirit dwelling and working in us; or else our best endeavors will be altogether sinful, and mere hypocrisy, notwithstanding all the help for which we trust upon him."[9]

Second, the activity of faith is not *for* life, but *from* life.[10] We do not act to gain life, but from and out of the fullness of life that is already ours in Christ. All of our disposition toward God and every activity is ultimately the result of His grace at work in us. We are called to faith in the gospel; God has provided a perfect salvation from beginning to end. Faith believes this reality and acts on the basis of it. Peter stated both God's provision and our responsibility in his second epistle:

> His divine power has given us everything we need for life and godliness through our knowledge of him who called us by his own glory and goodness. Through these he has given us his very great and precious promises, so that through them you may participate in the divine nature and escape the corruption in the world caused by evil desires. *For this reason, make every effort to add to your faith* goodness; and to goodness, knowledge; and to knowledge, self-control. . . (2 Peter 1:3-5, emphasis added).

Becoming What We Will Be

C.S. Lewis, a popular Christian writer and thinker, observed that faith causes us to "pretend" to be what we are not yet. A child, whose very nature is to grow up to be an adult grows by continually pretending to be grown up—playing soldier, fireman, teacher, and so on—and through it actually develops skills and reasoning powers. Similarly, the believer, whose very nature is a new creation alive with the indwelling Christ, by faith takes new steps of obedience in thought and act. And in doing so, grows and develops in the character and shape of Christ.[11]

If growth in sanctification can be described as growth in faith, then growth in faith comes through all of the same means that sanctification comes. Above all, growth in faith comes from knowing and meditating on the reality of God and His work for us, in us, and through us. Scripture affirms this, saying explicitly that faith comes through the Word of God (Romans 10:17). It's in the Word that we see God's works. We see the example of our Savior, "the author and perfecter of our faith" (Hebrews 12:2). We see the record of God's dealings with His people and examples of the faith expressed by some of those people (Hebrews 11). They are "a great cloud of witnesses," inspiring examples of those "who will testify that faith is worth it":[12]

> What more shall I say? I do not have time to tell about Gideon, Barak, Samson, Jephthah, David, Samuel and the prophets, who through faith conquered kingdoms, administered justice, and gained what was promised; who shut the mouths of lions, quenched the fury of the flames, and escaped the edge of the sword; whose weakness was turned to strength; and who became powerful in battle and routed foreign armies. Women received back their dead, raised to life again. Others were tortured and refused to be released, so that they might gain a better resurrection. Some faced jeers and flogging, while still others were chained and put in prison. They were stoned; they were sawed in two; they were put to death by the sword. They went about in sheepskins and goatskins, destitute, persecuted and mistreated— the world was not worthy of them. They wandered in deserts and mountains, and in caves and holes in the ground. These were all commended for their faith, yet none of them received what had been promised. *God had planned something better for us so that only together with us would they be made perfect* (Hebrews 11:32-40, emphasis added).

Indeed, "without faith it is impossible to please God" (Hebrews 11:6).

15

Growing in Holiness
Through Fellowship

*You are . . . fellow citizens with God's people and members
of God's household . . . with Christ Jesus himself as the chief
cornerstone. In him the whole building is joined together and
rises to become a holy temple in the Lord. And in him you
too are being built together to become a dwelling in which
God lives by his Spirit.*

—Ephesians 2:19-22

Leaving the pastorate to teach at Talbot School of Theology was a stretching experience for me (Neil). I loved being a pastor, and being involved with people and the various major events they experienced in their lives. The pastorate is the only profession that directly involves a person in every aspect of life from birth to death. A pastor is called upon to minister to people in both the high and low moments in life. His ministry takes place in the context of both physical and spiritual life as it is being lived.

By contrast, the seminary setting can be quite artificial. Most students commute to school and arrive just in time for class to begin. When the class is over, they leave. Very little community is established, and even less accountability. Some students will make an effort to build meaningful relationships with their colleagues and their professors, but sadly, many don't.

I was recruited to teach at Talbot by the late Dr. Glenn O'Neal, who was the dean at the time that I joined the staff. Shortly after I began teaching there, he asked me to go to a regional meeting of the Association of Theological Schools (ATS), which is the major accrediting body for all religious institutions, including Protestant, Catholic, and Jewish schools. I couldn't understand why he wanted me to attend this religious hodgepodge of liberal and conservative theologians; I suspected it was because he didn't want to go himself. Whatever the case, I was determined to make the most of his invitation because I was the new kid on the block.

While at the meeting, I had lunch one day with a Catholic theologian. He shared with me what the students at his school experienced during their stay. He explained that all the students lived together in a seminary community, and every student was personally assigned a spiritual mentor. The students were held accountable for their spiritual formation, and were asked weekly about their devotional life and their progress in school. I wondered if such a process could ever be applied to schools that had long used the more traditional academic approach to education.

Later, during a dinner break, I met a theologian from another school. He was also a pediatrician who maintained his medical license and continued a small practice on the side. During our time together, he shared with me that the best model for higher Christian education—a model that's more in line with biblical principles—was to be found in medical schools, not seminaries. I asked him to explain his perspective. He said that every medical school has a hospital. Thus the students don't just sit in classrooms and listen. They follow their instructor around the hospital as he calls on his patients and operates on them. Eventually the instructor watches the students as they practice what they've learned. No medical school will graduate a student who has merely taken courses but skipped the practical experience offered through a mentoring process and then an extended internship.

A medical school's mentoring process is very similar to the approach Jesus used when He discipled the Twelve, which could be summarized as follows: I'll do it; you come along and watch.

Then we will do it together. When I sense that you are ready, I'll let you do it, and I will watch and evaluate. Then you are ready to graduate or be commissioned to go into all the world and make disciples. You'll be ready to do the work I taught you.

That was the best three-year seminary program ever modeled, and all it cost the disciples was everything they had.

My experiences at the ATS meeting confirmed a conviction that I already had developed: The traditional approach to a seminary education was sorely lacking because it didn't include mentoring or a sense of community. It wasn't until after years of teaching at Talbot, however, that I had the opportunity to offer a four-week seminary class at a retreat center in Julian, California. My friend Dick Day, who established the center, believed that learning best takes place in the context of meaningful relationships. He had set up a 12-week program that accepted a maximum of 24 students, all of whom lived at the center. They had their meals together, and they all shared in the household chores. His program didn't meet during the month of January, so I brought a group of seminary students to Julian during that interim break, and my friend and I team-taught the students for four weeks.

That was my best learning experience ever as a professor, and I have never seen growth take place in the lives of students like I did during those four weeks. One student came merely to acquire head knowledge and never became personally involved in the experience. The rest of the students had life-changing encounters with God and each other. One couple fought the small-group process every afternoon for three weeks before they let down their defensive barriers and became participants in this wonderful experience.

The Need for Fellowship

In the preceding chapters, we have seen how God, through His Spirit, sanctifies His people when they appropriate His truth by meditating on His Word and obeying it in all that they do. But there is another vital aspect of Christian growth we don't want to miss: God conveys Himself and His truth to us through other believers. The British poet John Donne expressed an important truth about human nature when he said,

"No man is an island, entire of itself; every man is a piece of the continent, a part of the main."

According to Scripture, we are not designed to grow in isolation from other believers; God intends for us to grow together as part of a community. God's declaration, "It is not good for the man to be alone" (Genesis 2:18) is related to Christian growth as much as any other part of human life. Sanctification is not just a matter of I or me. The New Testament commonly speaks of holiness using the terms we and our. The word saint is used about 60 times in the plural, but only once in the singular. Christian community is God's idea, and a loving unity in the family of God is an integral part of growing in sanctification. It is also the means of sanctification. As one writer noted, community is one of the ways that God sanctifies His people: "By the concerted workings of His Word, His Spirit, and His people, God slowly but surely sanctifies His Children. . . ."[1]

From time to time, God may allow special circumstances in which a believer is forced into isolation from fellow Christians, as has been the experience of those who have encountered persecution or imprisonment as a result of their profession of faith. In such cases, God conveys His grace directly and sufficiently. But normally, He gives Himself to us corporately through His presence in the lives of others. Scripture reveals that our relationships with one another and with God are closely interwoven and sometimes difficult to separate. Our fellowship is both with God and with other believers (1 John 1:3). John also said that "if we love one another, God lives in us and his love is made complete in us" (1 John 4:12).

Sanctification, then, requires that we pay attention to the exhortation in Hebrews 10:24,25: "Let us consider how we may spur one another on toward love and good deeds. Let us not give up meeting together, as some are in the habit of doing, but let us encourage one another." The relationship between fellowship and growth toward holiness becomes more obvious when we consider 1) our real nature as human persons, and, 2) how our personal growth is intertwined with that of others.

Fellowship Restores Our True Nature

In sanctification we not only share in the holiness of God, but also our true nature as human beings is being restored. The true nature of our humanity, however, is realized only in community. Scripture gives us evidence that a person is destined to be fully human only in relationship to other people. It is clear from God's statement that "it is not good for the man to be alone" (Genesis 2:18) that we as humans were not designed to live in isolation from our fellow human beings (the root of the Hebrew word for "alone" means to "to separate, to isolate"). God's remedy for the first Adam's aloneness was to create another human being. While it's true that this remedy focuses on the marriage relationship between man and woman, it also affirms a truth about human beings. We were designed to live in relationships. To be human is to be co-human.

The Old Testament scholar G. Ernest Wright said, "According to Old Testament thought, the greatest curse which can befall a man is that he be alone."[2] The psalmist bemoaned his affliction, saying, "I am like a desert owl, like an owl among the ruins [owls are fond of the lonely environs of the desert and ruined places]. . . . I have become like a bird alone on a roof" (102:6,7). The British poet John Milton said, "Loneliness is the first thing which God's eye nam'd not good."

Our community nature as humans is also evident from the fact that we were created "in the image of God" (Genesis 1:26,27). According to Scripture, God is Triune: the Father, Son, and Holy Spirit—three Persons in one personal being. Although we cannot fully understand the Trinity, we can know with certainty that God is a social being. Involved in His one being is a fellowship of three Persons. And these Persons are what they are only in relationship to each other. For example, the Father would not be the Father except for His relationship to the Son and the Spirit. Likewise, the Son would not be the Son without being related to the Father and also the Spirit.

The fact that we were created "in the image of God"—in the image of a fellowship of three Persons—tells us that we were not created to live as isolated nomads. We were created to live in community—in fellowship with other humans. It is interesting that the very name "man" (Hebrew, *Adam*) is the name of both the first human person and of humanity. Man is both personal and corporate. If we are to grow as a person, we cannot grow in isolation from other people.

Fellowship Affirms Our Identity

Yet another indication that we were designed to live in fellowship is the realization that our personal identity comes from our relationships. In Western culture, where we emphasize individuality, we often surmise that individuality and sharing in a group are opposites—that our individuality is lost when we become part of a group. But in actuality, the opposite is true. We gain our true selfhood by sharing in community. Wright explains this basic concept:

> To belong to community is to share the life of a "people," and the conception of "people" arose from the understanding of starting in the father's household, extending to the family, and finally to all kinsmen who take part in the whole of the common history.[3]

We exist, then, not as separate entities, but as part of humanity. We cannot live the life for which we were created if we live in isolation from the rest of humanity. As the Danish scholar Pedersen says, "All life is common life. . . . no soul can live an isolated life. It is not only that it cannot get along without the assistance of others; it is in direct conflict with its essence to be something apart. It can only exist as a link of a whole, and it cannot work and act without working in connection with other souls and through them."[4]

Have you ever noticed that the uniqueness of our individual identity emerges as we build relationships with others? For example, individuality of a man and a woman becomes more apparent after they are joined in marriage. This is also apparent in the Bible's often-used metaphor of the church as a body. If we were to find a body part that was separated from the rest of the body and we have no knowledge of its relation to the body, we would not be able to identify what it really was—that is, its nature, purpose, and function. For example, a toe or kneecap by itself would appear to serve no useful purpose. We would simply identify it as a useless blob of flesh. It acquires its identity only in relation to the other parts of the body.

So our personal individuality—who we really are—comes only in relation to others, God, our family, and fellow believers.

Old Testament scholar L. Köhler said it well: *"Ein mensch ist kein mensch"* ("One man is no man").[5] Our human nature and divine purpose are not fully realized except in community.

It's important to note that sin disrupts community. When we choose to live independent of God, we not only alienate ourselves from the Creator but also from other humans. Sin brings an isolation that is the ruin of human community. The Jewish psychoanalyst Eric Fromm, in his work *The Art of Loving*, points to the destructiveness of such separation and the need for fellowship:

> Man is gifted with reason: he is life being aware of itself; he has awareness of himself, of his fellow man, of his past, and of the possibilities of his future. This awareness of himself as a separate entity, the awareness of his own short life span, of the fact that without his will he is born and against his will he dies, that he will die before those whom he loves, or they before him, the awareness of his aloneness and separateness, of his helplessness before the forces of nature and of society, all this makes his separate, disunited existence an unbearable prison. He would become insane could he not liberate himself from this prison and reach out, unite himself in some form or other with men, with the world outside.[6]

Our Oneness in Christ

If we require community to know fulfillment as humans, then Christian growth also requires community for us to reach our God-designed potential as born-again humans. Christian growth seeks the progressive conquering of the sin that alienates us so that God's intention of human community may be more fully realized. That is why Jesus prayed in the high-priestly prayer that we all be one as He and the Father are one (John 17:20-23). The book of Ephesians addresses this as well; it is God's goal to "bring all things in heaven and on earth together under one head, even Christ" (1:10). We as believers "in Christ" are the first phase of this overall purpose. Likewise, the most alienated people in New Testament times, the Jews and the Gentiles, were "in Christ" made into "one new man" (2:15).

Since the fall, every attempt to unite humanity on any basis other than Jesus Christ has ended in failure. God will continue to thwart the plans of man even as He did at the tower of Babel. People may try to become united for a common cause, but such efforts will last only for a season. As soon as the crisis that calls them together is resolved, they will fall apart and most likely re-align themselves to their ethnic identities, religious preferences, or class distinctions. Communism held Yugoslavia together by sheer force under the rule of Marshal Tito, but as soon as the external yoke was thrown off, the country splintered into Slovania, Croatia, Bosnia, and Serbia. Even the body of Christ becomes divided when we seek our identity in something other than Christ. Sectarianism, individualism, and denomination-alism will keep us divided and ineffective.

To put all this in terms of sanctification, our being set apart unto God not only clothes us with Christ, but it also makes us a new unified humanity. When we come to be in Christ personally, we find ourselves one with all others in Him (Galatians 3:28 says, "You are all one in Christ"). This oneness is not only with Christ, it is with one another: "We are members of one another" (Ephesians 4:25 NASB); "we, who are many, are one body in Christ, and individually members one of another" (Romans 12:5 NASB).

This oneness is expressed over and over again in the book of Ephesians by Paul's use of the preposition "with" (Greek, *syn*), which he attaches to many concepts. The Greek preposition *syn* is noted in the following verses in italic type:

- We are all "*fellow* citizens" (2:19).
- We are "joined *together* . . . to become a holy temple" and "built *together* to become a dwelling in which God lives by his Spirit" (2:21,22).
- The gospel has made us all "heirs *together*," "members *together*," and "sharers *together*" (3:6).

Living Out Our Unity

All those verses describe the reality that is ours in Christ. As soon as we are set apart, we are joined together in Christ by the Spirit. You'll recall that earlier we learned that our progressive sanctification is aimed at making real the truths of our positional sanctification. Thus at the beginning of his instructions about how we are to live, Paul exhorts us to live out the unity that is a reality in the body. He admonishes us:

> Be completely humble and gentle; be patient, bearing with one another in love. Make every effort to keep the unity of the Spirit through the bond of peace. There is one body and one Spirit—just as you were called to one hope when you were called—one Lord, one faith, one baptism; one God and Father of all, who is over all and through all and in all (Ephesians 4:2-6).

Becoming One Mature Man

Even more pointedly, Paul expresses the goal of sanctification as the attaining "to the unity of the faith, and of the knowledge of the Son of God, to a mature man" (4:13 NASB). The goal is one "mature man." It is not that we all become perfect individuals or that everyone becomes perfect by themselves. Rather, it is that we all become one "mature man." Bible commentators have noted the contrast of this one "mature man" with the description of the *plural* "infants" who are in process of becoming this *one* man: "Out of the immaturity of individualism ($\nu\acute{\eta}\pi\iota o\iota$ ['infants']), we are to reach the predestined unity of the one full-grown Man ($\epsilon\acute{\iota}\varsigma$ $\check{\alpha}\nu\delta\rho\alpha$ $\tau\acute{\epsilon}\lambda\epsilon\iota o\nu$ [one mature man])."[7]

The epitome of love in the believer's sanctification also leads to the conclusion that unity is the goal, for love binds together: "Beyond all these things put on love, which is the perfect bond of unity" (Colossians 3:14 NASB).[8] Paul even prays, "May the God who gives endurance and encouragement give you a spirit of unity among yourselves as you follow Christ" (Romans 15:5). Many of the metaphors used in Scripture to describe the church reveal that unity in the body of Christ is an essential part of the sanctifying process in us. The church is *one body*. It is *the bride*. It is *a temple*. Despite the fact that a body and a building have many parts, they are one because the parts are joined together in unity. "There is all the difference in the world between a great heap of bricks and those same bricks carefully fitted together and built into a beautifully designed building."[9]

Together for Eternity

Finally the biblical picture of life in eternity is not one of individual living. The difficulty of living with people now because of sinful self-centeredness may make us hope that heaven is a beautiful place where each of us gets to live alone under our own fig tree. But while heaven will no doubt be beautiful and spacious, our eternal home is pictured as a city, the New Jerusalem, where all of God's people live in the richness of human community (*see* Revelation chapters 21-22). For some people that may seem more like hell because they have been hurt so badly by the sinful activities of others. But in heaven there will be a total absence of sin, and the unconditional love and acceptance that we find in our heavenly Father will finally be perfected in us.

We live in a day of individualism that too often inserts itself into the concept of spiritual growth. We usually seek to edify our*selves*, and this may cause us to desire little attachment to the community of believers. And sometimes the attachment we do seek is motivated by a desire to enrich ourselves!

The biblical concept of true humanity as co-humanity and God's goal to restore this through salvation and sanctification declares that personal spiritual growth is designed to take place not in isolation, but in close fellowship with a community that is growing together to become one "mature man" of God.

The Role of Relationships

A Harvard professor who worked with top executives noticed three characteristics that were evident in all those who encountered failure in their careers. First, they became more and more autonomous. They became more independent in their work and isolated themselves from any sense of community and accountability. Second, they became increasingly authoritarian. And third, they all ended up committing adultery. We have seen those same characteristics manifest in Christian leaders who have fallen. The devil begins this process by encouraging us to isolate ourselves from the rest of the Christian community so that we have no accountability, and sin is inevitable once we start to live independently of God and each other.

At a men's retreat, after I (Neil) spoke on the importance of being willing to forgive others, two brothers approached me. Both had once been married and had remarried, and one of the brothers hadn't been to church for seven years. He said, "Neil, my problem is canonicity [a reference to the process by which early Christian leaders could determine which books belonged in the Bible]. I have read seven books on the closing of the canon, and I just can't accept what evangelicals say about this." I had no idea there were seven books on the subject, but I also knew that his real struggle had nothing to do with the closing of the canon. I got off the subject as fast as I could and got to what he was really struggling with, which turned out to be his need to come to terms with his past. He had never known his birth father, and his stepfather had never spent time with him. Thus he had never had a father. The result was that he had never developed close relationships with anyone. The same was true about his brother.

Those men are not alone; there are many people who have never learned to relate to others on a personal basis. I soon learned that the brothers had never experienced any sense of intimacy with their spouses or with other Christians, much less God. For them, church was an academic exercise, and marriage was nothing more than two people living in the same house. One brother had already left the church and both were in danger of losing their second marriages—all because they had never known any bonding relationships. When I explained the necessity of relating intimately with God and one another, the one brother who hadn't left the church decided the conversation was getting too personal. So he left. The other brother knew in his heart that intimacy was what he had lacked in his church experience and his present as well as failed marriage.

That night he had an encounter with God in a way he had never known before. The next morning he was still red-eyed from repenting, forgiving, and connecting with His heavenly Father. He asked to share his heart with the rest of the men through music. By the time he was done, there wasn't a dry eye in the camp. This dear man, like too many children of God, had kept other Christians and family members at arm's length.

When we do that, we rob ourselves and others of what God has given to the body of Christ, which can be received only as we relate to one another.

Relationships and Growth

In Scripture, it is easy to see that spiritual growth means growth in our ability to live in harmony with others. In one way or another, almost all the "deeds of the flesh" (Galatians 5:19-21) cause discord, while the "fruit of the Spirit" (Galatians 5:22,23) encourages harmonious relationships. Growth in our spiritual life, then, means growth in relationships. This social growth is not simply the goal of individual growth, as if a person could first grow in isolation and then get along with others better.

Consider this illustration of the importance of fellowship: A wooden tub requires good staves to hold water. If the individual staves are shrunken and dried up, the tub can no longer serve its purpose. Similarly, the church must have healthy members in order to be unified and fulfill its purpose. Keep in mind that it's not enough for the wood staves to each be healthy; they must work together toward a unified effort: keeping the water inside the tub. God's design for us in His plan of salvation is that we become healthy not only individually through direct personal relationship with Him, but also through vital relationships with others.

The truth that sanctification or spiritual growth takes place as a result of relationships between believers is a strong theme in Scripture. One of the key concepts used to speak of spiritual progress is "building up" or "edification." Outside of the one debated verse that mentions the tongue speaker who edifies himself (1 Corinthians 14:4), all of the key expressions used to speak of genuine edification are oriented toward other people. We are encouraged to build up our neighbor (Romans 14:2), and to edify "the other" (1 Corinthians 14:17). "Mutual edification," or the building up of "each other," is also commanded (Romans 14:19; 1 Thessalonians 5:11).

Most often the concept of edification or building up is used in relation to the functioning community. Spiritual gifts that edify or build up the church are to be commended (1 Corinthians 14:4,12). The metaphors of the church as a building and a body clearly teach growth in relationships. When Paul said that we "are being built together to become a dwelling in which God lives by his spirit" (Ephesians 2:22), he was not talking about people who are growing individually, but a group of believers who are unified through relationships. Peter described us as "living stones" all united to "the living Stone" being built into one "spiritual house" (1 Peter 2:4,5).

When I (Neil) was a pastor, I started a small-group ministry. I asked the group leaders to use the first three weeks to do nothing but get acquainted with everyone and focus on establishing meaningful relationships. We met some interesting resistance from some group participants who just wanted a Bible study. At the end of a year, however, everyone agreed that the group was the best Bible *learning* experience they had ever had in a church, even though the primary focus of the ministry was to build up, support, and pray for one another.

The dynamic of sanctification in relation to other people is clearly evident in the Bible's picture of the church as a body. We know that in our own physical bodies, the various parts grow only as they are in union with the rest of the body. Likewise, union with the body of Christ—other believers—is indispensable to the growth of every individual believer.

Relationships and Bearing Fruit

Further evidence of the necessity of relationships among believers is seen in the fruit of the Spirit (Galatians 5:22,23). For the most part, this fruit cannot be experienced by one person alone. As Michael Griffiths notes, "Love, patience, kindness, generosity, gentleness and self-control all demand the presence of at least one other human being. Solitary sainthood is unknown to the New Testament."[10]

Relationships and Knowledge

Finally, the knowledge of spiritual matters is not gained alone. Rather, it is gained through interaction with other believers. Paul prayed that we as believers "may have power, *together with all the saints*, to grasp how wide and long and high and deep is the love of Christ, and to know this love that surpasses knowledge—that you may be filled to the measure of all the fullness of God" (Ephesians 3:18,19, emphasis added). John Stott comments on the meaning of Paul's prayer:

> The isolated Christian can indeed know something of the love of Jesus. But his grasp of it is bound to be limited by his limited experience. It needs the whole people of God to understand the whole love of God, *all the saints* together, Jews and Gentile, men and women, young and old, black and white, with all their varied backgrounds and experiences.[11]

In Ephesians 4:12-16, Paul once again talks about how maturity in faith and knowledge takes place when those in the body of Christ are involved in building up one another. As each of us contributes our part to the rest of the body, we come to a better understanding of the spiritual matters that help to nourish our life and growth.

Spiritual growth, then, is more than personal; it is communal. God conveys Himself to each of us not only through our personal relations with Him and our practice of the spiritual disciplines, but also through other believers as we fellowship with them.

Now that we understand the truth that fellowship contributes to our growth, let's look at the specifics of *how* this happens.

How Relationships Bring Growth

The Call to Mutual Ministry

The manner in which we grow through relationships can be seen clearly in Paul's picture of the growing body in Ephesians chapter 4. Paul begins his discussion of our growth by saying that "each one of us" (verse 7) has received a grace-gift from God. The nature and purpose of those gifts becomes evident when he describes the purpose of giving us evangelists and pastor-teachers (verse 11). These gifted people are called "to prepare God's people for works of service [ministry], so that the body of Christ may be built up" (verse 12). This tells us that the building up of the body of Christ is the result of the ministry of *all* believers.

The dynamics of believers ministering to each other is explained in verses 15,16:

> We are to grow up in all aspects into Him, who is the head, even Christ, from whom the whole body, being fitted and held together by that which every joint supplies, according to the proper working of each individual part, causes the growth of the body for the building up of itself in love (NASB).

The phrase "by that which every joint supplies" is literally "through every joint of supply." The word translated "joint" suggests points of contact, or it can refer to ligaments that bind members together. It refers to close interaction among the members in the body. As commentator Charles Hodge explains, "the vital influence received from Christ the head" is conveyed "through the very joint or band which is the means of supply."[12]

The Bible's analogy of the body becomes even more interesting when we consider that nearly every cell in our physical body will die over a certain span of time. Within a time frame of seven years, every cell in our physical body is completely replaced except for those in our brain and spinal cord, which constitutes our central nervous system. On the spiritual side of the analogy, Christ is the head of the body and the Holy Spirit completes the central nervous system. They never change and they ensure the proper provision and direction for the rest of the body, which is being renewed continuously. The church body would cease being a living organism without their presence.

This same truth is portrayed in Paul's discussion of spiritual gifts in 1 Corinthians 12. There, he talks about the various members of the body and how they are all needed not only for the proper functioning of the entire body, but also for the proper functioning of each other. "The eye cannot say to the hand, 'I don't need you!' And the head cannot say to the feet, 'I don't need you!'" (verse 21). Just as the parts of our physical bodies need each other, so also do the members of Christ's body need each other. We are designed and equipped by God to minister what God has given to each of us for the health and growth of other believers. We cannot grow properly apart from our contact with them.

The Closeness of Mutual Ministry

Returning to Ephesians, we notice that Paul describes the body as "being fitted and held together" through the ministry of each member (4:16 NASB). Both verbs tell us something about what happens in mutual ministry. The Greek work for "fitted" describes the process of continually becoming more compact through mutual adjustment.[13] Paul's use of this same term to describe the process of constructing the church as a building helps us see more of what is involved. In the New Testament era, builders used an elaborate process to fit stones together. They cut and then rubbed the surfaces on the stones together to remove any rough edges or protrusions that might keep them from fitting together perfectly. Then holes were drilled and dowels prepared so that the stones could be even more solidly joined together.

Along with the architectural concept of being "fitted" together, Paul adds that we are "held together." (In Colossians 2:19, the NASB translates this same Greek word as "knit together.") The term "held together," frequently used in the context of reconciliation, "befits living beings capable of interlacing or fusing themselves spiritually."[14]

Taken together, the two verbs Paul uses—which are both in the present tense, describing continual action—forcefully teach that the growth of the body *and its members personally* must be involved in "a process of continual mutual adjustment."[15]

The Goal of Mutual Ministry

God's goal for humanity is not simply a number of perfected individuals, but a perfected and unified humanity. And the source of all growth is God Himself communicated through His Son, the Head of the body. But God does not simply communicate life and nourishment directly to each member. He also distributes His grace-gifts in diverse portions to each member

(Ephesians 4:7) so that spiritual growth necessitates fellowship. The ancient church Father Chrysostom rightly observed, "If we wish to enjoy the spirit which comes from the head, let us cling to one another."[16]

Thus growth is at once personal and communal. The whole design is aptly summed up by Montague: ". . . Christ diffuses His own eminent perfection in a myriad of different graces so that in and through their diversity, He may bring His members, and they may bring one another, to His own perfection (εἰς ἄνδρα τέλειον [one mature man])."[17]

The Means of Encouraging Growth

How does the communication of Christ's life and our spiritual growth actually take place in the fellowship of believers? In general terms, this can be seen to happen through the practice of all the "one anothers" in the New Testament. For example, believers are told to "encourage one another" (1 Thessalonians 5:11; Hebrews 3:13); "spur one another on toward love and good deeds" (Hebrews 10:24); comfort one another (2 Corinthians 1:3-7; 1 Thessalonians 4:18 NASB); "admonish one another" (Romans 15:14 NASB); "serve one another in love" (Galatians 5:13); "carry each other's burdens" (Galatians 6:2); and "confess your sins to each other and pray for each other" (James 5:16).

One important way we can minister to each other is through prayer. Jesus Himself prayed for others (for example, He prayed for Peter in Luke 22:31,32, and for all believers in John 17:9-24). Paul also prayed constantly for others (Ephesians 3:14-19; Colossians 1:9-11; 1 Thessalonians 1:2). Although many of Scripture's instructions about prayer may refer to private prayer, the context of many of those passages suggest corporate prayer as well (for example, Romans 12:10-13; 1 Thessalonians 5:14-17; James 5:13-16; 1 Peter 4:7-10). Corporate prayer helps us to avoid praying selfishly because it makes us focus on others and God's work in general.

Many of the "one another" instructions are no doubt performed through speech, but Scripture also sees them operating through corporate singing. It is the mark of Spirit-filled believers to "speak to one another with psalms, hymns and spiritual songs"

(Ephesians 5:19; *see also* Colossians 3;16). The effect of such ministry was once demonstrated to me in a most remarkable way. A college student had asked me (Neil) to immediately visit her dying grandmother, who was not a Christian. She had slipped into a coma that she was not expected to come out of, and she was given only a few more days to live because the family had given permission to remove all the life-support systems.

I could hear the grandmother's labored breathing as I entered her room. My student was supposed to meet me there, but she hadn't arrived yet. The grandmother's eyes were crossed, and every attempt to communicate with her was met with no response. I silently prayed for wisdom because I had no idea what to do. Then the Holy Spirit distinctly impressed upon my mind that I should sing to her. His prompting was clear, and I was glad there was no one else in the room. Feeling a little self-conscious, I knelt by the elderly woman's bed and began to sing Christian songs. Suddenly her eyes came together, and I could sense that she was consciously hearing me. During the next few minutes I had the privilege of leading this dear woman to Christ. Then her granddaughter came into the room, returning from the cafeteria, where she had been with her mother. I shared with them what had just happened. We were all praising God as we looked at the mother/grandmother, who was smiling at us with tears rolling down her cheeks. She lived for two more years. The family asked me to speak at the funeral service, which resulted in many more people coming to Christ.

Obviously that was not a normative experience, but it does show the powerful ministry that we can have on other people's lives. We are told to do good to all, but especially to those in the family of believers (Galatians 6:10). We are also to practice hospitality (1 Peter 4:9), which is a love of strangers.

Corporate giving is another way that we can minister to one another for the growth of all. In Eugene Peterson's paraphrased New Testament *The Message*, we read that the people in the early church "committed themselves to the teaching of the apostles, the life together, the common meal, and the prayers" (Acts 2:42). These practices all took place in the context of a church body.

The Benefits of Fellowship

The dynamics at work in the fellowship of believer with believer are much the same as those with any group of people, except that the interaction is not merely human. Rather, in such fellowship, the supernatural life of Christ is being shared through the power of the Spirit. It is because of Christ's life that we receive spiritual nourishment.

Fellowship Provides Strength

There is a strengthening of faith when it is shared in common with others. It is too difficult for us to stand alone and be bombarded with the lies of the world. Sharing mutual beliefs and values with one another in close fellowship provides the strength that we need individually.

How strong is mutual faith? An interesting picture is provided for us in the "shield of faith" (Ephesians 6:16), which is part of each believer's armor against the attacks of the enemy. The Roman soldiers in the New Testament era used a huge, door-shaped body shield that could provide much individual protection. But even more protection was offered when the soldiers came together as a compact unit and held these large shields side-by-side in front of them or above them. If they stood apart and held their shields individually, their sides were exposed, but when they brought their shields together, they were fully protected.

Fellowship Provides Learning

Learning is another aspect of spiritual growth that best takes place in the context of Christian fellowship. We can gain helpful insights from the teaching of gifted individuals whom God has given to the church. We can also benefit from the sharing of truth by all believers. No one person has all the spiritual gifts, nor can any one person thoroughly perceive God's truth on his or her own. We can learn and grow from one another's experiences and perspectives. Learning can also take place through observation; to see the truth modeled in another life can be more powerful than simply knowing it intellectually.

Fellowship Provides Accountability

The writer to the Hebrews exhorts us to "encourage one another daily . . . so that none of you may be hardened by sin's deceitfulness" (3:13). As Dietrich Bonhoeffer notes, sin is much more dangerous to our growth when it can get us alone:

> Sin demands to have a man by himself. It withdraws him from the community. The more isolated a person is, the more destructive will be the power of sin over him, and the more deeply he becomes involved in it, the more disastrous is his isolation.[18]

Larry Crabb says that an important part of our responsibility to each other in the body of Christ is "to give feedback lovingly and to receive feedback non-defensively. . . . Healthy group dynamics don't happen automatically, they grow in the rich soil of time, prayer, and trust."[19] Michael Griffiths said:

> Love, patience, kindness, generosity, gentleness and self-control all demand the presence of at least one other human being. Solitary sainthood is unknown to the New Testament. It is when two or three saints are put together that problems begin to develop! We sometimes help each other because we are easy and beautiful to live with. We sometimes help each other because we are difficult to live with and quite unintentionally, therefore, we sanctify one another! Richard Baxter in his *Christian Directory* speaks of the wife's being a chief instrument in her husband's sanctification and of her husband's being a chief instrument in his wife's sanctification! Both the difficulties and the resultant blessings are mutual. So it is with the new Christian community.[20]

The Preeminence of Relationships

The sequence in which Paul presented the information in his epistles reveals another important truth about our sanctification in the context of relationships: God works in our lives primarily through committed relationships. We can see this as we see the ultimate conclusion of Paul's logical progression in the book of Colossians. First he presents the finished work of Christ, then he talks about establishing God's people in Christ, and finally he discusses moving Christians on toward maturity. We learn in the first two chapters that we are transferred into the kingdom of Christ, forgiven, established in Him, and that the devil has been defeated. Chapter 3 begins with the admonition to set our eyes on the things of above, and to put off the old man and put on the new man, "which is being renewed in knowledge in the image of its Creator. Here there is no Greek or Jew, circumcised or uncircumcised, barbarian, Scythian, slave or free, but Christ is all, and is in all" (Colossians 3:10,11). In other words, there should be no racial, religious, social, or cultural barriers in the body of Christ. We are unified in Him.

After establishing our identity in Christ, Paul gives us instructions for developing character. These are followed by guidelines for family and work relationships, which were the two most committed types of relationships at that time.

Notice that Paul's instructions about character (in Colossians 3:12-14) are all relationship-oriented:

> As God's chosen people, holy and dearly loved, clothe yourselves with compassion, kindness, humility, gentleness and patience. Bear with each other and forgive whatever grievances you may have against one another. Forgive as the Lord forgave you. And over all these virtues put on love, which binds them all together in perfect unity.

The Keys to Great Fellowship

Someone once said that living in the context of committed relationships is like living in Noah's ark: "We wouldn't be able to stand the stink inside if it weren't for the storm outside!" There may be some truth to that, but living together would be a lot easier if we would all fulfill two key responsibilities:

1. *Confo]rm to the image of God.* We cannot blame other people for hindering us from becoming the person God created us to be. We must assume our own responsibility for our character. According to Paul, that is essentially God's will for our lives: "It is God's will that you should be sanctified" (1 Thessalonians 4:3).

From Proverbs we know that "as iron sharpens iron, so one man sharpens another" (27:17). There is always going to be friction when iron sharpens iron, but the sparks that fly are a sign that the rough edges are being smoothed out.

2. *Love one another.* We do this by accepting one another as Christ accepted us (Roman 15:7), and laying down our lives for one another as Christ laid down His life for us (1 John 3:16).

Imagine what would happen in our homes and churches if everybody assumed their responsibility for their own growth in character, and everybody made a commitment to meet one another's needs? Our homes and churches would be more like heaven than Noah's ark, and we would all be more like Jesus.

16

The Struggle of Sanctification

Brethren, we are under obligation, not to the flesh, to live according to the flesh—for if you are living according to the flesh, you must die; but if by the Spirit you are putting to death the deeds of the body, you will live. For all who are being led by the Spirit of God, these are sons of God.

—Romans 8:13,14 (NASB)

Every child of God is a diamond in the rough. However, we begin our Christian walk looking more like a lump of coal. But given enough time and pressure, every lump of coal will eventually become a brilliant diamond.

It's interesting to note that if you remove coal from the pressures of the earth and introduce impurities into its chemical composition, it will never achieve its potential. Staying pure and remaining under pressure is what makes a diamond out of coal. The same is true for us as Christians, but unlike coal, we have a part to play in the process of growing up.

The fact that sanctification is a supernatural work could lead us to believe that we should simply be passive—that we should "let go and let God." Like a lump of coal, we could relinquish any effort or responsibility on our part and let God control us while we rest in His power. Such a perspective is partially attractive because, ultimately, sanctification is God's work. Victory over sin is possible only through the finished

309

work of Christ. Progressive sanctification takes place when we abide in Christ and live by the power of the Holy Spirit. God is the one who causes growth (1 Corinthians 3:6), and there is a certain rest for the believer in the finished work of Christ. For instance, we don't need to strive for God's acceptance. In light of all that, however, Scripture presents the process of Christian growth as far more than a restful passivity.

A Determined Pursuit

Paul's exhortation is to "work out your salvation with fear and trembling" even as God "works in you to will and to act according to his good purpose" (Philippian 2:12,13). God prepared our "good works . . . in advance for us to do," but we are to do them (Ephesians 2:10).

Working out our salvation is a rigorous process that involves sacrifice and suffering. It is more like an athletic event than a tea party. Paul said the Christian life is like a race, and that we should run so as to win: "Forgetting what is behind and straining toward what is ahead, I press on toward the goal to win the prize for which God has called me heavenward in Christ Jesus" (Philippians 3:13,14). The Greek word for "press" is the same one used elsewhere for "persecute," and suggests a determined pursuit. In 1 Corinthians 9:24-27, Paul spoke like a coach rallying his team to victory in the game of life:

> Do you not know that in a race all the runners run, but only one gets the prize? Run in such a way as to get the prize. Everyone who competes in the games goes into strict training. They do it to get a crown that will not last; but we do it to get a crown that will last forever. Therefore I do not run like a man running aimlessly; I do not fight like a man beating the air. No, I beat my body and make it my slave so that after I have preached to others, I myself will not be disqualified for the prize.

Every major league baseball player has to attend spring training. Even the veterans are drilled again and again in the basics of their sport. Can we do no less in the game of life for the glory of God? Paul said, "Train yourself to be godly"

(1 Timothy 4:7). We get the English word "gymnasium" from the Greek word for *train*, which, in 1 Timothy 4:7, suggests rigorous exercise in things related to godliness. Sanctification requires us to ground ourselves in the basics of our faith and then discipline ourselves to live according to what God says is true.

An Ongoing Battle

Whether we like it or not, we are in a battle against evil forces (Ephesians 6:10-16)—a battle that is described as a "struggle" (verse 12), or literally, a "wrestling." The Greek word describes a "hand-to-hand fight."[1] Paul wrote to Timothy, "I give you this instruction in keeping with the prophecies once made about you, so that by following them you may fight the good fight" (1 Timothy 1:18). Later he added, "You, man of God, flee from all this, and pursue righteousness, godliness, faith, love, endurance and gentleness. Fight the good fight of the faith" (1 Timothy 6:11,12). In his second epistle to Timothy, he said, "Endure hardship with us like a good soldier" (2 Timothy 2:3). Then at the end of his ministry, Paul said, "I have fought the good fight, I have finished the race" (2 Timothy 4:7).

Those instructions and metaphors reveal that the Christian life is not at all an effortless lifestyle. We are to enter into a lifestyle that follows the example of our Lord in struggling against sin in all its forms. At the cross, Christ won the decisive battle over the powers of sin, but in God's providence and plan, the defeated enemies have not yet been judged. They still wage war against God, and in a real sense the battleground for the ongoing war between Christ and sin is now in our lives. Our coming to Christ means enlistment in His army to do battle against sin.

We are able to enter the fray armed with Christ's victory because we wage war "in Christ." Our ultimate victory is certain, but that does not eliminate the present battle. In fact, the closer we grow to Christ, the more the battle is likely to intensify. Bible commentator C.E.B. Cranfield rightly says:

> . . . the man in whom the power of sin is really being
> seriously and resolutely challenged, in him the power of
> sin is clearly seen. The more he is renewed by God's Spirit,

the more sensitive he becomes to the continuing power of sin over his life and the fact that even his very best activities are marred by the egotism still entrenched within him.[2]

We struggle against sin as it opposes us in the active process of growing spiritually. But we also struggle with the impersonal effects of sin—effects such as the suffering of various physical sicknesses and diseases, grief and death, and the emotional turmoil that is part of our spiritual growth and helping others to grow. That's what Paul was talking about in 2 Corinthians 6:3-10:

> We put no stumbling block in anyone's path, so that our ministry will not be discredited. Rather, as servants of God we commend ourselves in every way: in great endurance; in troubles, hardships and distresses; in beatings, imprisonments and riots; in hard work, sleepless nights and hunger; in purity, understanding, patience and kindness; in the Holy Spirit and in sincere love; in truthful speech and in the power of God; with weapons of righteousness in the right hand and in the left; through glory and dishonor, bad report and good report; genuine, yet regarded as impostors; known, yet regarded as unknown; dying, and yet we live on; beaten; and yet not killed; sorrowful, yet always rejoicing; poor, yet making many rich; having nothing, and yet possessing everything.

The Flesh: The Traitor Within

Scripture reveals that one of the opponents of our Christian growth is very close at hand. In fact, it is within us! Our "flesh" has sinful desires that oppose God. Paul wrote, "With my flesh [I am serving] the law of sin" (Romans 7:25 NASB; *see also* verse 18). The desires of the flesh are antithetical to those of the Spirit of God within us (Galatians 5:16). They are also antithetical to us and our sanctification. Peter said that we are to "abstain from fleshly lusts, which wage war against the soul" (1 Peter 2:11).

Defining the Flesh

The term "flesh" has many meanings in Scripture. It can refer simply to the physical body. Paul spoke of having a thorn in the flesh or a weakness of the flesh (2 Corinthians 12:7; Galatians 4:13). In both cases he is referring to the physical body (*see also* Galatians 2:20). Flesh can also refer to the entire human person, as the parallel in the following verse shows: "Cursed is the one who trusts in man, who depends on flesh for his strength" (Jeremiah 17:5). The prophet Isaiah declared that "all flesh" will see the glory of the Lord, but then went on to say that "all flesh is grass . . . the grass withers" (40:5-7). The Son of God's willingness to take on humanity is described as "the Word [became] flesh" (John 1:14).

In those preceding uses of the word "flesh," there is no concept of sinfulness or evil. The common element is weakness and transitoriness. Compared to the spirit, which denotes life and power, the flesh is weak. This is clear in God's chiding of His people for seeking help from the Egyptian armies instead of Himself: "The Egyptians are men and not God; their horses are flesh and not spirit" (Isaiah 31:3). The weakness of the flesh is seen also in the psalmist's fearlessness of man: "In God I have put my trust; I shall not be afraid. What can mere man [literally, flesh] do to me?" (56:4 NASB).

It is this concept of weakness that develops into the use of the term "flesh" for that which is sinful and contrary to God. Man, as flesh, is not only frail as a creature, but also morally. Apart from God, man is no match for the power of sin and consequently comes under its bondage. This is hinted at in the Old Testament; God judges the world with a flood because "all flesh had corrupted their way upon the earth" (Genesis 6:12 NASB). That verse points to man's moral frailty and the propensity of the flesh to sin. Man, as a creature prone to sin, also finds the presence of the holy God unendurable (Deuteronomy 5:26).[3]

Living in the Flesh

The use of "flesh" in reference to man's propensity to sin is explicit and prominent in the New Testament, especially in the writings of Paul. It may be defined very simply as existence apart from God—a life that is dominated by sin or a drive opposed to God. A person who walks by the flesh lives according to a natural, secular, humanistic philosophy and worldview. His life is self-centered rather than God-centered. In short, the flesh seeks life on human terms and standards rather than God's. It is the human tendency to rely on self rather than God. The apostle spoke of some people (including himself at one time) who "put confidence in the flesh" (Philippians 3:3,4). It is those same people who also boast "in the flesh," for man tends to boast about or glory in his own accomplishments. Paul eventually came to realize that the only proper ground for boasting was in "the cross of our Lord Jesus Christ" (Galatians 6:14).

"Flesh," as mankind apart from God and dominated by sin, is the term that characterizes the old humanity (the "old [corporate] man"). In a sense it characterized the history of fallen humanity before Christ and the coming of the new creation in "the new man," which is characterized by the Spirit.[4] Salvation in Christ brings a radical change in our relation to the flesh, but it doesn't eliminate it as a foe. In fact, we will experience more intense struggles with our flesh as the enemy of God and our soul.

According to Scripture, the person outside of Christ lives "in the flesh." Alienated from God, he lives in bondage to a sinful, self-centered existence as his own god. He not only lives in the flesh, but he also walks according to the flesh, meaning that his actions and attitudes all bear the characteristics of the flesh. Those who are "according to the flesh set their minds on the things of the flesh. . . . the mind set on the flesh is hostile toward God; for it does not subject itself to the law of God, for it is not even able to do so; and those who are in the flesh cannot please God" (Romans 8:5,7,8).

Breaking the Power of the Flesh

For believers who are "in Christ," sin's dominion through the flesh has been broken. We "are not in the flesh but in the Spirit" (Romans 8:9 NASB). In our death with Christ we have made a radical break with the flesh. Paul said that "those who belong to Christ have crucified the flesh with its passions and desires" (Galatians 5:24).

This brings us to a question that many Christians have struggled with: If the flesh has been crucified, why do we still have trouble with it? It is important to recognize that our crucifixion of the flesh is not the same as the crucifixion of the "old man" or "old self" (Romans 6:6; *see also* Galatians 2:20). The latter took place when, through faith, we were joined to Christ in His death. That actually happened to us—that is, "our old self was crucified" (Romans 6:6). "I" as an old creation belonging to the old humanity was made a new creature and part of the new humanity by God when "I" became joined to Christ. In all of this, "I" died, yet "I" live in newness of life in Christ (Galatians 2:20).

In the case of the flesh, however, "we" are said to have crucified it, not God. It is not that we died, but rather that we put the flesh to death. We denied our self-centered existence when we came to Christ. John Stott puts it this way:

> When we came to Jesus Christ, we repented. We "crucified" everything we knew to be wrong. We took our old self-centered nature, with all its sinful passions and desires, and nailed it to the cross. And this repentance of ours was decisive, as decisive as a crucifixion.[5]

Yet the reality of our actions is experienced only in accord with the faith in which it is done. As Stott says, we crucified "everything we knew to be wrong." And it might be added that we did it with all the faith that we had at the time. But our faith (which in reality includes knowledge), while sincere and genuine, was not yet mature and complete. As Scripture says, we are born again as babies, alive and designed to grow (*see* 1 Peter 2:2). We grow as we appropriate more and more of Christ's life by the power of the Spirit. And as we grow, the reality of what we did totally in principle—namely, crucify the flesh and its old self-centered influence—becomes increasingly more real in our experience.

As believers, we no longer live "in the flesh." Sin's reign over us through the passions and desires of the flesh has been broken. We have decisively said no to the old god-playing existence of the flesh and yes to Christ and the Spirit. The flesh is no longer the dominant controlling characteristic of our lives. There is a new "I" that, at its core, is God-oriented. But all of this is in the process of growing. The new "I" has not yet been perfected in faith to continually walk by the Spirit. The characteristics of the old man are still present, albeit no longer representing our true identity. We live in the situation of the "already/not yet." The new creation to which we belong has been inaugurated by the work Christ did at His first coming. But the old man has not yet been judged and removed and the perfection of the new man made complete.

In a very real sense the reality of the "already/not yet" of God's salvation belongs to the believer personally in this life as well as to the broader history of salvation. Only with final glorification will the new man be perfected. In the meantime the flesh, with its sinful passions and desires, is present to tempt us to indulge in self-centered attitudes and actions. That's why we are exhorted to "walk by the Spirit, and [we] will not carry out the desire of the flesh" (Galatians 5:16 NASB).

What the Flesh Does

Since the old propensity within us was to enthrone self and live autonomously, the flesh continually tempts the believer to live accordingly. In reality, it is sin that seeks to continue its domination over us through the flesh. As Chamblin notes, "The *sarx* [flesh] has sworn its allegiance to another. . . ."[6] The flesh is thus the traitor within us whose self-centered desires and passions are the expressions of sin's tempting power.

Since human life is many-faceted, the flesh's temptations to gain life apart from God takes multiple forms. A legalistic life of religiosity and good works *and* an immoral, lawless, pleasure-seeking life are both fleshly. They both hold out false promises of gaining life on the basis of man's values and effort. The apostle Paul said that before he came to Christ, he attempted to gain life according to the flesh:

> If anyone else thinks he has reasons to put confidence in the flesh, I have more: circumcised on the eighth day, of the people of Israel, of the tribe of Benjamin, a Hebrew of Hebrews; in regard to the law, a Pharisee; as for zeal, persecuting the church; as for legalistic righteousness, faultless (Philippians 3:4-6).

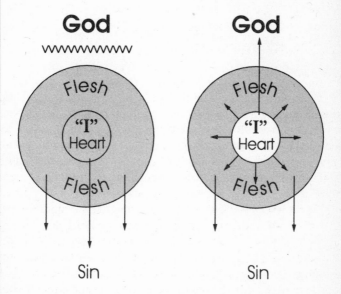

The Old Man

Total person is dominated by the flesh and oriented toward sin.

The New Man

The believer is oriented toward God, but still has remnant of propensity toward self-autonomy (flesh). This can be overcome by the power of the Spirit.

The old "I" died with Christ and has risen a new "I" with a new heart and a new orientation. This new orientation radiates outward to increasingly minimize the propensity of the flesh. This happens in the power of the Spirit, who dwells in the new heart and seeks to fill (control) the entire person.

After Paul became a Christian, instead of putting his "confidence in the flesh," he gloried in Christ (Philippians 3:3) and boasted in the cross (Galatians 6:14).

The other form of lawless fleshliness is well described in Paul's picture of people in the last days, where love of self, arrogance, lack of self-control, and unloving acts toward others dominate (2 Timothy 3:1-5).

The flesh within us, in relation to the power of sin, is open to the influence of the world system around us—a system that is dominated by evil powers (Ephesians 2:1-3) and the direct operation of evil spirits (Ephesians 6:12). The flesh is the pull within us to any and every form of action that is not from God. We might not be at the extremes of fleshly religiosity or uncontrolled living, but when we see within ourselves any desire to exalt self in any form, we can know with certainty that the flesh is still present within us. Simply stated, the flesh is the constant propensity to avoid living life through the cross or gaining true life through giving up our self-centeredness.

Scripture clearly shows that we are vulnerable to the sinful desires of the traitor within—the flesh. That's why the Bible is filled with exhortations to avoid the attitudes and actions of the flesh both in our personal and church life. But because we are no longer dominated by the flesh, we do not have to succumb to its desires.

Correctly Responding to the Flesh

The believer's response to the flesh must begin with the recognition that the power to resist the self-centered life cannot come from self. It must come from a power beyond ourselves. We as Christians cannot break the power of sin through the flesh any more than we could as a non-Christian. We are powerless against sin, and must depend upon a power greater than ourselves. Victory is available solely through the power of the Spirit.

The counterpart to the flesh is the Holy Spirit. We are told to put to death the fleshly deeds of the body "by the Spirit" (Romans 8:13). Only when we walk by the Spirit will we not "carry out the desire of the flesh" (Galatians 5:16 NASB; see also verses 17-26). It is only as we live in union with Christ by the power of the Spirit that we can overcome the temptations of the flesh.

Only the victorious life of Christ lived in us by the Spirit is suf-ficient for the task.

Living by the Spirit requires us to believe all that we have and are is in Christ and in the reality of the supernatural power resident within us. But it also takes obedient action. Two spe-cific actions related to the flesh are given in Scripture.

Resisting the Flesh

The first action we're to take against the flesh is found in Romans 8:13: "If by the Spirit you put to death the misdeeds of the body, you will live." The Spirit is the power by which the evil desires of the flesh can be resisted, but we have to partici-pate with Him. We are to be actively and continually putting to death practices that we know are sinful (in Romans 8:13, Paul wrote in the present tense to imply continuous action). The focus is on the activities that the flesh carries out through the body. The preceding context reveals the primary place where the battle is fought:

> Those who live according to the sinful nature [flesh] have their minds set on what that nature desires; but those who live in accordance with the Spirit have their minds set on what the Spirit desires. The mind of sinful man is death, but the mind controlled by the spirit is life and peace (Romans 8:5,6).

Have you ever noticed that people with addictive behaviors have no peace of mind? In fact, many people drink to drown out the bothersome thoughts that are plaguing them. Others simply obey the "voices" in their head by indulging the flesh in order to gain some temporary respite. By contrast, crucifying the flesh begins by taking every thought captive to the obedience of Christ (2 Corinthians 10:5).

Seek the Things Above

The other action we are to take against the flesh is given in Colossians 3:5: "Put to death, therefore, whatever belongs to your earthly nature: sexual immorality, impurity, lust, evil desires and greed, which is idolatry." The preceding context again tells us how we are to do that:

> If then you have been raised up with Christ, keep seeking the things above, where Christ is, seated at the right hand of God. Set your mind on the things above, not on the things that are on earth. For you have died and your life is hidden with Christ in God (Colossians 3:1-3 NASB).

If we mentally focus on earthly things, we will likely carry out the desires of the flesh.

One lady who attended one of Neil's seminars described well the struggles we can encounter:

> I struggled for my whole Christian life with bizarre thoughts. These thoughts were too embarrassing to share with anyone. How could I admit to someone in the church what had just crossed my mind? I didn't know yet what it meant to take every thought captive to the obedience of Christ. I tried to do it one time, but I was unsuccessful because I still blamed myself for my struggles. I always had a terrible cloud hanging over my head because of this, and consequently I never thought I was righteous because I never felt righteous.
>
> As a result of abuse, I was taught not to think for myself. This set me up for Satan's mind games. I used to fear taking control of my mind because I didn't know what would happen. I believed that I would lose my identity because I wouldn't have anyone to tell me how to live. But now that I have taken control of my mind, I have gained my identity for the first time. I no longer believe my mother's lies about me, nor the garbage that Satan feeds me. Now I know that I am a child of God. I used to worry about whether a thought came from me or from Satan. Now I realize that is not the issue. I just need to examine the thought according to the Word of God, and then choose the truth.

Replacing Fleshly Thoughts with Truth

Fixing "our eyes on Jesus, the author and perfecter of our faith" (Hebrews 12:2) and learning to discipline our minds to choose the truth greatly determines our progress in sanctification. Only when we know the truth and the character of Christ do we see the ugliness of the flesh. The sanctified heart will always choose freedom over bondage. Only then can we ruthlessly root out and put an end to all the manifestations of the self-centered life. John Stott explains that is

> . . . neither masochism (taking pleasure in self-inflicted pain), nor asceticism (resenting and rejecting the fact that we have bodies and natural bodily appetites). It is rather a clear-sighted recognition of evil as evil, leading to such a decisive and radical repudiation of it that no imagery can do it justice except "putting to death."[7]

Look at it this way: How do you get an old bone away from a hungry dog? You don't want to grab the bone because the dog will fight for it. He will become even more protective of that bone. Throw him a steak, and he will spit out the bone. Chances are that the dog will bury the old bone so he will have something to return to if life becomes a little lean. He may be tempted to dig it up again to make sure it's still available in case he gets hungry again. As Christians, we need to bury the deeds of the flesh and take a good look at Jesus when we are tempted to dig them up. Nothing else will satisfy like Jesus: "Blessed are those who hunger and thirst for righteousness, for they shall be satisfied" (Matthew 5:6 NASB).

Paul tells us in Romans 13:14 (NASB), "Put on the Lord Jesus Christ, and make no provision of the flesh in regard to its lusts." The Greek term translated "make . . . provision" basically refers to caring for, being concerned about, and taking thought for.[8] We are not to think of or do anything that would aim at or tend to the gratification of the flesh's sinful desires. Letting our thoughts dwell on negative things or immoral subjects can stir up fleshly attitudes of anger, envy, bitterness, and despair, and lead to immoral actions. If we try to avoid thinking wrong thoughts, however, we will usually end up defeated. Instead, we have to think right thoughts. We are to overcome the lie by choosing the truth. Just renouncing the lie will not help us.

Avoiding Fleshly Situations

If we want to avoid making provision for the desires of the flesh, we need to avoid situations and entanglements that can stimulate fleshly behavior. Having a hidden bottle of liquor or a secret stash of pornographic magazines somewhere in your house is making provision for the flesh. We make provision as well when we entertain thoughts or make plans for when the deeds of the flesh can be carried out in secret. Paul told young Timothy, "Flee the evil desires of youth, and pursue righteousness, faith, love and peace, along with those who call on the Lord out of a pure heart. Don't have anything to do with foolish and stupid arguments, because you know they produce quarrels" (2 Timothy 2:22,23).

Notice that Paul's exhortation deals with more than just avoiding sensual temptations. He also said that in our relations with other people, we are to avoid situations and actions that tend to stir up improper assertions and defenses of self. Rather, we are to pursue the things of the Spirit in the fellowship of others. Fellowship with others is important because we're more vulnerable to sin when we are alone. One way of not making provision for the flesh is to stay in ongoing fellowship with other believers.

When I was in the navy, I saw more than one sailor return to the ship all beat up and stripped of his money. This happened to sailors who had ventured out alone to a bar during shore leave. I never saw that happen to anyone who had gone with a group of friends to the Christian servicemen's center or the gym on the navy base. Likewise, as Christians, we have a choice of either avoiding compromising situations or putting ourselves into them. "Do not be misled: Bad company corrupts good character" (1 Corinthians 15:33).

The World: Opposition from Outside

Defining the World

Not only do we have to contend with the flesh, which is the traitor within, but we also need to stand against the world, which represents the opposition without. In the New Testament, the term "world" (Greek, *kosmos*) basically means "order" or "system." *Kosmos* is used in Scripture in reference to the entire created universe (Acts 17:24), the earth (Mark 8:36, John 1:1); and frequently for the world of mankind (John 3:16,19). In addition, because the world of mankind is under the dominion of sin, a further meaning arises: "the world" is a term used to speak of the complex system of humanity apart from God. This concept of the world has been well defined as ". . . the whole system of humanity (its institutions, structures, values, and mores) as organized without God."[9]

Another Greek term, *aion*, which basically means "a long time" or "an age," is used in some instances to designate "the course of the world apart from Christ."[10] As such it encompasses the idea of human history in all of its dimensions under the domination of sin (*see* the parallel in 1 Corinthians 1:20 and 3:19). The two Greek terms are brought together when Paul speaks of the sinful "course [*aion*] of this world [*kosmos*]" (Ephesians 2:2 NASB).

The evil character of the world and its animosity toward God and His salvation is seen in what Jesus said to His disciples: "If the world hates you, keep in mind that it hated me first." (John 15:18,19). The wisdom of the world looks at the cross of Christ as foolishness and is antithetical to the wisdom of God (1 Corinthians 1:18-24). The evil nature of the world is seen also in the fact that it is the domain of Satan's rule. He is "the prince of this world" (John 12:31; 16:11) and the "god of this age [or world]" (2 Corinthians 4:4). "The whole world is under the control of the evil one" (1 John 5:19). Not only the devil, but his evil spirit allies are spoken of as "the rulers . . . the authorities . . . [and] the powers of this dark world" (Ephesians 6:12).

The Elements of Worldliness

The true characteristics of the world are seen in 1 John 2:16: "All that is in the world, the lust of the flesh and the lust of the eyes and the boastful pride of life, is not from the Father, but is from the world" (NASB). The "lusts of the flesh" are the sinful desires of our fallen human nature—those that leave God and His will out. The "lusts of the eyes" relate to looking only on the outward appearance of someone or something without seeing the real value of him or it. As one person said, it is "the love of beauty divorced from love of goodness. . . ."[11] In the Bible, we read that Eve saw the forbidden fruit as "pleasing to the eye" (Genesis 3:6). Achan "saw" the forbidden spoils of war and hid them in his tent (Joshua 7:21). David looked on the beauty of Bathsheba and sinned grievously.

Finally, 1 John 2:16 (NASB) mentions "the boastful pride of life" as characteristic of this world. The Greek term for "boastful" describes "one who makes more of himself than the reality justifies." It denotes in this description of the world "the attitude of the cosmic man who does not ask concerning the will of the Father but tries to make out that he himself may sovereignly decide concerning the shape of his life. . . ."[12] This worldly boastfulness is seen in those who say, "Today or tomorrow we will go to this or that city, spend a year there, carry on business and make money" (James 4:13). James then says we can't foresee what will happen in the future. Our life is but "a mist that appears for a little while and then vanishes" (verse 14). Thus we ought to say, "If it is the Lord's will, we will live and do this or that" (verse 15). The worldly boastfulness James talks about is not limited to the braggart; 1 John 2:16 indicates it is the attitude of anyone who lives his life apart from the Father.

When John wrote about the lust of the flesh, the lust of the eyes, and the pride of the world, he said that those characteristics come "not from the Father but from the world" (1 John 2:16). He was showing that the danger of worldliness in our lives is not simply a matter of doing certain things and avoiding others. Rather, he was talking about the attitude we have in life. Is God included in all that we do? If not, it is "from the world."

The world is also characterized by its own "wisdom," which originates from both arrogant human reasoning (1 Corinthians 1:19-31) and "the devil" (James 3:15). It is a wisdom that asserts knowledge but does not really change life. James asked, "Who is wise and understanding among you? Let him show it by his good life, by deeds done in humility that come from [true] wisdom" (3:13).

Friendship with God or the World?

The constant danger for us as Christians is that we might let our affections be drawn to the world. Thus we are warned, "Do not love the world or anything in the world. If anyone loves the world, the love of the Father is not in him" (1 John 2:15). As Christians, we are betrothed to Christ as His bride. But we are tempted to commit adultery with the world: "You adulterous people, don't you know that friendship with the world is hatred toward God? Anyone who chooses to be a friend of the world becomes an enemy of God" (James 4:4). Demas is an example of someone who failed in his walk as a believer; because "he loved this world," he deserted Paul (2 Timothy 4:10).

The world constantly seeks to pull our love away from Christ by appealing to our flesh, which desires to live after the world's values. The connection between our flesh and the world is evident in Paul's description of those who "followed the ways of this world. . . . gratifying the cravings of our sinful nature [literally, our flesh] and following its desires and thoughts" (Ephesians 2:2,3). James tells us that both fighting and quarreling—which characterize the world and result from selfishness—come from "your desires that battle within you" (James 4:1). Sometimes we bring worldly prayer requests to God so that we may spend what we get on our pleasures (verse 3). The great temptation of the world is to satisfy our pleasures and not seek that which pleases God. Only the latter, of course, is ultimately life-giving and truly fulfilling.

Correctly Responding to the World

The world system promotes self-sufficiency, and this message is found everywhere in our society and culture—the media, the workplace, the education system, economic circles, and so on. Despite being surrounded by the world system and having within us the flesh, which is attracted to the world's allurements, we have all the resources we need "in Christ" to withstand these threats.

As Christians, having a love for God is possible because in Christ we are overcomers of the world: "This is love for God: to obey his commands. And his commands are not burdensome, for everyone born of God overcomes the world" (1 John 5:3,4). In that passage, the verb "overcomes" is present tense, indicating not that the believer never succumbs to the temptations of the world, but that the life of the believer is generally characterized by victory rather than defeat.

John then shares that the means of victory is our faith in God: "This is the victory that has overcome the world, even our faith. Who is it that overcomes the world? Only he who believes that Jesus is the Son of God" (1 John 5:4,5). The tenses John uses in that statement are interesting. In the first sentence, the phrase "has overcome" is in the Greek aorist tense, which suggests that the action is *finished*. This is consistent with the truth that when we came to Christ, we were joined to the One who could say, "Take heart! I have overcome the world" (John 16:33). Christ's decisive triumph over the powers of sin belongs to every believer "in Him." When we placed our faith in Christ, we in a very real sense became overcomers. We have overcome the evil spirit of the world "because the one who is in [us] is greater than the one who is in the world" (1 John 4:4).

In the second sentence, the verb "overcomes" is in the present tense, suggesting an *ongoing* overcoming—that is, the daily experiencing of our victory over the world because we are in Christ. In summary, then, it is our initial faith in Christ that made us overcomers, and it is our continuing faith ("who believes" is literally "the one who continually believes") that wins the battle on a daily basis. One Bible commentator said this:

> To the natural man the power of evil appears uncontrollable, and to the weak Christian the force of temptation appears irresistible. It requires a firm belief in Jesus to enable us to dismiss this appearance of irresistible, uncontrollable evil as being merely appearance. . . . Such faith is far from being wish-fulfillment or sheer illusion. On the contrary, it rests foursquare on the fact that Jesus Christ has defeated death, and anybody who can defeat death can defeat anything.[13]

Faith's Role in Overcoming the World

Recall that we were born into this world physically alive but spiritually dead. We had neither the presence of God in our lives nor the knowledge of His ways. So our minds were programmed by the world, which conditioned our flesh to live our lives independent of God. Because we as Christians still live in the world, it can continue to shape us. That is why the apostle Paul said, "Do not conform any longer to the pattern of this world, but be transformed by the renewing of your mind" (Romans 12:2). The focus of renewing our minds has to be on Christ, the author and perfecter of our faith, because He is the way and the truth. Elsewhere, Paul cautions, "See to it that no one takes you captive through hollow and deceptive philosophy, which depends on human tradition and the basic principles of this world rather than on Christ" (Colossians 2:8). We can protect ourselves from the world with the help of all biblical truth, but there are several specific truths that are particularly useful for combating the world.

James appeals to his readers by letting them know that worldliness is absolutely antithetical to their relationship with God: "Don't you know that friendship with the world is hatred toward God? Anyone who chooses to be a friend of the world becomes an enemy of God" (4:4). We cannot serve two masters or love two wives; we must continually recognize how much the world hates God and God hates the sin of the world.

Friendship with the world is not only antithetical to God, it is antithetical to our identity as believers. The apostle Paul speaks for all believers when he says, "May I never boast except in the cross of our Lord Jesus Christ, through which the world has been crucified to me, and I to the world" (Galatians 6:14). Faith in Christ means faith in the cross. The world hates the cross because it reveals the ultimate error of the world's attitude that man is adequate and capable of finding life on his own terms. But the believer loves the cross. His confidence is in the cross alone, and thus his boast. Through the cross he became a radically new creature that no longer belongs to the world or lives according to it. He has a new identity, which has absolutely nothing to do with the world. As a result of our crucifixion with Christ, "we and the world have parted company.

Each has been 'crucified' to the other. . . . Previously we were desperately anxious to be in favor with the world. But now that we have seen ourselves as sinners and Christ crucified as our sin-bearer, we do not care what the world thinks or says of us or does to us."[14]

Our new identity is not only separate from the world, it also has new propensities, new desires, new passions, new values. The faith in the One who overcame the world never forgets the cross and the new identity that is made possible through His work—an identity completely antithetical to the values and characteristics of the world system.

In simple terms, resistance to the world is simply right-mindedness, and worldliness is the epitome of stupidity. To love the world is to deliberately plan for doom. "The world and its desires pass away [present tense, "are in the process of passing away"], but the man who does the will of God lives forever" (1 John 2:17). Jesus said that to build life on the sands that drift is to invite disaster. To lay up treasures that moths and rust and burglary can take from us is to face final bankruptcy. So to love the things that are even now in the process of passing away is to determine beforehand that the heart will ultimately be left barren and bereaved.

Making the Right Choice

A physically attractive couple came to the church I (Neil) pastored, hoping to find an answer for their crumbling marriage. They drove an expensive sports car and were immaculately dressed. They had everything the world could offer them. He was an engineer who had a law degree, and he had climbed the corporate ladder to what the world would call success. But their marriage was on the rocks because of his sexual attraction to another woman. In the process of counseling, the wife became a Christian, but the husband didn't. To show that he was cooperating in the effort to resolve their marriage problems, he continued to come to church with her.

Then he made an appointment with me. He told me that people in the church were urging him to become a Christian because he would be such a good testimony! A testimony to what? His own accomplishments without Christ? What had all those worldly attainments actually gotten him? The man was miserable. He was smart enough to see through what the people were saying, and he also knew the choices that were confronting him. He had climbed the ladder of success and discovered that it was leaning against the wrong wall. What he wanted to do was to push the ladder over to the right wall and stay on the top rung, but he couldn't do it. He wanted the best of both worlds, but he couldn't have it. He had to begin all over again on the bottom rung like everyone else. As Jesus said, "It is easier for a camel to go through the eye of a needle than for a rich man to enter the kingdom of God" (Matthew 19:24). This rich young ruler was not willing to give up the false security and fleshly indulgences of this world. Eventually he left his wife to satisfy his lust, and his security remained in his worldly possessions.

When the disciples asked Jesus who was the greatest in the kingdom, "He called a little child and had him stand among them. And he said; 'I tell you the truth, unless you change and become like little children, you will never enter the kingdom of heaven. Therefore, whoever humbles himself like this child is the greatest in the kingdom of heaven'" (Matthew 18:2-4). Humility is confidence properly placed in Christ. We are to put no confidence in the flesh (Philippians 3:3).

Is your ladder to success leaning on the right wall? The world and the flesh are formidable foes that we cannot take lightly. "There is a way that seems right to a man, but in the end it leads to death" (Proverbs 14:12).

In his earlier years, Moses was no good for God in Pharaoh's court. After being humbled for 40 years on the back side of the desert, he became the instrument through whom God worked to set His people free. Author and speaker Chuck Colson was no good for God in the White House, but he became useful when he was put in prison. We don't need what the world can offer; we need Christ. Any position in the world pales in comparison to being seated with Christ in the heavenlies.

17

The Warfare of Sanctification

But I am afraid, lest as the serpent deceived Eve by his crafti-
ness, your minds should be led astray from the simplicity and
purity of devotion to Christ.

—2 Corinthians 11:3 (NASB)

It is thanksgiving time, and do I ever have a lot to be
thankful for! I'm free! I'm free! I'm free! Chalk up another
pastor delivered from the terrible bondage of deception to
freedom in Christ. I could match story for story, personal
testimony for personal testimony, gross experience for
gross experience with many of the letters that you share. If
it would help other defeated pastors, I would be happy to
share my specific freedom from sexual sins, eating disor-
ders, and inability to read and concentrate on the Word of
God. When I read *Victory Over the Darkness*, the light
started to shine and I began to experience God's freedom
as the truth of His Word began to enter my mind and drive
out the lies. When I prayed through the "Steps to Freedom
in Christ" at your conference, I knew I was free! Free from
satanic deception, free to enjoy my relationship with God
as His son, and free to think clearly again!

That is just one of hundreds of unsolicited letters that we
have received from people who have truly submitted to God

331

and resisted the devil (James 4:7) by using the "Steps to Freedom in Christ." The "steps" don't set you free, of course. *Who* sets you free is Christ, and *what* sets you free is your response to Him in repentance and faith. The "Steps to Freedom" is just a tool that helps people to resolve personal and spiritual conflicts that are keeping them from enjoying a vibrant relationship with God.[1] It is a comprehensive process of repentance that takes into account the reality of the spiritual forces of evil, the third and ultimate enemy of sanctification. (We saw the other two enemies—the flesh and the world—in the previous chapter.)

Engaged in a Real Battle

The one who lies behind and utilizes both the world and the flesh in his opposition against the plan of God is "the ruler of this world" (John 14:30 NASB), the "prince of the power of the air" (Ephesians 2:2 NASB). John says, "We know that we are children of God, and that the whole world is under the control of the evil one" (1 John 5:19).

Unfortunately, many Christians aren't aware of that. They don't know who they are in Christ nor why that is even important to know, and even fewer know in a practical sense that "our struggle is not against flesh and blood, but against the rulers, against the authorities, against the powers of this dark world and against the spiritual forces of evil in the heavenly realms" (Ephesians 6:12).

The real battle is between the Christ and the antichrist; between the One who is the truth and the father of lies; between the kingdom of light and the kingdom of darkness; between the Spirit of truth and deceiving spirits; and ultimately between life and death. Apparently many people will never receive the abundant life that Jesus offered because "the god of this age has blinded the minds of unbelievers, so that they cannot see the light of the gospel of the glory of Christ, who is the image of God" (2 Corinthians 4:4).

Acknowledging a Real Enemy

Saying that we as Christians believe in a personal devil has always been part of the doctrinal statement of the historical church. Commenting on the devil as mentioned in Ephesians 6:11, Andrew T. Lincoln says, ". . . the forces of evil that lie behind human activity are seen as having a personal center."[2] In the beginning of time Satan deceived Eve by his craftiness (2 Corinthians 11:3), and in the last days he will be a key foe, according to the book of Revelation.

The reality of this enemy is seen in Peter's words: "Your enemy the devil prowls around like a roaring lion looking for someone to devour" (1 Peter 5:8). Satan's goal is nothing less than the "devouring" of believers. Just before Jesus was arrested and crucified, He warned Peter, "Satan has asked to sift you as wheat" (Luke 22:31). Through the events up to and following the cross, Satan was going to try to destroy the faith of the disciples (we know this because the word "you" in Luke 22:31 is plural, referring to all of the disciples—not just Peter). Satan hoped that they, like Judas, would be "blown away like chaff."[3]

Satan's opposition to God and His children is evident in the names and descriptions ascribed to him. In addition to the name "devil," which means "slanderer," this chief enemy is known as "Satan," which means "adversary." His character is also evident in the names "the evil one" and "the great dragon," which denotes a terrible monster; and "serpent," which symbolizes his cunning and seducing deceitfulness.

Satan's Schemes

Temptation Through Deception

Although the devil is explicitly called "the tempter" in only two instances (Matthew 4:3; 1 Thessalonians 3:5[4]), Jesus identified him as being related to all temptation when He taught His model prayer: "And lead us not into temptation [that is, temptation that would overpower us], but deliver us from the evil one" (Matthew 6:13; see also 1 Corinthians 7:5;

Revelation 2:10).[5] Every believer has to face and overcome the tempter, and it *is* possible to overcome him, according to 1 Corinthians 10:13:

> No temptation has seized you except what is common to man. And God is faithful; he will not let you be tempted beyond what you can bear. But when you are tempted, he will also provide a way out so that you can stand up under it.

Earlier in this book we learned that true life and growth come from incorporating God's life into our lives via faith in His Word, His truth. The opposite of that is also true: Death and destruction come from that which opposes God—the lie. If we are sanctified by faith as the Holy Spirit leads us into all truth, then Satan's primary strategy for destroying mankind is to counter God's truth with lies. He knows that people will not always live according to what they *profess*, but by what they choose to *believe in their hearts*. Satan, then, can succeed in leading people away from God and away from His righteous principles by getting them to believe a lie. That is why God struck down Ananias and Sapphira when they lied to the Holy Spirit (Acts 5:3). He wanted to send a strong message to the early church about the danger of succumbing to Satan. The devil's primary strategy is to tempt us to believe and consequently live out his lies—that's how he leads us to our destruction.

It Began with a Lie

The first sin was the result of Satan's temptation through a lie (Genesis 3:4,5). This original lie reveals to us the nature of his lies: He wants to get us to doubt God's infinite love and goodness. He wants us to believe that God is somehow limiting the fullness of our lives, and that God's will is not best for us. He wants to get us to believe that we can have richer and fuller life living apart from God. In fact, *all* temptation is an attempt to get us to live our lives independent of God.

After declaring that it is the truth in Him that breaks the bonds of sin and sets us free, Jesus says to those that sought to kill Him, "You belong to your father, the devil. . . . He was a murderer from the beginning, not holding to the truth, for there is no truth in him. When he lies, he speaks his native language, for he is a liar and the father of lies" (John 8:44). It is noteworthy that murder and all other sins stem from not knowing the truth and choosing to believe the lie.

The fact that deception is the real weapon in all of Satan's temptations aimed at believers is evident at the end of Scripture. Revelation 20 tells us of a time when Satan will be locked up in an abyss for 1,000 years. The result of his absence reveals the nature of his attack. It is "to keep him from deceiving the nations anymore until the thousand years were ended" (Revelation 20:3). After the 1,000 years are completed, he will be released for a brief time, and again the nature of his work is clear: "Satan will be released . . . and will go out to deceive the nations in the four corners of the earth" (20:7).

No wonder Jesus prayed in His high priestly prayer,

> I have given them your word and the world has hated them, for they are not of the world any more than I am of the world. My prayer is not that you take them out of the world but that you protect them from the evil one. . . . Sanctify them by the truth; your word is truth. As you sent me into the world, I have sent them in the world. For them I sanctify myself, that they too may be truly sanctified (John 17:14-19).

A Crafty Enemy

As we might suspect, the enemy's tactic of deceit includes his method of operation. We are to put on the armor of God so that we can stand against the devil's "schemes" (Ephesians 6:11). The Greek word translated "schemes" refers to cunning and deceit. Satan's attacks do not always come as obvious frontal assaults; he "employs cunning and wily stratagems designed to catch believers unawares."[6] His cleverness caused Paul to warn against being outwitted (or cheated, defrauded) by the devil (2 Corinthians 2:11).

In 2 Corinthians 11:3, Paul refers to the "cunning" or "craftiness" of our enemy using a Greek term (a combination of "all" and "work") that signifies "a cunning readiness to adopt any device or trickery for the achievement of ends which are anything but altruistic."[7]

Much like hunters will use concealed traps to snare an animal, Satan "traps" believers through his cunning, deceitful tactics. "Satan himself masquerades as an angel of light" (2 Corinthians 11:14).

Thomas Brooks, the seventeenth-century English preacher and pastor, wrote about many of Satan's clever strategies in his classic work entitled *Precious Remedies Against Satan's Devices*. Among them he notes that Satan, as he did to Eve in the garden, presents the pleasure and profit of sin, but hides the misery that will follow. He paints sin with virtuous colors; for example, he presents covetousness as good economy. He diminishes sin by saying, "It is just a little pride, a little worldliness"; minimizes the fear of sin by presenting only the great mercy of God; makes the soul confident that it can walk close to the occasions of sin and not get hurt; discourages the person by focusing on the sorrows and losses of a life of holiness; incites comparison with those thought to be worse; causes us to mind our sins more than our Savior; and makes us believe that we are no good because we were beset by temptation and cannot enjoy God as we once did.[8]

The moment we give in to temptation, Satan immediately changes his strategy and becomes the accuser. He is specifically called "the accuser of our brothers, who accuses them before our God day and night" (Revelation 12:10). Although that verse speaks of accusations brought before God (as in Jobs' case—*see* Job 1:6-12; 2:1-5), Satan also hurls accusations at us via our thoughts in order to beset us with discouragement and depression.

Satan Knows Our Weaknesses

Satan's schemes are more dangerous than we realize because in his superhuman knowledge, he knows where each of us is prone to sin and uses that knowledge to his advantage. As Brooks points out:

> If David be proud of his people, Satan will provoke him to number them, that he may be yet prouder, 2 Samuel xxiv. If Peter be slavishly fearful, Satan will put him upon rebuking and denying Christ, to save his own skin, Matthew xvi. 22, chapter xxvi. 69-75. If Ahab's prophets be given to flatter, the devil will straightway become a lying spirit in the mouths of four hundred of them, and they shall flatter Ahab to his ruin, 1 Kings xxii. If Judas will be a traitor, Satan will quickly enter into his heart, and make him sell his master for money, which some heathens would never have done, John xiii. If Ananias will lie for advantage, Satan will fill his heart that he may lie, with a witness, to the Holy Ghost, Acts v. 3. Satan loves to sail with the wind and to suit men's temptations to their conditions and inclinations. If they be in prosperity, he will tempt them to deny God, Proverbs xxx. 9; if they be in adversity, he will tempt them to distrust God; if their knowledge be weak, he will tempt them to have low thoughts of God; if their conscience be tender, he will tempt to scrupulosity; if large, to carnal security; if bold-spirited, he will tempt to presumption; if timorous, to desperation; if flexible, to inconstancy; if still, to impenitency.[9]

Satan tempts believers to sin through a wide variety of means. Rarely does he expose his hand, and seldom does he attack in an obvious way. His demons are like cockroaches. They come out at night and scurry for cover when the light comes on. His activities are far more covert than overt. As Brooks said, "So doth Satan more hurt in his sheep's skin than by roaring like a lion."[10]

Temptation Through the World System

The approach Satan used to tempt Jesus shows that many of Satan's temptations are mediated through others in the world system about us. Just before the beginning of Jesus' public ministry, Satan directly assaulted Jesus in the wilderness. Afterward, "when the devil had finished all this tempting, he left [Jesus] until an opportune time" (Luke 4:13). Apparently Satan continued to tempt Jesus when favorable opportunities arose. And because there are no other Scripture references that say Satan directly tempted Jesus, we can assume that those temptations came through other means. No doubt they included the questions Jesus' opponents asked in an effort designed to trap Him (Luke 20:20) and Peter's attempt to discourage Jesus from going to the cross (which Jesus saw as inspired by Satan—Matthew 16:21-23). Most likely those temptations included the struggle Jesus endured in Gethsemane when He was faced with suffering on the cross. Jesus' concern over the possibility that His disciples would be tempted in that hour, no doubt, also applied to Himself. In all of those situations and more, Jesus was offered to do that which would be easy and pleasing to Him and the world rather than doing the will of His Father. He was "tempted in every way, just as we are" (Hebrews 4:15), and Luke 4:13 suggests that the devil was involved in those temptations.

The devil's involvement in temptations that originate from other people or sources is clearly seen in James's caution to his readers:

> If you harbor bitter envy and selfish ambition in your hearts, do not boast about it or deny the truth. Such wisdom does not come down from heaven but is earthly, unspiritual, of the devil. For where you have envy and selfish ambition [or, strife], there you find disorder and every evil practice (3:14-16).

We can't escape James's conclusion that the lies coming from the god of this world are the cause of envy, selfish ambition, and strife, all of which affect our relationships with other people. Remember what we learned in chapter 10: Our emotions are primarily a product of our thought life. This includes Christians, as Bible commentator Simon Kistemaker says: "The letter of James leaves the impression that the devil employed some of the members of the church."[11] James's rebuke against worldliness and pride, which evidently brought about slander and sinful judgment of believer against believer, is also clearly related to the devil (James 4:1-12).

In James 4:6,7 and 1 Peter 5:6-8, the devil and pride are mentioned together. Florence Allshorn observed that the devil, unlike the Christian, "takes pride seriously, knowing that as long as he can affect human pride he can frustrate God's purposes, if but temporarily . . . for the devil's purpose a proud Christian is of much more use than an atheist or a pagan."[12]

Satan's temptation of believers by using other people is also clear in his incitement of persecution. Peter's warning about the devil, who seeks to devour believers, is given to believers who were enduring suffering through persecution: "Resist him, standing firm in the faith, because you know that your brothers throughout the world are undergoing the same kind of sufferings" (1 Peter 5:8,9). The apostle John adds, "The devil will put some of you in prison to test you, and you will suffer persecution" (Revelation 2:10).

Whether through physical pain or various forms of emotional hurt, the devil will tempt us to deny or distrust God, and he will do this through persecution from those who belong to the world system. When you talk to Christians who have been victimized by godless people, you will find that many of them, as a result of their persecution, are struggling with thoughts that question the existence or care of our Lord.

Deception Through Direct Thoughts

Scripture also reveals that Satan can deceive us by putting certain thoughts in our minds. For example, in the Old Testament, we read that "Satan rose up against Israel and incited David to take a census of Israel" (1 Chronicles 21:1). David went ahead and counted the Israelites even though Joab protested and pointed out that to do so was sin. Although David later confessed that he had done wrong, 70,000 men of Israel still died as a result of David's sin.

In John 13:2 we read that the devil had prompted Judas Iscariot to betray Jesus. We may be tempted to dismiss Judas's betrayal as just a bad decision that came from the flesh, but Scripture clearly says that his thoughts about betraying Jesus originated from Satan. When Judas realized what he had done, he took his own life. That affirms the end result of all that Satan does: "The thief comes only to steal and kill and destroy" (John 10:10).

In the early church, Satan "filled" the heart of Ananias to lie to the Holy Spirit (Acts 5:3). We believe that F.F. Bruce, the New Testament scholar, is right when he says that Ananias was a believer.[13] Bible commentator Ernst Haenchen says Ananias was "a Jewish Christian," and offers this observation:

> Satan has filled his heart. Ananias has lied to the Holy Spirit, inasmuch as the Spirit is present in Peter (and in the community). Hence in the last resort it is not simply two men who confront one another, but in them the Holy Spirit and Satan, whose instruments they are."[14]

In relation to the devil and our thoughts, Martin Luther said, "The devil throws hideous thoughts into the soul—hatred of God, blasphemy and despair." Concerning himself he said:

> When I awake at night, the devil tarries not to seek me out. He disputes with me and makes me give birth to all kinds of strange thoughts. I think that often the devil, solely to torment and vex me, wakes me up while I am actually sleeping peacefully. My nighttime combats are much harder for me than in the day. The devil understands how to produce arguments that exasperate me. Sometimes he has produced such as to make me doubt whether or not there is a God.[15]

David Powlison, who states that demons cannot invade believers, acknowledges that Satan can put thoughts into a person's mind:

"Voices" in the mind are not uncommon: blasphemous mockeries, spurts of temptation to wallow in vile fantasy or behavior, persuasive lines of unbelief. Classic spiritual warfare interprets these as coming from the evil one. . . .[16]

Thomas Brooks, in his discussion about Satan's devices, continually talked of Satan presenting thoughts to the souls of believers.[17] I (Neil) have counseled hundreds of believers who experienced struggles in their thought life. Some people had difficulty concentrating on and reading their Bible, while others actually heard "voices" or struggled with accusing and condemning thoughts. With few exceptions, those thoughts were proven to be spiritual battles for the mind.

Deception Through False Teachers

Demons are also behind false teachings that lead believers from the truth. Paul wrote in 1 Timothy 4:1, "The Spirit clearly says that in later times some will abandon the faith and follow deceiving spirits and things taught by demons." He then added that such demonic teaching comes through human teachers. Similarly, those who oppose the truth and are involved in false teachings are said to be in "the trap of the devil" (2 Timothy 2:25,26).

It is possible that Paul viewed evil spirits as being behind legalistic teachings that hold people in bondage. In Colossians 2:8 he warned, "See to it that no one takes you captive through hollow and deceptive philosophy, which depends on human tradition and the basic principles [Greek, *stoicheia*] of this world rather than on Christ" (*see also* Galatians 4:9). While some interpreters understand the Greek term *stoicheia* as referring to "basic principles" (as in the NIV and NASB), it's more likely that we're to understand the term as a reference to evil spirits who exercise power over the world. That's how the RSV and NEB Bibles interpret the term: "the elemental spirits of the universe."[18] In other words, the teachings of these "spiritual confidence tricksters" were really "a tool in the hands of . . . demonic personal forces which sought to tyrannize over the lives of men."[19]

Peter warned us, "There were also false prophets among the people, just as there will be false teachers among you" (2 Peter 2:1). John said it is our responsibility to test the spirits:

> Dear friends, do not believe every spirit, but test the spirits to see whether they are from God, because many false prophets have gone out into the world. . . . They are from the world and therefore speak from the viewpoint of the world, and the world listens to them (1 John 4:1,5).

Notice that we aren't to test the false prophets, but rather test the spirits that they are in bondage to. This requires mature spiritual discernment because there are "false apostles, deceitful workmen, masquerading as apostles of Christ" (2 Corinthians 11:13). One telltale sign that these false prophets sometimes exhibit is that they "despise authority" (2 Peter 2:10).

Deception Through Physical Attacks and Miracles

At least 25 percent of all the healings recorded in the Gospels are actually the result of the Lord freeing people from spiritual attacks—such as the woman described as a daughter of Abraham, "who had been crippled by a spirit for eighteen years" (Luke 13:11). Even the apostle Paul said, "There was given me a thorn in my flesh, a messenger of Satan, to torment me" (2 Corinthians 12:7). Even though this messenger of Satan was allowed by God to work in Paul's flesh for his spiritual good, keeping him from pride, that was certainly not Satan's goal. Rather, Satan wanted to move Paul to unbelief—which is what he tried to do with Job as well.

The Bible tells us that the coming of the Antichrist "will be in accordance with the work of Satan displayed in all kinds of counterfeit miracles, signs and wonders, and in every sort of evil that deceives those who are perishing" (2 Thessalonians 2:9). In the end times, "false prophets will appear and perform great signs and miracles to deceive even the elect—if that were possible" (Matthew 24:24). Early church father Irenaeus said, "The devil, however, as he is the apostate angel, can only go to this length, as he did at the beginning, to deceive and lead astray the mind of man into disobeying the commandments of God, and gradually to darken the hearts."[20]

Satan, the Flesh, and the World

Three Sources of Temptation

How does Satan's work relate to the attacks of our other enemies—the world and the flesh? Is Satan the cause of our temptations, or is the world, or our own sinful flesh? Scripture reveals that it is difficult—if not impossible—to separate the temptations that arise from these three sources, and to do so may be erroneous. We have seen that Satan is the "god of this age," "the prince of this world." The world is under his control. Something of what this means is seen when the apostle Paul describes Satan as "the spirit who is now at work in those who are disobedient"[21]—that is, those who follow "the ways of this world" (Ephesians 2:2).

What is significant is that the Greek word for "works in" (ἐνεργεῖν), which describes Satan's activity in those in the world, is the same word used to speak of God's working in His people. In fact, whenever the agent of the "working" is directly stated, it is either divine or satanic—most often the former (*see also* its use in Ephesians 1:11,19). By using both the words "spirit" and "work in" in Ephesians 2:2, Paul seems to be purposefully suggesting a rivalry between the satanic spirit and God's Spirit.[22]

An interesting use of "works in" appears in Philippians 2:13, where God is the One who "works in you [believers] to will and to act according to his good purpose." Without suggesting that evil spirits indwell unbelievers in exactly the way that the Holy Spirit indwells believers, Paul seems to be saying that those who are dominated by the world are also under the powerful influence of Satan and demons.[23]

After talking about the satanic inspiration of the world system in the first two verses of Ephesians 2, Paul goes on to tie in the flesh. Describing us before our salvation, Paul says, "We too all formerly lived in the lusts of our flesh, indulging the desires of the flesh" (verse 3 NASB). In other words, walking according to the world system is the same as living according to the desires and passions of the flesh. The propensities of the flesh to find life apart from God are the very things that the world system values and lures the flesh to go after. Thus, according to Ephesians 2:2, the world and the flesh operate "according to the prince of the power of the air, of the spirit that is now working in the sons of disobedience."

A similar relationship of flesh, world, and demonic is seen in the epistle of James. In chapter 1, James points to the origin of our sin as following the temptation of the flesh: "Each one is tempted when, by his own evil desire [of the flesh], he is dragged away and enticed. Then, after desire has conceived, it gives birth to sin" (verses 14,15). Later James reveals that demonic powers lie behind our personal evil desires. The "wisdom" that promotes the fleshly acts of "bitter envy and selfish ambition" and "disorder and every evil practice" (3:14,16) is ultimately "of the devil" or demonic in origin (verse 15). Finally, when James warns against friendship with the world (4:4-6) his antidote is to "resist the devil" (verse 7). Again the world, the satanic, and the flesh are all tied together in our battle with the power of sin.[24]

In summary, all three of our enemies are involved in temptation's pull for us to live apart from God. Satan utilizes the power of sin (which also controls him) to control mankind, thus forming a world system structured on values opposed to God's principles of righteousness. He then uses this worldly system, which surrounds all people and confronts them on every side, in order to pull at the old propensities of the flesh, which still linger in the believer—propensities that are oriented toward worldly values.

Who Is Ultimately Responsible?

Even though three enemies are involved in attempting to pull us away from God, it is important to note that the final responsibility for our sin rests on us. No one can say, "The devil made me do it" or, "The attraction of the world was too powerful; I couldn't help myself." God always provides for us a way of escape (1 Corinthians 10:13). We are the agents of our own choice to sin. Despite the flesh, the world, and the underlying powerful influence of the god of this world, those who choose to sin are credited with responsibility for their actions: "You were dead in your trespasses and sins . . . you . . . walked according to the course of this world. . . . we formerly lived [actively 'walked'] in the lusts of our flesh . . ." (Ephesians 2:1-3 NASB, emphasis added). Similarly, James says that despite the world and the devil, sin is born when "each one . . . is carried away and enticed by his own lust" (1:14). Satan "filled" the heart of Ananias to lie, but Peter asked, "Why is it that you have conceived this deed in your heart?" (Acts 5:4 NASB).

This, of course, does not necessarily mean that all sinful thoughts originate within us. If it's true that Satan can plant thoughts in our minds, then their original source is alien. But when those thoughts issue in sin, they become ours. They become our own fleshly thoughts, which we've allowed to turn into a desire that issues in a sinful act. As believers in Christ, we are indwelt by the Spirit of God and freed from the bondage of sin, and we must make the responsible choice to serve our Lord rather than give in to the temptations to sin.

The Extent of Satan's Attacks

We as Christians are no longer in the kingdom of darkness and are freed from Satan's power, but we can still enslave ourselves by the choices we make. Scripture teaches that we have been delivered from Satan's power (Acts 26:18; Colossians 1:12,13) just as we have been delivered from sin's power. Our Savior has already defeated the god of this world (John 12:31; 16:11) and all the evil spiritual powers (Colossians 2:15). We have been joined to Christ in the heavenly realm, where He is "far above all rule and authority, power and dominion" (Ephesians 1:20,21). We are fully and adequately equipped to wage victorious warfare against Satan and all of his evil spiritual forces (Ephesians 6:11-18). Nothing, including demons, can separate us from the love of God that is in Christ Jesus our Lord (Romans 8:38,39).

Opening Ourselves to Satan's Influence

Having said all this, however, Scripture indicates that believers can still give themselves over to sin and evil powers and become enslaved to them. Scripture clearly states that our freedom is real, but we are commanded to make it real in our life experiences. That happens when we exercise, through faith in God's truth, what is ours "in Christ." We are no longer slaves, but we can still choose to live like one.

Paul warned us to avoid letting sin "reign" in our "mortal bodies" by using our bodies as instruments of unrighteousness (Romans 6:12-23). That passage and other portions of Scripture affirm that we can allow Satan and demons to exert their influence upon us. This influence can have a varied extent of control over us. The basic biblical picture of man is that he is open to outside influence, which is ultimately either from God or evil spirits. The soul was never designed to function as its own master; we will either serve God or mammon (Matthew 6:24). Jesus and those who wrote the Scriptures viewed man as a being who is open to external supernatural forces. The Holy Spirit and Satan are part of a world of spirits who are active outside man.

Commenting on Satan's filling of Ananias's heart, Bible commentator Richard Rackham says:

In Hebrew psychology the heart, the center of life, corresponds most to our will or purposes. The heart of man is not however an absolutely independent and self-determining agent. It is open to influence from without; or to use another figure, like a "house empty, swept and garnished," it can and will be occupied by a spirit—either the Spirit of God or the spirit of evil. Those outside the sphere of the Spirit are in "the power of Satan." When men sin wilfully it is because in the place of the Holy Spirit *the heart is filled with Satan*, or speaking impersonally, "guile and villainy." This is both S. Luke's and S. John's explanation of the sin of Judas. But this does not free man from his personal responsibility. He is responsible for keeping his heart. *Why didst thou put this in thy heart*, suffer Satan to enter thy heart? asks S. Peter. As yet the entrance of Satan has not destroyed the individual personality, for—*thou didst lie*.[25]

Scripture reveals that believers can, to a varied extent, come under the influence of Satan and demons. In 2 Corinthians 2:10,11 we are urged to forgive because we are not ignorant of Satan's schemes. Commenting on this verse, C.K. Barrett said, "It is Satan's object to seize Christian believers and make them his own; this he would succeed in doing if the offender were *swallowed up in excessive sorrow*, and despaired; equally, if Paul and the Corinthians were unforgiving."[26] Similarly, Philip Hughes said, ". . . to show an unforgiving spirit would be to grant Satan an entry where he has no right."[27]

Even Christians Are Susceptible

Paul's hope for those who oppose the Lord's servants is that God would "grant them repentance leading them to a knowledge of the truth, and that they will come to their senses and escape from the trap of the devil, who has taken them captive to do his will" (2 Timothy 2:25,26).

To apply that passage to pagans only is to miss the point of the epistle and deny that Christians, even good ones, can be deceived. J.N.D. Kelly said, ". . . Paul has in mind the constructive re-education of misguided Christian brethren."[28] Patrick Fairbairn also sees Paul referring to "persons within the professing church, but who, taking up some false notions, or misled by perverted counsels, set themselves to withstand the pure teaching and goodly order of Christ's kingdom."[29] Commentator George Knight sees these individuals "either as false teachers themselves or as those influenced by false teachers," which certainly could include believers. The trap of "the intellectual allurement of error" set by the devil has actually "taken them captive," expressing "the decisive hold that the devil has."[30]

The possibility that a believer can be trapped by the evil one is seen in 1 Timothy 3, where Paul lists the qualifications of a church leader: He is to have "a good reputation with outsiders, so that he will not fall into disgrace and into the devil's trap" (verse 7). Note that the trap is one set *by* the devil, not *for* him. As the verse above indicates, those held captive need "to come back to their senses," so a person without a good testimony from outsiders could "'lose his head' or 'senses' when he fell into reproach and thereby be ensnared to obey the evil one and disobey God."[31]

Additional affirmation that believers can be influenced is seen in these words from Paul: "In your anger do not sin: Do not let the sun go down while you are still angry, and do not give the devil a foothold" (Ephesians 4:26,27). The word "foothold" (Greek, τόπος) literally means "a place." Karl Braune says that to "'give place' designates, as in Romans 12:19, affording free play, wide space, of course in the heart. . . . Sinful anger brings even the Christian's heart into the power of Satan, from whom he was freed, destroying the fellowship with the Redeemer and His grace."[32] Markus Barth says, "The warning of 4:26,27 can be summed up this way: the devil will take possession of your heart if your wrath endures."[33] Finally, John Eadie says of this passage, "Envy, cunning, and malice are the preeminent feelings of the devil, and if wrath gain the empire of the heart, it lays it open to him, and to those fiendish passions which are identified with his presence and operations."[34]

Clearly the matter of a believer's sin is not simply a matter of the flesh; it is also that of the devil as well, as William Hendriksen points out:

> The devil will quickly seize the opportunity of changing our indignation, whether righteous or unrighteous, into a grievance, a grudge, a nursing of wrath, an

unwillingness to forgive. Paul was very conscious of the reality, the power, and the deceitfulness of the devil, as 6:10 shows. What he means, therefore, is that *from the very start* the devil must be resisted (James 4:7). No *place* whatsoever must be given to him, no room to enter or to stand.[35]

Charles Hodge said, "Anger when cherished gives the Tempter great power over us, as it furnishes a motive to yield to his evil suggestions."[36]

Some Crucial Distinctions

How far can the enslavement of believers go? Can it include their actual demonization? Before discussing that question, a word about terminology is necessary.

Defining the Terms

The traditional term for what we are talking about has been "demon possession." The English dictionary has some very valid meanings to describe this reality: "to enter into and control firmly: Dominate. . . ." In fact, Webster's dictionary's first definition of the adjective "possessed" is: "influenced or controlled by something (as an evil spirit or a passion)."[37]

But because confusion is often introduced by the fact that the word *possess* also carries the meaning of ownership, it is best not to use it in relation to demons and believers. Those who are believers have been purchased by God with the precious blood of Christ (Acts 20:28; Revelation 5:9). They don't even belong to themselves (1 Corinthians 6:19), let alone to Satan or demons. They belong to God. Biblically, it is impossible for Satan to possess a believer in the sense of ownership.

What has traditionally been called "demon possession" is, in Scripture, simply "demonized" (Greek, *diamonizomai*), or "having a demon."[38] Scripture's use of those terms is reserved for those people who are severely influenced or controlled by demonic forces. Perhaps it is best to simply use the term *demonized* for such people. But it is important to recognize that the degree of control over those same people varies greatly. In some instances, such as with the demoniac of Gadarenes, the demons exercised almost total control of their victim so that he returns to "his right mind" after Jesus casts them out (Mark 5:1-15). On the other hand, Satan is said to have "entered" Judas (Luke 22:3), and there is no indication that this caused him to act radically different outwardly. In fact, both Jesus and John the Baptist were accused of "having demons" (Jesus—Mark 3:22; John 7:20; 8:48,52; John—Matthew 11:18), which clearly shows that being demonized was not always accompanied by an obvious loss of self-control or overt demonical behavior.

Responding to an Objection

Some Christians object to the idea that believers can be internally affected by a demon. Their objection is that believers are indwelt by the Spirit, who, by virtue of His holiness, cannot share residence with a sinful demon. This objection, however, is undermined when we realize that the Spirit lives with our own human spirit, which can still commit grievous sins that bring deep grief and hurt to the Holy Spirit, but not His departure (see Ephesians 4:30).

A second response to that objection is that demons need not be conceived as dwelling in the same place and in the same way as the Holy Spirit. Even in cases where a demon takes control of a person's body and uses it to express his own will, the demon need not be seen as residing in the very center of the person. Bible commentator Franz Delitzsch describes how demonization simply involves demons intruding themselves between the person's own spirit and body and taking over the person's nervous system in order to express demonic actions, thereby limiting the person's expression of his or her real self.[39]

Examining the Possibilities

According to Scripture, the Holy Spirit comes into the very core of the believer—namely, his heart (Galatians 4:6). Thus any demonic invasion is not a residence at the same depth as the Holy Spirit. In addition, because the Holy Spirit lives in the heart, He will always have the most power over the believer—for it is out of the heart that life is lived (Proverbs 4:23).

The question, then, is this: How far can a believer—even with the Holy Spirit's presence in his heart—allow sin to dominate his life . . . his thoughts and actions? We know both from Scripture and personal experience that the presence of the Holy Spirit does not prevent a believer from sinning. In fact, it is difficult to draw a line at what sin or depth of sin a believer is not permitted to go—short of the sin of apostasy or the radical rejection of Christ from the heart. What we do know is that believers can allow sinful practices to dominate their lives. If we accept the possibility that a believer might actually take his own life, that would seem to be an ultimate domination by sin. There are many kinds of addictions—including those of alcoholism and drugs—that have on occasion exerted strong power over believers' lives. That would seem to allow the possibility that a believer could sinfully relinquish control over his life to the power of sin in various forms.

Could this not also include the possibility of control by an evil spirit—control exercised from within the body in some way? As we have seen, that which is demonic generally is related to our own sinful flesh. By our own fleshly actions we can "give place to the devil," and allow him to exert his influence and take advantage of us.

As for the devil working inside us, it's difficult to limit a spirit to some specific locality within us. We do know he can put thoughts in our minds. That seems to involve an inward action, although it might be argued that this is different than residency. Perhaps more to the point is the matter of false prophecy or other forms of speech that are demonically inspired. In 1 Corinthians 12:3, Paul warns, "No one who is speaking by the Spirit of God says, 'Jesus be cursed,' and no one can say, 'Jesus is Lord,' except by the Holy Spirit." Although some Bible interpreters reject the possibility that believers could actually say, "Jesus be cursed," many see this as most likely what had taken place at Corinth.

Ellis explains this possibility by looking at the practice of prophetic speech—that is, speech that was conveyed through a human being and inspired by an outside spirit:

> Both assertions refer to pneumatic, i.e., "prophetic" utterances and apparently presuppose that a pneumatic person may give voice to at least two kinds of spirits, evil and good. The charism of "discernment [διακρίσεις] of spirits," which is mentioned a few verses later (1 Corinthians 12:10), probably is to be understood within this context. That is, the plural refers (at least) to a good and an evil spirit. This interpretation finds a measure of support in Thessalonians, where, with reference to manifestations of the Spirit, Paul instructs his readers to test all things (πάντα δοκιμάζετε, 1 Thessalonians 5:12) and to disregard any prophecy through a spirit (διὰ πνεύματο) that the day of the Lord has come (2 Thessalonians 2:2).[40]

The possibility that 1 Corinthians 12:3 refers to demonic inspiration is also expressed by James Dunn:

> We may assume from the implied rebuke of 12:2 that this frequently involved the assembly (or certain members) working themselves up into a state of spiritual excitement, leaving themselves open to passions and power (spirits?) which swept them away . . . in an outpouring of glossalalic ecstasy. . . .[41]

Similarly, Aust and Müller state:

> In 1 Corinthians 12:3 the issue is to distinguish between ecstasy which is the work of the Spirit of God and ecstasy which issues from demonic influence. Persons in ecstacy who pronounce the *anathema* on Jesus, who in uttering the ban deliver Jesus to annihilation by God, cannot possibly speak by the Holy Spirit. Such persons have become the mouth and instrument of demonic powers.[42]

All that should make us cautious about seeking spiritual power or experience. If demonic activity is present within the church in 1 Corinthians 12:3, how much more would it seem possible to be present in the case of believers who deliberately get involved in occultic practices?

Our entire discussion of Satan's attack upon believers has demonstrated that this attack from personal evil spirits is usually related to the sins that stem from the evil desires of our own flesh. Satan takes advantage of our weak, sinful flesh to push his influence over us. Thus yielding to the flesh is also yielding to the influence of Satan and his demons. That such influence can reach the point of enslavement is also taught in Scripture. Yet *how* he does this is not fully clear to us.

Correctly Responding to Satanic Attacks

Repenting of Our Sins

If we find that we have succumbed to Satan's influence, our first response has to be repentance, as Paul indicated in 2 Timothy 2:25,26: "If perhaps God may grant them repentance leading to the knowledge of the truth, and they may come to their senses and escape from the snare of the devil, having been held captive by him to do his will" (NASB). This may require the help of another person (as described in Neil's book *Helping Others Find Freedom in Christ*). An unrepentant person is like a house in which the garbage has piled up for months. That is going to attract a lot of flies. The primary answer, however, is not to get rid of the flies, but rather, the garbage. It's not necessary for us to study the flight patterns of the flies, or determine their names and rank structure. The answer has and always will be repentance and faith in God.

Taking a Stand in the Faith

When we're faced with satanic attacks, the critical issue is our relationship with God. Once that is established, we can stand against the evil one. "Submit yourselves, then, to God: Resist the devil, and he will flee from you" (James 4:7). "Be self-controlled and alert. Your enemy the devil prowls around like a roaring lion looking for someone to devour. Resist him, standing firm in the faith" (1 Peter 5:8,9). The Greek word for "resist" in both verses is literally "stand against." We are to take our stand in Christ against the devil and his demons.

Standing firm in the faith (1 Peter 5:9) is not so much a matter of holding to true doctrine, but rather, it's more of "personal or communal commitment."[43] "A flint-like resolution is what he calls for here."[44] There is no place for passivity in the Christ walk. We must actively take our place in Christ.

You cannot passively put on the armor of God:

> Therefore *put on* the full armor of God, so that when the day of evil comes, you may be able to stand your ground, and after you have done everything, to stand. Stand firm then, with the belt of truth buckled around your waist, with the breastplate of righteousness in place, and with your feet fitted with the readiness that comes from the gospel of peace (Ephesians 6:13-15, emphasis added).

Putting on the armor of light (Romans 13:12) is the same as putting on the Lord Jesus Christ (Romans 13:14). The only sanctuary we have is "in Christ." Commenting on James 4:7, Peter Davids says, "To resist the devil is to commit oneself to follow God or to draw near."[45]

Choosing the Truth

Choosing the truth is our first line of defense; therefore, "we take captive every thought to make it obedient to Christ" (2 Corinthians 10:5). We're not supposed to try to analyze whether a thought came from the television set, another person, our own memories, or from the pit. We are to take "every thought" captive. Does that mean we should rebuke every negative thought? No, because we'll find ourselves doing that for the rest of our lives. Instead, we are to overcome the father of lies by choosing the truth. We are not called to dispel the darkness; we are called to turn on the light.

Making Ourselves Humble

Commitment to God means making ourselves low before Him. Both James 4:6 and 1 Peter 5:5 say, "God opposes the proud but gives grace to the humble." Humility is confidence properly placed. Like Paul, we should "put no confidence in the flesh" (Philippians 3:3). Rather, we should place all our confidence in God. Pride makes us vulnerable to the devil; it is his own sin. English preacher Thomas Brooks said:

> Humility keeps the soul free from many darts of Satan's casting, and snares of his spreading; as the low shrubs are free from many violent gusts and blasts of wind, which shake and rend the taller trees. The devil hath least power to fasten a temptation on him that is most humble. He that hath a gracious measure of humility, is neither affected with Satan's proffers nor terrified with his threatenings.[46]

The exhortation that we are to merely *resist* the devil means that we should not be out looking for him to engage him in hostile action. We should never let the devil set the agenda. The Holy Spirit is our guide, not the devil. Yet at the same time, we should "be self-controlled and alert" (1 Peter 5:8). We are to be aware of Satan's schemes (2 Corinthians 2:11). Ignorance is not bliss, it is defeat.

Arming Ourselves with Spiritual Weapons

Spiritual warfare against a spiritual foe requires spiritual weapons. Paul says, "The weapons we fight with are not the weapons of the world. On the contrary, they have divine power to demolish strongholds" (2 Corinthians 10:4). Elsewhere we are told to "put on the full armor of God" (Ephesians 6:11). The Lord himself used only spiritual weapons (that is, the Word of God) against the devil. We can stand against the power of Satan only by the power of the One who has overcome him—namely, Christ. Thus, abiding in Christ and walking by the Spirit are required for victory in spiritual warfare against the demonic enemy.

Spiritual warfare rests on immediate communion with God for fresh power. Thomas Brooks says, "Ah, souls! remember this, that your strength to stand and overcome must not be expected from graces received, but from the fresh and renewed influences of heaven."[47] At the same time that we are watchful, and resisting the devil, and fighting with spiritual weapons, we are to pray for God's help: "Lead us not into temptation, but deliver us from the evil one" (Matthew 6:13). Similarly, Paul concludes his words about standing against the enemy with God's armor by saying, "Pray in the Spirit on all occasions with all kinds of prayers and requests. With this in mind, be alert and always keep on praying for all the saints" (Ephesians 6:18). The grammatical structure of the original Greek text shows that the exhortations to "pray in the Spirit" [literally, "praying at all times in the Spirit"] and "keep alert" are connected to the main command to "stand firm" (verse 14).[48] Our standing firm is to be constantly undergirded by prayer and alertness.

Remembering That Victory Is Assured

We should be comforted in the knowledge that Satan's attacks have limitations. As Brooks puts it, "Satan must have a double leave before he can do anything against us. He must have leave from God, and leave from ourselves, before he can act anything against our happiness."[49] Satan can do only what God permits (see Job 1:11,12; 2:3-5; Luke 22:31), and "the battle is the LORD'S" (1 Samuel 17:47). It is not our personal battle. It is part of an ongoing war between good and evil. And we are led by the Unconquerable One, who has already won the decisive battle. Christ Himself said, "Take heart! I have overcome the world" (John 16:33). In praise, Paul exclaimed, "Thanks be to God! He gives us the victory through our Lord Jesus Christ" (1 Corinthians 15:57).

As we stand firm in our faith at the end of the twentieth century, we are standing with the church fathers who fought the same fight of faith. Writing to those who question the reality of the spiritual world, early church father Tertullian wrote:

> Mock as you like, but get the demons if you can to join in your mocking; let them deny that Christ is coming to judge every human soul. . . . Let them deny that, for their wickedness condemned already, they are kept for that very judgment day, with all their worshipers and their works. Why, all the authority and power we have over them is from naming the name of Christ, and recalling to their memory the woes with which God threatens them. . . . Fearing Christ in God, and God in Christ, they become subject to the servants of God and Christ. So at our touch and breathing, overwhelmed by the thought and realization of those judgment fires, they leave at our command the bodies they have entered, unwilling and distressed.[50]

18

The Suffering and Triumph in Sanctification

Truly, truly, I say to you, unless a grain of wheat falls into the earth and dies, it remains by itself alone; but if it dies, it bears much fruit.

—John 12:24 (NASB)

Practicing the Christian life begins with being a good steward of everything that God has entrusted to us, including our own lives. Of course, we can commit to God only what we know about ourselves, which is not everything there is to know. Paul says in 1 Corinthians 4:1-5:

> Let a man regard us in this manner, as servants of Christ, and stewards of the mysteries of God. In this case, moreover, it is required of stewards that one be found trustworthy. But to me it is a very small thing that I should be examined by you, or by any human court; in fact, I do not even examine myself. For I am conscious of nothing against myself, yet I am not by this acquitted; but the one who examines me is the Lord. Therefore do not go on passing judgment before the time, but wait until the Lord comes who will both bring to light the things hidden in

the darkness and disclose the motives of men's hearts; and then each man's praise will come to him from God (NASB).

This passage, which tells us that God will reveal our hearts at the final judgment on the Day of the Lord, clearly reveals that we don't have total knowledge of ourselves. In response to Paul's words, Professor Gerd Thiessen of the University of Heidelberg says:

> If the text is taken literally, it allows for the possibility of unconscious forces and impulses within us. . . . This exegesis has a long tradition. . . . Precisely the three basic elements within human beings are combined in this text: God's knowledge of the heart; the limited nature of human self-knowledge; and the significance of inner reality."[1]

Other Bible passages show that the revealing of our hearts takes place not only at the last day, but also in our present lives. The psalmist prayed, "Search me, O God, and know my heart; test me and know my anxious thoughts. See if there is any offensive way in me, and lead me in the way everlasting" (Psalm 139:23,24). A similar request is found in Psalm 26:2: "Test me, O LORD, and try me, examine my heart and my mind." David was asking God "to prove the state of his mind, and, if it be not as it appears to his consciousness, to make this clear to him. . . ."[2]

God also used His prophets to reveal the "secrets" of people's hearts (1 Corinthians 14:24,25). The effect of prophetic revelation, as Charles Hodge explains it, is that a person's "real character and moral state, with regard to which he was before ignorant, are made known to him."[3] Indeed the Word of God reveals people's hearts:

> The word of God is living and active. Sharper than any double-edged sword, it penetrates even to dividing soul and spirit, joints and marrow; it judges the thoughts and attitudes of the heart. Nothing in all creation is hidden from God's sight. Everything is uncovered and laid

bare before the eyes of him to whom we must give account
(Hebrews 4:12,13).

Christian maturity thus includes the process of God revealing to us unconscious thoughts or the unconscious contents
of the heart. Augustine spoke of God revealing the things of a
man's heart of which he is unconscious and unaware.[4] The early
church father Irenaeus referred to the Spirit revealing in a ben-
eficial way the hidden things of human hearts.[5]

Growth and Transparency

In the words of Thiessen, Scripture teaches "a conception of
an unconscious dimension within the human being. Within
this dimension lie not only repressed unconscious deeds but also
unconscious plans and motives."[6] With this in mind, you could
divide the Christian into four quadrants as follows (as we dis-
cuss this diagram, keep in mind that we are talking about character—that is *who* we are rather than what we do):

	You see	You don't see
I see	transparent self	pride
I don't see	blind spots	hidden self

In every one of us is a part that is totally transparent. That's
the part of our lives that we have knowledge of, and so does the
rest of the world. Then there is a part of us that we know but
don't want others to know. This is a conscious cover-up of ourselves. By way of illustration, let's suppose someone recognizes a
Hollywood celebrity as he steps into an elevator. The person
asks, "Are you the real (name)?" As the elevator doors close,
the celebrity responds, "Only when I'm alone."

Just as the celebrity has a hidden side that no one knows, we too have a hidden side. There are some things about ourselves we just don't want to share with others. What keeps us from being totally transparent people? Probably the fear of rejection, or perhaps pride is involved. Whatever the case, we usually try to project an image of ourselves that is not indicative of who we really are.

Our Christian growth will always be inhibited to the degree that we cover up who we really are. That's because we're allowing ourselves to become more concerned with how we look to other people rather than to God. God, however, calls us to "walk in the light as He Himself is in the light" (John 1:7 NASB), and He wants us to lay aside falsehood and speak the truth with our neighbors because we are members of one another (Ephesians 4:25). "Speaking the truth in love, we are to grow up in all aspects into Him, who is the head, even Christ" (Ephesians 4:15 NASB). Every Christian should make a conscious effort to live in this way in every area of his life; it is very disconcerting to see a saint function well in society and then find out he is a monster at home.

We are conscious of everything above the middle line in the diagram on page 361, but there are some things below the line that others know about us yet we aren't even aware of. These are our blind spots, and we all have them. It doesn't take much maturity for us to see the character defects in other people. But we are not supposed to judge other people's character; in fact, we are commanded not to. We are supposed to accept one another as Christ has accepted us (Romans 15:7). Nothing frees a person more for growth than the love and acceptance of others. However, *don't* confuse judgment with discipline. There is a difference: discipline is always based on observed behavior, whereas judgment is always related to character.

The last quadrant in the diagram is that which only God knows. He has total knowledge of us; He even knows how many hairs we have on our heads.

Now, let's tie all this together as it relates to Christian growth. Take a careful look at the following diagram.

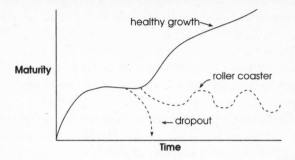

In 1 Corinthians 4:3-5, Paul said there are times when we can say, "It is a very small thing that I should be examined by you, or by any human court; in fact, I do not even examine myself. I am conscious of nothing against myself, yet I am not by this acquitted; but the one who examines me is the Lord."

Paul was saying that we shouldn't be concerned about what others think of us because the One who examines us is the Lord. Paul had already examined himself and knew of nothing against himself. To his knowledge, he had no unresolved conflicts. He had nothing more to confess, and there was nobody he needed to forgive or ask forgiveness of. Even in light of all that, he still said that he was "not by this acquitted." Although he had at that point reached a plateau in his Christian walk (as we all do at times), he knew he still hadn't arrived. These plateaus are the good times in the process of being sanctified. We don't feel convicted by anything, and our conscience is clean.

Growth and Suffering

No plateau, however, lasts forever. God has a way of letting us know that we are not yet qualified to be a member of the Trinity! Usually the way we interact with people reveals how stubborn and immature we really are. The Lord is clearly involved in reproving us: "Whom the LORD loves He reproves" (Proverbs 3:12 NASB). God can also reprove us when we study His Word: "All Scripture is inspired by God and profitable for teaching, for reproof, for correction, for training in righteousness" (2 Timothy 3:16 NASB). And, from the Old Testament wisdom literature we read, "He who regards reproof is prudent. . . . He who hates reproof will die" (Proverbs 15:5,10).

There are three basic responses to the reproofs of life. One option is to drop out, which is what most people do. They don't come to church because they don't want to hear the truth. They don't want to be convicted, nor do they want to change themselves or their lifestyles. So they stay away from anything that will make them feel guilty.

Another option is to hang in there but never grow up. This is the classic roller-coaster Christian. To this believer, God may appear to be saying, "You didn't learn from that experience, so I will have to take you through that situation again. You still didn't learn? I'll take you through the situation again. You still didn't learn? Through the situation again . . . and again . . . and again!"

What should we do when we find ourselves falling short of the glory of God? That brings us to our third option: When you come under conviction in the course of living, then own up to your "something less than Christlike character." When you realize that you reacted to someone impatiently or unkindly, admit it. Don't blame someone else or rationalize your attitude or behavior. Just walk in the light by agreeing with God that perfection has still eluded you. Admit what you did, apologize, ask for forgiveness, forgive or do whatever Scripture requires you to do, and most important of all, be honest with God and the people around you. A mistake is never a failure unless you fail to learn from it. Someone once said that to stumble and fall is not failure. Even if you stumble and fall again, that is not failure. Failure comes when you say you were pushed. In other words, the reproofs of life don't cause us to fail; rather, they just reveal who we really are.

God's Design in Suffering

Paul's attitude toward the trials and tribulations of life is seen in Romans 5:3-5:

> We also exult in our tribulations, knowing that tribulation brings about perseverance; and perseverance, proven character; and proven character, hope; and hope does not disappoint, because the love of God has been poured out within our hearts through the Holy Spirit who was given to us (NASB).

We have a God of hope, but unfortunately people have a tendency to say, "This job or ministry or marriage is hopeless," and they think the solution is to change jobs or ministries or spouses. What we should do instead is hang in there and grow up! There may be times when it is appropriate for us to change jobs or ministries, but if our motivation is to avoid our present trials and tribulations, then the change won't do us any good. Our problems will always follow us no matter where we go.

When we are faced with difficulties, our hope lies in proven character. God's intention is that we come through the trials and tribulations of life a better person than we were before. Nothing can keep us from becoming the person that God wants us to be!

The humble way of bringing about this kind of growth is to deny yourself, pick up your cross daily, and follow Him (Matthew 16:24); and the key is to do it daily. Let us illustrate: In Southern California, where we both have taught for a number of years, there are many earthquake faults. Most of them, like the renowned San Andreas Fault, run in a north-south direction below the surface of the earth. Because the earth's giant subterranean plates are moving slowly under the crust, we frequently have very minor quakes that reflect small adjustments being made along the affected fault lines. They usually shake up the population a little and remind us of God's sovereignty or our mortality, but they do very little damage. But in places where the fault lines refuse to adjust to the movements of the subterranean plates, a great amount of pressure is created. Eventually the pressure becomes so great that the fault snaps—thereby creating a large quake. Usually, the longer the pressure has built up, the bigger the earthquake can be.

Such is the case with us as Christians. God has no other plan for us more important than our sanctification. If we fail to grow over time, we may find ourselves brought against a major adjustment that God uses to get our attention. He may go so far as to sacrifice our career if we fail to conform to His image. The Lord was patient with David after he sinned with Bathsheba. God gave him at least nine months to own up to his sin. David was under heavy conviction, but he did not acknowledge his sin so the Lord spoke to him through a prophet. The end result? David lost the child he had with Bathsheba, and his sons slept with his wives on the rooftops of Israel. In hindsight, David's counsel to us is this: "I will instruct you and teach you in the way you should go; I will counsel you and watch over you. Do not be like the horse or the mule, which have no understanding but must be controlled by bit and bridle" (Psalm 32:8,9).

Though many of us may face major adjustments in life at one time or another, these adjustments aren't always easy to see. They're more obvious in extreme cases, such as a person who is struggling with alcohol. Let's say this person turned to alcohol as a means of coping with the pressures with life or dealing with pain. This stymies his spiritual growth, and along the way he finds that he needs more and more alcohol as his tolerance level increases. As his life continues to disintegrate, he refuses to admit he has a problem. Finally a big adjustment comes. God allows him to lose his health, his family, or his job. God knows it won't be enough just to get this person to stop drinking because his spiritual needs have become so great. He has overwhelming needs that only Christ can meet, and he needs to get back on the track of conforming to the image of God.

When Paul rebuked the Corinthians for their worldly behavior, he concluded by saying, "What do you prefer? Shall I come to you with a whip, or in love and with a gentle spirit?" (1 Corinthians 4:21). If you are a parent, wouldn't you prefer to discipline your children by talking to them rather than having to use a rod (Proverbs 22:15)? Good parents will not spare the rod if they have to, but most parents, like God, would prefer to discipline with love and a spirit of gentleness. When we ourselves need to be reproved, would we want God to use a rod or gently discipline us? The choice is ours.

The suffering we face as we grow from sin toward holiness is inevitable. Yet we can take comfort in knowing that one of the great themes of Scripture is glory through suffering. Jesus walked the path of suffering to glory, and so did His disciples. The apostle Paul knew that if he wanted to experience the power of Christ's resurrection as the dynamic force that transformed his life, then he had to endure "the fellowship of sharing in [Christ's] sufferings, becoming like him in his death" (Philippians 3:10). Paul said to the Colossian believers, "I fill up in my flesh what is still lacking in regard to Christ's afflictions" (1:24). He was saying that his sufferings were part of the measure of sufferings that must be endured en route to the final state of perfection. Every believer participates in this great drama of suffering that leads to glory.

Sanctification involves warfare, and warfare always means that we will suffer. Suffering, for the believer, is always related to the cosmic struggle between God and Satan. Yet we need not despair; we can have the same attitude as the apostles in the early church, who rejoiced "because they had been counted worthy of suffering disgrace for the Name" (Acts 5:41).

The Necessity of Suffering

There are many terms used in Scripture to talk about suffering—"affliction," "anguish," "distress," "grief," "misery," "pain," "tribulation," "chastisement," and so on. Various metaphors also depict suffering, including refining fire (Isaiah 48:10; 1 Peter 1:6,7), overflowing waters (Isaiah 43:2), and birth pangs (John 16:20-22; Romans 8:18-22). All of these come to us in the experience of suffering, which has been concisely and aptly defined by theologian J.I. Packer as "getting what you do not want while wanting what you do not get. . . ."[7] Such experience is the lot of all people in this life, and, according to Scripture, it plays a significant role in helping us to grow toward holiness.

The necessity of suffering is made clear to us in Scripture. We will share in the glory of Christ only if we "share in his sufferings" (Romans 8:17). "If we endure [in suffering (2 Timothy 2:9,10)], we will also reign with him" (2 Timothy 2:12). "For just as the sufferings of Christ flow over into our lives, so also through Christ our comfort overflows" (2 Corinthians 1:5).

Much of the suffering faced by believers is a result of living for Christ in a hostile world. "Trials" are destined to come "in spreading the gospel of Christ" (1 Thessalonians 3:2,3). The various trials that bring suffering as a Christian should not be surprising or thought "as something strange" (1 Peter 4:12). Acts 4:22 tells us, "We must go through many hardships to enter the kingdom of God."

As we have already seen, suffering can come in the form of chastisement from God when we're involved in sin. When David sinned, he felt the heavy hand of God in physical and mental suffering (Psalm 32:3-5). Even apart from sin, our Father will put us through discipline in order to help us grow. Christ, even though He was sinless, was nevertheless perfected through suffering (Hebrews 2:9,10; see also 5:8).

Finally, suffering can come simply from our human frailty as part of a fallen world. One Bible commentator says that when Paul spoke about the decaying of the "outer man" and the accompanying afflictions, he was referring to his moral existence in the present life "subject to a thousand troubles and under sentence of death."[8] One of the more profound sufferings of this kind is the pain of broken love. Bonds of intimacies, if not broken through sin, are surely broken through death.

Despite our natural aversion to suffering, Scripture tells us that we can expect it and, in fact, it is a necessity for spiritual growth. In the words of J.I. Packer, "suffering Christianly is an integral aspect of biblical holiness, and a regular part of business as usual for the believer."[9]

The Value of Suffering

Suffering Motivates Change

Physical pain is a necessary warning signal. As one physician states, "Pain is a sign that action should be taken; it implies that if action is not taken, the survival chances of the organism are going to decrease."[10] Even lack of proper bodily nourishment is felt as pain. Similarly, pain (or suffering) in the Christian life can be a sign of spiritual sickness and serve as a warning that further deterioration is inevitable unless something is changed. God may allow suffering to motivate us to change, as C.S. Lewis's well-known statement suggests: "God whispers to us in our pleasures, speaks in our conscience, but shouts in our pains."[11]

Sometimes it takes great suffering to get our attention. "Small trials often make us *beside* ourselves, but great trials bring us again back *to* ourselves." Such was the case of the prodigal son. It was only after he ran out of food and said, "I am starving to death!" that he "came to his senses [literally, to himself]" and repented and returned to his father (Luke 15:17-20).

Suffering Builds Righteous Character

That suffering is necessary for building character is one of the clearest truths of both life and Scripture. Jesus Himself is the greatest example. Apart from the suffering He endured to pay the consequences of our sin, He knew suffering that helped produce something in His own life. He was made perfect through suffering (Hebrews 2:9,10), and "he learned obedience from what he suffered" (5:8). These statements do not suggest that Christ was in some way disobedient or sinful. Rather, the growth He knew through suffering was a growth from immaturity to maturity. His experience made Him a compassionate High Priest who could identify with and come to the aid of suffering people (Hebrews 4:15,16). Suffering also taught Christ the fullness of what it meant to obey and determine to follow His Father's will, no matter how high the cost. Jesus, as a human being, had to learn the chain of moral values that develop as a result of adversity: "We know that suffering produces perseverance; perseverance, character; and character, hope" (Romans 5:3,4). If it was "fitting that God . . . should make the author of [our] salvation perfect through suffering" (Hebrews 2:10), how much more fitting it is that He should perfect us through suffering. Hebrews 12:10,11 tells us:

> Our fathers disciplined us for a little while as they thought best; but God disciplines us for our good, that we may share in his holiness. No discipline seems pleasant at the time, but painful. Later on, however, it produces a harvest of righteousness and peace for those who have been trained by it.

All godly human character is somehow summed up in love, according to Paul's description of love in 1 Corinthians 13. And love flows only from those who have died to self-centeredness and live for others. When we put to death the old self, we'll feel pain. The old self does not die easy, and there is no painless way to die to ourselves. Growth in true character, which is the expression of love, inevitably entails suffering. C.S. Lewis said that "to render back the will which we have so long claimed for our own, is in itself, wherever and however it is done, a grievous pain."[12]

Suffering Draws Us to God

Complete holiness—which is the same as complete humanness and fullness of life—is to love God Himself with all our heart. Our love of God, however, is often tinted with our love of the good things that He gives us. Suffering helps to strip away any pretense in our relationship with God. It weans us from all that is not God so that we might learn to love Him for who He is and not for what He gives us.

Augustine said, "God wants to give us something, but cannot, because our hands are full—there's nowhere for Him to put it." Suffering empties our hands so that God can give us Himself, the true treasure of life. C.S. Lewis said:

Now God, who has made us, knows what we are and that our happiness lies in Him. Yet we will not seek it in Him as long as He leaves us any other resort where it can even plausibly be looked for. While what we call "our own life" remains agreeable, you will not surrender it to Him. What then can God do in our interest but make "our own life" less agreeable to us, and take away the plausible sources of false happiness?[13]

Suffering Helps Us Understand God

We live in a world of moral conflict. The battle between good and evil, which is the story of biblical history, reveals that evil has brought a suffering that even God shares. He suffers because of what sin has done to His creation. Isaiah said that God also suffers in the suffering of His people: "In all their distress he too was distressed" (63:9). This reality of evil and the true nature of God's love for us would not be known except through the experience of suffering: ". . . the only way in which moral evil can enter into the consciousness of the morally good, is as suffering."[14] Lewis says, "A bad man, happy, is a man without the least inkling that his actions do not 'answer,' that they are not in accord with the laws of the universe."[15]

Suffering Promotes Ministry and Unity

Whether our suffering is physical pain, poverty, or spiritual turmoil, all of these provide opportunities for us to minister to each other and not only to give blessing, but also to receive blessing through service (see, for example, 2 Corinthians 1:5-7, where suffering provides the opportunity to minister comfort). Such ministry serves to bring people together and promotes unity among believers, which, as we have seen, is the goal of sanctification. Suffering also has a way of binding people together; that is, shared suffering creates community bonding as perhaps little else can.

Our suffering can also serve God in ways that we will never know in this life. For example, nowhere in the book of

Job do we see that Job ever knew exactly why he suffered. But from our viewpoint, knowing the entire story, we know that his suffering brought glory to God. Our suffering can also provide us an opportunity to let other people see God's sustaining grace in our own lives. Both believers and unbelievers who see God's sustenance may end up being drawn closer to God. Perhaps you have heard about doctors or nurses whose lives were touched by godly patients who held up well under suffering and faced death without fear.

Our Response to Suffering

Suffering is inevitable. It may come from the antagonism and hostility of the anti-Christian world around us. If we are Christ's disciples, we can expect to be persecuted: "If they persecuted me, they will persecute you also" (John 15:20). Thus Peter tells the suffering church of his day, "Do not be surprised at the painful trial you are suffering, as though something strange were happening to you" (1 Peter 4:12).

We live in a world that is conditioned by sin. The creation from God's good hand was a creation of order and harmony. All the elements of the material and spiritual worlds were in proper relationship. But sin has infected every realm with disorder and improper relationships, and physical, emotional, and spiritual pain are the result. Thus we can expect pain in all three realms.

Three Key Truths

Scripture tells us that we cannot escape from suffering in this life. "In fact, everyone who wants to live a godly life in Christ Jesus will be persecuted" (2 Timothy 3:12). The proper response for us, then, is to let suffering work toward our sanctification. We must always view suffering in the light of our loving heavenly Father. That is made possible when we keep in mind three key truths about suffering:

1. *God is always in control of our suffering.* No matter what the source of our suffering—whether directly from God's discipline, or from the hand of another person, or simply from the

evil that is part of the fallen world—it is all under the control of God. In His omniscient wisdom and infinite love, He allows suffering to come our way for His ultimate glory. He allows suffering either for our own transformation or so that He can glorify Himself before other people. Peter Kreeft suggests some possibilities that we may find helpful to keep in mind when we suffer:

> Perhaps we suffer so inordinately because God loves us so inordinately and is taming us. Perhaps the reason why we are sharing in a suffering we do not understand is because we are the objects of a love we do not understand. . . . Perhaps we are even becoming more real by sharing in sufferings that are the sufferings of God, both on earth, as part of Christ's work of salvation, and in heaven, as part of the eternal life of the Trinity, which is the ecstatic death to self that is the essence of both suffering and joy.[16]

We may never know fully the reasons for all the sufferings we endure in this life. But when we recognize that God can use our suffering for our good or His, we then can let suffering contribute to our growth and ultimately to God's perfect glory.

2. God always has a limit on the amount of suffering He allows for each of us. Just as God clearly set limits on the suffering that Satan could bring to Job, so also does He set limits for our suffering. Some saints obviously have broader shoulders that enable them to suffer more for righteousness' sake, such as Job and Paul.

When we suffer, we're usually tempted to respond either in despondency and say, "God has forsaken me and there is no hope," or in anger and say, "God, I hate you for letting this happen, so forget You! I'm going to go my own way from now on."

But our heavenly Father assures us that He will allow no suffering that we cannot bear.

No temptation [or "testing," "trial"] has seized you except what is common to man. And God is faithful; he will not let you be tempted beyond what you can bear [or, "beyond your strength"]. But when you are tempted, he will also provide a way out so that you can [or, "have strength to"] stand up under it (1 Corinthians 10:13).

This promise assures us that God places a limit on our suffering. He knows how much we can bear in each circumstance. He knows the strengths and weaknesses in every area of our life— bodily, emotionally, and spiritually—and says that He will not allow any suffering on any occasion that we cannot handle with His grace. Thus we can be confident that the will of God will never take us where the grace of God will not sustain us.

3. *God will always provide "a way out" so that we can "stand up under" our suffering.* The phrase "stand up under" tells us that God doesn't simply bring about an immediate cessation of the sufferings. What we *can* count on is that God will give us the grace we need to stand under our suffering until it is removed. It is our trust in God's faithfulness and His promise of a way out that gives us the strength to endure suffering.

Nowhere in Scripture are we ever promised that God will keep us from all suffering or remove it quickly when it comes. Rather, He promises to provide grace that enables us to faithfully endure in it. The psalmist did not say, "Cast your cares on the Lord and go free from care," but rather, "Cast your cares on the LORD and he *will sustain you*" (55:22). Similarly, Paul does not tell us that the causes of our anxieties will be removed, but that in their midst we can be garrisoned with God's peace (Philippians 4:6,7). When Paul was in prison and on trial, he testified that "the Lord stood at [his] side and gave [him] strength" (2 Timothy 4:17).

A Key Promise

God's comfort is also made available to us in our sufferings. He is "the Father of compassion and the God of all comfort, who comforts us in all our troubles" (2 Corinthians 1:3,4). The Greek word for "comfort" may also be translated "encouragement." It is used herein in its basic sense of "standing beside a person to encourage him when he is undergoing severe testing."[17] The present tense of the verb tells us that our God comforts us at *all* times, constantly and unfailingly in *all* of our sufferings. Consider these words from the hymn "Be Still, My Soul":

> Be still, my soul: The Lord is on thy side;
> Bear patiently the cross of grief or pain;
> Leave to thy God to order and provide;
> In every change He faithful will remain.
> Be still, my soul: the best thy heavenly Friend
> Thro' thorny ways leads to a joyful end.

Rejoicing in Our Sufferings

James gives us one of Scripture's most profound statements about suffering, which is often difficult to obey: "Consider it pure joy, my brothers, whenever you face trials of many kinds" (James 1:2). Now, the idea of joy as a result of trials and suffering is not unique to this verse. In Romans 5:3, Paul says, "We also rejoice in our sufferings." Similarly, Peter says, "Rejoice that you participate in the sufferings of Christ, so that you may be overjoyed when his glory is revealed" (1 Peter 4:13). All of those verses share something of Jesus' pronouncement of a state of blessedness on the poor, the mourning, the hungry, and the persecuted (Matthew 5:3,4,6,10-12).

It's important to recognize that we are to express joy or experience blessedness in trials—not because of the suffering itself, but because of the outcomes usually associated with suffering. For example, the various sufferings endured by the listeners of Jesus' beatitudes shows that they are rightly related to God and thus can know the joy that comes from being a part of God's eternal kingdom. This makes them "blessed" even in the midst of their suffering. In 1 Peter 4:13, Peter spoke of having joy in our present sufferings with the knowledge that even greater joy is in store for us in the future.

Joy in trials is possible because we are to know that "the testing of [our] faith develops perseverance." Knowing this, we are to let "perseverance . . . finish its work so that [we] may be mature and complete, not lacking anything (James 1:3,4; *see also* Romans 5:3). Peter tells us that trials produce a genuine faith like gold from a refiner's fire, which will result "in praise, glory and honor when Jesus Christ is revealed" (1 Peter 1:6,7).

For us to know joy in our suffering, we must have an appreciation and even gratitude for what God is doing. John White says:

> You must thank God in the midst of your pain. Tell Him you trust Him. Praise Him for what He can do, for what He is doing. As you do so pressures will lift. You will be given a garment of praise to replace a spirit of heaviness."[18]

We can sense a deep joy in the midst of our trials not only because we know that they are helping produce godly characteristics within us, but also because we know that God's power is at work in us. Notice what Paul said about God's power in relation to the thorn in his flesh:

> I will boast all the more gladly about my weaknesses, so that Christ's power may rest on me. That is why, for Christ's sake, I delight in weaknesses, in insults, in hardships, in persecutions, in difficulties. For when I am weak, then I am strong (2 Corinthians 12:9,10).

Paul was not rejoicing over his sufferings in the sense that he was seeking more. Rather, he was rejoicing because he knew that through his sufferings, God's power was on display. Sufferings reveal our weaknesses, and thus are opportunities for God to display His sustaining strength and comfort.

It goes without saying that we cannot find joy in the midst of trials unless we have hope. Paul, Peter, and James all indicated that joy can be present in our trials because we have the promise of future glory. The right attitude in suffering, then, is to focus on the hope that is before us.

Some people think that hope is wishful thinking. In actuality, it is the present assurance of some future good. Even though we live in a valley of tears, we can have hope because we know this is not the end. There is a new day coming for the Christian—a day that is described as fullness of joy, where there will be "no more death or mourning or crying or pain, for the old order of things [with its trials and sufferings] has passed away" (Revelation 21:4).

It is suffering itself that helps us to cultivate a perspective of hope, which is so very useful in the midst of suffering. Let me (Robert) illustrate: Several years ago my wife Nancy and I lost our youngest daughter. I remember it vividly. With no indication of any health problems, she suddenly collapsed and died of heart failure when she was only 28 years old. As Neil put it to me one day, it was like being hit with a .45 slug. If I had seen this happen to another family, I would have said to myself, as I had on several occasions, "I don't think I could take it if that happened to me." But now it had happened to me, and God's grace was sufficient. Against the darkness of the suffering, the light of the hope that Scripture offered me was almost tangible. Heaven became more real to me with a reality that I'm sorry to say was not there before. And that hope has continued to shape my life ever since. Yes, there was pain in my heart, but in the depth of that pain I also found a certain sweetness of joy, which I know was brought there by God as a result of meditating on the hope that He offers to all believers. God truly does prepare a table of blessing for us even in the midst of our enemies (see Psalm 23:5).

In Romans 5, Paul presents this twofold connection of hope in relation to our suffering. Because of salvation in Christ he declares, ". . . we rejoice in the hope of the glory of God" (verse 2). As believers we are armed with hope as we enter trials and suffering. But then Paul goes on to say, "Not only so, but we also rejoice in our sufferings, because we know that suffering produces perseverance; perseverance, character; and character, hope" (verses 3,4). Hope thus not only undergirds our steadfastness in trials and enables joy, but it is also strengthened by such trials. As John Murray says, "We glory in tribulations because they have an eschatological orientation— they subserve the interest of hope."[19] We can more easily accept the sufferings that come our way if we understand they serve a purpose and if we know that God will make everything right in the end.

When Suffering Comes

What would you do if for some reason you could no longer sense God's presence, and for some reason He suspended His visible blessings in your life? What would you do if, in the course of faithfully following God, all your external circumstances suddenly turned sour? Job was enjoying the benefits of living righteously, then one day all that he had was taken away. Health, wealth, and even his family were taken from him. If we were in Job's circumstances, our minds would spin with questions: What did I do to deserve this? Did I miss a turn in the road? Is this what I get for living a righteous life? Where is God? God, why are you doing this to me? Like Job, you would be tempted to curse the day you were born.

That has happened twice to me (Neil) and my family. If we had not known the truth shared in Isaiah 50:10,11, I'm not sure we would have survived those trials:

> Who is among you that fears the LORD, that obeys the voice of His servant, that walks in darkness and has no light? Let him trust in the name of the LORD, and rely on his God. Behold, all you who kindle a fire, who encircle yourselves with firebrands, walk in the light of your fire, and among the brands you have set ablaze. This you will have from My hand, and you will lie down in torment (NASB).

In that passage, Isaiah was talking about a believer who obeys God yet walks in darkness. He was not talking about the darkness of sin, nor even the kingdom of darkness. Rather, he was talking about the darkness of uncertainty—a blanket of heaviness that settles in as though a black cloud has drifted over a believer's very being. The assurance of yesterday has been blanketed by the uncertainties of tomorrow. God has suspended His conscious blessings. Even attending church may be a dismal experience. Friends may have become more of a bother than a blessing.

What should we do when we find ourselves in such oppressive circumstances?

Keep on Walking

First, keep on walking by faith in the light of God's previous revelation. This light comes from God, and it helps us to see the next step, to see that the path ahead is clear. That light helps us to discern a friend from an enemy and determine where the obstacles are. Even though our natural instincts tell us to drop out, sit down, or stop, we are told by Isaiah to keep on walking. Never doubt in darkness what God has already clearly shown you in the light.

That brings me (Neil) to the first period of darkness for my family.[20] When I was a pastor, our church became involved in an exciting building program. God had clearly guided us to a new property, and enabled us to build new facilities. Within months after those buildings were completed, I was nearing the completion of my doctoral studies, and facing the major task of writing a dissertation. I also knew that my seminary education was not quite complete.

Sensing God's release, I resigned from the pastorate and began one of the most difficult years of my education. In one year I completed 43 semester units (17 of those units were Greek and Hebrew), took my comprehensive exams, completed my research, and wrote my dissertation. During that year I also taught part-time at Talbot School of Theology. We started that year with the assurance that $20,000 would be made available to us as an interest-free loan. I was confident that everything would work out, and that upon completing my education, God would have a place for us in His kingdom plans. For the next six months all our life's plans were going well, and then God turned out the light.

We were told that the second half of the $20,000 loan would not be coming to us. Having no other source of income, our cupboards became bare. I had no job, and at that time, my educational goals were only half completed. I had always endeavored to faithfully care for my family, but now I was on the brink of not being able to do so. I had been so certain of God's calling six months earlier, but now my confidence was being shaken.

I looked into a couple of ministry opportunities, but they weren't for me, and I knew I couldn't accept them. The problem wasn't an unwillingness to work; I would have sold hotdogs to provide for my family. Yet I knew I had to wait upon God's will. The tension to create my own light during that time was overwhelming. It was as though God had dropped me into a funnel, and things became darker and darker as I descended. When I thought my circumstances couldn't get much darker, I hit the narrow part of the funnel. At our darkest hour, God dropped us out of the bottom of that funnel, and everything became clear.

Nothing changed circumstantially, but everything changed internally. I woke up in the middle of one night with such a sense of joy and peace that I knew the trial was over. I had a conscious awareness of God in a remarkable way. There were no audible voices or visions, only God in His quite and gentle way renewing my mind. The thoughts He brought to my mind went something like this: "Neil, do you walk by faith, or do you walk by sight? Can you walk by faith now? You believed Me last summer; do you believe Me now? Neil, do you love Me, or do you love My blessings? Do you worship Me for who I am, or do you worship Me for the blessings I bring? Even if I suspend my conscious presence in your life, will you still believe in Me?"

I knew I could. In my spirit I responded, "Lord, you know I love You, and I walk by faith, not by sight. Lord, I worship You because of who You are, and I know that You will never leave me nor forsake me. Forgive me, Lord, that I ever doubted Your place in my life or questioned Your ability to provide all our needs."

Such precious moments can't be planned or predicted. They're never repeatable. What we have previously learned from the Bible becomes incarnate during such times. Our worship is purified, and our love is clarified. Faith moves from a textbook definition to a living reality. Trust is deepened when God puts us in a position where we have no other choice but to trust. We will either trust Him or compromise our faith. The Bible gives us the infallible rules of faith and gives us knowledge about the One in whom we should place our faith—but we still have to learn to live by faith in the arena of life. That's especially true when our circumstances are not working favorably for us.

On the very next day, the dean at Talbot School of Theology called to ask if I had taken another job position elsewhere. I had not, and that Friday afternoon he offered me the faculty position I had formerly held for over ten years. That same evening, a man from my previous ministry visited us. I half-jokingly asked him if he'd like to buy our house and he said, "Maybe I would." The next Tuesday, he and his parents made an offer on our house, which we accepted. Our financial crisis was over with, and with my faculty position secured, we knew the destination of our next move.

God can change in a moment what circumstances can never change. That's one reason my wife and I have committed ourselves to never making a major decision when we are down. That commitment alone has kept me from resigning from my ministry after facing difficult board meetings or preaching messages that bombed.

Again, we should never doubt in darkness what God has clearly shown us in the light. We are to keep on walking in the light of God's previous revelation. If what He showed me was true six months ago, it's still true today. If we are serious about our walk with God, He will test us to determine if we love Him or His blessings. He may purposely cloud our future so we will learn to walk by faith instead of by sight or feelings.

Walk in God's Light Only

Returning to what Isaiah said about handling oppressive circumstances, the second principle is that we're not to light our own fire. We're not to create our own light. The natural tendency when we don't see things God's way is to do things our way. But Isaiah said, "Behold, all you who kindle a fire, who encircle yourselves with firebrands, walk in the light of your fire." He wasn't talking about a fire of judgment; he was talking about a fire that creates light. Notice what happens when people create their own light: "Walk in the light of your fire and among the brands you have set ablaze. This you will have from my hand, you will lie down in torment." Go ahead: Do it your way. God will allow it; but misery will follow.

To illustrate, God called Abraham out of Ur into the Promised Land. In Genesis 12, God made a covenant promising Abraham that his descendants would be more numerous than the sands of the sea or the stars in the sky. Abraham lived his life in the light of that promise, then God turned out the light. So many months and years passed that Abraham's wife, Sarah, could no longer bear a child by natural means. God's guidance had been clear before, but now it looked like Abraham would have to assist God in the fulfillment of His promise. Abraham created his own light, and Sarah supplied the match by offering her handmaiden to Abraham. Because of that union, the whole world lives in torment. Jew and Arab have not been able to dwell together peacefully to this day.

We find yet another example in Moses. God superintended Moses' birth and provided for his preservation. Moses was raised in the home of Pharaoh, and was given the second most prominent position in Egypt. But God had put into Moses' heart a burden to set his fellow Israelites free. Impulsively Moses pulled out his sword, and God turned out the light. Abandoned to the back side of the desert, Moses spent 40 years tending his father-in-law's sheep. Then one day Moses turned aside to see a burning bush that wasn't being consumed, and God turned the light back on.

Now, I'm not suggesting that we may have to wait 40 years to come out the other end of a period of darkness. In the shorter lifespans of today, that would be more time than an average person's faith could endure. But it's possible that the darkness may last for weeks, months, and possibly even years. God is in charge, and He knows exactly how big a knothole He can pull us through. When we are stretched to our limit, He pulls us out the other side. We will never return to the shape we were before. In Isaiah 45:7, God tells us, "The One forming light and creating darkness, causing well-being and creating calamity; I am the LORD who does all these."

Our second period of darkness was far more difficult than the first. A number of years ago, my wife Joanne developed cataracts in both eyes and slowly lost her eyesight. In those days, doctors wouldn't do lens implants unless you were over 60 years old. So she had to be fitted with cataract glasses, and finally contacts. Five years later, she found out she could have implants because of improvements made in the materials used for implants. The surgery was successful, but Joanne awoke from the anesthetic emotionally disturbed. She became fearful and depressed. For months she went from doctor to doctor. Because she was 45 years old, most of the doctors wanted to make a head or hormone case out of her. She was neither. She was ill and was hospitalized five times, but we could not find the cause of her illness.

Our medical insurance coverage ran out, and we had to sell our house to pay the medical bills. I struggled with my role in Joanne's conflict. Was I her pastor, or counselor, and/or her husband? I decided there was only one role I could fulfill in her life, and that was to be her husband. If someone was going to restore my wife, it would have to be someone other than myself. My role was to hold her every day and say, "Joanne, someday this will pass." I thought her trial would end after a matter of weeks or months, but it turned into a long, 15-month ordeal. The funnel got narrower and darker. During these days, Isaiah 21:11,12 grew to have a great deal of meaning for me.

One keeps calling to me from Seir, "Watchman, how far gone is the night? Watchman, how far gone is the night?" The watchman says *"Morning comes* but also night" (NASB).

I base my ministry on the hope that "morning comes." No matter how dark the night, morning will come. And it's always darkest just before dawn.

In our darkest moment, when I wasn't even sure if Joanne was going to make it, we had a day of prayer at Biola University. I had nothing to do with the program other than setting aside special times for prayer in my own classes. Our undergraduate students had a communion service that evening. Normally I wouldn't have attended the service, but because work had detained me on campus I decided to participate. I sat on the gym floor with the students and took communion. I'm sure nobody in the student body was aware that I was going through one of the loneliest and darkest times of my life. However, I was deeply committed to doing God's will, and I was walking as best as I could in the light of previous revelation—even though I felt abandoned.

I can honestly say that during those months, I never once questioned God nor felt bitter about my circumstances. Somehow I knew that the nature of my ministry was related to what my family was going through, but I didn't know what to do about it. Should I back out of that ministry to spare my family? God was blessing my ministry, but not me. He had stripped me and Joanne of everything we owned. All we had left was each other and our relationship to God. And when there was no where else to turn, morning came!

God spoke to my heart in that communion service. His words didn't come by way of the pastor's message or the testimonies of the students, but in the context of taking communion. Guided by the Holy Spirit, my thoughts went something like this: "Neil, there's a price to pay for freedom. It cost My Son His life. Are you willing to pay the price?"

I responded, "Dear God if that's the reason, I'm willing, but if it's some stupid thing I'm doing, then I don't want to be a part of it anymore." I left the communion service with the inward assurance that our ordeal was over. Our circumstances hadn't changed, but in my heart I knew that morning had come.

Within a week, Joanne woke up one morning and said, "Neil, I slept soundly last night." Sixteen days previously she had visited a family doctor who specialized in treating clinical depression. He took Joanne off all the medication that had been prescribed by the other doctors and treated her chemical imbalance with proper nutrition and medication. From that point onward, she knew she was on the road to recovery. She never looked back, but continued on to regaining her full health. At the same time, our ministry took a quantum leap forward.

What was the purpose for all that? In God's ministry of darkness, you learn a lot about yourself. Whatever was left of my old nature's inclination to give hurting people simplistic advice such as, "Why don't you read your Bible?" or, "Just work harder" or, "Pray more" was mercifully stripped away. People going through dark times don't need pious platitudes. They need someone to wrap his or her arms around them and just be there.

In God's ministry of darkness, we learn compassion. We learn to wait patiently with people and weep with those who weep. We learn to respond to the emotional needs of people who have lost hope, knowing that the time for instruction will come later.

What Job needed in his hour of darkness was a few good friends who would just sit with him. Three of his so-called friends visited him for one week, and then their patience ran out. Joanne and I also had friends like that who tried to advise us in our time of darkness, and I can tell you, it hurts. The help that meant the most to us we received from certain people in our church—people who just stood by us and prayed. Though God had taken away all our external blessings, we still had some meaningful relationships, and as a result of our experience, we now have a greater appreciation for good friends. Finally, in the end, God replaced everything we had lost, only this time our blessings were far better in terms of home, family, and ministry. Be encouraged that God makes everything right in the end.

Another reason God allows times of darkness in our lives is to bring us to the end of our resources so that we may discover His. Unfortunately, we don't hear many sermons about brokenness in our churches these days. It's the great omission, and that's why we can't fulfill the great commission. In all four Gospels, Jesus taught us to deny ourselves, pick up our cross daily, and follow Him. When the time came for the Son of Man to be glorified, He said, "Truly, truly, I say to you, unless a grain of wheat falls into the earth and dies, it remains by itself alone; but if it dies, it bears much fruit" (John 12:24 NASB).

I don't know of any painless way to die to ourselves. But I do know that it's necessary, and that it's the best possible thing that could ever happen to us. Paul confirmed that when he said, "We who live are constantly being delivered over to death for Jesus' sake, that the life of Jesus also may be manifested in our mortal flesh" (2 Corinthians 4:11 NASB).

"No pain, no gain," says the bodybuilder. Is it also true in the spiritual realm? "No discipline seems pleasant at the time. Later on, however, it produces a harvest of righteousness and peace for those who have been trained by it" (Hebrews 12:11). Proven character comes from persevering through the tribulations of life.

Trust God Completely

The third point Isaiah makes in Isaiah 50:10,11 appears in verse 10: "Let him trust in the name of the LORD and rely on his God." Yet another reason that God allows us to walk in darkness is to help us learn to trust Him. Every great period of personal growth in my own life and ministry has always been preceded by a major time of testing.

Generally our times of testing will be followed by a time of reward or blessing. Yet we should be grateful for our trials not because of what we might receive in the end, but because they help to strengthen our character. In fact, possibly the greatest sign of spiritual maturity is the ability to postpone rewards. The ultimate test would be to receive nothing in this lifetime and wait to receive our reward in the life to come. Hebrews 11:13 talks about that in relation to many great Old Testament saints:

> All these died in faith, without receiving the promises, but having seen them and having welcomed them from a distance, and having confessed that they were strangers and exiles on this earth. For those who say such things make it clear that they are seeking a country of their own (NASB).

Verse 39 adds, "And all these, having gained approval through their faith, did not receive what was promised, because God had provided something better for us, so that apart from us they should not be made perfect" (NASB).

Growth and God's Reward

If I had known beforehand what my family would have to go through to get where we are today, I probably wouldn't have come this way. But looking back, we all say, "We're glad God took us down the paths that He did." God doesn't show us what's on the other side of the door for that reason. Remember, God makes everything right in the end, yet our reward may not be in this lifetime, as it wasn't for the heroes mentioned in Hebrews 11. I believe with all my heart that when our life on earth is done, all those who have remained faithful will say that the will of God is good, acceptable, and perfect (Romans 12:2).

Suffering is the crucible in which faith and confidence in God is developed. Suffering for the sake of righteousness is intended to make us into the people that God wants us to be. To remember the dark times when God stood by us and finally made a "way of escape" is a source of nourishment to continue in faith. In fact, Hebrews 10:32-39 encourages us to think back to previous times of suffering when we find ourselves entering difficult times:

> Remember those earlier days after you had received the light, when you stood your ground in a great contest in

the face of suffering. Sometimes you were publicly exposed to insult and persecution; at other times you stood side by side with those who were so treated. You sympathized with those in prison and joyfully accepted the confiscation of your property, because you know that you yourselves had better and lasting possessions.

So do not throw away your confidence; it will be richly rewarded. You need to persevere so that when you have done the will of God, you will receive what he has promised. For in just a very little while, "He who is coming will come and will not delay. But my righteous one will live by faith. And if he shrinks back, I will not be pleased with him." But we are not of those who shrink back and are destroyed, but of those who believe and are saved.

Indeed, we are those who willingly accept the Refiner's fire . . . so that we who are common may become holy.
Like Him.

NOTES

CHAPTER ONE

1. Although this reference describes the goal of the corporate community of believers, it obviously applies to each individual believer. Compare this with Colossians 1:28, where the apostle expresses a similar goal of maturity for each believer.

2. Thomas E. McComiskey, "קָדַשׁ; (qadash) be hallowed, holy, sanctified; to consecrate, sanctify, prepare, dedicate," *Theological Wordbook of the Old Testament*, vol. 2, edited by R. Laird Harris, Gleason L. Archer, Jr. and Bruce K. Waltke (Chicago: Moody Press, 1980), pp. 786-88.

3. That "holy" does not at the outset denote moral purity is evident in its use for those dedicated to pagan gods and religions. For example "shrine prostitute" in Deuteronomy 23:17 is literally "the holy one" (*see also* Genesis 38:21,22; 1 Kings 14:24; Hosea 4:14).

4. Eugene Peterson, *The Message* (Colorado Springs: NavPress, 1995), p. 663.

CHAPTER TWO

1. Neil T. Anderson, *Living Free in Christ* (Ventura, CA: Regal Books, 1993), pp. 56-58.

2. Georg Fohrer, "σώζω κτλ.," *Theological Dictionary of the New Testament*, edited by Gerhard Friedrich, vol. 7 (Grand Rapids: Eerdmans, 1971), p. 973.

3. Charles Hodge, *The Way of Life*, edited by Mark A. Noll (Mahwah, NJ: Paulist Press, 1987), pp. 217-18.

CHAPTER THREE

1. See the article by Karl Heinrich Rengstorf in the *Theological Dictionary of the New Testament*, vol. 1, edited by Gerhard Kittel (Grand Rapids: Eerdmans, 1964), pp. 327-28, and the commentary by George W. Knight, *The Pastoral Epistles* (Grand Rapids: Eerdmans, 1992), p. 101.

2. George W. Knight, *The Pastoral Epistles* (Grand Rapids: Eerdmans, 1992), p. 102.

3. Confrontation with the righteousness and holiness of God frequently brought deep acknowledgment of a person's own sinful condition. Peter's recognition of himself before the Lord as a "sinful man" is not uncommon among the saints (Luke 5:8, *see also* Genesis 18:27; Job 42:6; Isaiah 6:5; Daniel 9:4). Though the believer is sinful, Scripture does not seem to define his identity as a sinner.

4. Louis Berkhof, *Systematic Theology* (Grand Rapids: Eerdmans, 1941), p. 527.

5. Maximos the Confessor as paraphrased by John Meyendorff in *Christ in Eastern Christian Thought*, p. 210; cited by Michael C.D. McDaniel, "Salvation as Justification and *Theosis*," in *Salvation in Christ: A Lutheran-Orthodox Dialogue*, edited by John Meyendorff and Robert Tobias (Minneapolis: Augsburg Press, 1992), p. 80.

6. J.I. Packer, *Rediscovering Holiness* (Ann Arbor, MI: Servant Publications, 1992), p. 26.

7. Chris Brain and Robert Warren, "Why Revival Really Tarries—Holiness," *Renewal* (June 1991), p. 35; cited by J.I. Packer, *Rediscovering Holiness*, pp. 27-28.

8. Hodge, *The Way of Life*, p. 211.

CHAPTER FOUR

1. Horatius Bonar, *God's Way of Holiness* (New York: Robert Carter & Brothers, 1865), p. 23.

2. C. David Needham, *Alive for the First Time* (Sisters, OR: Multnomah Books, 1995), p. 34.

3. Christian Mauer, "ὑπόδικος," *Theological Dictionary of the New Testament*, vol. 8, edited by Gerhard Friedrich (Grand Rapids: Eerdmans, 1972), p. 558.

4. Bonar, *God's Way of Holiness*, p. 93.

5. The being "made righteous" in this verse may refer to the future final future ratification of the righteous standing of the believer. But whether present or future, our justification is always finally based on the obedience or righteousness of Christ and not our own works of obedience.

6. Bonar, *God's Way of Holiness*, pp. 56-57.

7. Neil Anderson, *Living Free in Christ* (Ventura, CA: Regal Books, 1993), pp. 39-40.

8. Bonar, *God's Way of Holiness*, pp. 69-70.

9. Ibid., p. 71.

10. Ibid.

11. See John Murray, "Definitive Sanctification" and "The Agency in Definitive Sanctification" in *Collected Writings of John Murray*, 2 vols. (Carlisle, PA: Banner of Truth Trust, 1977), 2:227-93.

12. Bonar, *God's Way of Holiness*, p. 52.

13. Ibid., p. 58.

CHAPTER FIVE

1. The other uses of ἄνωθεν (John 3:31; 19:11,23) all carry the meaning of "from above." John tends to describe man's birth in terms of its origin and not simply the idea of another birth. Birth is either from God (or the Spirit) or the flesh (*see* John 1:13; 1 John 2:29; 3:9; 4:7; 5:18).

2. E.K. Simpson and F.F. Bruce, *Commentary on the Epistles to the Ephesians and the Colossians* (Grand Rapids: Eerdmans, 1957), p. 273.

3. Colossians 3:11 begins with a Greek word that denotes "place." It is therefore easier to see the "new man" as the "new humanity," or the sphere of Christ in which all distinctions have been removed, rather than as the individual Christian or his new nature as in some translations (cf. NIV, RSV).

4. For the various meanings of the Greek term used, see D.G. James Dunn, *Romans 1-8*, Word Biblical Commentary, vol. 38A (Dallas: Word Books, 1988), p. 319.

5. Peter T. O'Brien, *Colossians, Philemon*, Word Biblical Commentary, vol. 44 (Waco, TX: Word Books, 1982), pp. 27-28.

6. According to Hans Wolff, "The most important word in the vocabulary of Old Testament anthropology is generally translated 'heart.'" *Anthropology of the Old Testament* (Philadelphia: Fortress, 1974), p. 40.

7. Bernard Ramm, *Offense to Reason: The Theology of Sin* (San Francisco: Harper & Row, 1985), p. 41.

8. Robert Jewett, *Paul's Anthropological Terms* (Leiden: E.J. Brill, 1971), p. 313. Compare also Laidlaw's description of the heart as "the workplace for the personal appropriation and assimilation of every influence" [John Laidlaw, *The Bible Doctrine of Man* (Edinburgh: T. & T. Clark, 1895), p. 122].

9. D.A. Carson, "Matthew," in *The Expositor's Bible Commentary*, edited by Frank E. Gaebelein, vol. 8 (Grand Rapids: Zondervan, 1984), p. 177.

10. O'Brien, *Colossians, Philemon*, p. 28.

11. Jewett, *Paul's Anthropological Terms*, pp. 322-23.

12. John Calvin, *Institutes of the Christian Religion*, II, iii, 6.

13. Franz Delitzsch, *A System of Biblical Psychology* (Grand Rapids: Baker, 1966, rpt.), p. 416.

14. J. Pedersen, *Israel: Its Life and Culture*, vol. 1-2 (London: Oxford University Press, rpt., 1973), p. 166.

15. D.G. James Dunn, "Romans 7:14-25 in the Theology of Paul," *Theologische Zeitschrift* (September/October 1975) 31:257-73.

16. For a brief sketch of this latter interpretation, see N.T. Wright, *The Climax of the Covenant* (Minneapolis: Fortress, 1992), pp. 196-200.

17. C.E.B. Cranfield, *A Critical and Exegetical Commentary on the Epistle to the Romans*, vol. 1 (Edinburgh: T. & T. Clark, 1975), pp. 358-59.

18. D.G. James Dunn, *Romans 1-8*, Word Biblical Commentary, vol. 38A (Dallas: Word Books, 1988), p. 389.

19. Delitzsch, *A System of Biblical Psychology*, p. 438; Delitzsch goes on to give a helpful description of the interaction between the believing ego opposed to sin and the power of sin. Referring to the sin of unchastity, he says sin "is possible only when the might of temptation succeeds either in over-mastering, or even in interesting, the Ego of the man. At times there are mingled in the range of man's thoughts impure thoughts which he acknowledges as not less thought by his Ego than the pure ones which it opposed to them in order to dislodge them. Sometimes temptation succeeds in drawing in the man's Ego into itself; but in the midst of the sinful act, the man draws it back from it, full of loathing for it. Sometimes, moreover, the Ego, in order to complete the sinful act unrestrainedly, is voluntarily absorbed into unconsciousness, and does not until after its completion return in horror to recollection of itself; and the spirit with shame becomes conscious of its having been veiled by its own responsibility."

20. J. Knox Chamblin, *Paul and the Self* (Grand Rapids: Baker, 1993), pp. 173-74.

21. Charles Hodge, *The Way of Life*, edited by Mark A. Noll (Mahwah, NJ: Paulist Press, 1987), pp. 211-12.

CHAPTER SIX

1. Some commentators understand the reference to "sin" in verse 8 to mean "sin nature," but the following statement about the need to confess "sins" (verse 9), however, suggests that the claim of no "sin" (verse 8) involves actual sins (cf. I. Howard Marshall, *The Epistles of John*, New International Commentary on the New Testament (Grand Rapids: Eerdmans, 1978), pp. 114-15.

2. John Calvin, *The Institutes of the Christian Religion*, III, iii, 10.

3. Ibid., III, iii, 11.

4. The Greek form (aorist participles) of the words translated "taken off" and "put on" may be used in an imperative sense, meaning that here Paul is exhorting the Colossian believers to "take off the old man" and "put on the new man."

5. The putting off and putting on in Ephesians 4:22-24 can also be interpreted like Romans 6:6 and Colossians 3:9,10 in the sense that these actions have already taken place in the past. The Greek infinitives translated "to put off" (verse 22) and "to put on" (verse 24) can be understood as "explanatory infinitives" expressing the content and result of that which the believers had been "taught" in the past (verse 21). Van Roon says, "For the believer the fact that he has rejected the old man and embraced the new man is a fact of reality. The aoristic infinitives in 4:22 and 24 give a secondary suggestion of instant accomplishment and characterize the action as having taken place in the past. They do not (indirectly) record a demand on the faithful. The sentence of 4:20-24 has the motivating force of an admonition but is not, in fact, either an admonition or a command. It is presumed in the sentence that when Christ was divulged to the addressees and they were taught about him, they became aware that they had put off the old man and put on the new man.

   "This act of having put aside the old man and put on the new is truth ἐν τῷ Ἰησοῦ only when people have been instructed 'as the truth is in Jesus' have they 'learned τὸν Χριστόν' in the right way. In 4:21 the author links to this ἐν τῷ Ἰησοῦ not only the proclamation of Christ but also the fact of having put off the old man and put on the new." A. Van Roon, *The Authenticity of Ephesians* (Leiden: E. J. Brill, 1974), p. 336; cf. also John Murray, *Principles of Conduct* (Grand Rapids: Eerdmans, 1957), pp. 214-19.

6. Andrew T. Lincoln, *Ephesians*, Word Biblical Commentary, vol. 42 (Dallas: Word Books, 1990), pp. 285-86.

7. Richard N. Longenecker, *Galatians*, Word Biblical Commentary, vol. 41 (Dallas: Word Books, 1990), p. 156.

8. D.G. James Dunn, *Romans 9–16*, Word Bible Commentary, vol. 38b (Dallas: Word Books, 1988), p. 791.

9. F.F. Bruce, *The Epistle to the Galatians*, The New International Greek Testament Commentary, (Grand Rapids: Eerdmans, 1982), p. 186.

10. Neil T. Anderson, *Victory Over the Darkness* (Ventura CA: Regal Books, 1990), pp. 45-47.

11. Werner Foerster, *Theological Dictionary of the New Testament*, edited by Gerhard Kittel (Grand Rapids: Eerdmans, 1964), pp. 379-80.

12. Lincoln, *Ephesians*, p. 59.

13. Ibid., p. 235.

14. Markus Barth, *Ephesians 4–6*, The Anchor Bible (Garden City, NY: Doubleday & Co., 1974), p. 454.

15. J. Behm, *Theological Dictionary of the New Testament*, vol. 4, edited by Gerhard Kittel (Grand Rapids: Eerdmans, 1967), p. 759.

16. Cited by Dunn, *Romans 9–16*, p. 712.

17. John Calvin, *Institutes of the Christian Religion*, III, iii, 20.

18. Glenn E. Hinson, "The Contemplative View," in *Christian Spirituality*, edited by Donald L. Alexander (Downers Grove, IL: InterVarsity Press, 1988), p. 177.

19. Henry Scougal, *The Life of God in the Soul of Man* (Philadelphia: Westminster Press, 1948), p. 49.

20. Peter Kreeft, *The God Who Loves You* (Ann Arbor, MI: Servant Books, 1988), p. 50.

21. Ibid., pp. 50-51.

22. Scougal, *The Life of God*, p. 38.

23. Kreeft, *The God Who Loves You*, pp. 140-41.

24. Ibid., p. 112.

25. Scougal, *The Life of God*, p. 38.

26. Ibid., p. 52.

CHAPTER SEVEN

1. Richard N. Longenecker, *Galatians*, Word Biblical Commentary, vol. 41 (Dallas: Word Books, 1990), p. 93.

2. Robert C. Tannehill, *Dying and Rising with Christ* (Berlin: Alfred Töpelmann, 1967), p. 19.

3. D.G. James Dunn, *Jesus and the Spirit* (Philadelphia: Westminster Press, 1975), p. 342.

4. F.F. Bruce, *1 & 2 Thessalonians*, Word Biblical Commentary, vol. 45 (Waco, TX: Word Books, 1982), p. 191.

5. Walter Bauer, *A Greek–English Lexicon of the New Testament and Other Early Christian Literature*, trans. W.F. Arndt and F.W. Gingrich, 2d ed. rev. and augmented by F.W. Gingrich and F.W. Danker from Bauer's 5th ed. (1958) (Chicago: University of Chicago Press, 1979), p. 421.

6. Moses Silva, *Philippians* (Grand Rapids: Baker Book House, 1992), p. 139.

7. Ibid., p. 202.

8. John Murray, *Redemption: Accomplished and Applied* (London: Banner of Truth, 1961), pp. 148-49.

9. In Andrew T. Lincoln, *Ephesians*, Word Biblical Commentary, vol. 42 (Dallas: Word Books, 1990), p. 116.

10. H. Wheeler Robinson, *The Christian Doctrine of Man* (Edinburgh: T. & T. Clark, 1926), p. 22.

11. Hans Wolff, *The Anthropology of the Old Testament* (Philadelphia: Fortress, 1974), p. 46.

12. *See also* Psalm 73:21,22; Proverbs 6:32; Hosea 4:11.

13. Wolff, *The Anthropology*, p. 47.

14. *See also* Proverbs 14:33; 16:21,23.

15. According to Harder, "*nous* [mind, reason, intellect] is found only 24 times, *noeo* [apprehend, perceive, understand] and *katanoeo* [notice, consider, contemplate] 14 times each, and the other associated terms even less often" (G. Harder, "Reason, Mind, Understanding," *New International Dictionary of New Testament Theology*, edited by Colin Brown, vol. 3 (Grand Rapids: Zondervan, 1978), p. 126.

16. Ibid., pp. 124, 127.

17. Robert Jewett, *Paul's Anthropological Terms* (Leiden: E.J. Brill, 1971), p. 327.

18. *See also* Psalm 119:36, incline=have desire for; Romans 1:24; 10:1; resolves, plans, etc., Genesis 6:5; Exodus 35:5; 1 Chronicles 29:16-18; Isaiah 10:7; John 13:2; Acts 5:4; 1 Corinthians 4:5; 2 Corinthians 9:7.

19. Further examples of the use of "heart" for various emotions include: love or hate (Deuteronomy 19:6; Leviticus 19:17; 2 Samuel 6:16; Romans 5:5; Philippians 1:7; 2 Corinthians 7:3; 1 Timothy 1:5); joy or sorrow (Deuteronomy 28:47; Psalm 13:2; 109:22; Proverbs 25:20; John 16:6; Acts 2:46; 14:17; Romans 9:2; 2 Corinthians 2:4); peace (Proverbs 15:30); courage or lack of it

(Deuteronomy 20:8; 2 Samuel 7:17; Daniel 11:25); anxiety (Proverbs 12:25); fear (Deuteronomy 28:67).

20. J. Pedersen, *Israel: Its Life and Culture*, vol. 1–2 (London: Oxford University Press, rpt., 1973), p. 106.

21. O.A. Piper, "Knowledge," *The Interpreter's Dictionary of the Bible* (Nashville: Abingdon, 1962), 3:43. For other instances showing the relation of knowledge to behavior, see Jeremiah 4:22; Hosea 4:1-2.

22. Pedersen, *Israel: Its Life and Culture*, p. 125.

23. Robert Durback, ed., *Seed of Hope, A Henri Nouwen Reader* (New York: Bantam Books, 1990), p. 197.

CHAPTER EIGHT

1. The theology and practical application of the "Steps to Freedom in Christ" are given in Neil's book *Helping Others Find Freedom in Christ*, published by Regal Books. It is a comprehensive discipleship counseling process of repentance that takes into account the reality of the spiritual world.

2. This illustration of the computer is not intended to deny that we are all born with a bent away from God. We have a clean slate only as far as information from outside. But we are born with a program that structures the input during our developmental years into habits and patterns of living for self independently of God.

CHAPTER NINE

1. Andrew T. Lincoln, *Ephesians*, Word Biblical Commentary, vol. 42 (Dallas: Word Books, 1990), p. 288.

2. John Eadie, *Commentary on the Epistle to the Ephesians* (Grand Rapids: Zondervan, n.d., rpt. of 1883 edition, T. & T. Clark), p. 346.

3. Jerome Murphy-O'Connor, "Truth: Paul and Qumran," in *Paul and Qumran: Studies in New Testament Exegesis* (London: Geoffrey Chapman, 1968), p. 206.

4. Frederick Dale Bruner, *Matthew*, vol. 2 (Dallas: Word Books, 1990), p. 548.

5. Dallas Willard, *In Search of Guidance* (San Francisco: Harper, 1993), p. 141.

6. Horatius Bonar, *God's Way of Holiness* (New York: Robert Carter & Brothers, 1865), pp. 41-42.

7. Henry Scougal, *The Life of God in the Soul of Man* (Philadelphia: Westminster Press, 1948), p. 38.

8. Sinclair Ferguson, "The Reformed View," in *Christian Spirituality*, edited by Donald L. Alexander (Downers Grove, IL: InterVarsity Press, 1988), p. 60.

9. Neil T. Anderson, *Victory Over the Darkness* (Ventura, CA: Regal Books, 1990), pp. 57-59.

10. Peter Kreeft, *Heaven: The Heart's Deepest Longing* (San Francisco: Ignatius, 1989), p. 183.

CHAPTER TEN

1. Trent C. Butler, *Joshua*, Word Biblical Commentary, vol. 7 (Waco: TX: Word Books, 1983), p. 3.

2. H. Ringgren, "הָגָה *haghah*," *Theological Dictionary of the Old Testament*, vol. 3, edited by G. Johannes Botterweck and Helmer Ringgren (Grand Rapids: Eerdmans, 1978), p. 321.

3. Ibid., "הָגָה *haghah*," p. 323.

4. A. Negoita, "הָגָה *haghah*," *Theological Dictionary of the Old Testament*, vol. 3, edited by G. Johannes Botterweck and Helmer Ringgren (Grand Rapids: Eerdmans, 1978), p. 323; citing H.J. Franken, *The Mystical Communion with JHWH in the Book of Psalms* (Leiden, 1954), p. 21.

5. Franz Delitzsch, *Biblical Commentary on the Psalms* (Grand Rapids: Eerdmans, 1959, rpt.), III, 259.

6. W.E. Vine, *An Expository Dictionary of New Testament Words* (Old Tappan, NJ: Fleming H. Revell, 1966), vol. 3, p. 70.

7. Wolfhart Pannenberg, *Anthropology in Theological Perspective* (Philadelphia: The Westminster Press, 1985), p. 259; referring to Augustine, *Enarr. in Ps. 94,2*.

8. Jonathan Edwards, *Religious Affections* in *The Works of Jonathan Edwards*, vol. 2, edited by John E. Smith, general editor Perry Miller (New Haven: Yale University Press, 1959), pp. 101-02.

9. Ibid., p. 97.

10. Evelyn Underhill, "The Place of Will, Intellect, and Feeling in Prayer," from *The Essentials of Mysticism* in *The Fellowship of the Saints*, compiled by Thomas S. Kepler (New York: Abingdon-Cokesbury, 1948), p. 626.

11. Robert Law, *The Emotions of Jesus* (New York: Charles Scribner & Sons, 1915), pp. 90-91.

12. Dietrich Bonhoeffer, *Meditating on the Word*, translated and edited by David Gracie (Cambridge, MA: Cowley Publications, 1986), p. 19.

13. Richard Benson, *The Way of Holiness: An Exposition of Psalm CXIX Analytical and Devotional*, p. vi; cited by Bonhoeffer, *Meditating on the Word*, p. 19.

14. G. Fred Bergin (compiler), *Autobiography of George Müller* (London: J. Nisbet and Co., 1905), pp. 152-53.

15. Paul Meier, "Spiritual and Mental Health in the Balance," in *Renewing Your Mind in a Secular World*, edited by John D. Woodbridge (Chicago: Moody Press, 1985), pp. 26-28.

16. Horatius Bonar, *God's Way of Holiness* (New York: Robert Carter & Brothers, 1865), pp. 197-98.

CHAPTER ELEVEN

1. Peter T. O'Brien, *Colossians, Philemon*, The Word Biblical Commentary, vol. 44 (Waco, Tx: Word, 1982), p. 23.

2. Gary A. Anderson, *A Time to Mourn, A Time to Dance: The Expression of Grief and Joy in Israelite Religion* (University Park, PA: Pennsylvania University Press, 1991), p. 14.

3. Ibid., p. 20.

4. Ibid., see Deuteronomy 14:26; 16:11,14-15; 26:11; 27:7.

5. For other occasions on which eating and joy are associated, see 2 Samuel 6:12; 1 Chronicles 12:41; 2 Chronicles 30:21,23,25; Ezra 6:22; Nehemiah 12:43; Esther 8:15-17; 9:17-19,22; Joel 1:16.

6. See Anderson, *A Time to Mourn*, pp. 37-45.

7. Ibid., p. 48.

8. Ibid., p. 49.

9. Martin Bolt and David G. Myers, *The Human Connection* (Downers Grove, IL: InterVarsity Press, 1984), p. 13.

10. The following evidence comes from David G. Myers, *The Human Puzzle* (San Francisco, Harper & Row, 1978), pp. 94-104.

11. Ibid., p. 97.

12. O.A. Piper, "Knowledge," *The Interpreter's Dictionary of the Bible*, edited by George Arthur Buttrick (Nashville: Abingdon Press, 1962), 3:44.

13. Cited in Bolt and Myers, *The Human Connection*, p. 19.

14. Dietrich Bonhoeffer, *The Cost of Discipleship* (New York: Macmillan, 1963), pp. 69, 86.

15. J. Goetzmann, "Mind," *The New International Dictionary of New Testament Theology*, vol. 2 (Grand Rapids: Zondervan, 1976), p. 617.

16. Peter T. O'Brien, *The Epistle to the Philippians* (Grand Rapids: Eerdmans, 1991), p. 507, citing V.P. Furnish, *Theology and Ethics in Paul* (Nashville: Abingdon Press, 1968), p. 89.

17. George Fohrer, "σοφία κτλ.," *Theological Dictionary of the New Testament*, vol. 7, edited by Gerhard Friedrich (Grand Rapids: Eerdmans, 1971), p. 487.

18. Johannes Pedersen, *Israel (I-IV) Its Life and Culture*, vol. 1–2 (London: Oxford University Press, rpt., 1973), pp. 126-27.

19. Gerhard Wallis, "אָהֵב; 'ahabh; אַהֲבָה 'ahbhah; אַהַב 'ahabh; אֹהֵב 'ohabh," *The Theological Dictionary of the Old Testament*, vol. 1, edited by G. Johannes Botterweck and Helmer Ringgren (Grand Rapids: Eerdmans, 1974), p. 105.

20. Ibid., p. 115.

21. Derek Kidner, *The Proverbs*, Tyndale Old Testament Commentaries (Downers Grove; IL: InterVarsity Press, 1969), p. 68.

22. Georg Fohrer, "σοφία κτλ.," *The Theological Dictionary of the New Testament*, vol.7, edited by Gerhard Friedrich (Grand Rapids: Eerdmans, 1971), p. 487.

23. James Adamson, *The Epistle of James* (Grand Rapids: Eerdmans, 1976), p. 130.

24. Cited by Bruce Larson, *A Call to Holy Living*.

25. Bob Benson, *Laughter in the Walls* (Nashville: Impact Books, 1969), p. 46.

CHAPTER TWELVE

1. See Horatius Bonar, *God's Way of Holiness* (New York: Robert Carter & Brothers, 1865), pp. 115-60.

2. A. van Selms, "Law," *The New Bible Dictionary*, edited by J.D. Douglas (Grand Rapids: Eerdmans, 1962), p. 718.

3. W.J. Harrelson, "Law in the OT," *The Interpreter's Dictionary of the Bible*, edited by George A. Buttrick (Nashville: Abingdon, 1976), 3:77.

4. Jerome Murphy-O'Connor, "Truth: Paul and Qumran," in *Paul and Qumran: Studies in New Testament Exegesis* (London: Geoffrey Chapman, 1968), pp. 189-90.

5. Peter C. Craige, *The Book of Deuteronomy*, New International Commentary on the Old Testament (Grand Rapids: Eerdmans, 1976), p. 170.

6. While "the Law" in Matthew 5:17 is a reference to the Old Testament law, the meaning of Christ being a fulfillment of the Old Testament law also encompasses all of God's law, including that written in the hearts of all people, even those who had no written law (*see* Romans 2:15). For a good brief discussion on the meaning of Christ as the "fulfillment" and "end" of the law, see Douglas J. Moo, "The Law of Moses or the Law of Christ," in *Continuity and Discontinuity*, edited by John S. Feinberg (Westchester, IL: Crossway Books, 1988), pp. 203-18.

7. Richard N. Longenecker, *Galatians*, Word Biblical Commentary, vol. 41 (Dallas: Word Books, 1990), p. 148.

8. Richard N. Longenecker, *Paul, The Apostle of Liberty* (New York: Harper and Row, 1964), pp. 125-26.

9. Bonar, *God's Way of Holiness*, p. 120.

10. W.F. Lofthouse, "The Old Testament and Christianity," in *Record and Revelation*, edited by H.W. Robinson (Oxford: Clarendon Press, 1938), p. 467.

11. Bonar, *God's Way of Holiness*, pp. 41-42.

12. Douglas J. Moo, "The Law of Moses or the Law of Christ," in *Continuity and Discontinuity*, edited by John S. Feinberg (Westchester, IL: Crossway Books, 1988), p. 217.

13. Herman N. Ridderbos, *Paul: An Outline of His Theology* (Grand Rapids: Eerdmans, 1975), p. 285.

CHAPTER THIRTEEN

1. Neil's books *Helping Others Find Freedom in Christ*, *The Christ-Centered Marriage*, and *Setting Your Church Free* are designed to help individuals, marriages, and churches become free in Christ through personal and corporate repentance so that He can be the center of people's lives, marriages, and ministries.

2. John Calvin, *The Institutes of the Christian Religion*, edited by John T. McNeill (Philadelphia: Westminster Press, 1960), III, i, 1.

3. Andrew T. Lincoln, *Ephesians*, Word Biblical Commentary, vol. 42 (Dallas: Word Books, 1990), p. 206. Rather than taking the indwelling of Christ in our hearts as the result of the empowering of the Spirit (as translated in NIV, NASB), some interpreters understand the indwelling of Christ as a parallel thought elaborating on the empowering of the Spirit. The thought is similar either way.

4. Frederick Louis Godet, *Commentary on the Gospel of John* (Grand Rapids: Zondervan, rpt. from orig., 1893), II, 282.

5. We have chosen to use the NASB throughout this discussion of abiding in Christ because it uses the word "abide" rather than "remain" as in the NIV. "Abide" is more accurate at this point and does add something of intimacy and dynamic that is not clear in "remain."

6. Raymond E. Brown, *The Gospel According to John (i-xii)*, The Anchor Bible, vol. 29 (Garden City, NY: Doubleday, 1966), pp. 510-11. Karlfried Munzer, "Remain," *The New International Dictionary of New Testament Theology*, vol. 3, edited by Colin Brown (Grand Rapids: Zondervan, 1971), p. 225.

7. Rudolph Bultmann, *The Gospel of John* (Philadelphia: Westminster Press, 1971), pp. 535-36.

CHAPTER FOURTEEN

1. Adapted from Neil T. Anderson, *Walking in the Light* (Nashville: Thomas Nelson, 1992), pp. 173-74.

2. F.J. Helfmeyer, "הָלַךְ; *halakh*." *Theological Dictionary of the Old Testament*, edited by G. Johannes Botterweck and Helmer Ringgren, vol. 3 (Grand Rapids: Eerdmans, 1978), p. 390.

3. Claus Westermann, *Genesis 12-15: A Commentary* (Minneapolis: Augsburg Publishing House, 1985), p. 259.

4. E. Edmond Hiebert, *The Thessalonian Epistles* (Chicago: Moody Press, 1971), p. 244. For more on the general applicability of this command, *see also* Leon Morris, *The First and Second Epistles to the Thessalonians*, rev. ed. (Grand Rapids: Eerdmans, 1991), p. 176.

5. Gerhard Delling, "πλήρης, κτλ.," vol. 6, *Theological Dictionary of the New Testament*, edited by Gerhard Friedrich (Grand Rapids: Eerdmans, 1968), p. 291.

6. A.W. Tozer, *Gems from Tozer* (Camp Hill, PA: Christian Publications, 1969), pp. 68-69.

7. Walter Marshall, *The Gospel-Mystery of Sanctification* (Grand Rapids: Zondervan, 1954), p. 156.

8. John White, *The Fight* (Downers Grove, IL: InterVarsity Press, 1976), p. 98.

9. Marshall, *The Gospel-Mystery*, p. 171.

10. Ibid., 172.

11. For a fascinating discussion about how what we are as Christians is practically lived out through "pretending" on both our part and that of God, see C.S. Lewis, *Mere Christianity* (New York: Macmillan, 1960), pp. 146-51.

12. White, *The Fight*, p. 108.

Chapter Fifteen

1. J. Knox Chamblin, *Paul and the Self* (Grand Rapids: Baker, 1993), p. 168. For more on the place of "the people of God" in the sanctification process, *see also* Larry Crabb, *Inside Out* (Colorado Springs: NavPress, 1988), pp. 153-70.

2. G. Ernest Wright, *The Challenge of Israel's Faith* (London: SCM Press, 1946), p. 92.

3. G. Ernest Wright, *The Biblical Doctrine of Man in Society* (London: SCM Press, 1954), p. 51.

4. J. Pedersen, *Israel: Its Life and Culture*, vol. 1-2 (London: Oxford University Press, 1926), p. 308.

5. L. Köhler, *Theologie des Alten Testaments* (Tübingen, 1947), p. 113; cited by G. Ernest Wright, *The Biblical Doctrine of Man in Society*, p. 47.

6. Eric Fromm, *The Art of Loving* (New York: Harper & Row, 1956), pp. 6-7.

7. J. Armitage Robinson, *St. Paul's Epistle to the Ephesians* (London: James Clarke & Co, n.d.), p. 183.

8. The NASB rendering is probably the correct rendering as opposed to the NIV ("Over all these virtues put on love, which binds them all together in perfect unity"). As O'Brien notes, the apostle nowhere else speaks of love as uniting other virtues. Rather, love is what binds believers together in the body of Christ. "Paul is concerned with the readers' corporate life and the perfection he sets before them is not something narrowly individual. It is attained only as Christians, in fellowship, show love to one another" [Peter T. O'Brien, *Colossians, Philemon*, Word Biblical Commentary, vol. 44 (Waco, TX: Word Books, 1982), p. 204].

9. Michael Griffiths, *God's Forgetful Pilgrims* (Grand Rapids: Eerdmans, 1975), p. 37.

10. Ibid., p. 65.

11. John R.W. Stott, *God's New Society* (Downers Grove, IL: InterVarsity Press, 1979), p. 137.

12. Charles Hodge, *A Commentary on the Epistle to the Ephesians* (Philadelphia: Presbyterian Board of Publication, 1856), p. 84.

13. George T. Montague, *Growth in Christ* (Kirkwood, MO: Maryhurst Press, 1961), p. 158.

14. Ibid.

15. Andrew T. Lincoln, *Ephesians*, Word Biblical Commentary, vol. 42 (Dallas: Word Books, 1990), p. 262.

16. In George T. Montague, *Growth in Christ*, p. 160.

17. Ibid., p. 161.

18. Dietrich Bonhoeffer, *Life Together* (San Francisco: Harper & Row, 1954), p. 112.

19. Larry Crabb, *Inside Out* (Colorado Springs: NavPress, 1988), p. 167.

20. Griffiths, *God's Forgetful Pilgrims*, p. 65.

Chapter Sixteen

1. Markus Barth, *Ephesians 4–6*, The Anchor Bible, vol. 34A (Garden City, NY: Doubleday, 1974), p. 763.

2. C.E.B. Cranfield, *A Critical and Exegetical Commentary on the Epistle to the Romans*, vol. 1 (Edinburgh: T. & T. Clark, 1975), pp. 341-42.

3. Hans Walter Wolff, *Anthropology of the Old Testament* (Philadelphia: Fortress Press, 1974), pp. 30-31.

4. During the period before Christ, believers such as Abraham, Moses, and David were surely related to "flesh" somewhat differently than those who lived in rebellion against God. Yet they were not freed from the dominion of sin in the same way as we are today through participation in the death and resurrection of Christ and the regeneration that belongs to the new covenant of final salvation inaugurated through the work of Christ. (See the discussion on the change of dominions in chapter 4.)

5. John R.W. Stott, The Message of Galatians (London: InterVarsity Press, 1968), p. 151.

6. J. Knox Chamblin, Paul and the Self (Grand Rapids: Baker, 1993), p. 50.

7. John R.W. Stott, Romans: God's Good News for the World (Downers Grove, IL: InterVarsity Press, 1994), p. 228.

8. J. Behm, "προνοέω," Theological Dictionary of the New Testament, vol. 4, edited by Gerhard Kittel (Grand Rapids: Eerdmans, 1967), p. 1010.

9. Peter H. Davids, The Epistle of James (Grand Rapids: Eerdmans, 1982), p. 161.

10. Joachim Guhrt, "Time," The New International Dictionary of New Testament Theology, vol. 3, edited by Colin Brown (Grand Rapids: Zondervan, 1978), p. 831.

11. Robert Law, The Tests of Life: A Study of the First Epistle of St. John, 3d ed. (Grand Rapids: Baker Books, rpt. 1968), p. 151.

12. Gerhard Delling, "ἀλαζών, ἀλαζονεία," Theological Dictionary of the New Testament, vol. 1, edited by Gerhard Kittel (Grand Rapids: Eerdmans, 1964), pp. 226-27.

13. I. Howard Marshall, The Epistles of John (Grand Rapids: Eerdmans, 1978), p. 229.

14. Stott, The Message of Galatians, p. 180.

CHAPTER SEVENTEEN

1. The theology and practical application of this discipleship counseling process is given in Neil's book Helping Others Find Freedom in Christ (Ventura, CA: Regal Books, 1995).

2. Andrew T. Lincoln, Ephesians, World Biblical Commentary, vol. 42 (Dallas: Word Books, 1990), p. 443.

3. Norval Geldenhuys, Commentary on the Gospel of Luke (Grand Rapids: Eerdmans, 1951), p. 566.

4. Hiebert says, "The present participle ["the tempter" in 1 Thessalonians 3:5] pictures him as persistently engaged in the effort to destroy the faith of the Thessalonians through temptation. He never gives up his sinister efforts" [D. Edmond Hiebert, The Thessalonian Epistles (Chicago: Moody Press, 1971), p. 142].

5. Most interpreters see "evil" as personal, that is, "evil one." In Matthew it would be naturally associated with Satan, who is called "the tempter" (4:3).

6. Lincoln, Ephesians, p. 443.

7. Philip Edgcumbe Hughes, Paul's Second Epistle to the Corinthians (Grand Rapids: Eerdmans, 1962), p. 123.

8. Thomas Brooks, Precious Remedies Against Satan's Devices with The Covenant of Grace (N.p.: Sovereign Grace Publishers, 1960), pp. 12-113. For an excellent discussion of these and other devices Satan uses to attack believers, see the entire work.

9. Ibid., pp. 3-4.

10. Ibid., p. 12.

11. Simon J. Kistemaker, James and I-III John, New Testament Commentary (Grand Rapids: Baker Books, 1986), p. 120.

12. In James B. Adamson, The Epistle of James (Grand Rapids: Eerdmans, 1976), p. 174.

13. F.F. Bruce, Commentary on the Book of Acts (Grand Rapids: Eerdmans, 1954), p. 114.

14. Ernst Haenchen, The Acts of the Apostles (Philadelphia: Westminster Press, 1971), p. 237.

15. Martin Luther, Table Talk, IV, 5097 (cited by Father Louis Coulange, pseud. [Joseph Turmel]), The Life of the Devil (London: Alfred A. Knopf, 1929), pp. 147-48; for other references of the devil putting thoughts into the minds of noted saints, see pp. 150ff.

16. David Powlison, Power Encounters: Reclaiming Spiritual Warfare (Grand Rapids: Baker Books, 1995), p. 135.

17. Brooks, Precious Remedies Against Satan's Devices.

18. For support of *stoicheia* as personal spirits, see Clint Arnold, *Powers of Darkness: Principalities and Powers in Paul's Letters* (Downers Grove, IL: InterVarsity Press, 1992), pp. 53-54.

19. Peter T. O'Brien, *Colossians, Philemon*, Word Biblical Commentary, vol. 44 (Waco, TX: Word Books, 1982), pp. 132-33.

20. Irenaeus, *Against Heresies*, V. 24.3.

21. The term "spirit" in Ephesians 2:2 is taken to refer directly to Satan (*see* Markus Barth, *Ephesians 1–3*, Anchor Bible [Garden City, NY: Doubleday, 1974], pp. 228-29), or to the evil spiritual power over which Satan rules (Lincoln, *Ephesians*, pp. 96-97), or as "a term describing the empire of spirits over whom Satan presides" (John Eadie, *Commentary on the Epistle to the Ephesians*, 1883 [Grand Rapids: Zondervan, rpt., 1883], p. 123). In any case, it refers to the evil spirit power at work in those who belong to the world.

22. J. Armitage Robinson, *St. Paul's Epistle to the Ephesians* (London: James Clarke, n.d.), p. 155.

23. Note also 1 Corinthians 2:12, where the spirit of the world is contrasted to the Spirit from God.

24. Other passages that connect the flesh and demonic influence are seen throughout Scripture. Evil thoughts come from our own heart (Matthew 15:19). Yet they also stem from Satan, as we have seen in the cases of David and Ananias. Satan tempts the believer to lack of self-control in the area of sexuality, which, in some passages, refers to the desires of the flesh (for example, 1 Corinthians 7:5). As Grosheide explains, ". . . the incontinence exists always and everywhere and seeks expression. Satan uses it by urging people to give it an illicit expression. And then sin is near" [F.W. Grosheide, *Commentary on the First Epistle to the Corinthians* (Grand Rapids: Eerdmans, 1953), p. 158]. David Powlison notes, "Satan's congruence with the fallen human heart operates in every passage that deals with moral evil. See Ephesians, 1 Peter, 1 Timothy 3:6, 1 Corinthians 10:6-11, and 1 John 3:1-10 and 5:16-21" (Powlison, *Power Encounters*, p. 159, n. 17).

25. Richard Belward Rackham, *The Acts of the Apostles* (London: Methuen & Co., 1922), p. 66.

26. C.K. Barrett, *A Commentary on the Second Epistle to the Corinthians* (New York: Harper & Row, 1973), p. 93.

27. Hughes, *Paul's Second Epistle to the Corinthians*, p. 72.

28. J.N.D. Kelly, *A Commentary on the Pastoral Epistles* (London: Adam & Charles Black, 1963), p. 190.

29. Patrick Fairbairn, *Commentary on the Pastoral Epistles* (Grand Rapids: Zondervan, 1874, 1956 rpt.), p. 358.

30. George W. Knight III, *The Pastoral Epistles*, New International Greek Testament Commentary (Grand Rapids: Eerdmans, 1992), pp. 424, 426.

31. Ibid., p. 166.

32. Karl Braune, "The Epistle of Paul to the Ephesians," in *Commentary on the Holy Scriptures Critical, Doctrinal and Homiletical—Galatians*, vol. 11, by John Peter Lange (Grand Rapids: Zondervan, 1960 rpt.), p. 170.

33. Markus Barth, *Ephesians 4–6*, The Anchor Bible, vol. 34A (Garden City, NY: Doubleday, 1974), p. 515.

34. John Eadie, *Commentary on the Epistle to the Ephesians* (Grand Rapids: Zondervan, n.d.), p. 350.

35. William Hendriksen, *Ephesians*, New Testament Commentary (Grand Rapids: Baker Books, 1967), s.v. *possessed*.

36. Charles Hodge, *An Exposition of Ephesians* (Wilmington, DE: Associated Publishers and Authors, Inc., n.d.), p. 94.

37. *Webster's New Collegiate Dictionary* (Springfield, MA: B. & C. Merriam Co., 1980), s.v. *possessed*.

38. The parallel use of "have a demon" (John 10:20) and "demonized" (John 10:21) shows that the meaning of both terminologies is essentially the same.

39. Delitzsch describes demonic possession thusly: " . . . the specific character of possession consists in this, that demons intrude themselves between the corporeity—more strictly, the nervous body—and the soul of man, and forcibly fetter the soul together with the spirit, but make the bodily organs a means of their self-attestation full of torment to men" [Franz Delitzsch, *A System of Biblical Psychology* (Grand Rapids: Baker, 1966, rpt. of 1899 edition), p. 354].

40. E. Earl Ellis, *Prophecy and Hermeneutic in Early Christianity* (Tübingen: J.C.B. Mohr [Paul Siebeck], 1978), p. 29.

41. D.G. James Dunn, *Jesus and the Spirit* (Philadelphia: Westminster Press, 1975), p. 234. Dunn goes on to say, "It would be difficult to deny that this verse [1 Corinthians 12:3] provides one particular rule of thumb for evaluating spiritual utterances. It is quite likely, though many disagree, that during the Corinthian worship some member(s) of the assembly had cried out under inspiration, 'Jesus be cursed!' Possibly there were those in Corinth influenced by gnostic ideas of the fundamental impurity of matter who consequently maintained a distinction between the man Jesus and the heavenly spiritual being Christ: to identify this Christ with the physical human being Jesus seriously dishonoured Christ and put the whole (gnostic) way of salvation in question, hence, 'Jesus be cursed!')" (p. 234).

42. Hugo Aust and Dietrich Müller, "Curse," in the *New International Dictionary of the New Testament*, vol. 1, edited by Colin Brown (Grand Rapids: Zondervan, 1975).

43. J. Ramsey Michaels, *1 Peter*, Word Biblical Commentary, vol. 49 (Waco, TX: Word Books, 1988), p. 300.

44. Edward Gordon Selwyn, *The First Epistle of St. Peter* (London: Macmillan, 1961), p. 238.

45. Peter H. Davids, *The Epistle of James*, New International Greek Testament Commentary (Grand Rapids: Eerdmans, 1982), p. 166.

46. Brooks, *Precious Remedies Against Satan's Devices*, p. 159.

47. Ibid., p. 162.

48. Lincoln, *Ephesians*, Word Biblical Commentary, vol. 42, p. 451.

49. Brooks, *Precious Remedies Against Satan's Devices*, p. 153.

50. In Everett Ferguson, *Demonology of the Early Christian World* (New York: The Edwin Mellen Press, 1984), pp. 130-31.

CHAPTER EIGHTEEN

1. Gerd Thiessen, *Psychological Aspects of Pauline Theology* (Philadelphia: Fortress, 1983), pp. 61-62.

2. Franz Delitzsch, *Biblical Commentary on the Psalms*, vol. 1 (Grand Rapids: Eerdmans, 1959), p. 350.

3. Charles Hodge, *An Exposition of the First Epistle to the Corinthians* (Grand Rapids: Eerdmans, 1953), p. 298.

4. William Watts, *St. Augustine's Confessions*, vol. 2 (Cambridge, MA: Harvard University Press, 1912), p. 85.

5. A. Roberts and J. Donaldson, *Ante-Nicene Fathers*, 1:531.

6. Thiessen, *Pyschological Aspects*, p. 66.

7. J.I. Packer, *Rediscovering Holiness* (Ann Arbor, MI: Servant Publications, 1992), p. 249.

8. C.K. Barrett, *A Commentary on the Second Epistle to the Corinthians* (New York: Harper & Row, 1973), p. 146.

9. Packer, *Rediscovering Holiness*, p. 250.

10. Gordon R. Lewis, "Suffering and Anguish" in *Zondervan Pictorial Encyclopedia of the Bible*, edited by Merrill C. Tenney (Grand Rapids: Zondervan, 1976), 5:532.

11. C.S. Lewis, *The Problem of Pain* (New York: Macmillan, 1962), p. 93.

12. Ibid., p. 91.

13. C.S. Lewis, *The Joyful Christian: 127 Readings from C.S. Lewis* (New York: Macmillan, 1977), p. 210.

14. H.W. Robinson, *Suffering: Human and Divine* (New York: Macmillan, 1939), p. 139.

15. C.S. Lewis, *The Problem of Pain*, p. 93.

16. Peter Kreeft, *Making Sense Out of Suffering* (Ann Arbor, MI: Servant Books, 1986), p. 78.

17. Philip Edgcumbe Hughes, *Paul's Second Epistle to the Corinthians* (Grand Rapids: Eerdmans, 1962), p. 11.

18. John White, *The Fight* (Downers Grove, IL: InterVarsity Press, 1976), p. 116.

19. John Murray, *The Epistle to the Romans*, vol. 1 (Grand Rapids: Eerdmans, 1959), p. 164.

20. The following story is condensed from chapter 14 of my (Neil's) book *Walking in the Light* (Nashville: Thomas Nelson, 1992).